Three Best Friends
HEIRLOOM DOLL CLOTHES

By Martha Campbell Pullen, Ph. D.

May God Bless You
Martha Pullen

This book is dedicated to mothers, grandmothers, aunts,
godmothers and very special friends who love to bring great joy to someone's life by sewing doll clothes.

Proverbs 31:26
She opens her mouth with wisdom,
and the teaching of kindness is on her tongue. NRSV

Book Team

Book Design and Layout
Kelly Chambers

Contributing Sewing Designers
Sue Pennington, Charlotte Potter, Patty Smith,
Beverley Sheldrick, Jena Blair, Craig Sharp, Starlette Picket,
Kathy McMakin and Elda Bratager

Construction Consultants
Kathy McMakin, Charlotte Potter, Louise Baird and Patty Smith

Illustrated By
Kris Broom, Suzy Peterson and Angela Pullen

Photography
Jennifer & Company

Photo Styling
Charlotte Potter and Claudia Newton

© 1998 Martha Pullen Company

All Rights Reserved.
No part of this book may be reproduced or transmitted in any
form or by any means, electronic or machanical, including
photocopying, recording, or any information storage and retrieval
system, without permission in writing from the publisher.

Printed By
Lithographics, Inc.
Nashville, TN

Published and Distributed By
Martha Pullen Company, Inc.
518 Madison Street
Huntsville, Alabama 35801-4286
Phone 256-533-9586
Fax 256-533-9630

Library of Congress Catalog Card Number 98-68284

ISBN 1-878048-15-5

Table of Contents

GENERAL DIRECTIONS — 4
THREE BEST FRIENDS DRESSES
- Blue Batiste Dress — 11
- White and Ecru Dress — 15
- Velvet Dress — 17
- Flip-Flop Border Dress — 19
- Two Tone Pink Scalloped Dress — 21
- Fancy Collar Bib Dress — 24
- Mardi Gras Dress and Bonnet — 27
- Pintucked Diamonds Dress — 32
- English Flower Girl Dress — 35
- English Netting Blue Bow Dress — 37
- Seaside Garden Dress — 39
- English Netting Dress with Pink Rose — 42
- Smocked Bodice Dress — 44
- White Smocked Yoke Dress — 47
- Lady Bugs Smocked Yoke Dress — 50
- Dusty Pink Antique Middy — 53
- Middy Bow Dress — 56
- Peach and Pink Linen Middy — 59
- Red, White and Blue Sailor Middy — 62
- Blue Plaid School Dress — 64
- School Days Pinafore — 66
- Pointed Collar Dress — 68
- Floral Dress with Detachable Collar — 70
- Robin's Egg Blue Tiered Dress — 72
- Pink Silk Dress — 74

BONNET — 76
PARIS BONNET — 77
NIGHTGOWN — 79
INTIMATE APPAREL
- Half Slip — 81
- Waisted Slip — 82
- Dropped-waist Slip — 83
- Short Bloomers and Long Bloomers — 84
- Straight Legged Pantaloons — 86
- Camisole — 87

PADDED DOLL HANGERS
- Heirloom Oval Hanger — 88
- Bullion Hanger — 89
- Pink Heirloom Hanger — 90
- Ladybug Hanger Cover — 91

SILK RIBBON BED ENSEMBLE
- Silk Ribbon Quilt — 93
- Dust Ruffle — 95
- Pillow and Pillow Case — 96
- Bolster — 97
- Sheet — 98

TECHNIQUES
- Beginning French Sewing Techniques — 99
- Machine Entredeux — 101
- Puffing — 103
- Basic Pintucking — 104
- Lace Shaping Techniques — 107
- Shaping Lace Diamonds — 108
- Shaping Flip-Flopped Lace Bows — 111
- Tied Lace Bows — 113
- Hearts-Fold Back Miter Method — 113
- Scalloped Skirt — 115
- French Seam — 117
- Extra-stable Lace Finishing — 118
- Making Baby Piping — 118
- Ribbon Rosettes — 119
- Shaped Puffing — 120
- Embroidery Techniques — 121

ABOUT THE AUTHOR — 126

General Directions

The General Directions contain instructions for plackets, neck, and sleeve finishes that are used repeatedly in garment construction. The Specific Directions found under each garment title give special embellishment instructions for that particular garment. Portions of the General Directions are referred to periodically throughout the Specific Directions.

ALL PATTERN PIECES CAN BE FOUND ON THE PULL-OUT PAGES.

A. Placket

a. Continous Lap Placket

1. Cut a slit down the center back of the skirt for the back placket to the following measurement:

	13"	17½"	18" & 19½"
Yoke	3"	3½"	4"
Mid-Yoke	2½"	3"	3½"
Waist and Dropped Waist	2"	3"	3"

2. Cut a strip of fabric down the selvage ¾" wide by the length listed below:

Placket Measurement Chart

	13"	17½"	18" & 19½"
Yoke	6½"	7½"	8½"
Mid-Yoke	5½"	5½"	7½"
Waist and Dropped Waist	4½"	6½"	6½"

3. Pull the slit in the skirt apart to form a "V". Place the right side of the strip to the right side of the skirt slit. The stitching will be done from the wrong side with the skirt on top and the placket strip on the bottom. The placket strip will be straight and the skirt will form a "V" with the point of the "V" ¼" from the edge of the placket. Stitch, using a ¼" seam. As you stitch, you will just catch the tip (a few fibers) at the point of the "V" (fig. 1).
4. Press the seam toward the selvage edge of the placket strip. Turn the selvage edge to the inside of the dress, enclosing the seam allowance. Whip by hand or stitch in place by machine (fig. 2).
5. Match the top edges of the skirt and find the center of the placket. Stitch the lower edges of the placket together in a dart, starting about ¼" above the end of the placket (refer to fig. 3).
6. The back of the dress will lap right over left. Fold the right side of the placket to the inside of the skirt and pin. Leave the left back placket open (fig. 4).
7. Run two rows of gathering in the top edge(s) of each side of the skirt piece at ⅛" and ¼" (fig. 4).

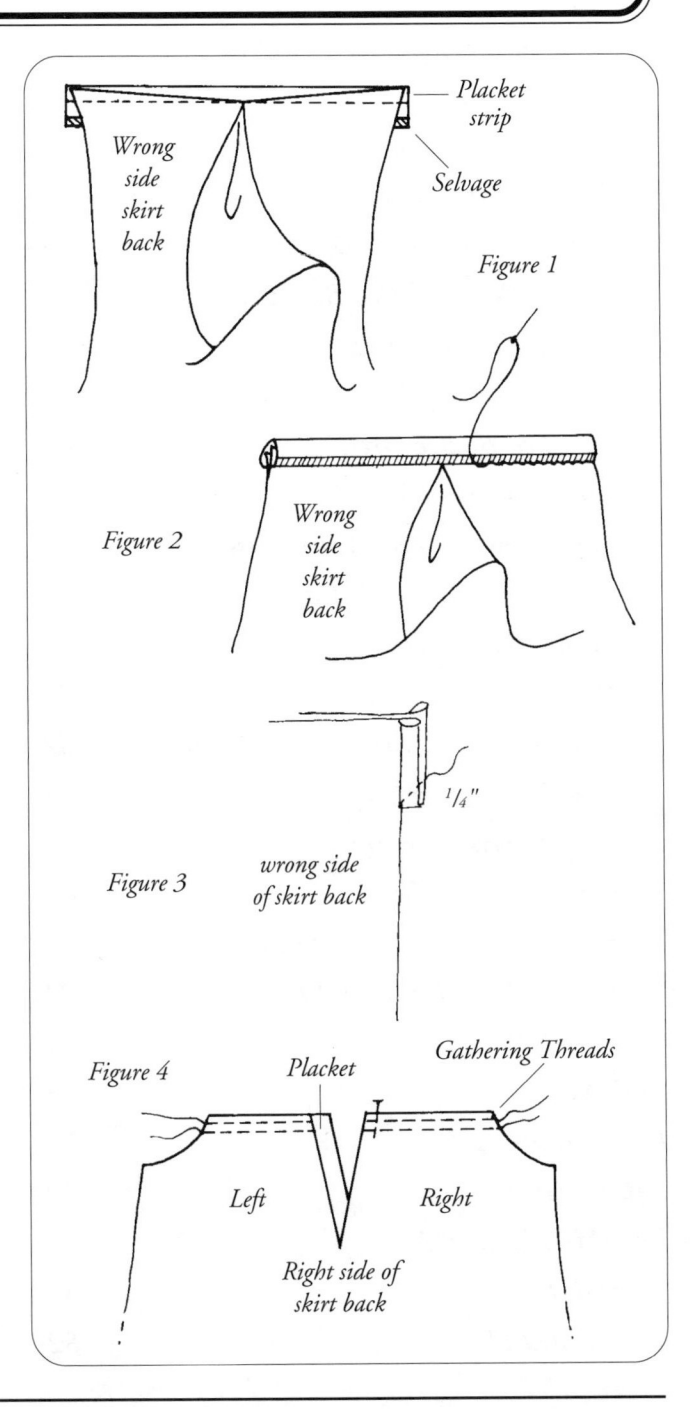

Figure 1

Figure 2

Figure 3

Figure 4

b. Placket in a Seam

1. Place the backs of the skirt, right sides together. Start stitching from the bottom of the skirt using a $1/4$" seam, stopping at the measurement listed below. Backstitch (fig. 5).

	13"	17 $1/2$"	18" & 19$1/2$"
Yoke	3"	3$1/2$"	4"
Mid-Yoke	2$1/2$"	3"	3$1/2$"
Waist and Dropped Waist	2"	3"	3"

2. Place a clip straight across the seam allowance at the top of the stitching. Press the seam allowance open if the seam allowance included the selvages. If the seam allowance does not include the selvages, finish the raw edges of the seam with a zigzag or serger (fig. 6).

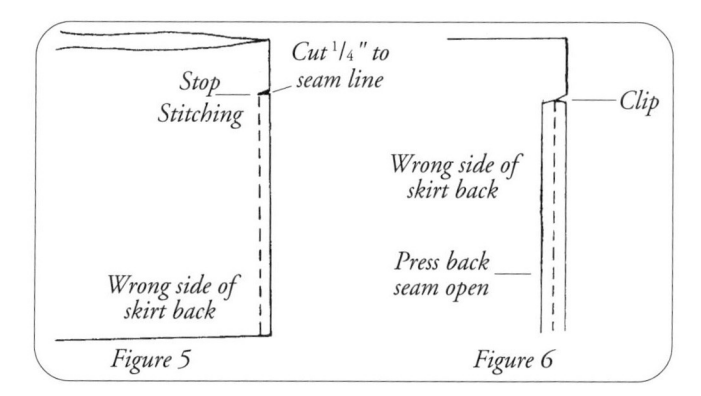

Figure 5

Figure 6

3. Cut a strip of fabric down the selvage $3/4$" wide by the length listed below:

   Placket Measurement Chart

	13"	17$1/2$"	18" & 19$1/2$"
Yoke	6$1/2$"	7$1/2$"	8$1/2$"
Mid-Yoke	5$1/2$"	5$1/2$"	7$1/2$"
Waist and Dropped Waist	4$1/2$"	6$1/2$"	6$1/2$"

4. Pull the back edges of the skirt apart above the stitching to create a straight line. The clipped edges will come together. Place the right side of the strip to the right side of the opening, with the cut edges of the placket meeting the edge of the opening. The stitching will be made from the wrong side, with the garment on top and the placket strip on the bottom. Stitch, using a $1/4$" seam catching a few fibers at the back seam line (fig. 7).

5. Press the seam toward the selvage edge of the placket strip. Turn the selvage edge to the inside of the dress, enclosing the seam allowance. Whip by hand or stitch in place by machine to the seam line (fig. 8).

6. Match the top edges of the skirt and find the center of the placket. Stitch the lower edges of the placket together in a dart, starting about $1/4$" above the end of the placket (fig. 9).

7. The skirt will lap right over left. Fold the right side of the placket to the inside of the dress and pin. Leave the left back placket open (fig. 10).

8. Run two rows of gathering in the top edge(s) of each side of the skirt piece at $1/8$" and $1/4$" (fig. 10).

Figure 7

Figure 8

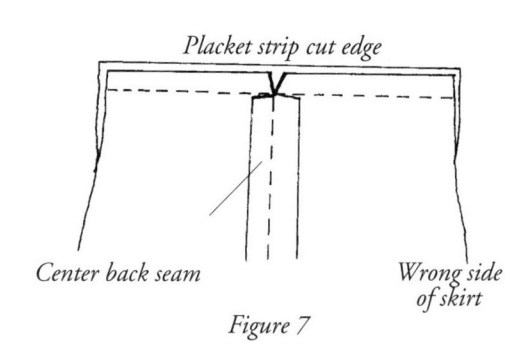

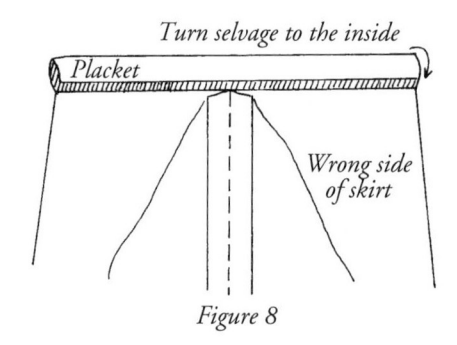

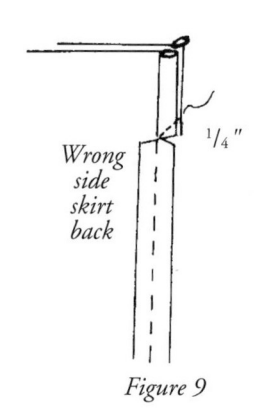

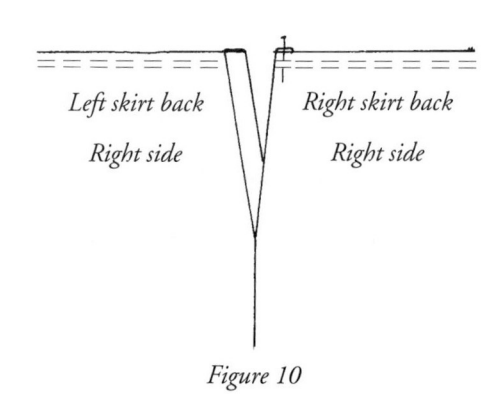

Figure 9

Figure 10

General Directions — *Three Best Friends*

B. Sleeves and Sleeve Finishes

1. Cut two sleeves using the desired sleeve pattern.

   Option: Decorate two squares of fabric larger than the sleeve pattern. Cut sleeves from the embellished fabric. Refer to the specific directions for the sleeve embellishment of each specific dress.

2. Stitch two gathering rows in the top and bottom of each sleeve piece, at 1/4" and 1/8".
3. Gather the bottom of the sleeve to the measurements given of the sleeve band chart.

Sleeve Band Chart

	13"	17 1/2"	18"	19 1/2"
Elbow Length Sleeve	3 3/4"	5"	5 1/4"	5 1/2"
3/4 Length Sleeve	3 1/2"	4"	4 3/4"	4 3/4"
Long sleeve	3 1/2"	4"	4 1/2"	4 5/8"

a. Entredeux to Gathered Edging Lace

1. Cut two strips of entredeux to the desired measurement given on the sleeve band chart. Cut two pieces of edging lace twice the length of the entredeux.
2. Gather the edging lace to fit the entredeux. Stitch together using the technique "entredeux to gathered lace" (fig. 11).
3. Gather the bottom of the sleeve to fit the entredeux/edging lace band. Stitch the band to the sleeve, right sides together, using the technique "entredeux to gathered fabric" (fig. 12).

b. Entredeux to Flat Lace

1. Cut two strips of entredeux to the desired measurement given on the sleeve band chart.
2. Cut two pieces of edging lace the length of the entredeux.
3. Attach the entredeux to the lace edging using the technique "lace to entredeux" (fig. 13).

c. Entredeux and a Fabric Lace Ruffle

1. Cut two strips of entredeux or entredeux beading to the measurement on the sleeve band chart. Cut two pieces of edging lace twice the length of the entredeux and two pieces of fabric twice the length of the entredeux and 3/4" wide for 13" dolls and 1" wide for 17 1/2", 18" and 19 1/2" dolls.
2. Attach edging lace to one long side of each ruffle piece using the technique "lace to fabric" (fig. 14).
3. Run two gathering rows in the top edge of the fabric/lace ruffle strip at 1/8" and 1/4". Gather the strip to fit the entredeux or entredeux beading pieces. Attach the ruffle to the entredeux or entredeux beading using the technique "gathered fabric to entredeux" (fig. 15).
4. Gather the bottom of the sleeve to fit the entredeux/ruffle band. Stitch the band to the sleeve, right sides together, using the technique "entredeux to gathered fabric" (see fig. 15).

Entredeux to Gathered Edging Lace

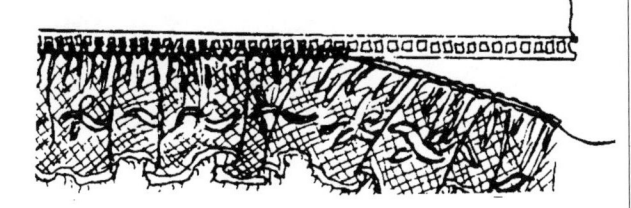

Figure 11

Entredeux or Entredeux Beading and Gathered Edging Lace

Figure 12

Entredeux to Flat Lace

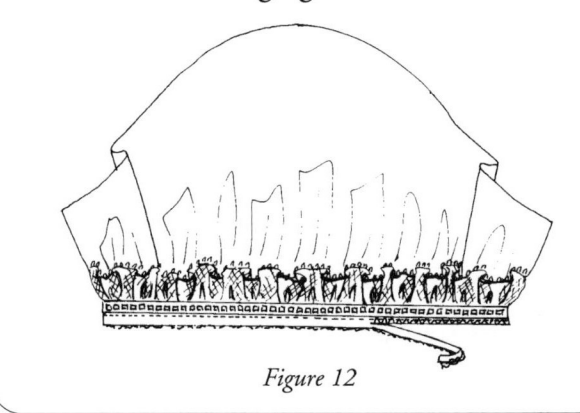

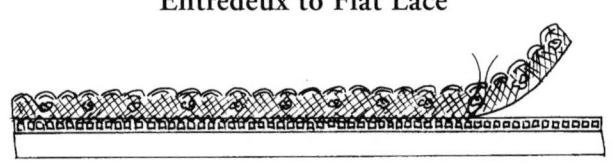

Figure 13

Entredeux and a Fabric Lace Ruffle

Figure 14

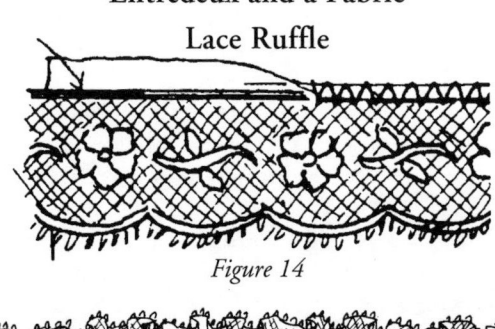

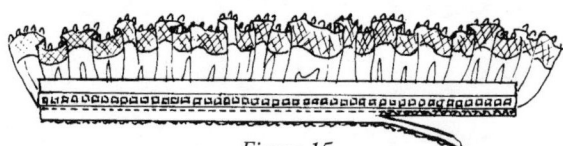

Figure 15

d. Bias Sleeve Bindings

1. Cut two bias strips of fabric 1" wide by the desired measurement given on the sleeve band chart.
2. Gather the bottom of the sleeve to fit the bias band. Stitch the band to the sleeve, right sides together, using a $1/4$" seam (fig. 16). Fold the lower edge of the band to the inside $1/4$" (fig. 17). Place the folded edge just over the seam line on the inside of the sleeve, enclosing the seam allowance, creating a $1/4$" band. Hand stitch or machine stitch the folded edge of the band to the seam line (fig. 18).

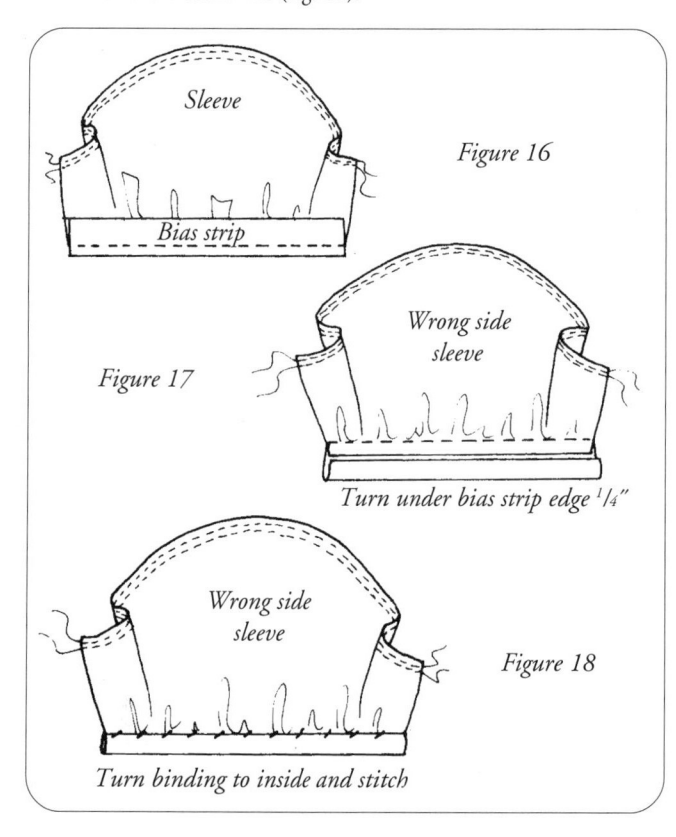

Figure 16
Sleeve
Bias strip

Figure 17
Wrong side sleeve
Turn under bias strip edge $1/4$"

Figure 18
Wrong side sleeve
Turn binding to inside and stitch

e. Gathered Sleeve with Elastic and Lace

1. Stitch a strip of edging lace along the bottom of each sleeve using the technique "lace to fabric" (fig. 19).
2. Measuring from the scalloped lace edge on the wrong side of the sleeves, draw a line with a fabric marker at the following measurement: 1" for 13" dolls and $1 1/4$" for $17 1/2$", 18" and $19 1/2$" dolls (fig. 20).
3. Start with two pieces of $1/8$" elastic 1" longer than the measurement given on the sleeve band chart. The longer measurement will aid in attaching the elastic. Place a dot $3/4$" from each end of the elastic.
4. Place one elastic piece on the drawn line of one sleeve with the dot at the side edge of the sleeve. Stitch the elastic in place with several tiny straight stitches (fig. 20). Continue stitching with a loose zigzag that encloses the elastic but does not catch the elastic. Pull the elastic until the second dot is at the side edge of the sleeve. Tack in place with several tiny straight stitches (fig. 21). Trim the elastic even with the sides of the sleeve. Repeat for other sleeve.

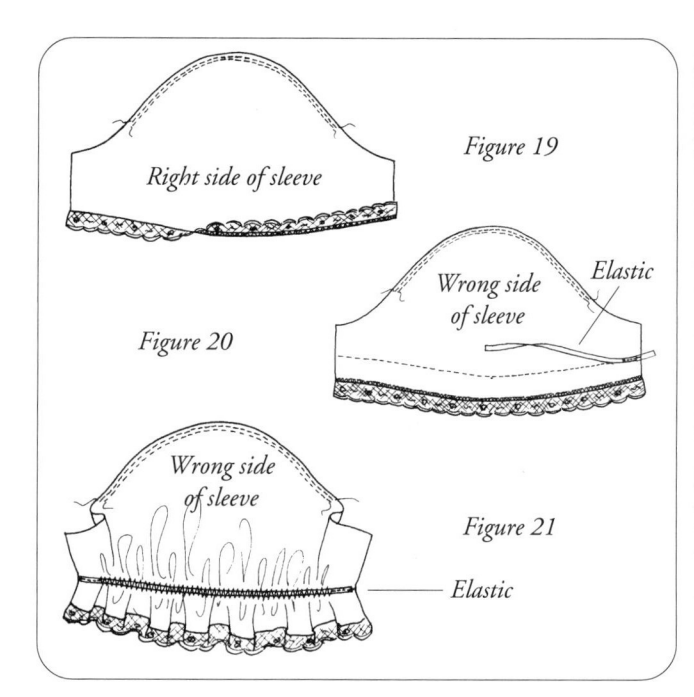

Figure 19
Right side of sleeve

Figure 20
Wrong side of sleeve
Elastic

Figure 21
Wrong side of sleeve
Elastic

f. Gathered Sleeve with Elastic and Ribbon

1. Cut sleeves $5/8$" longer for this technique.
2. Cut two pieces of $1/2$" ribbon the length of the sleeve bottom.
3. Place the ribbon across the bottom edge of the wrong side of the sleeves. The ribbon can be stitched in place along the top edge of the ribbon or held in place with wash-away basting tape (fig. 22).
4. Flip the ribbon to the right side of the sleeve. Press. Stitch along the top and bottom edges of the ribbon (fig. 23).
5. Refer to steps 2 to 4 in section e. above to attach the elastic to the sleeves.

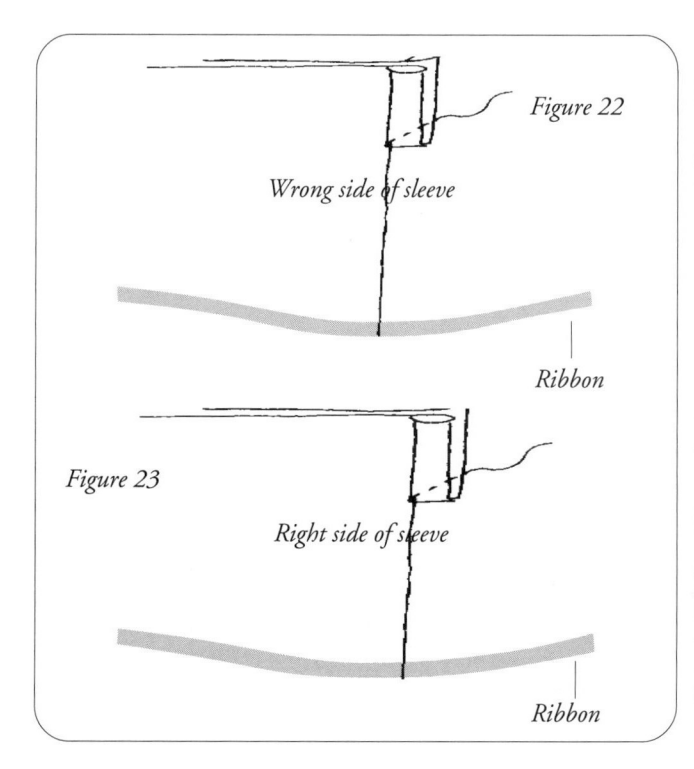

Figure 22
Wrong side of sleeve
Ribbon

Figure 23
Right side of sleeve
Ribbon

g. Sleeve Band

1. Cut two strips of fabric 1" wide by the measurement given on the sleeve band chart for your specific doll body.
2. Fold the strip in half lengthwise and press (fig. 24).
3. If decorative stitching or piping is used, refer to your specific directions for instruction.
4. Gather the lower edge of the sleeve with two rows of machine stitching $1/8$" and $1/4$" from the lower edge.
5. Pull up the gathers to fit the sleeve band. Refold the bands if needed from step 3 and pin the bands to each sleeve with the cut edges together.
6. Stitch the band to the sleeve with a $1/4$" seam (fig. 25).

h. Attaching the Sleeves

1. Place the sleeves to the arm openings, right sides together, matching the center of each sleeve to the shoulder seam of the bodice.
2. Gather the sleeves to fit the openings with the gathers falling $3/4$" - $1 1/2$" on each side of the shoulder seam.
3. Stitch in place (fig. 26).

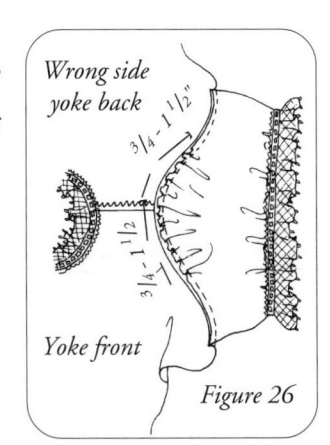

Figure 24

Figure 25

Figure 26 — Wrong side yoke back; Yoke front

C. Neck Finishes

Neck Band Chart

Doll Size	13"	$17 1/2$"	18"	$19 1/2$"
Neck Band Measurement	$6 3/4$"	7"	$7 3/4$"	8"

a. Entredeux to Gathered Edging Lace

1. Cut a strip of entredeux to the neck band measurement given in the chart for the specific doll.
2. Cut a piece of edging lace twice the length of the entredeux. Gather the edging lace to fit the entredeux strip.
3. Trim away one side of the entredeux fabric and attach the gathered edging lace to the trimmed entredeux using the technique "entredeux to gathered lace" (refer to fig. 11).
4. If the fabric edge remaining on the entredeux is not already $1/4$", trim to $1/4$". Clip this fabric so that it will curve along the neck edge of the dress (fig. 27). Place this strip to the neck (back plackets extended - not folded) of the dress, right sides together. Attach neck band using the technique "entredeux to fabric" (fig. 28).
5. Press the seam allowance toward the dress. Using a tiny zigzag, tack the seam allowance to the dress. This stitching will keep the entredeux/gathered lace standing up at the neck (fig. 29).
6. Finish the back edge of the lace with a small zigzag stitch.

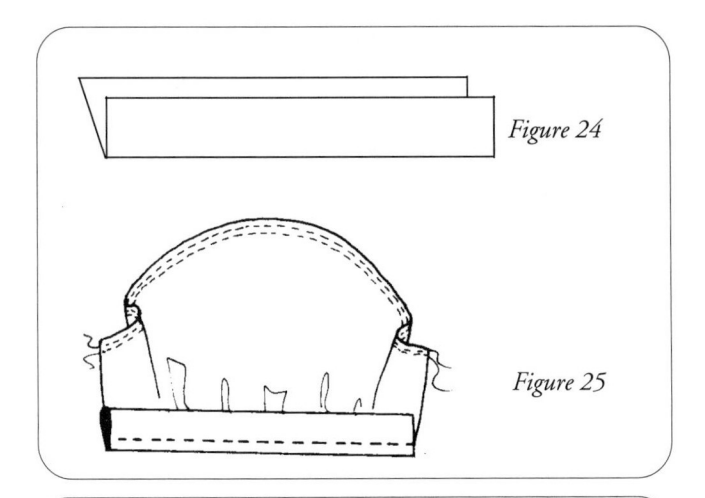

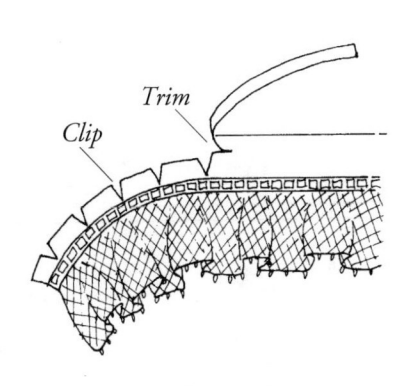

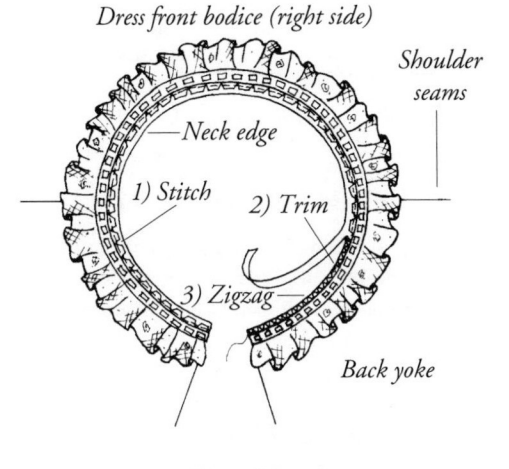

Figure 27 — Trim; Clip

Figure 28 — Dress front bodice (right side); Shoulder seams; Neck edge; 1) Stitch; 2) Trim; 3) Zigzag; Back yoke

Figure 29 — Wrong side bodice; Zigzag over seam allowance

Three Best Friends — *General Directions*

b. Entredeux to Flat Edging Lace

1. Cut a strip of entredeux and a strip of narrow lace to the neck band measurement given in the chart for the specific doll.
2. Trim away one side of the entredeux fabric and attach the edging lace to the trimmed entredeux using the technique "entredeux to lace" (refer to fig. 13).
3. If the fabric edge remaining on the entredeux is not already $1/4$", trim to $1/4$". Clip this fabric so that it will curve along the neck edge of the dress (see fig. 27). Place this strip to the neck (back plackets extended - not folded) of the dress right sides together. Attach using the technique "entredeux to fabric" (see fig. 28).
4. Press the seam allowance toward the dress. Using a tiny zigzag, tack the seam allowance to the dress. This stitching will keep the entredeux/lace standing up at the neck (see fig. 29).

c. Bias Binding

1. Trim $1/4$" from the edge of the neck. Fold the back edges of the back bodice to the inside along the fold lines. Press.
2. Measure around the neck with the back folds in place and add $1/2$" to this measurement. Cut a bias strip 1" wide by this measurement. Fold each long side of the bias strip to the inside $1/4$". Press in place (fig. 30). Open out one side of the bias strip and stitch to the neck using a $1/4$" seam (stitch in the fold) (fig. 31). The bias strip will extend $1/4$" beyond the folded plackets of the back. Flip the bias up, toward the seam allowance, fold the ends to the inside and pull the upper folded edge of the bias strip over the seam allowance. Press. Hand stitch or machine stitch in place.

d. Bias Binding with Gathered Edging Lace

1. Finish the neck of the dress with a bias binding using the directions found in section C. c. above.
2. Cut a piece of edging lace three times the length of the neck binding.
3. Turn each cut edge of lace to the inside $1/4$" and $1/4$" again. Gather the edging lace to fit the neck of the dress.
4. Hand stitch the gathered lace to the inside of the neck binding (fig. 32).

e. Bias Facing

1. Cut a bias strip 1" wide by the length of neck band measurement given in the neck band chart. Fold the bias strip in half along the length and press. Place the cut edges of the strip to the neck of the dress. Cut the ends of the strip $1/4$" from each side of the back bodice edges.
2. Flip the back edges of the bodice to the outside along the fold lines. Place these folds under the bias strip. Stitch the bias strip to the neck edge using a $1/4$" seam. Trim the seam allowance to $1/8$". Clip the curves (fig. 33). Flip the bias strip and the back bodice edges to the inside of the bodice. Hand stitch the bias strip in place, finishing the neck edge (fig. 34).

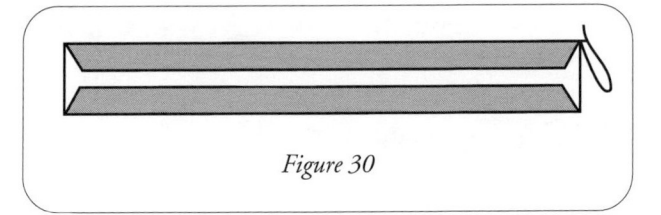

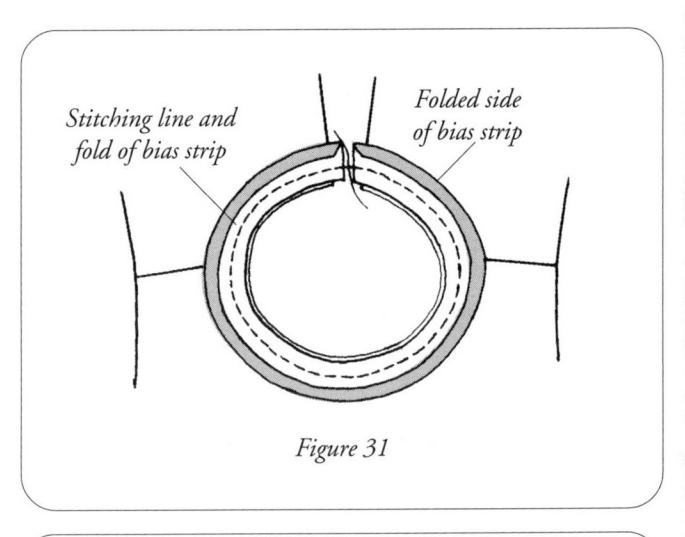

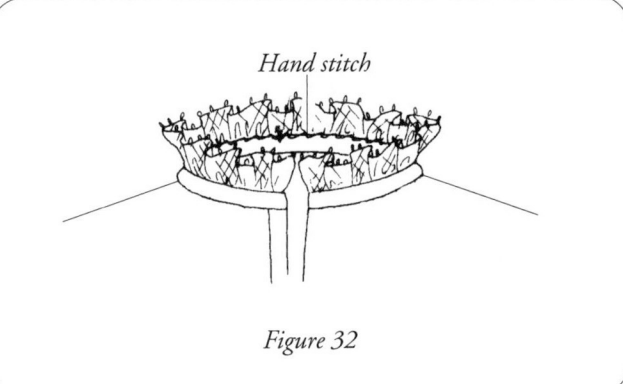

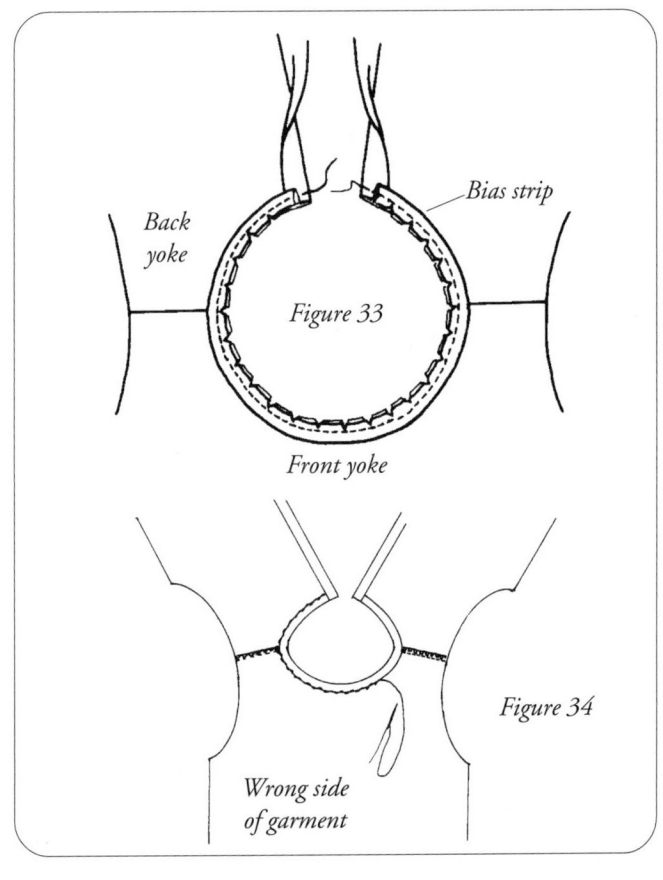

Figure 30

Figure 31 — Stitching line and fold of bias strip; Folded side of bias strip

Figure 32 — Hand stitch

Figure 33 — Back yoke; Bias strip; Front yoke

Figure 34 — Wrong side of garment

General Directions   *Three Best Friends*

f. Attaching A Collar with a Bias Facing

1. Place the wrong side of the collar to the right side of the dress. Pin in place.
2. Cut a bias strip 1" wide by the length of neck band measurement given in the neck band chart. Fold the bias strip in half and press. Place the cut edges of the strip to the neck of the collar/dress. Cut the ends of the strip $3/8$" from each side of the back bodice edges.
3. Flip the back bodice edges to the outside along the fold lines. Place these folds under the folded bias strip. Stitch the bias strip to the neck edge using a $1/4$" seam (fig. 35). Trim the seam allowance to $1/8$", clip. Flip the bias strip and the back bodice edges to the inside of the bodice. Hand stitch the bias strip in place finishing the neck edge (refer to fig. 34).

e. Stand-Up Collar

1. Cut a straight strip of fabric 1" wide by the length given on the neck band chart for the specific doll.
2. Fold each long side of the fabric to the wrong side $1/4$", press. This will create two creases along each side $1/4$" from the edge (fig. 36).
3. With the back bodice placket edges extended, open one side of the bias and place the strip to the neck edge, right sides together. Stitch the strip to the neck using a $1/4$" seam. You will be stitching in one of the creases. Clip the curve along the seam allowance (fig. 37).
4. With the top edge folded, place the top fold just past the seam, enclosing the seam allowance. Pin the folded strip in place and stitch the lower edge of the strip to the neck by hand or machine (fig. 38).
5. Zigzag along the ends of the neck strip even with the edges of the back bodices. Trim off any excess beyond the zigzags (fig. 39).
6. Fold the bodice/neck strip to the inside of the bodice along the back fold lines and press (fig. 40).

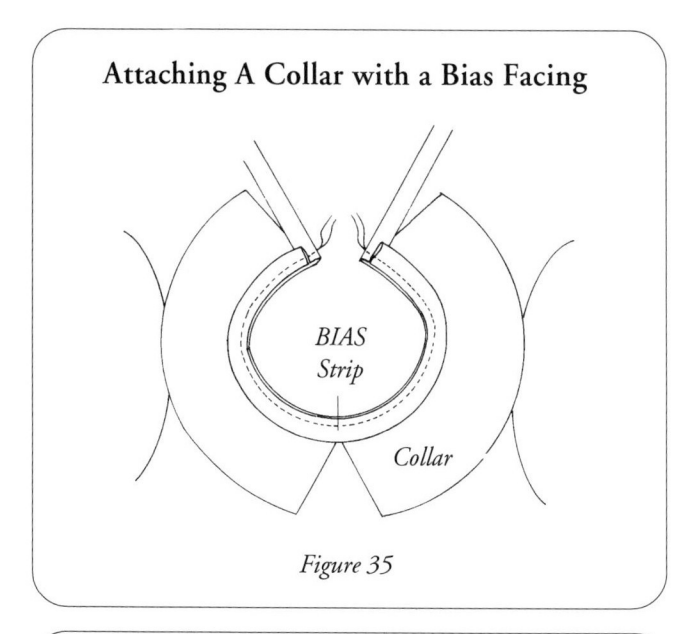

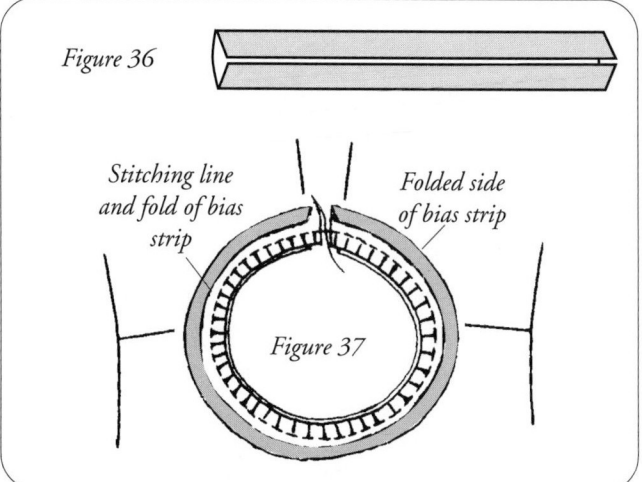

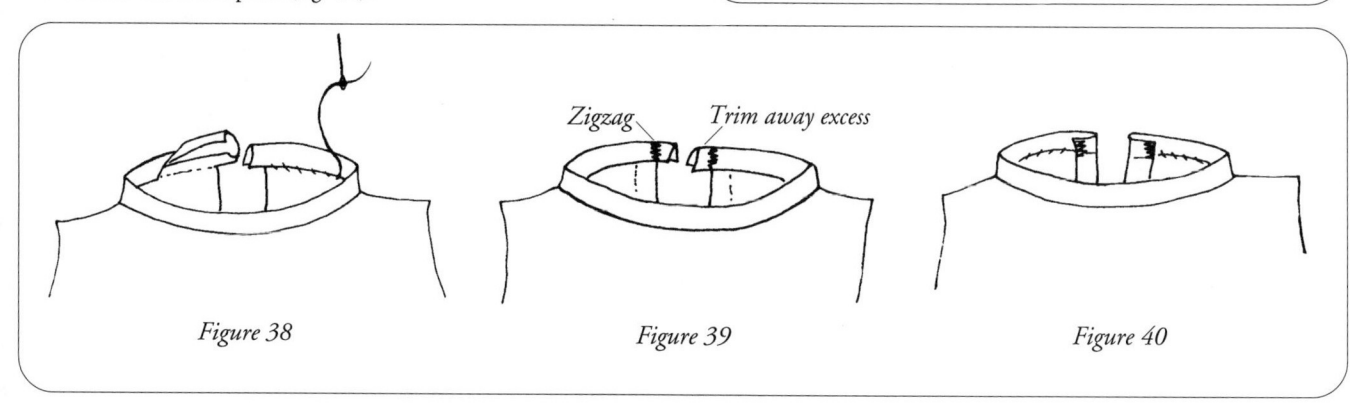

Attaching A Collar with a Bias Facing

Figure 35

Figure 36

Stitching line and fold of bias strip

Folded side of bias strip

Figure 37

Figure 38

Zigzag *Trim away excess*

Figure 39

Figure 40

Blue Batiste Dress

Featuring baby blue Nelona Swiss batiste, this dress is a dream to behold. The double collar is of batiste with white French lace on the edge of both collars. The sleeves are so precious with the piece of insertion and gathered lace in the middle. The bottoms of the sleeves feature entredeux and gathered white French edging. The overskirt has scalloped insertion with gathered French lace edging. The underskirt has a fancy band of entredeux, two rows of insertion, entredeux, and a gathered batiste ruffle edged with French edging. The back closes with Velcro™. Two ribbon rosettes or Fru Frus are found on the shoulder.

Fabric Requirements

Fabric Requirements:

	13"	17 1/2", 18 and 19 1/2"
Fabric - Blue Swiss batiste	3/4 yard	1 yard
Lace edging (1")	9 1/4 yards	9 3/4 yards
Lace insertion (3/4")	5 yards	5 1/4 yards
Entredeux	3 yards	3 yards

Notions

Lightweight sewing thread, Velcro™, snaps or tiny buttons, 2mm silk ribbon

Directions

All seams 1/4" unless otherwise indicated. Finish all seams with a zigzag or serge to finish the fabric edges.

Please read through both the General Directions and the Specific Directions before starting the dress. The General Directions can be found on page 4 and give instructions for plackets, neck, and sleeve finishes. These Specific Directions give instructions for the special details concerning this particular dress and the sequence of the construction.

The following pattern pieces needed for this dress are found on the pull-outs: mid-yoke front, mid-yoke back, and elbow-length sleeve.

The sleeve template and the overskirt template are found on page 14.

A. Constructing the Dress

1. Cut out two mid-waist backs from the selvage, one mid-waist front on the fold and two sleeves. Refer to the chart below for the size to cut the following pieces: two strips for the collar (one A and one B), two strips for the ruffle, one skirt piece and one skirt piece for the overskirt.

	13"	17 1/2"	18 1/2"	19 1/2"
Collar Strip A	1 1/2" by 22"	1 3/4" by 22"	2" by 22"	2" by 22"
Collar Strip B	2" by 22"	2 1/2" by 22"	2 1/2" by 22"	2 3/4" by 22"
Ruffle Strips (2)	1 1/2" by 45"	2" by 45"	2" by 45"	2" by 45"
Skirt Piece	3 1/4" by 45"	5 5/8" by 45"	6 5/8" by 45"	6 5/8" by 45"
Overskirt Piece	3 5/8" by 45"	5 1/8" by 45"	6 1/8" by 45"	6 1/8" by 45"

2. Place the shoulders of the front bodice and back bodice right sides together and stitch (fig. 1).
3. Cut a piece of lace edging 2 times the length of Collar Strip A and Strip B. Gather the lace to fit the collar strips and attach the lace referring to the technique "lace to fabric". Finish the ends of each collar strip with a narrow hem (fig. 2).
4. Place the unfinished edges of the collar strips together with the narrower collar piece on top and treat them as one piece. Run two rows of gathering stitches 1/8" and 1/4" from the edge (fig. 3). Pull up the gathers to fit the neckline and attach the collar to the bodice neck edge using the General Directions, C. Neck Finishes, f. Attaching a Collar with a Bias Facing.

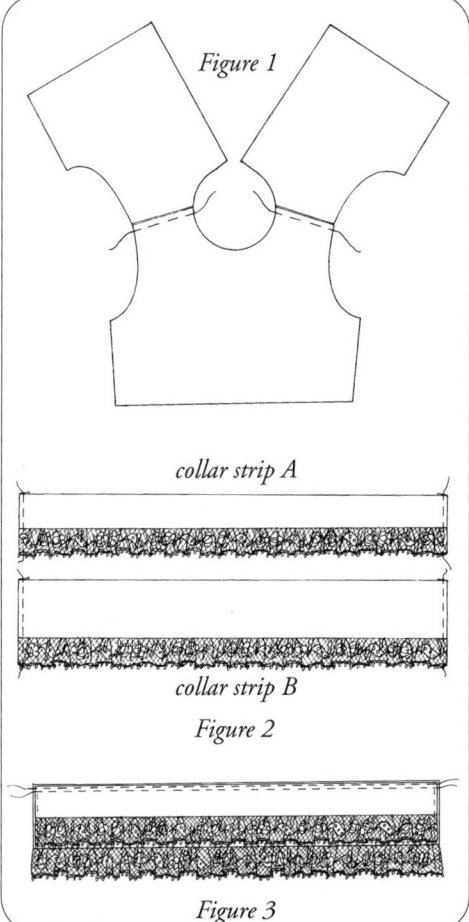

Blue Batiste Dress

Figure 1

collar strip A

collar strip B

Figure 2

Figure 3

Figure 4 — marking lines

Figure 5 — trim away fabric from behind lace

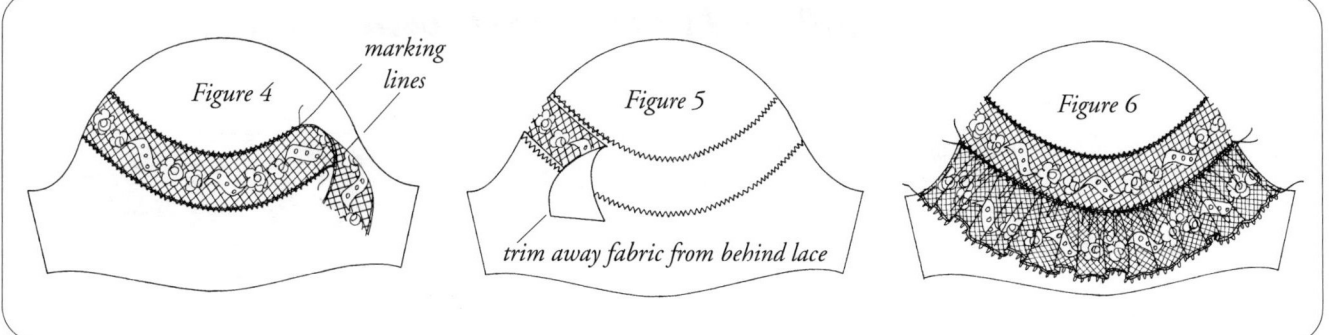

Figure 6

5. Place the sleeves onto the sleeve template and trace the lace placement line with a wash-out marker. Refer to the lace shaping section and attach the lace to each sleeve (fig. 4). Trim the fabric from beneath the lace (fig.5). Measure the bottom edge of the lace curve, cut a piece of lace edging twice this length. Gather the lace edging and stitch in place with a small zigzag stitch along the lower edge of the lace insertion on the sleeve. At each end of the lace edging, baste the lace to the raw edge of the sleeve (fig.6).
6. Finish the bottom edge of each sleeve referring to the General Directions, B. Sleeves and Sleeve Finishes, a. Entredeux to Gathered Edging Lace.
7. Refer to the General Directions, B. Sleeves and Sleeve Finishes, h. Attaching the Sleeves and attach the sleeves to the bodice (fig. 7).
8. Place the sides of the dress right sides together, matching the ends of the sleeves, the underarm seams and the lower edges of the bodice. Stitch in place (fig.8).
9. Using the technique "lace to lace", construct a fancy band for the underskirt by sewing two pieces of 45" long lace insertion together. Add entredeux on each side using the technique "lace to entredeux" (fig.9).
10. To form the ruffle strip for the bottom of the fancy band, cut one of the 45" ruffle strips in half, then sew one on each side of the other 45" strip to form a 90 continuous piece (22 $1/2$" + 45" + 22 $1/2$").
11. Attach lace edging to one long side of the ruffle referring to the technique "lace to fabric". Gather the unfinished edge of the ruffle by running two rows of gathering stitches $1/8$" and $1/4$" from the edge (fig. 10). Pull up the gathers to fit the entredeux on one side of the lace band created in step 9 and attach the ruffle referring to the technique "entredeux to gathered fabric" (fig. 11).
12. Attach the skirt piece to the top of the fancy band using the technique "entredeux to flat fabric".
13. Fold the overskirt piece in half to find the center front. Trace the scallop design from

Figure 7

Figure 8

Figure 10 — gathering threads at $1/8$" and $1/4$"

Figure 11

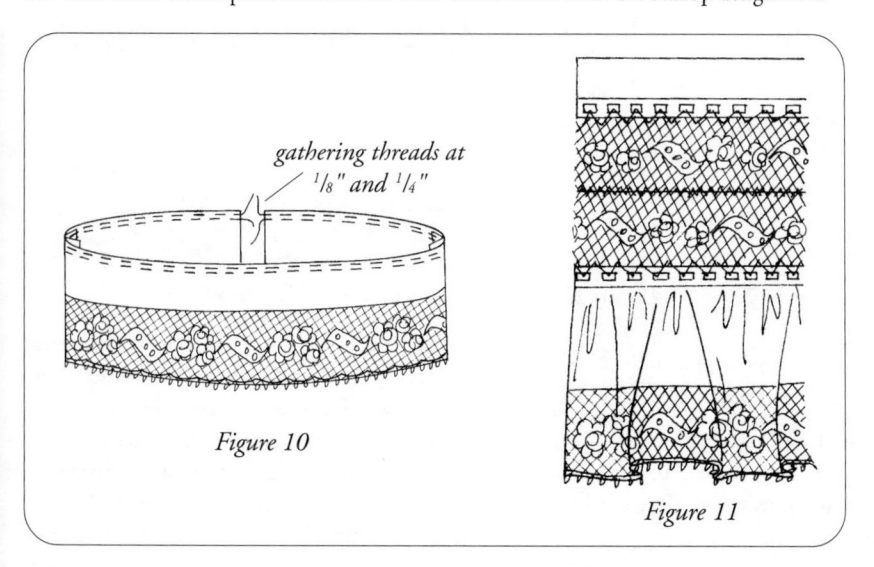

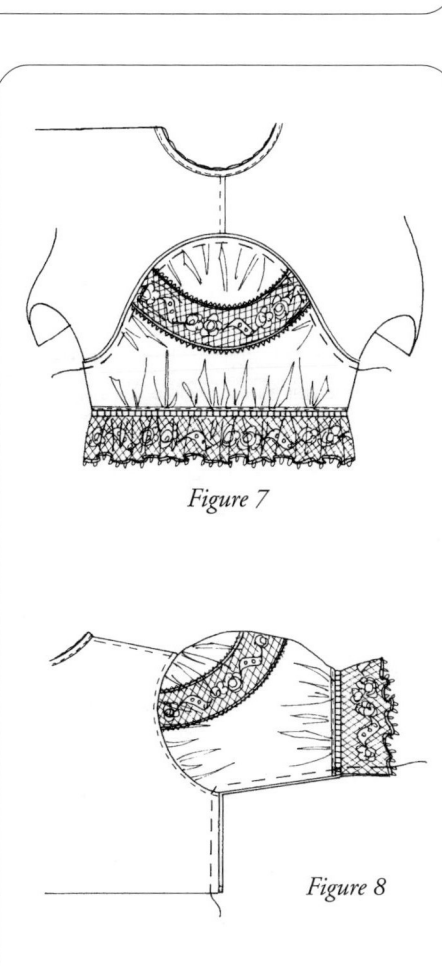

Figure 9

the overskirt scallop template, start the template with a point in the center front and the bottom of the template $1/2$" from the edge of the fabric (fig 12). Refer to the technique "lace shaping" and shape the lace along the drawn line. Stitch the top edge of the lace and trim the excess fabric from behind the lace (fig. 13). Stitch the miters of the scallops with a tiny zigzag and trim the excess lace away. Cut a piece of edging lace 90" long, gather the lace edging to fit the lower edge of the lace scallop. Refer to the technique "gathered lace to lace" and stitch the two laces together leaving 2" of the gathered lace not stitched at each end of the skirt piece. Stitch these after the skirt back seam is stitched so the gathered lace edging is not caught in the seam (fig.14).

14. Lay the overskirt on top of the underskirt placing the bottom edge of the lace edging just above the entredeux at the top of the ruffle and the top edges even (fig. 15). Stitch two gathering rows, through both skirt pieces treating them as one, at $1/8$" and $1/4$" on the top edge of the skirts (fig. 15). Fold the skirt in half and mark the center front, fold again to find the quarters and mark. Match the center front mark to the center front of the bodice and the quarter marks to the side seams. Pull up the gathers to fit the bottom edge of the bodice. Stitch the skirt to the bodice, right sides together (fig.16).

15. Match the back edges of the skirt treating the two skirt pieces as one and sew back together, stopping 3 $1/2$" from the neck edge for the 13" doll and 5 $1/2$" from the neck edge for the larger sizes. Do not catch the gathered lace edging in the seam and match the scallops (fig.17). When the seam is complete, place the gathered lace edging along the lower curve of the insertion lace. Fold under one side of the lace and lap over the other to create a seam in the lace edging. Zigzag this lace seam in place through the lace only and trim the excess lace from behind the seam. Zigzag the gathered lace to the curve to complete the back (fig. 18).

16. Close with Velcro™, snaps, or small buttons and buttonholes along each side of the back bodice.

17. Refer to the technique "Ribbon Rosettes" and make two rosettes. Add extra streamers underneath the rosette to hang down the front of the dress.

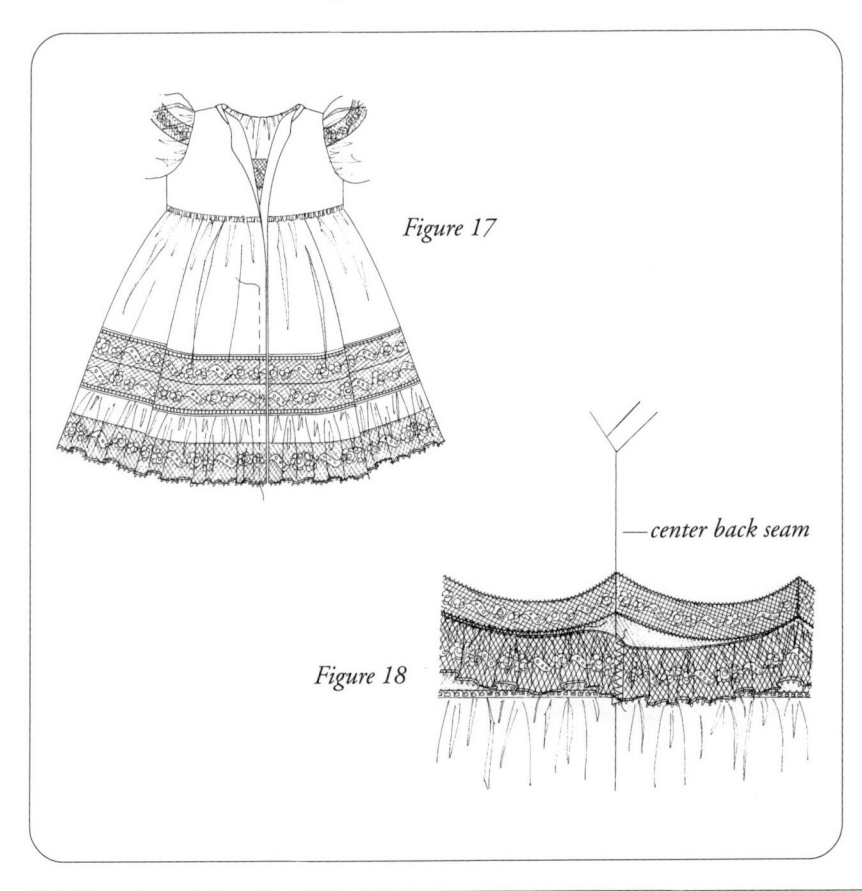

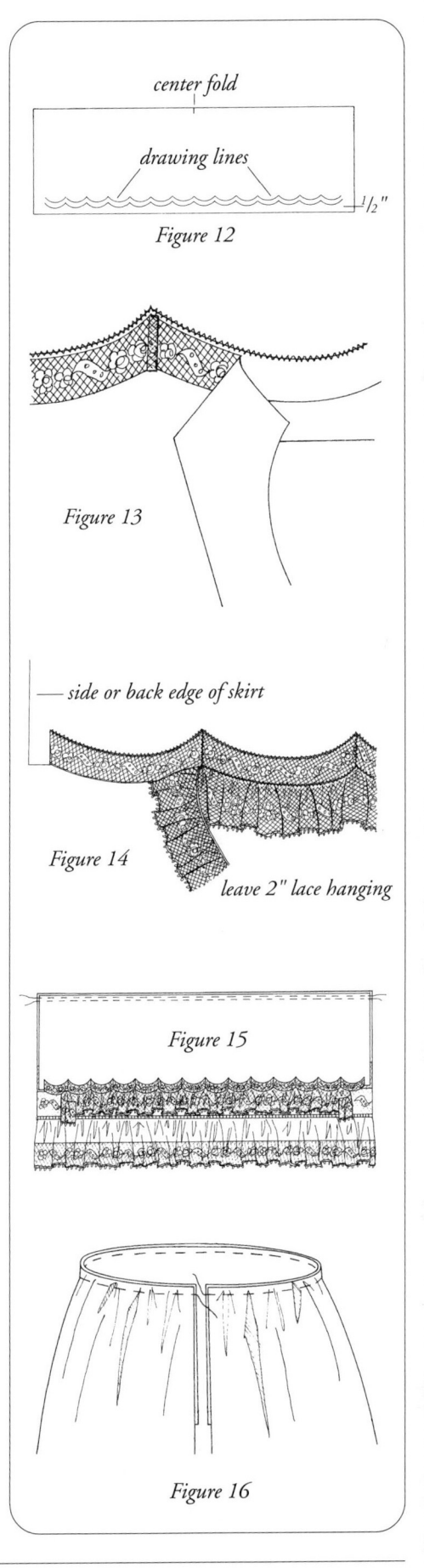

Figure 12

Figure 13

Figure 14

Figure 15

Figure 16

Figure 17

Figure 18

Dresses — Three Best Friends

Blue Batiste Dress Templates

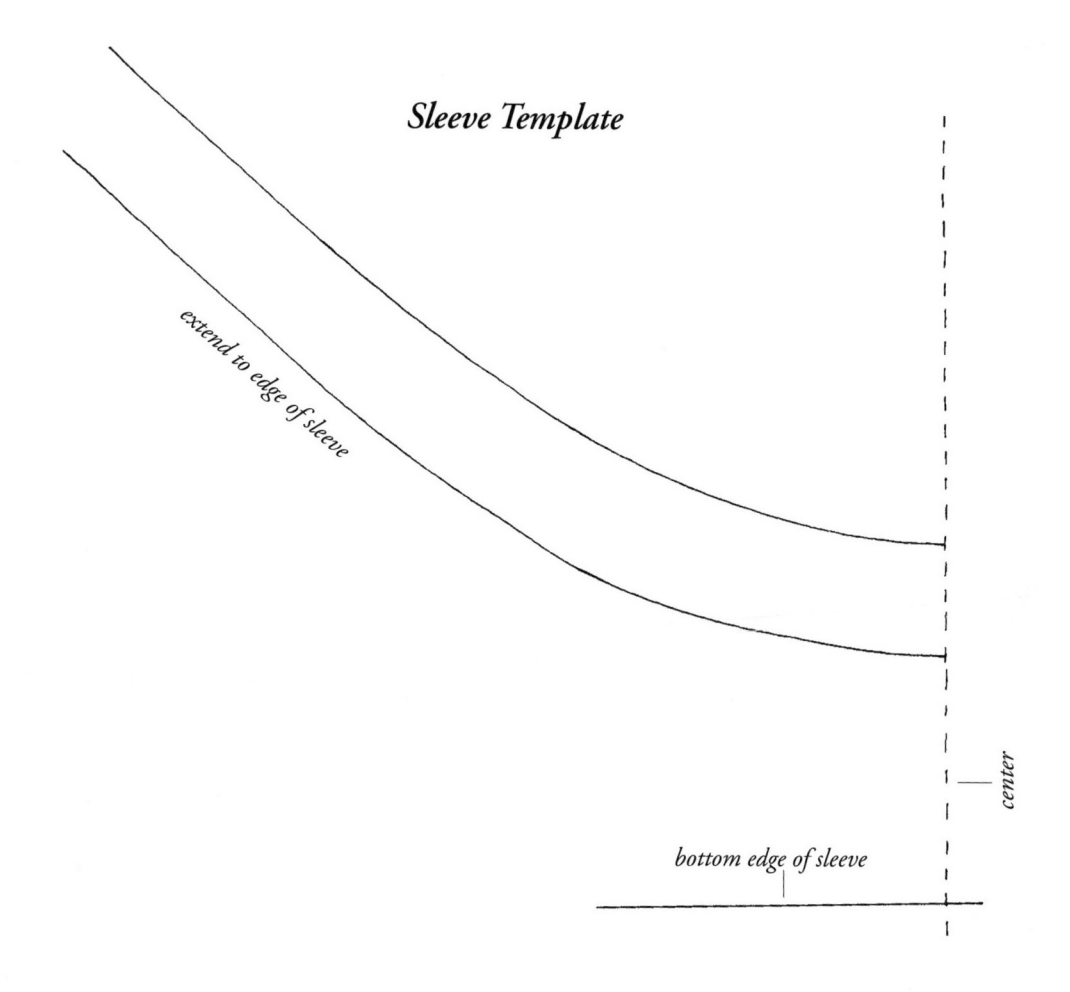

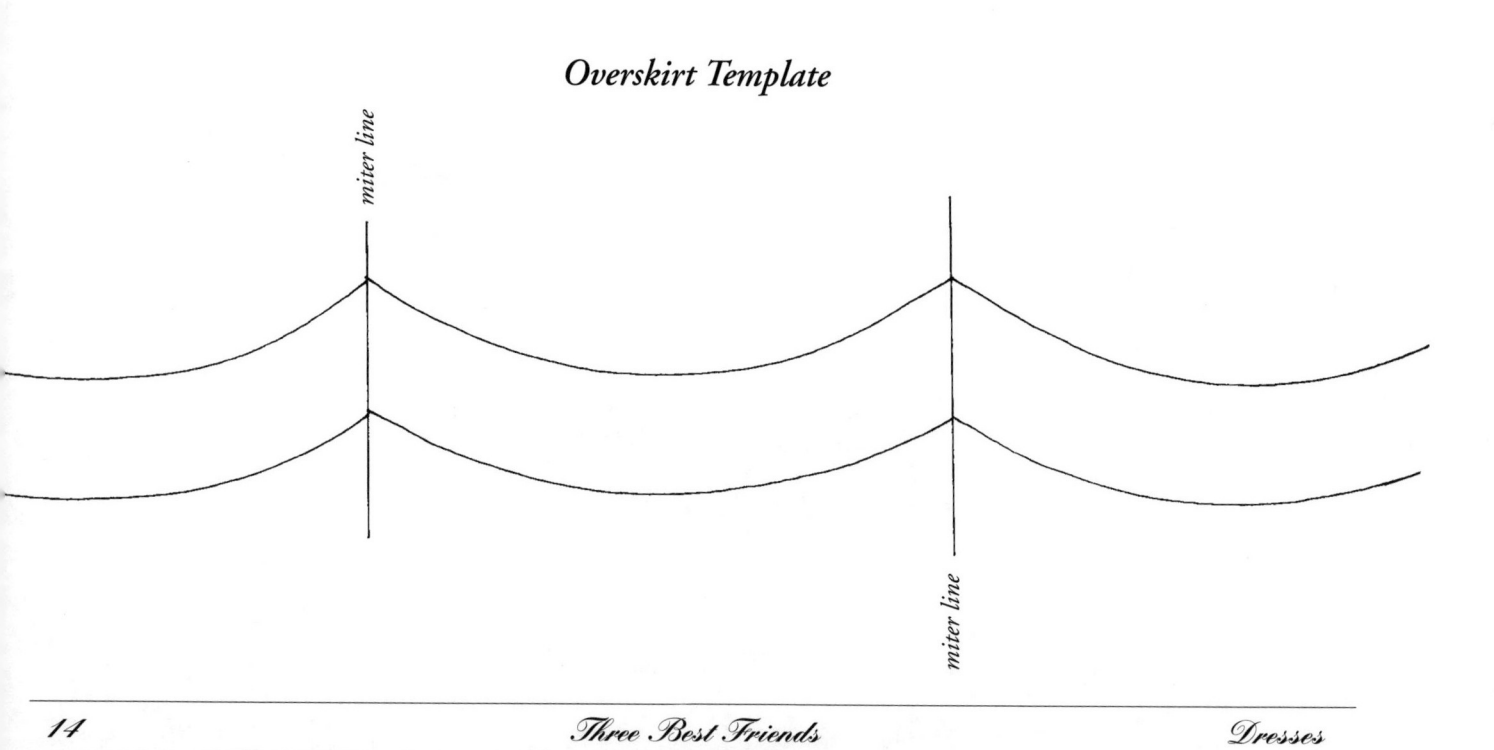

Sleeve Template

extend to edge of sleeve

center

bottom edge of sleeve

Overskirt Template

miter line

miter line

White and Ecru Dress

Ecru stitching and ecru lace on white fabric is one of the most beautiful combinations in heirloom sewing. The use of the wing needle entredeux stitch creates a beautifully decorated fabric to construct the bodice and sleeves of this dainty little dress. An intricate pattern of the entredeux stitch embellishes the skirt and adds body to the lower portion of the dress. A band of lace insertion and lace edging, applied flat, edges the hem of the skirt in a "V" pattern. A satin ribbon sash is the finishing touch to make this friend's dress a masterpiece for you to create.

Fabric Requirements

Fabric Requirements:

	13"	17 1/2", 18" and 19 1/2"
Fabric - Swiss Batiste	1/2 yd	5/8 yd
Lace Edging (3/8")	3 1/2 yds	3 3/4 yds
Lace Insertion (5/8")	2 1/2 yds	2 1/2 yds
Satin Ribbon (1 1/2")	1 yd	1 yd
Entredeux	5/8 yd	3/4 yd

Notions

Lightweight sewing thread, Wing tip needle, Velcro™, snaps or tiny buttons

Directions

All Seams 1/4" unless otherwise indicated. Finish all seams with a zigzag or serge to finish the fabric edges.

Please read through both the General Directions and the Specific Directions before starting the dress. The General Directions can be found on page 4 and give instructions for neck, sleeves and hem finishes. These Specific Directions give instructions for the special details concerning this particular dress and the sequence of the construction.

The following pattern pieces found on the pull-outs, are needed for this dress: waisted front, waisted back and elbow-length sleeve. The bodice and sleeve template and the skirt template are found on the pull-outs.

A. Preparing the Dress Pieces

1. From the Swiss batiste cut the following: two back bodices from the selvage, and one skirt piece 45" wide by the following length:
13" doll	6"
17 1/2" doll	8 1/4"
18" doll	9"
19 1/2"	9"

   One block 6" by 8" for bodice front for all sizes.
   Two blocks for the sleeves 6" by 10" for 13" doll and 8" by 12" for all others.
2. Preparing the bodice and sleeve blocks: Heavy starch or stabilizer may be used to do the wing needle entredeux stitch. Refer to the Technique on Machine Entredeux. Treat the blocks for the bodice and sleeves and the skirt pieces in the same manner.
3. With a wash-out marker, trace the grid pattern from the bodice/sleeve template lining up the edge of the fabric along the placement line onto the block for the bodice and blocks for both sleeves. You will need to reposition the grid to complete the pattern.
4. Using the appropriate settings for your machine stitch the entredeux stitch along the lines of the grid pattern.
5. Rinse away all blue marks and starch.
6. Press the blocks. Fold the bodice block in the center and cut out one front bodice on the fold (fig. 1). Fold the sleeve blocks in the center and cut out two sleeves from the sleeve blocks.
7. Finish each sleeve referring to the General Directions, B. Sleeves and Sleeves Finishes, a. Entredeux to Gathered Edging Lace.
8. Trace the design from the skirt template onto the lower edge of the skirt piece lining up the edge of the fabric with the placement line on the template (fig. 2).

White and Ecru Dress

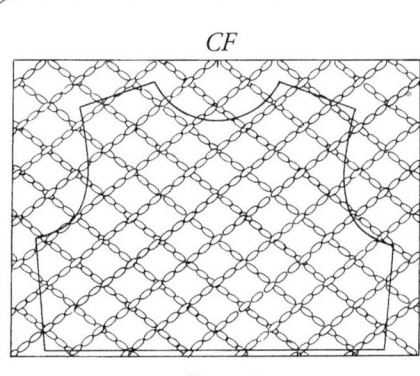

Figure 1

bottom edge of fabric

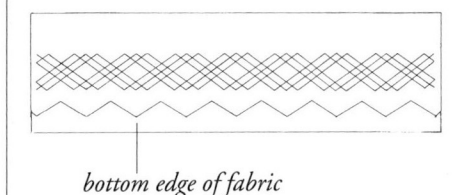

Figure 2

9. Using the same settings as for the bodice/sleeve blocks stitch the entredeux stitch along the lines of the design on the body of the skirt. Do not stitch the lower "V" edge at this time.
10. Using the technique "lace to lace" stitch 2 1/2 yards of the edging to the 2 1/2 yards of insertion.
11. Treating this strip as one lace, shape the lace along the "V" of the skirt. Refer to lace shaping technique. NOTE: the lace will be shaped below the "V" edge.
12. Attach the lace to the fabric using a pin stitch or zigzag. Trim away the excess fabric from beneath the lace (fig. 3).

Figure 3

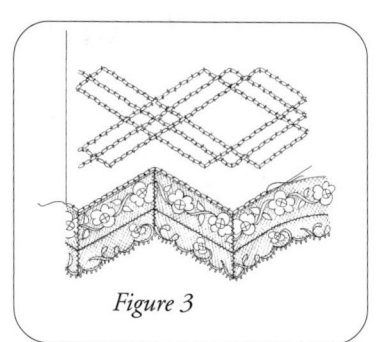

B. Constructing the Dress

1. Place the front bodice to the back bodice pieces, right sides together. Stitch the shoulder seams (fig. 4).
2. Finish the neck referring to the General Directions, C. Neck Finishes, a. Entredeux to Gathered Edging Lace.
3. Refer to the General Directions, B. Sleeves and Sleeve Finishes, h. Attaching the Sleeves and attach the sleeves to the bodice (fig. 5).
4. Cut the ribbon for the sash in half at a slant. Pleat the sash at the straight end and pin to the back bodice on each side even with the edges of the bodice side backs having the lower edge of each sash 1/4" above the bottom edge of back bodice to allow for the waist seam.
5. Place the sides of the bodice, right sides together, matching the ends of the sleeves, the underarm seams and the lower edges of the bodice. Stitch the side seams in place (fig. 6).
6. Fold the skirt in half to find the center. Mark at the top edge. Fold the skirt again to find the quarter points (fig. 7). Mark.
7. Create a placket in the skirt referring to the General Directions, A. Plackets, b. Placket in a Seam. Remember to stitch the center back seam so that the template design is continuous, any excess seam allowance can be trimmed away (fig. 8)
8. Place the back bodices to the skirt back, right sides together with the placket edges to the fold lines of the back bodices. Remember, one side of the placket will be folded to the inside of the skirt and pinned, while the other side will remain extended. Wrap each bodice back around the placket opening in the skirt. Gather the skirt to fit the bodice, matching the center of the skirt to the center front bodice and the quarter markings on the skirt with the side seams of the bodice. Stitch together (fig. 9). Flip the bodice away from the skirt (fig. 10).
9. Close the dress using Velcro™, snaps, or tiny buttons and buttonholes along each side of the back bodice.

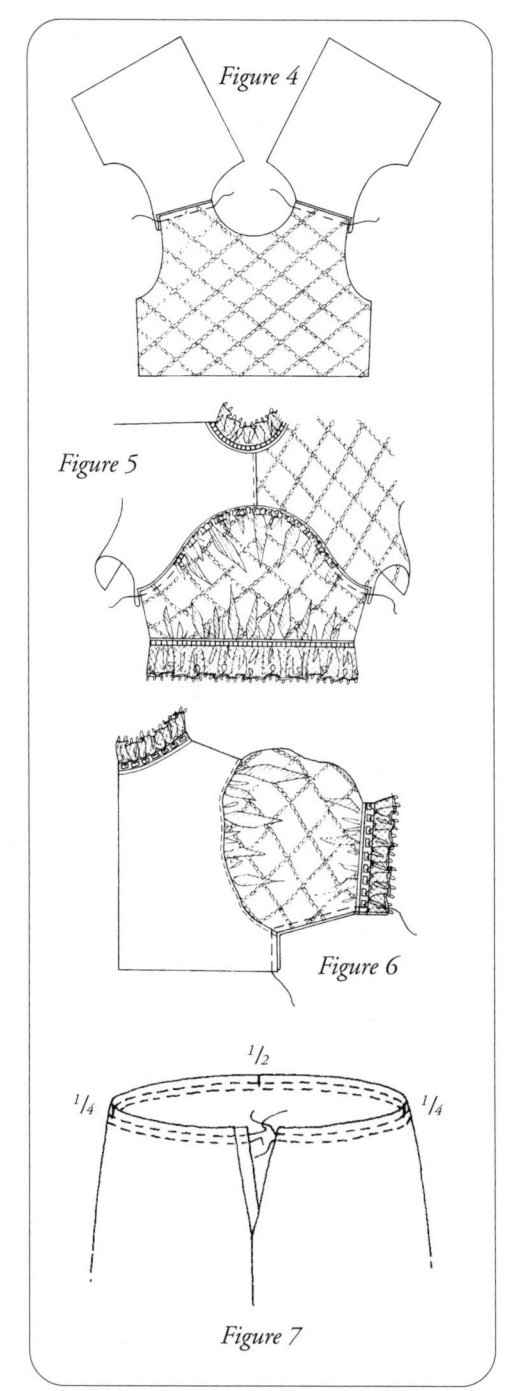

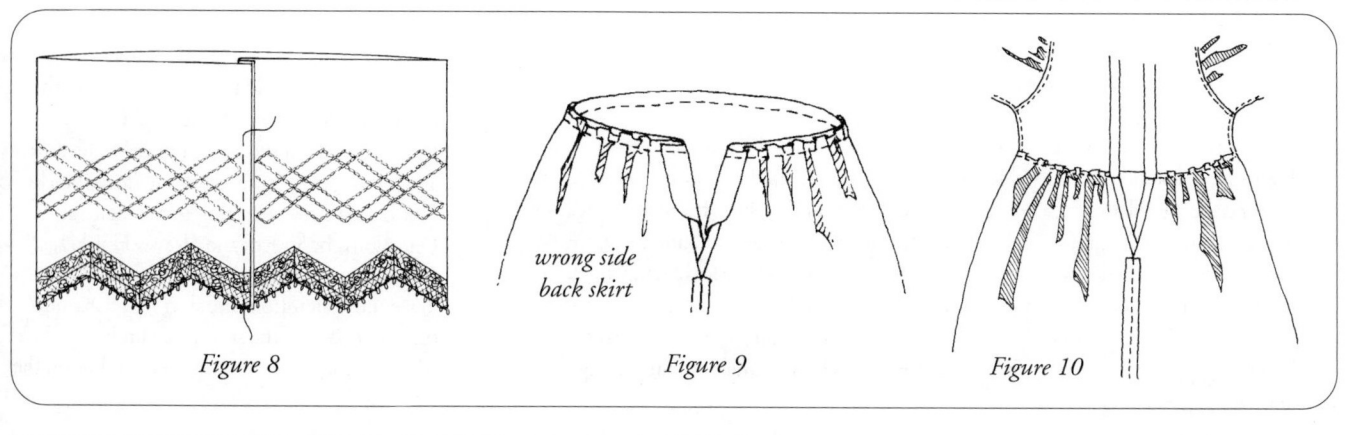

Figure 4

Figure 5

Figure 6

Figure 7

Figure 8

Figure 9

Figure 10

Three Best Friends — *Dresses*

Velvet Dress

Made of lucious purple velvet, this gorgeous dress will delight you and the friends. The neckline is finished with white entredeux, two rows of white French insertion, and edged with tiny tatting. The sleeves are finished with entredeux and tiny tatting in white. The bow on the front of the dress is made of a shiny organza ribbon and has flowers made of four lazy daisies in purple, three leaves in green, and a pearl in the center of each flower. The back of the dress is closed with snaps.

Fabric Requirements

Fabric Requirements:

	13"	17 1/2", 18" and 19 1/2"
Fabric - Velvet	1/2 yard	3/4 yard
Insertion Lace (1/2")	1 yard	1 1/4 yards
Tatted Edging Lace (1/4")	1 1/2 yards	1 3/4 yards
Entredeux	3/4 yard	1 yard
Organdy Ribbon (2")	1 yard	1 yard

Silk Ribbon (4mm) - lavendar and moss green, Small beads or small pearls

Notions

Lightweight sewing thread, paper, Velcro™, snaps or 3 or 4 tiny buttons

Directions

All Seams 1/4" unless otherwise indicated.

Please read through both the General Directions and the Specific Directions before starting the dress. The General Directions can be found on page 4 and give instructions for plackets, neck and sleeve finishes. These Specific Directions give instructions for the special details concerning this particular dress and the sequence of the construction.

The following pattern pieces needed for this dress are found on the pull-outs: waisted front, waisted back and elbow-length sleeve.

A. Cutting and Constructing the Dress

1. Cut two back bodices from the selvege, one front bodice from the fold and two elbow-length sleeves. Cut one skirt piece 45" by the following lengths:
   13" = 7 1/2"
   17 1/2" = 9 3/4"
   18" and 19 1/2" = 10 1/2"
2. Place the front bodice to the back bodice pieces, right sides together. Stitch the shoulder seams in place (fig. 1).
3. To create the collar piece, cut two pieces of lace insertion and one piece of tatted edging to the following measurement:
   13" = 16" long
   17 1/2", 18", and 19 1/2" = 18" long
4. Butt the two lace insertion pieces together and zigzag using the technique "lace to lace".
5. Butt the tatting to one edge of the lace insertion and zigzag in place using the technique "lace to lace" (fig.2).
6. Referring to the General Directions, C. Neck Finishes, a. Entredeux to Gathered Edging Lace (eliminate Step 2; Step 3. Trim away one side of the entredeux fabric. continue on with Steps 4 and 5) to finish the neck edge.
7. On the collar lace band you created in step 5, fold under 1/8" once and then again along the raw edge of each end. Stitch in place to finish the edges.
8. Pull a thread in the top edge of the collar fancy band and pull up the gathers to fit the neckline. The collar fancy band will be stitched from the fold of the facing on the right back bodice to 1/4" from the fold of the facing on the left back bodice. Place the band onto the right side of the bodice and zigzag into place catching the lace and hitting the holes of the entredeux (fig. 3).

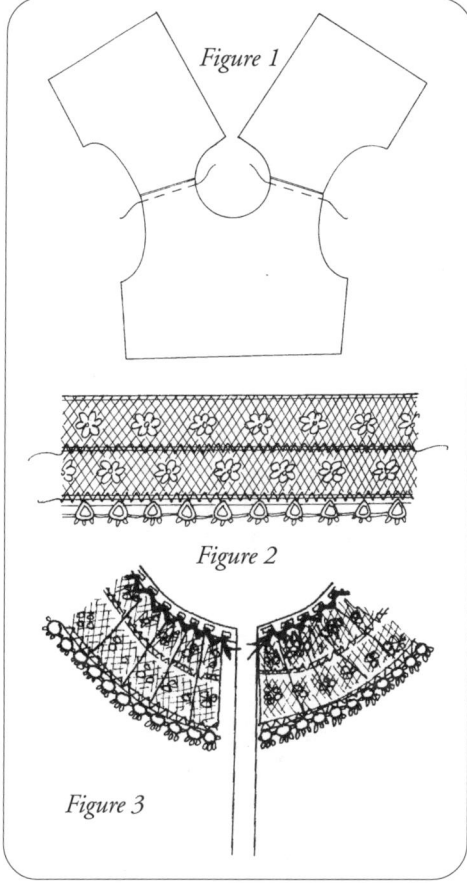

Velvet Dress

Figure 1

Figure 2

Figure 3

9. Refer to the General Directions, B. Sleeves and Sleeve Finishes (steps 2 - 3), b. Entredeux to Flat Lace to finish the sleeves.
10. Refer to the General Directions, B. Sleeves and Sleeve Finishes, h. Attaching the Sleeves to attach the sleeve.
11. Place the sides of the bodice together and stitch in place (fig. 4).
12. Fold the skirt in half to find the center. Mark at the top edge. Fold the skirt again to find the quarter points. Mark.
13. Refer back to the General Directions, A. Plackets, b. Placket in a Seam to create a placket in the skirt.
14. Place the back bodices to the skirt back, right sides together with the placket edges to the fold lines of the back bodices. Remember, one side of the placket will be folded to the inside of the skirt and pinned, while the other side will remain extended. Wrap each bodice back around the placket opening in the skirt. Gather the skirt to fit the bodice, matching the center of the skirt to the center front bodice and the quarter markings on the skirt with the side seams of the bodice. Stitch in place. Flip the bodice away from the skirt (fig. 5).
15. Serge or zigzag around the lower edge of the skirt. Turn the finished edge of the skirt to the inside of the dress 1$\frac{1}{2}$" and hem.
16. Close the dress using Velcro™, snaps, or tiny buttons and buttonholes along each side of the back bodice.

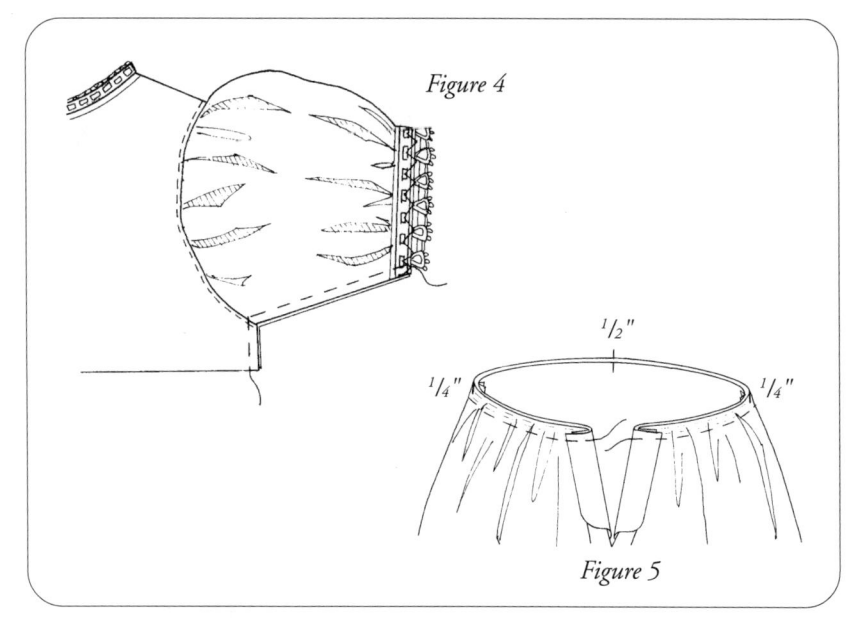

Figure 4

Figure 5

B. Creating the Bow

1. Cut two pieces of ribbon to the following measurements: 10" and 20" (fig. 6).
2. Fold each end of the 10" ribbon to the center overlapping the ends by $\frac{1}{2}$" (fig. 7). Zigzag along the center of the overlapped ribbon creating the top of the bow (fig. 8).
3. Place a line 8" from one end of the 20" ribbon. Fold each end of the ribbon to overlap the drawn line by $\frac{1}{4}$" (fig. 9). Zigzag along the line (fig. 10). This will become the "tails" of the bow.
4. Place the "bow" along the zigzaged line of the "tail" (fig. 11). Tie the "tail" around the bow to create a knot (fig. 12). Hand stitch the completed bow to the waist of the dress between the center front and the side. Stitch the ties of the bow in place with the shorter tail on top of the longer (see finished drawing).
5. Stitch three, four petal lazy daisy flowers to the top layer of each bow tail. Add Japaneese ribbon stitch leaves to each flower. Stitch a pearl or bead in each flower center (fig. 13). Refer to Embroidery Techniques.

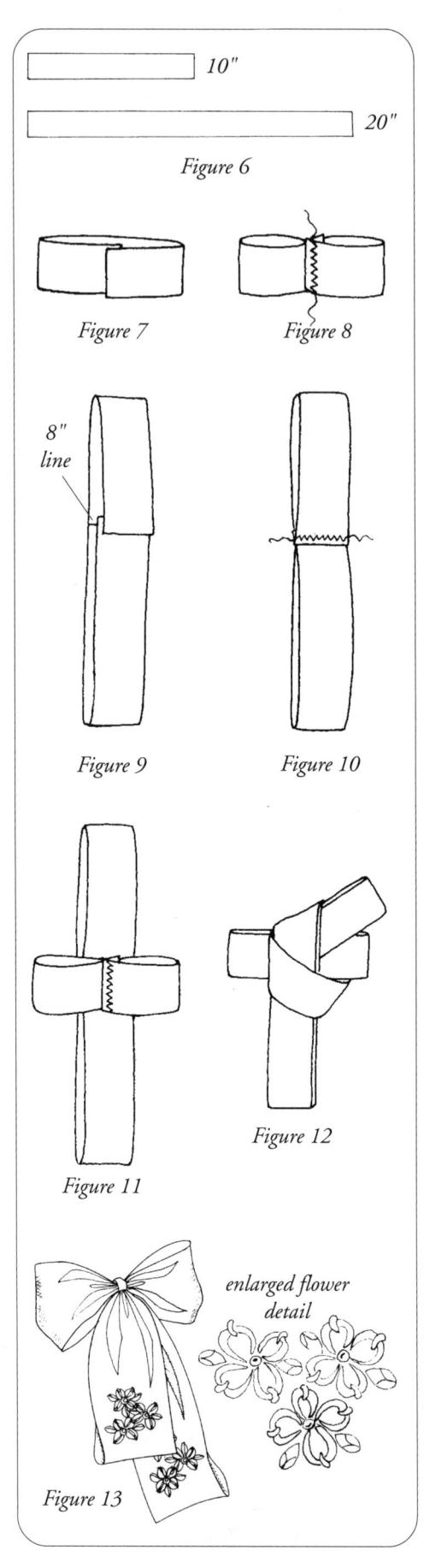

Figure 6

Figure 7 *Figure 8*

8" line

Figure 9 *Figure 10*

Figure 11 *Figure 12*

Figure 13 *enlarged flower detail*

Flip-Flop Border Dress

Flip-flopped ecru French lace perfectly trims the skirt of this spectacular dress. The fabric is red silk dupioni and with this beautiful ecru lace, this would be a beautiful Christmas dress for the friends. The neckline is finished with a bias binding and rows of French lace are found on the high yoke bodice. The very full sleeves are finished with entredeux and gathered ecru French edging. There is a piece of ecru French insertion stitched down the center of each sleeve. Ecru silk ribbon has been threaded through the entredeux on the bottom of the sleeves and tied on the top. The dress is closed with Velcro™.

Fabric Requirements

Fabric Requirements:

	13"	17 1/2", 18" and 19 1/2"
Fabric - Silk Dupioni	1/2 yard	5/8 yard
Insertion Lace (1-1/8")	3 1/2 yards	3 3/4 yards
Edging Lace (1-1/8")	1/2 yard	2/3 yard
Entredeux	1/4 yard	1/3 yard
Silk Ribbon	20"	24"

Flip-Flop Border Dress

Notions

Lightweight sewing thread, paper, Velcro™, snaps or 3 or 4 tiny buttons, wash-out marker

Directions

All Seams 1/4" unless otherwise indicated. Finish all seams with a zigzag or serge to finish the fabric edges.

Please read through both the General Directions and the Specific Directions before starting the dress. The General Directions can be found on page 4 and give instructions for neck, sleeves and hem finishes. These Specific Directions give instructions for the special details concerning this particular dress and the sequence of the construction.

The following pattern pieces needed for this dress are found on the pull-outs: high-yoke front bodice, high-yoke back bodice, armhole guide, elbow-length sleeve. The Flip-Flop lace template for the skirt can be found on the pull-outs.

A. Embellishing the Sleeves and Yoke

1. To alter the sleeve pattern to accommodate the box pleat with the "hidden" lace insertion, add 1 1/8" to the fold side of the sleeve pattern (fig. 1). Trace the new sleeve pattern on paper. Cut two sleeves from the fold using the new pattern. Mark the center of the sleeves and the original center on each layer.
2. Cut out one yoke front from the fold, two yoke back bodices from the selvage (trace the fold lines on each pattern piece) and two skirt pieces 23 1/4" wide by the following length (skirt length plus 2 1/2") :
   13" doll - 9 3/4"   17 1/2" doll - 13"
   18" doll - 13 3/4"   19 1/2" doll - 14 1/4"
3. Place a strip of lace insertion in the center of each sleeve. Stitch along each straight side of the lace using a zigzag or straight stitch (fig. 2).
4. Fold each side of the sleeve to the center, covering the lace, forming a box pleat. Press the pleat in place. Straight stitch across the top and bottom of the sleeve 1/8" from the edge to hold the pleat in place (fig. 3).
5. Measure the yoke from the highest point on the shoulder to the lower edge. Cut five pieces of lace 1/2" longer than this measurement. Butt the lace pieces together and zigzag using a small, tight stitch. These lace pieces form a rectangle.
6. Center the lace rectangle on the front yoke. Stitch the lace to the yoke 1/8" from the edge of the yoke. Trim away the excess lace (fig 4).

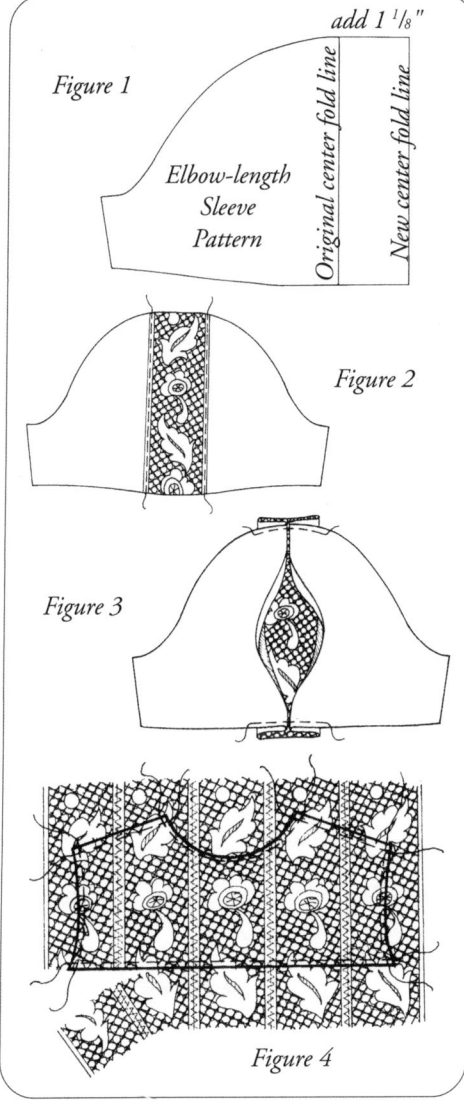

Figure 1 — add 1 1/8", Elbow-length Sleeve Pattern, Original center fold line, New center fold line

Figure 2

Figure 3

Figure 4

Dresses — Three Best Friends — 19

B. Constructing the Dress

1. Trace and cut out the armhole guide along the top, side edges of the skirt pieces.
2. Place a placket in the center of one skirt piece referring to the General Directions - A. Plackets - a. Continuous Lap Placket.
3. Run two gathering rows $1/8$" and $1/4$" in each side of the skirt back and along the skirt front (fig. 5).
4. Gather the skirt front to fit the yoke front. Place the skirt front to the yoke front, right sides together. Pin. Stitch using a $1/4$" seam (fig. 6).
5. Place the yoke backs to the skirt back, right sides together with the placket edges to the fold lines of the yoke backs. Remember, one side of the placket will be folded to the inside of the skirt and pinned, while the other side will remain extended (fig. 7). Wrap each yoke back around the placket opening in the skirt. Gather the skirt to fit the back yoke pieces (fig. 8). Stitch in place. Flip the yokes away from the skirt.
6. Stitch the front yoke to the back yoke at the shoulders.
7. Finish the neck of the dress referring to the General Directions - C. Neck Finishes - c. Bias Binding.
8. Finish the ends of the sleeves with entredeux and gathered edging lace. Refer to the General Directions - B. Sleeves and Sleeves Finishes (step 1 - 3) - a. Entredeux to Gathered Edging Lace.
9. Place the sleeves to the arm openings, right sides together, matching the center of each sleeve to the shoulder seam of the bodice. Gather the sleeves to fit the openings. Stitch in place.
10. Place the sides of the dress, right sides together, matching the ends of the sleeves, the underarm seams and the lower edges of the skirt. Stitch the side seams in place (fig. 9).
11. Cut the silk ribbon into 2 equal pieces. Thread the ribbon into a large tapestry needle and run through the holes of the beading, beginning and ending opposite the underarm seam. Tie the ends into a bow.
12. Turn the lower edge of the skirt to the inside $2^{1}/_{2}$". Press.
13. Trace the skirt template onto the skirt with the top of the template $2^{1}/_{4}$" from the fold of the hem. Shape the lace insertion along the template lines referring to Flip-Flop Lace (pg. 111). Pin the lace in place through the skirt and the hem (fig. 10).
14. Zigzag the lace in place along each side of the lace insertion. Trim the excess fabric from the hem close to the upper stitching (fig. 11).
15. Close the dress using Velcro™, snaps, or tiny buttons and buttonholes along each side of the back bodice.

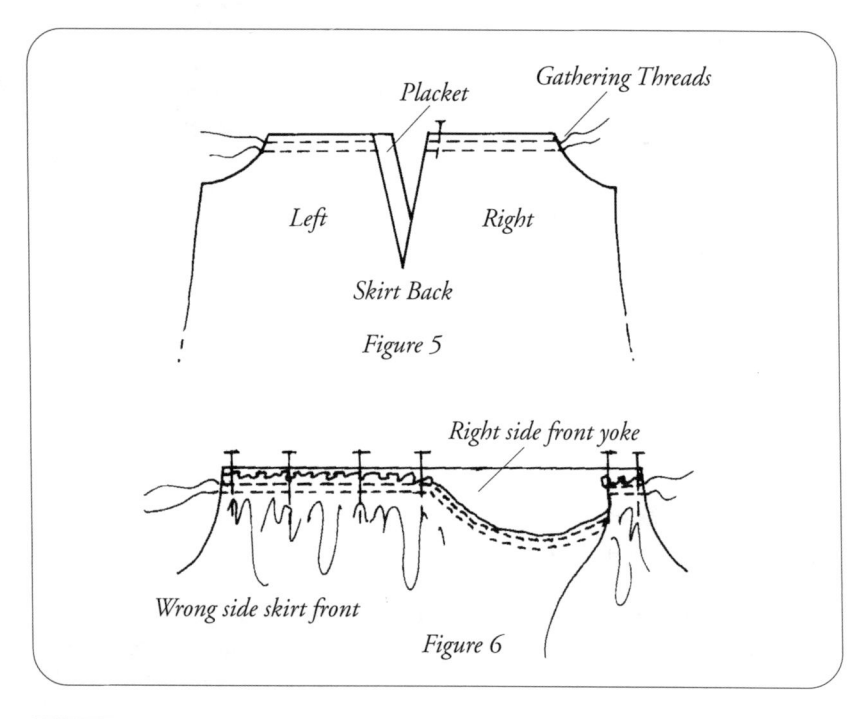

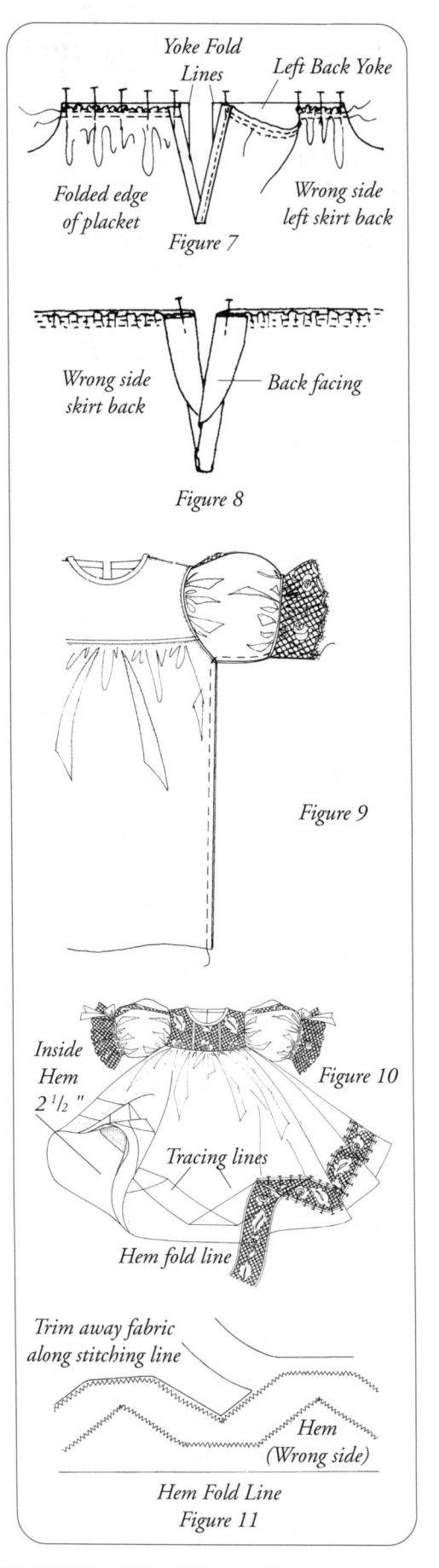

Figure 5

Figure 6

Figure 7

Figure 8

Figure 9

Figure 10

Figure 11

Two Tone Pink Scalloped Dress

If you have ever shaped scallops, you know they are so easy and fun to do. If you never have, this is the perfect dress to get you hooked on this technique. The use of two different shades of pink fabric in the scallops is so creative. The shaped insertion on the bodice with the wide edging attached creates a mock collar. Just tie a pretty pink ribbon in your friend's hair and she will be ready for that special party or social function.

Fabric Requirements

Fabric Requirements:

	13"	17 1/2", 18" and 19 1/2"
Fabric - Swiss Batiste White	5/8 yard	3/4 yard
Light Pink	1/8 yard	1/8 yard
Darker Pink	1/8 yard	1/8 yard
Lace Edging (1 1/2")	3/4 yard	1 yard
Lace Edging (3/4")	4 1/4 yard	4 1/4 yards
Lace Insertion (1/2")	6 1/8 yards	6 1/8 yards
Entredeux	1/2 yard	5/8 yard

Two Tone Pink Scalloped Dress

Notions

Lightweight sewing thread, tiny piping, wing needle, Velcro™, snaps or tiny buttons

Directions

All Seams 1/4" unless otherwise indicated. Finish all seams with a zigzag or serge to finish the fabric edges.

Please read through both the General Directions and the Specific Directions before starting the dress. The General Directions can be found on page 4 and give instructions for neck, sleeves and hem finishes. These Specific Directions give instructions for the special details concerning this particular dress and the sequence of the construction.

The following pattern pieces needed for this dress are found on the pull-outs: waisted front bodice, waisted back bodice, and elbow-length sleeve. The scallop template for the skirt can also be found on the pull-outs.

A. Preparing the Dress Pieces

1. From the white Swiss batiste cut the following: one front bodice from the fold, two back bodices from the selvage, two sleeves, a bias strip 15" long by 1 1/2" wide and one skirt piece 45" wide by the following length:

13" doll	6"
17 1/2" doll	8 1/4"
18" doll	9"
19 1/2"	9"

2. From dark pink batiste 3 1/2" by 45".
3. From light pink batiste 3 1/2" by 45".

B. Making Scalloped Skirt

1. Trace the scallop template on the bottom edge of the dark pink batiste having the dip of the scallop fall 1/2" above the bottom edge starting with a point in the center front (fig. 1). Refer to the techniques for shaping lace scallops.

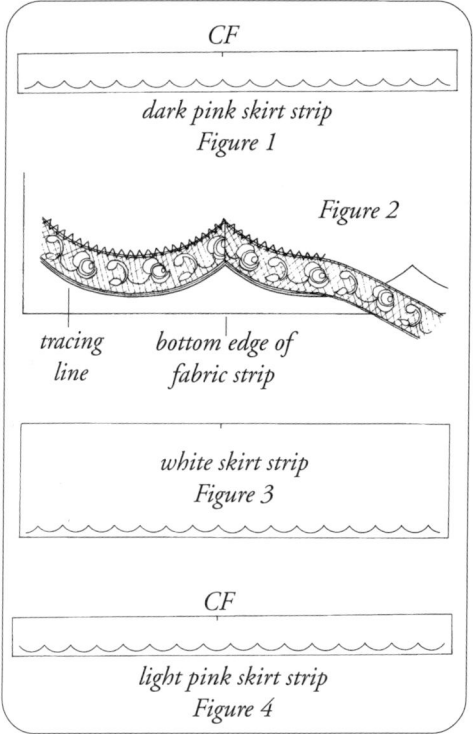

dark pink skirt strip
Figure 1

Figure 2
tracing line *bottom edge of fabric strip*

white skirt strip
Figure 3

light pink skirt strip
Figure 4

2. Shape the lace using the lace shaping techniques, using the scallop line as a guide for the lower edge of the lace.
3. Stitch the upper edge of the lace insertion to the fabric. Trim the excess fabric from behind the lace (fig 2). Zigzag the miters and trim away the excess lace.
4. Follow steps 1-3 with the white batiste (fig. 3).
5. Follow steps 1-3 with the lighter pink fabric with the following exception that the scallop will be started in the center front in the middle of a scallop (fig. 4).

Figure 5

Figure 6

Figure 7

Figure 8

Figure 9

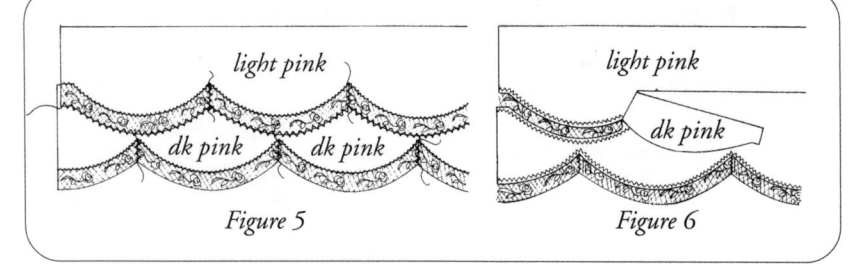

6. The skirt pieces are then put together. Pin the light pink scalloped strip to the dark pink scalloped strip starting in the center front with the bottom of the scallop of the light pink at the point of the scallop in the dark pink.
7. Zigzag the bottom edge of the lace scallop of the light pink to the dark pink fabric (fig. 5). Trim the dark pink from behind the lace (fig. 6).
8. The pink scallops will then be attached to the bottom of the white scalloped strip. Pin together starting in the center front with the point of the white scallop over the center of a scallop in the light pink and a point in the scallop of the dark pink.
9. Stitch the bottom edge of the lace scallop on the white to the light pink fabric (fig. 7). Trim the light pink fabric from behind the lace (fig. 8).
10. Refer to the General Direction, A. Placket, b. Placket in a Seam and close the back of the skirt matching the scallops at the center back (fig. 9).
11. Pull a thread in the lace heading and gather 2 ½ yards of the ¾" lace edging to fit the bottom edge of the skirt and attach to the bottom of the skirt using the technique "lace to lace" (fig. 9).
12. Measure the finished length of skirt and cut away any excess fabric from the top edge so the skirt is the following measurements:
   13"   6"
   17 ½   8 ¼"
   18" & 19 ½"   9"

C. Constructing the Dress

1. Place the front bodice to the back bodice pieces, right sides together. Stitch the shoulder seams (fig. 10).
2. Lay front and back bodice out flat and place small marks ⅝" from neck edge all around the neck starting and ending at the selvages (fig. 11).
3. Shape the lace insertion around the neck using the small marks as a guide for the top edge of the lace. Refer to lace shaping techniques. NOTE: You may wish to draw another line ½" (width of the insertions) from the dots to give you a lower line for shaping.
4. Stitch the top edge of the lace to the bodice using a small zigzag stitch. Secure the bottom edge of lace with a small zigzag.
5. Gather the 1½" edging to fit the bottom edge of the lace insertion. Sew the gathered

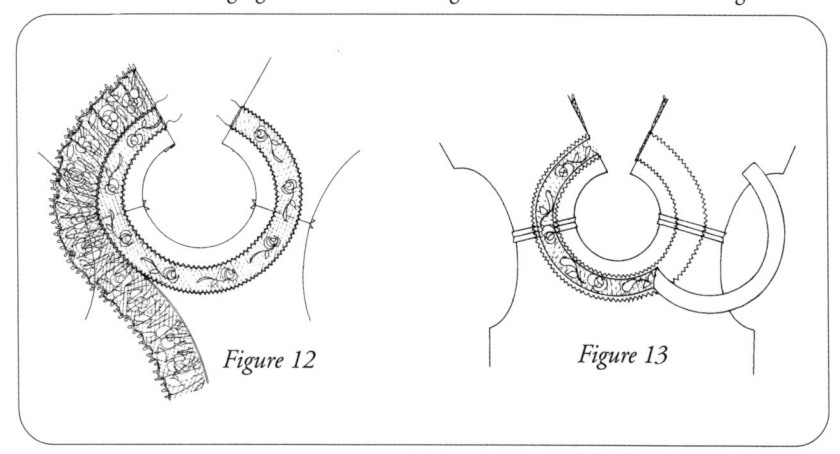

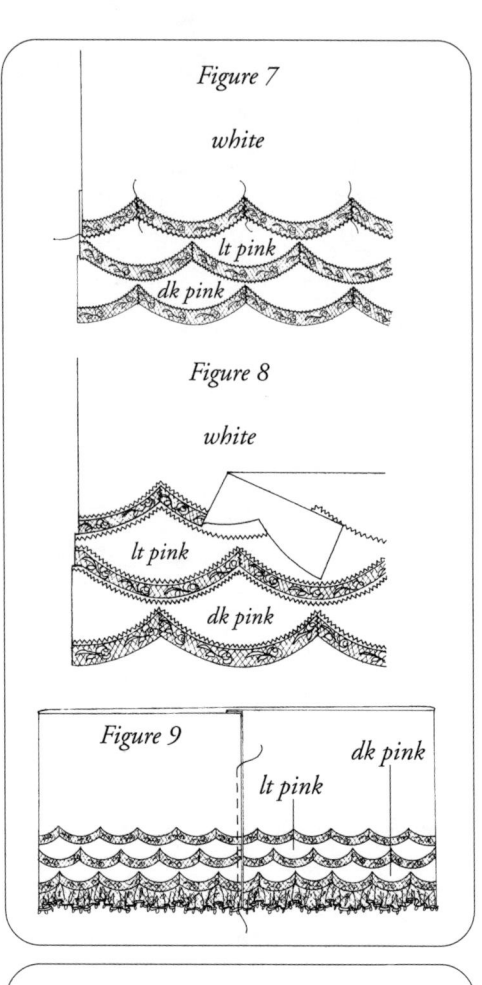

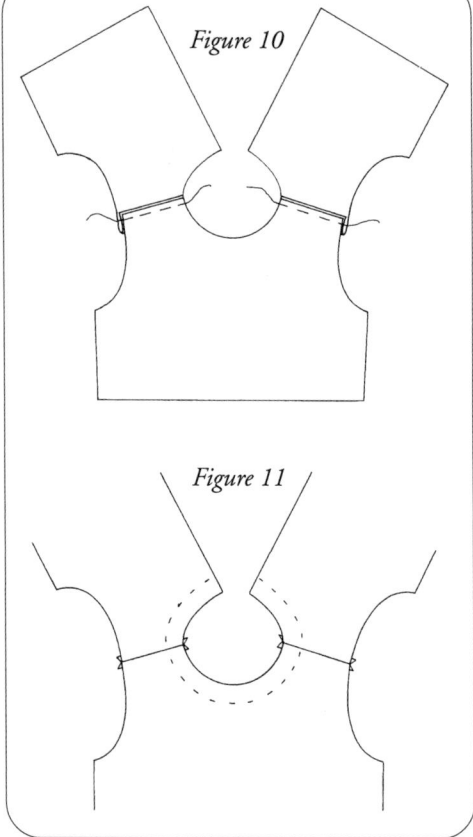

Figure 10

Figure 11

Figure 12

Figure 13

Three Best Friends — *Dresses*

lace edging to the lace insertion using a small zigzag or a entredeux stitch and a wing needle (fig. 12). Trim the fabric from behind the insertion lace (fig. 13)

6. Turn under the back facings and press.
7. Finish the neck referring to the General Directions, C. Neck Finishes, a. Entredeux to Gathered Edging Lace.
8. Refer to the General Directions, B. Sleeves and Sleeves Finishes, a. Entredeux to Gathered Edging Lace and finish bottom of sleeves.
9. Refer to the General Directions, B. Sleeves and Sleeves Finishes, h. Attaching the Sleeves and attach the sleeves to the dress (fig. 14).
10. Place the sides of the bodice, right sides together, matching the ends of the sleeves, the underarm seams and the lower edges of the bodice. Stitch the side seams in place (fig. 15).
11. Place a piece of small cord in the center of the bias strip and fold the strip in half enclosing the cord.
12. Using a pintuck foot (or any foot with a small groove in the bottom) place the covered cord in the groove of the foot. A zipper foot can also be used. Stitch close to the cord creating piping. Trim the seam allowance of the piping to $1/4$" (fig. 16).
13. Place the piping along the lower edge of the bodice (back folds extended) with raw edges even and stitch in place along the seam line. Trim the piping even with the back edge of the bodice. Using tweezers pull and cut about 1" of the cord from each side of the piping at the back edges of the bodice. This will eliminate bulk (fig. 17).
14. Fold the skirt in half to find the center. Mark at the top edge. Fold the skirt again to find the quarter points. Mark.
15. Place the back bodices to the skirt back, right sides together with the placket edges to the fold lines of the back bodices. Remember, one side of the placket will be folded to the inside of the skirt and pinned, while the other side will remain extended. Wrap each bodice back around the placket opening in the skirt. Gather the skirt to fit the bodice, matching the center of the skirt to the center front bodice and the quarter markings on the skirt with the side seams of the bodice. With the bodice on top, stitch the bodice to the skirt just inside the piping stitching line (fig. 18).
16. Flip the bodice away from the skirt, folding the back facings to the inside of the bodice.
17. Close the dress using Velcro™, snaps, or tiny buttons and buttonholes along each side of the back bodice.

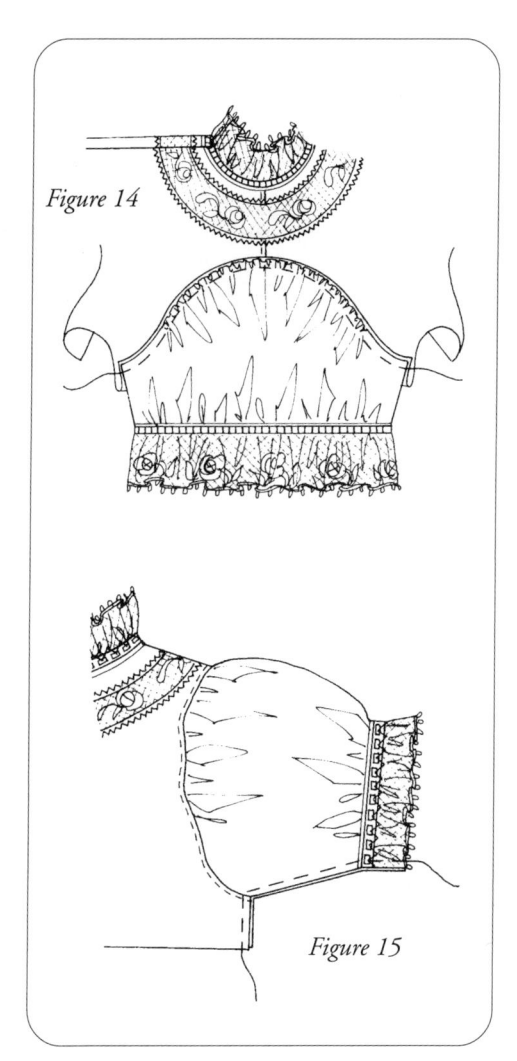

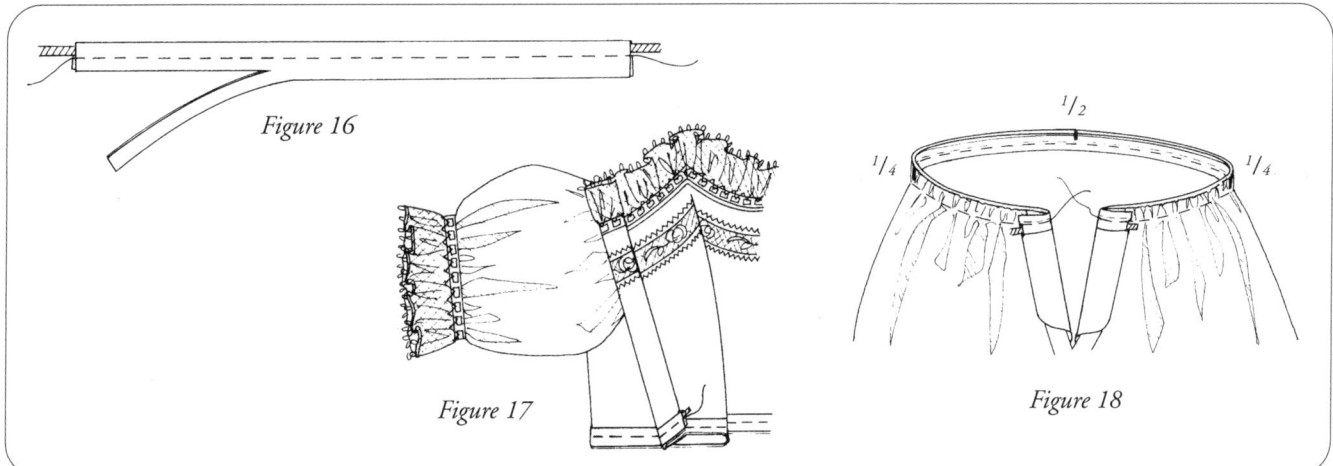

Figure 14

Figure 15

Figure 16

Figure 17

Figure 18

Fancy Collar Bib Dress

Our Three Best Friends love antique laces, especially when used on a delicate white Swiss batiste dress. The collar is scrumptious with its three rows of antique ecru laces with entredeux on each side. The collar ties at the sides to give the appearance of a collar bib. Entredeux and gathered antique ecru laces finish the outside of the collar and the neckline has an entredeux and gathered lace edging finish. The dress has a slightly lowered high yoke which comes under the armholes a little. The sleeves have the same three rows of antique lace insertion with entredeux on each side in the middle of the white batiste. The bottom of each sleeve is finished with entredeux and gathered French antique edging on the bottom. The fancy band has three rows of antique French ecru insertion with entredeux at the top and bottom. Gathered French antique edging is found at the bottom of the dress. The dress closes in the back with snaps; however, buttons have been sewn on the top so it appears to be closed with buttons.

Fancy Collar Bib Dress

Figure 1

Figure 2

Figure 3

Fabric Requirements

Fabric Requirements:

	13"	17½", 18 and 19½"
Fabric - Swiss Batiste	½ yard	⅝ yard
Insertion Lace A (¾")	4 yards	4 yards
Insertion Lace B (¾")	2 yards	2 yards
Edging Lace (1⅛")	8½ yards	8½ yards
Edging Lace (¾")	½ yard	½ yard
Entredeux	6 yards	6 yards
Silk Ribbon (2mm)	4 yards	4 yards

Notions

Lightweight sewing thread, Velcro™, snaps or tiny buttons(3), wash-out marker

Directions

All Seams ¼" unless otherwise indicated. Finish all seams with a zigzag or serge to finish the fabric edges.

Please read through both the General Directions and the Specific Directions before starting the dress. The General Directions can be found on page 4 and give instructions for neck, sleeves and hem finishes. These Specific Directions give instructions for the special details concerning this particular dress and the sequence of the construction.

The following pattern pieces needed for this dress are found on the pull-outs: mid-yoke front, mid-yoke back, square collar front, square collar back, elbow-length sleeve.

A. Creating the Lace Embellishment

1. Cut two pieces of entredeux, two pieces of lace insertion "A" and one piece of lace insertion "B" to 72".
2. Butt lace insertion "A" to each side of lace insertion "B" and zigzag in place using the technique "lace to lace".
3. Trim one fabric edge of the entredeux and attach to each side of the created lace band using the technique "entredeux to lace". This lace band will be used to embellish the collar bib, the sleeves and the skirt (fig. 1).
4. Cut 45" from the lace band and set aside for the skirt. The fabric edges of the entredeux will remain on this strip.
5. Trim both fabric edges from the **remaining** lace band. This will be used for the collar and the sleeves (fig. 2).

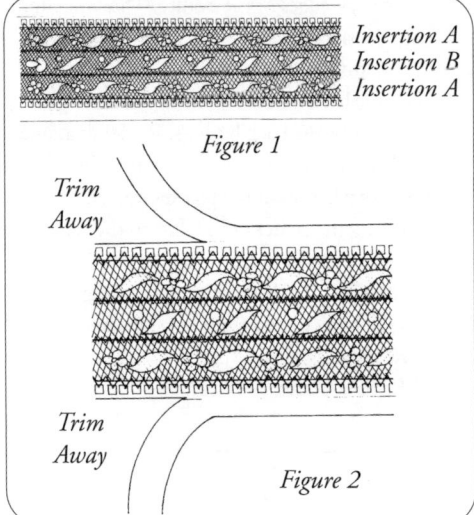

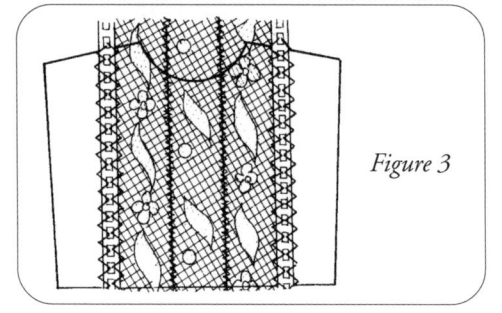

B. Embellishing the Collar and the Sleeves

1. Cut two sleeves, one collar front on the fold and two collar backs on the selvage.
2. Place the trimmed lace band to the center of the collar front with the lower edge of the band to the lower edge of the collar. Using an open zigzag, stitch along the outer edge of the entredeux ladder on each side of the lace band. Trace the outline of the neck and shoulder edges on the lace band (fig. 3).

Cut the fabric behind the lace band at the center front of the collar. Fold each side of the fabric to the stitching. Restitch the edge of the entredeux along each side of the lace band using a small, tight zigzag. Trim the excess fabric close to the stitching (fig. 4). This technique is much like "Extra-Stable Lace Finish" found on page 118.

3. Straight stitch just inside the drawn lines of the neck and shoulders. Cut the excess lace band from the collar along the drawn lines (fig. 5).
4. Place the trimmed lace band to the center of each sleeve piece. Stitch the band to the sleeves in the same manner (step 2 - 3).
5. Place the collar front to the collar backs, right sides together. Stitch and finish the seams (fig. 6).
6. Stitch the entredeux to the lower front collar edge and two lower back collar edges using the technique "entredeux to fabric". Press the entredeux away from the collar. Place entredeux to the sides of the collar using the technique "entredeux to fabric". Press the entredeux away from the sides of the collar (fig. 7).
7. Trim the fabric edge from the entredeux. Trim the excess entredeux at the corners of the collar to form a nice corner.
8. Measure around the edges of the collar. Cut a piece of wide edging lace two and one half times the length of the measurement. Gather the edging to fit the collar. Butt the edging to the entredeux and zigzag in place using the technique "gathered lace to entredeux". Set aside.
9. Finish each sleeve referring to the General Directions - B. Sleeves and Sleeves Finishes (steps 1 - 3) - a. Entredeux to Gathered Edging Lace.

C. Constructing the Dress

1. Cut one front bodice from the fold, cut two bodice backs from the selvage, and one skirt 45" wide by the following lengths: 13" doll = 3"; 17 $\frac{1}{2}$" doll = 6 $\frac{1}{4}$"; 18 and 19$\frac{1}{2}$" dolls = 7 $\frac{1}{4}$.
2. Place the front bodice to the back bodices at the shoulders, right sides together and stitch in place.
3. Place the sleeves to the arm openings, right sides together, matching the center of each sleeve to the shoulder seam of the bodice. Gather the sleeves to fit the openings with the gathers falling $\frac{3}{4}$" to 1$\frac{1}{2}$" on each side of the shoulder seam. Stitch in place (fig. 8).
4. Place the wrong side of the collar to the right side of the bodice. Fold the right collar back to the inside of the collar to match the fold line of the right bodice. Fold the left collar back with the fold of the collar $\frac{1}{4}$" from the fold line of the bodice. Pin the folded edges in place, remove the collar from the bodice and press the folds. Hand stitch or machine stitch the folds of the collar in place along the entredeux. Fold the cut edges of the edging lace under twice and stitch in place by hand or machine (fig. 9).
5. Place the wrong side of the collar to the right side of the bodice. Pin in place and treat the collar and the bodice as one layer. Finish the neck of the dress using the $\frac{3}{8}$" edging lace and referring to the General Directions - C. Neck Finishes - a. Entredeux to Gathered Edging Lace.

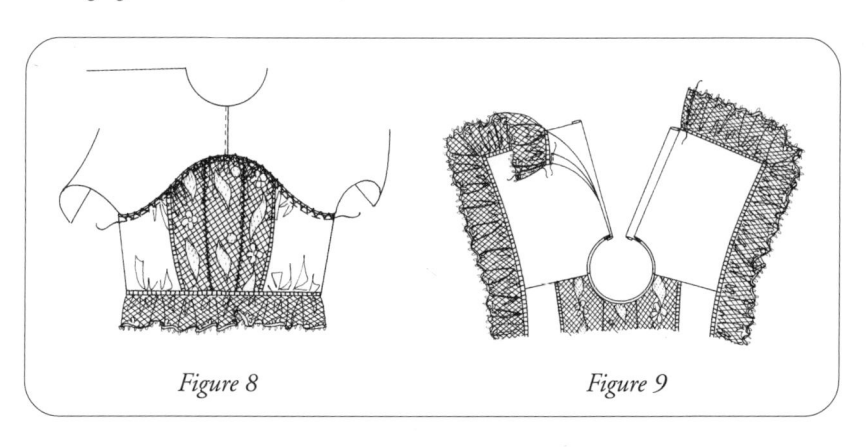

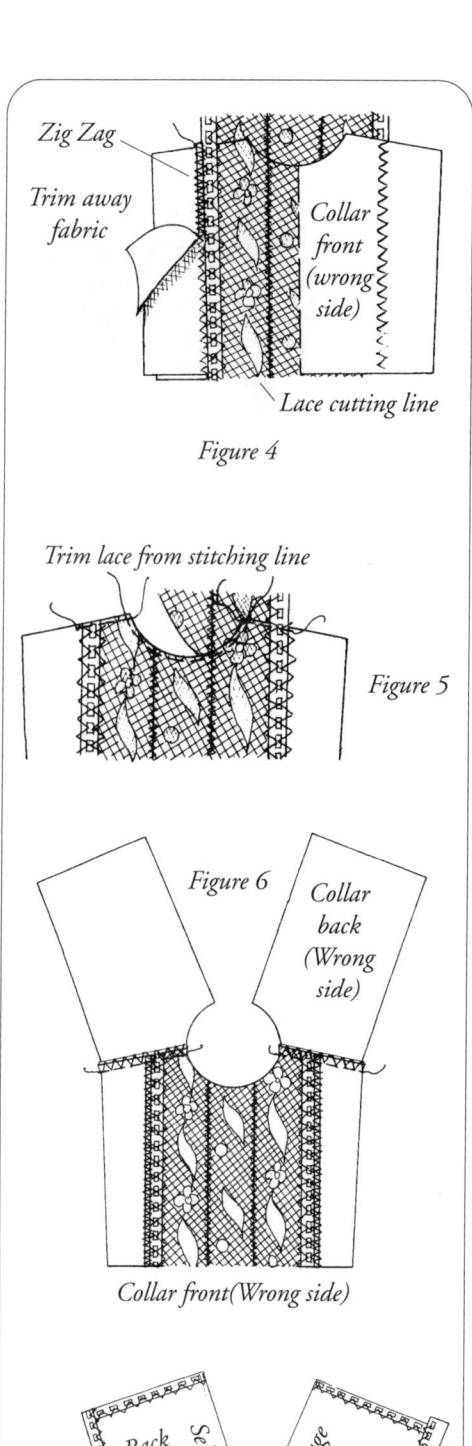

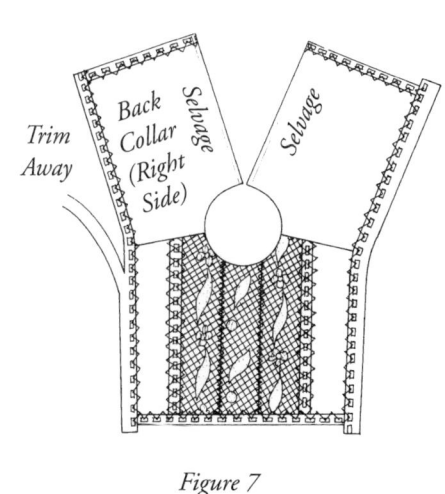

Figure 4

Figure 5

Figure 6

Figure 7

Figure 8

Figure 9

Figure 10

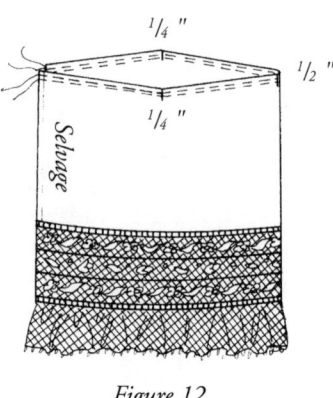

Figure 11 Trim away entredeux

Figure 12

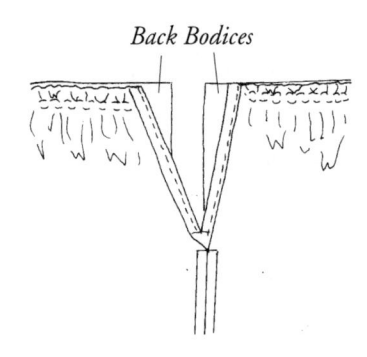

Figure 13 Back Bodices

Figure 14 Wrap back bodices around skirt

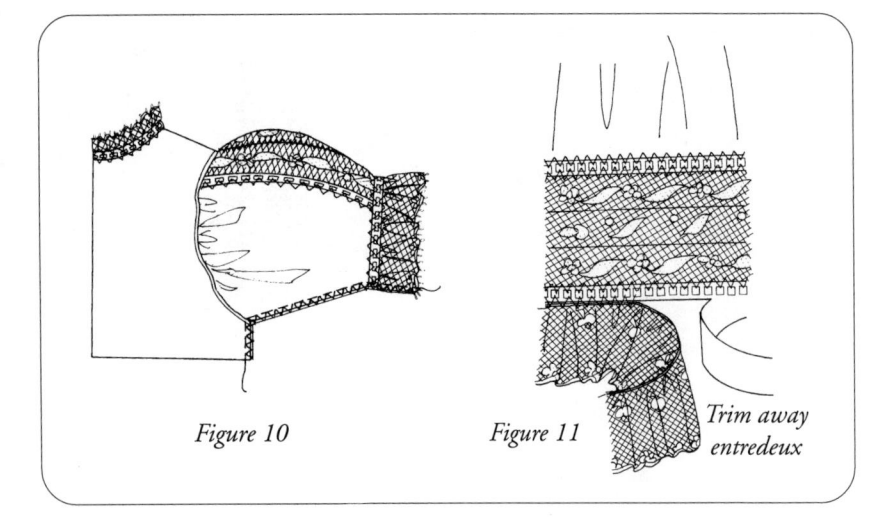

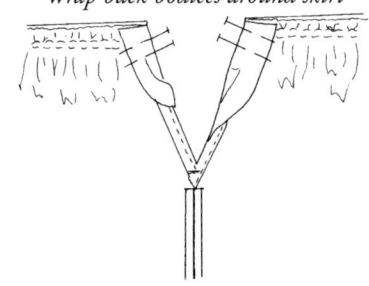

6. Place the sides of the bodice, right sides together, matching the ends of the sleeves, the underarm seams and the lower edges of the bodice. Stitch the side seams in place (fig. 10).
7. Attach the fabric skirt piece to the lace band constructed in section A. Creating the Lace Embellishment - step 4, using the technique "entredeux to fabric".
8. Trim the fabric edge from the lower edge of the entredeux on the lace band. Gather the remaining wide edging lace to fit the lower edge of the lace band. Butt the gathered lace to the entredeux and zigzag using the technique "gathered lace to entredeux" (fig. 11). Fold the skirt in half to find the center. Mark at the top edge. Fold the skirt again to find the quarter points. Mark. (fig. 12)
9. Create a placket in the skirt referring to the General Directions - A. Plackets - b. Placket in a Seam.
10. Place the back bodices to the skirt back, right sides together with the placket edges to the fold lines of the back bodices (fig. 13). Remember, one side of the placket will be folded to the inside of the skirt and pinned, while the other side will remain extended. Gather the skirt to fit the bodice, matching the center of the skirt to the center front bodice and the quarter markings on the skirt with the side seams of the bodice. Wrap each bodice back around the placket opening in the skirt (fig. 14). Stitch in place. Flip the bodice away from the skirt.
11. Close the dress using Velcro™, snaps, or tiny buttons and buttonholes along each side of the back bodice.
12. Use 2 yards of ribbon to create a ribbon rosette. Place dots on the ribbon 1¼" apart beginning and ending 8" from the ends of the ribbon. Tack the ribbon rosette to one side of the collar.
13. Cut the remining ribbon into four equal pieces. Hand stitch each ribbon piece to the corners of the underside of the collar. Tie together under the sleeve.

Mardi Gras Dress

In New Orleans, Mardi Gras is for very special costumes for dolls, children and grown ups alike. The underdress is peach silk dupioni. The trims are handmade tatting and there is English cotton netting used over and under nearly every area of this dress. The large round collar is made of peach silk dupioni with a scrunched white netting on the top. A shiny white trim goes around this collar, and it is edged with hand made tatting. Little pre-made white and green ribbon flowers are dotted all over the collar, both in the front and in the back. The sleeves are of peach silk dupioni with gathered netting on top; white faggoting finishes the bottom of the sleeves and they have a netting ruffle finished with white hand made tatting. There are three skirts on this dress. The top and shortest skirt is of white netting; it has circles of white netting trimmed with tatting and finished with a white and green flower in the center. The next skirt is of peach silk dupioni and it has wide hand tatted insertion with tatted edging on the bottom. The underskirt, which is the longest, is of English netting with white hand made tatting on the bottom. The dress is closed with Velcro™.

Fabric Requirements

Fabric Requirements:

	13"	17 1/2", 18" and 19 1/2"
Fabric - Silk Dupioni	1/2 yard	5/8 yard
English Netting	1 1/4 yards	2 yards
Tatting edging (1")	3/4 yard	1 yard
Tatting edging (5/8")	6 1/4 yard	6 1/2 yard
Tatting beading (3/4")	1 1/3 yard	1 1/3 yard
Victorian Fagotting	1/3 yard	1/3 yard
Roses on a ribbon	1 1/4 yard	1 1/2 yard
Trim for collar	3/4 yard	1 yard

Notions

Sewing thread, hand sewing needle Velcro™, snaps or tiny buttons

Directions

All Seams 1/4" unless otherwise indicated. Finish all seams with a zigzag or serge to finish the fabric edges.

Please read through both the General Directions and the Specific Directions before starting the dress. The General Directions can be found on page 4 and give instructions for plackets, neck, and sleeve finishes. These Specific Directions give instructions for the special details concerning this particular dress and the sequence of the construction.

The following pattern pieces needed for this dress are found on the pull-outs: waisted front bodice, waisted back bodice, elbow-length sleeve and round collar.

A. Constructing the Dress

1. Cut the following pieces from the netting: one waisted front bodice on the fold, two waisted bodice backs and the following pieces:

	13"	17 1/2"	18"	19 1/2"
Top Skirt 45" by	8"	12 1/2"	14"	14"
Bottom Skirt 45" by	11"	15 1/2"	17"	17"
Collar Block	7" by 18"	8" by 20"	8" by 24"	8 1/2" by 26"
2 Sleeve Blocks	5 1/2" by 20"	7" by 22"	7" by 24"	8" by 24"
Strip 1 1/2" wide to Total	65"	65"	70"	70"

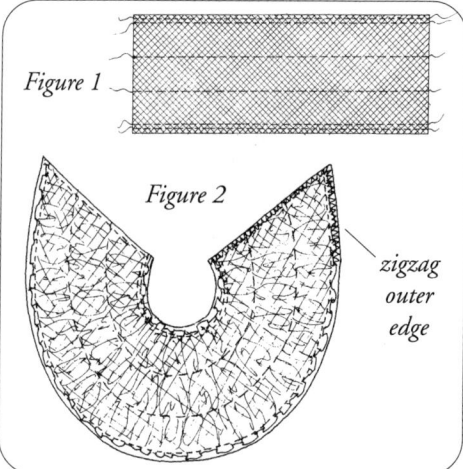

Mardi Gras Dress

Figure 1

Figure 2 — zigzag outer edge

2. Cut the following pieces from the silk dupioni, one waisted bodice front on the fold, two waisted bodice backs from the selvage, two elbow-length sleeves, one collar on the fold, and one skirt piece 45" wide by the following:

13"	6"
17 1/2"	8 1/4"
18" or 19 1/2"	9"

B. Collar

1. To prepare the collar block of netting for gathering, run 6 rows of gathering threads, two on the top and bottom edges at 1/8" and 1/4" from the edge and one 1/3 of the way down the strip and the other row 2/3 of the way down the strip (fig. 1). Gather these blocks of netting to fit the silk collar. Lay the gathered netting on top of the right side of the silk and stitch in place 1/8" from the edge of the silk collar. Trim off excess netting (fig. 2).

2. Finish the outer edge of the silk and netting collar piece with a small zigzag (fig. 2). Apply the 1" tatting to the outer edge of the collar using the technique "lace to fabric", starting the tatting at the back neck edge (fig. 3).
3. This seam and the zigzag finish are then covered by applying the trim for the collar on top of the zigzag stitches to finish off the collar. Apply the trim with either a straight or zigzag stitch (fig. 3).
4. Take 15" for 13 1/2" doll or 18" for larger dolls, of the roses on a ribbon and randomly place the roses on the collar attaching the roses in place by hand. Refer to the finished drawing for approximate placement. Remove gathering threads from the netting.

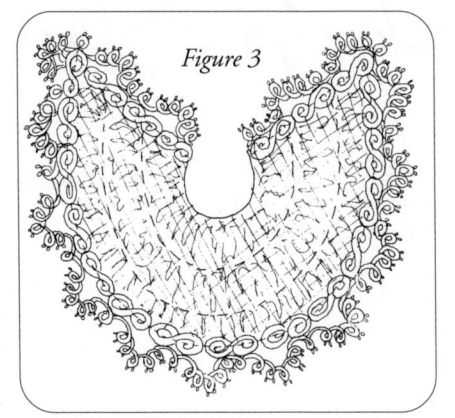

Figure 3

Figure 4

Figure 5

C. Sleeves

1. To prepare the sleeve blocks of netting for gathering, run 5 rows of gathering threads, two on the top and bottom edges at 1/8" and 1/4" from the edge and one in the center. Gather these blocks of netting to fit the silk sleeve. Lay the gathered netting on top of the right side of the silk and stitch in place 1/8" from the edge of the silk sleeve. Trim off excess netting (fig. 4).
2. Cut 5 of the roses from the rose strip and hand attach randomly on the right side of each sleeve. Remove the center gathering thread from the netting (fig. 5).
3. To create the netting and lace ruffle for the sleeves, cut two strips of the 1 1/2" netting strip twice the length of the sleeve band chart, refer to General Directions, B. Sleeves and Sleeve Finishes. Fold the netting strip in half so that it measures 3/4" wide. Using the technique "lace to lace" attach the 5/8" tatting to the folded edge of the strips, treating the netting as a lace (fig. 6).
4. Refer to the General Directions, B. Sleeves and Sleeve Finishes, c. Entredeux and a Fabric Lace Ruffle to finish the bottom of the sleeve, using the Victorian Fagotting in place of the entredeux (see finished drawing).

Figure 6

Figure 7

leave seam open 2" top and bottom

D. Skirt Construction

1. Take the netting cut for the top skirt and place short sides together and stitch leaving 2" unstitched at the top and bottom of the seam. Press the seam open (fig. 7).
2. Fold in half down the center of the 45" strip and press (fig. 8).
3. Using the technique "lace to lace" attach 5/8" tatting at the folded edge of the skirt starting at the center back seam finishing off tatting where it is joined together. The folded edge of the netting will be treated as lace (fig. 9).
4. Take netting cut for bottom skirt and follow the above steps 1, 2 and 3.
5. Place silk cut for skirt right sides together and sew the center back seam leaving 2" unstitched at top edge.
6. Press under 1/8" on bottom edge, turn up a 1" hem and stitch in place.
7. Using the technique "lace to lace" attach a 46" piece of beading and 5/8" tatting together.
8. The beading/tatting strip is sewn on the right side of the silk skirt bottom, using the sewn hem line as a guide. Place the top of the beading on the stitching line and using a small zigzag stitch, stitch beading to the skirt starting in the center back, finishing the beading/tatting where they overlap (fig. 10).
9. Place the top edges of the three skirts together layered top skirt, silk skirt and bottom skirt, matching the center back openings that were left in the skirts.
10. Run gathering threads at 1/8" and 1/4" from the top edge treating all three layers as one.

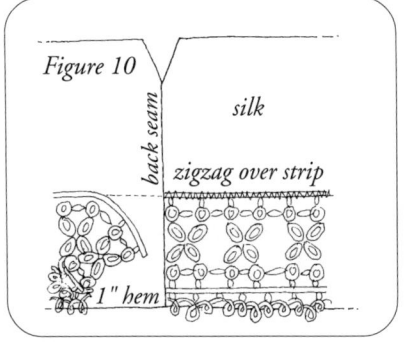

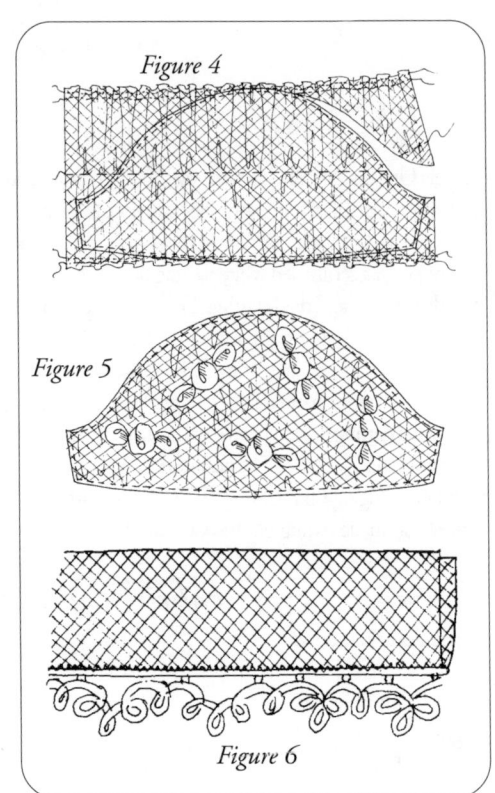

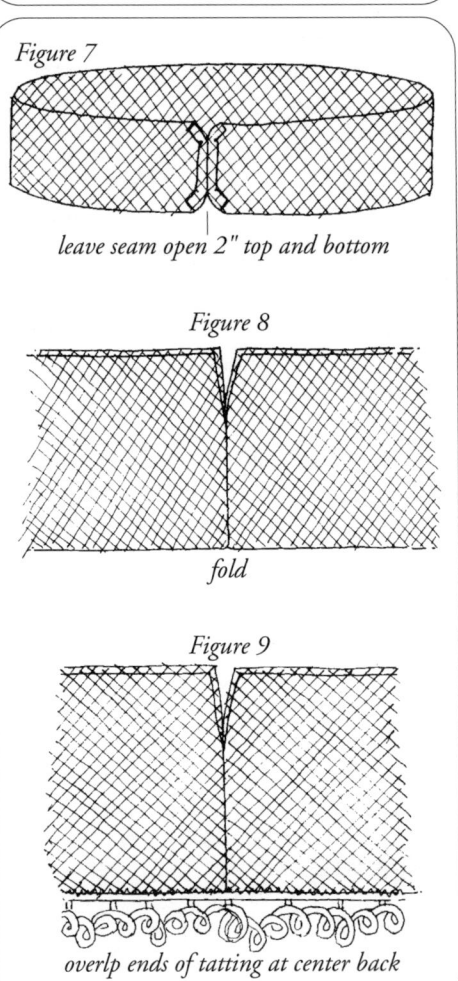

Figure 8

fold

Figure 9

overlp ends of tatting at center back

Figure 10

back seam
silk
zigzag over strip
1" hem

Three Best Friends — *Dresses*

E. Constructing Dress

1. Place the netting front and back bodice pieces on top of silk bodice pieces and stitch together around outer edge.
2. Press under at the fold lines on the center back. Stitch the dress front to the dress back at the shoulders (fig. 11).
3. Place the wrong side of the collar to the right side of the neck edge. Stitch the collar in place and finish the neck referring to the General Directions, C. Neck Finishes, f. Attaching a Collar with a Bias Facing.
4. Refer to the General Directions, B. Sleeves and Sleeve Finishes, h, Attaching the Sleeves and attach the sleeves to the dress. Stitch side seams in place (fig. 12).
5. Place the bodice to the skirt piece, right sides together. Pull up the gathers of the skirt to fit the bodice. The center back openings will come to the fold line on the left and right backs. Wrap the back facings around the skirt center back openings. Sew the bodice to the skirt (fig. 13).
6. Pull the bodice away from the skirt, folding the back facings to the inside of the bodice.
7. Cover the waist seam by zigzagging a strip of $5/8$" tatting on top of the waist seam wrapping unfinished edge of tatting to wrong side (see finished drawing).
8. Close the dress with Velcro, snaps, or tiny buttons and buttonholes along each side of the back bodice.

F. To Create Medallions

1. Fold the $1 1/2$" strip that was cut for the Medallions in half so that it measures $3/4$" wide. Using the technique "lace to lace" attach the $5/8$" tatting to the folded edge of the long strip, treating the netting as a lace (see fig. 6).
2. Cut the long strip into 8 strips each $5 1/2$" long. Run two rows of gathering threads in the long unfinished side one at $1/8$" and one at $1/4$" (fig 14).
3. Sew the short sides together, and pull the gathering threads to bring the center together and tie off the gathering threads tightly and hand sew the center to secure the gathers (fig. 15).
4. Cut 8 roses from the ribbon and attach one rose to each center by hand.
5. Space 7 medallions around the top netting skirt and attach by hand or machine.
6. Place one medallion at center back waist and attach by hand or machine.

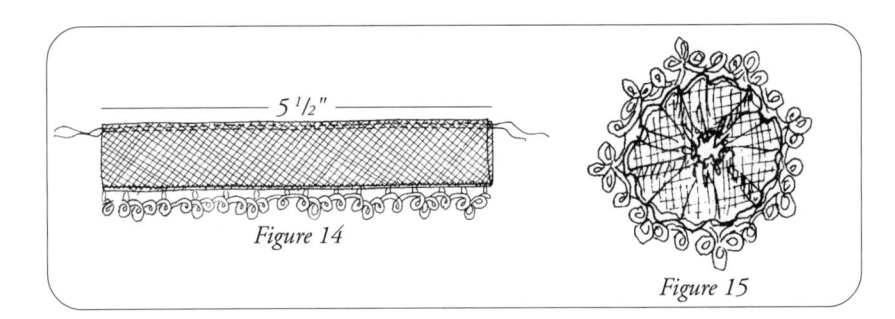

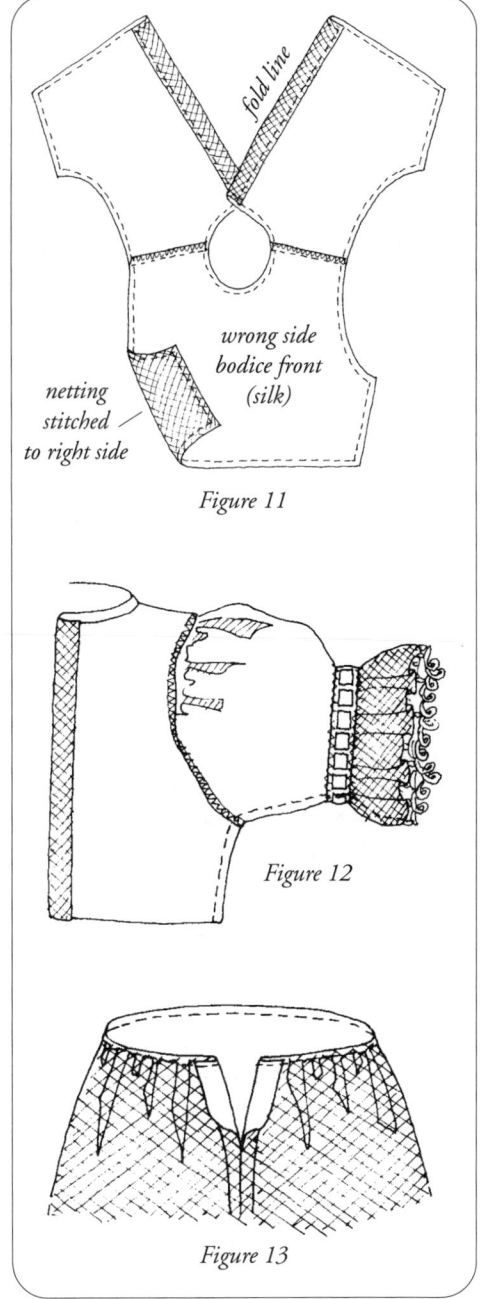

Figure 11

Figure 12

Figure 13

Figure 14

Figure 15

Mardi Gras Bonnet

This doll bonnet starts with a round circle for the base. The top layer has two rows of English netting and the center is scrunched with tatting and white and green flowers for the trim. There is a double ruffle, one on the top and one on the bottom of the circular base of the hat. The circular base is covered in the peach silk dupioni.

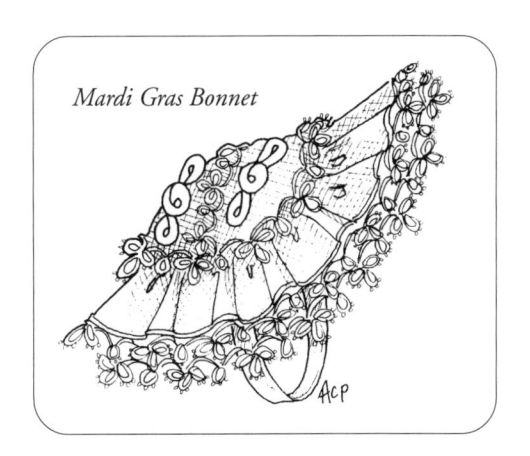

Mardi Gras Bonnet

Fabric Requirements

Fabric Requirements:

Netting	1/2 yard
Silk Dupioni	1/4 yard
Tatting edging (5/8")	3 1/4 yards
Tatting edging (1")	1 yard
Stiffening	1/3 yard
Roses on a ribbon	1/3 yard
Elastic (1/8")	1/3 yard

Notions

Sewing thread, hand sewing needle

Directions

The following pattern pieces are needed: Netting hat circle (found on page 31)

A. Constructing the Hat

1. Cut the following pieces from the netting:
   Two Strips 1 1/2" wide by 36"
   One Strip 1 1/2" wide by 24"
   One block 10" by 20"
2. Cut two Netting hat pattern pieces from the silk.
3. Cut three Netting hat pattern pieces from the stiffing.
4. Lay all three layers of the stiffing pieces one on top of the other. Put one silk piece on the top and one on the bottom of the stack of stiffing (fig. 1). Zigzag around the outer edges of the hat pattern piece to hold all layers together and to finish the outer edge (fig. 2).
5. Fold the 10" by 20" block in half to make a 10" by 10" square. Place the hat piece in the center of the square and draw the fabric up around the hat and tack together in the center, cutting off excess netting (fig. 3).
6. Attach the 1" edging to the outer edge of the hat using the technique "lace to lace" treating the netting edge as a lace. Secure the end of the edging (fig. 3)
7. Fold the two 36" strips in half to make them 3/4" wide. Using the technique "lace to lace" attach the 5/8" tatting to the folded edge of the strip, treating the netting as a lace (see fig. 14 - Mardi Gras Dress).
8. Run two rows of gathering threads in the unfinished edge of the strips, one at 1/8" and one at 1/4". Stitch the strips into a circle finishing the seam.
9. Pull up gathering threads so that one strip will fit around the outer edge of the hat. The unfinished edge of the ruffle will be stitched to the under side of the hat, the hat will extend out 1/4" over the edge of the ruffle (fig. 4).
10. To finish the edge in step 9, cover with the 5/8" tatting and secure the tatting in place with a zigzag stitch (fig. 4).
11. Pull up gathering threads so that the other strip will fit around the top outer edge of the hat. The unfinished edge of the ruffle will be stitched 1/4" in from the outer edge of the hat. Place 1" tatting around the top edge of the ruffle and zigzag in place (fig. 5).

B. Creating the Medallions

1. Fold the 1 1/2" by 24" strip that was cut for the Medallions in half so that it measures 3/4" wide. Using the technique "lace to lace" attach the 5/8" tatting to the folded edge of the long strip, treating the netting as a lace (see fig. 14 - Mardi Gras Dress).
2. Cut the long strip into 4 strips each 5 1/2" long. Run two rows of gathering threads in the long unfinished side one at 1/8" and one at 1/4" (see fig. 14 - Mardi Gras Dress).

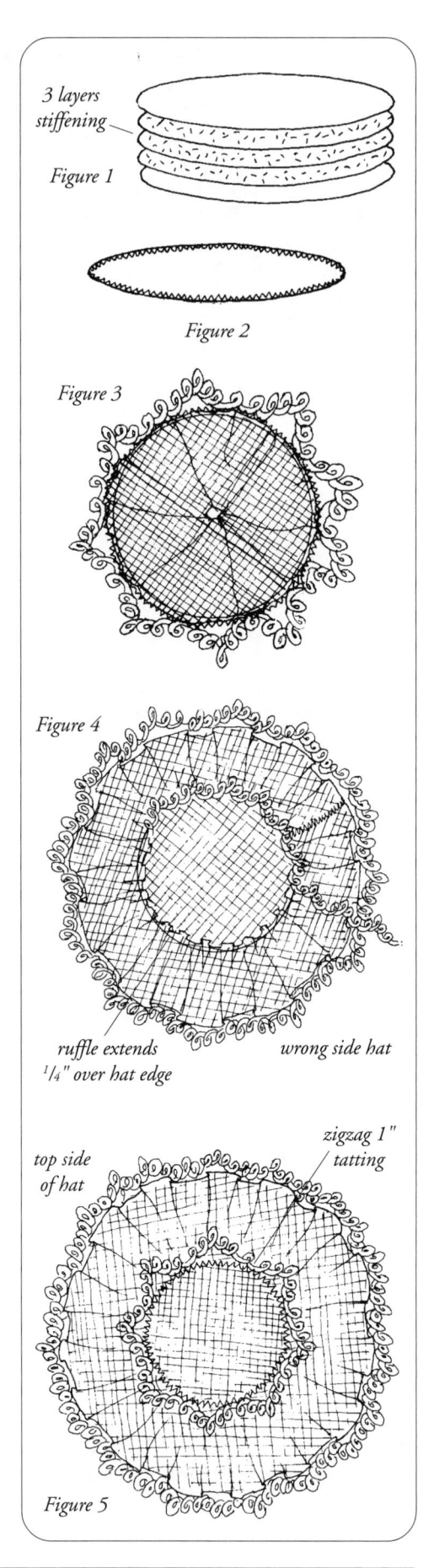

3 layers stiffening

Figure 1

Figure 2

Figure 3

Figure 4

ruffle extends 1/4" over hat edge   *wrong side hat*

top side of hat   *zigzag 1" tatting*

Figure 5

3. Sew the short sides together, and pull the gathering threads to bring the center together and tie off the gathering threads tightly and hand sew the center to secure the gathers (see fig. 14 - Mardi Gras Dress).
4. Cut 4 roses from the ribbon and attach one rose to each center by hand.
5. Lay the four medallions on the top of the hat. Refer to the drawing for placement (fig. 6). The tatting on the medallions will overlap each other and the inner edge of the ruffle.
6. Bar tack in place through all layers of the hat. Each medallion will need several bar tacks.

Finishing

1. On the back of the hat, pinch up two ½" tucks and secure in place with a bar tack. Refer to the template for placement.
2. Take a 6" piece of elastic and secure in place on each side of hat.

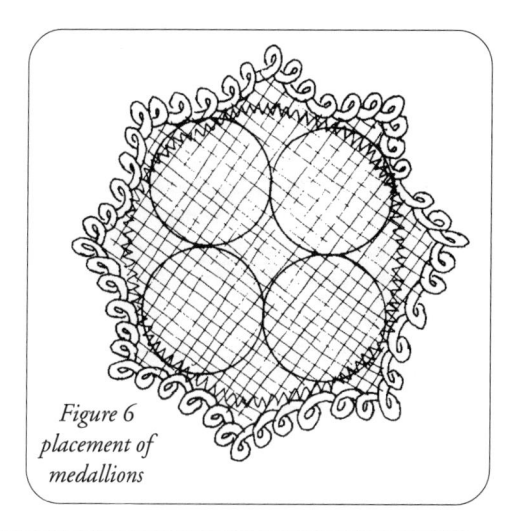

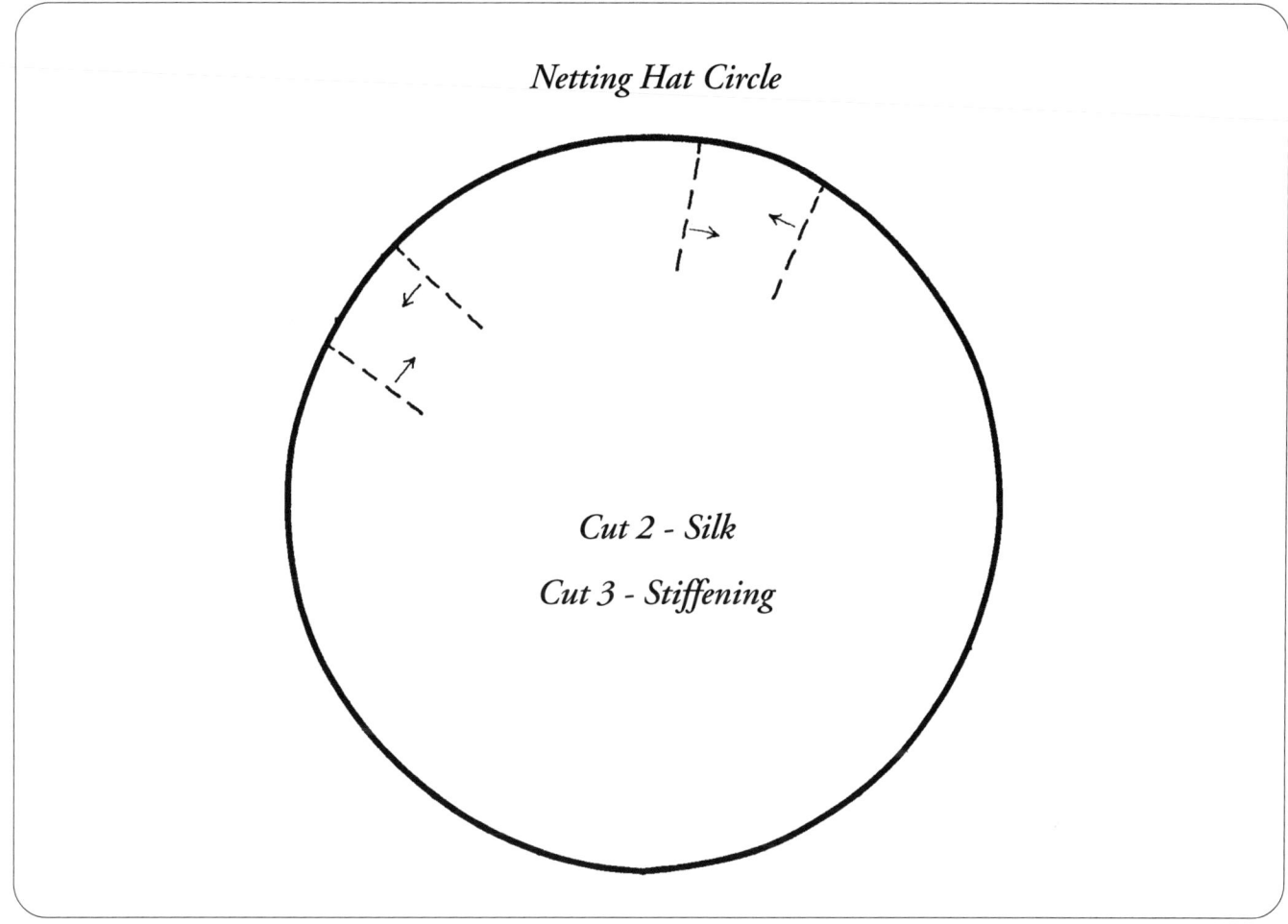

Figure 6 placement of medallions

Netting Hat Circle

Cut 2 - Silk

Cut 3 - Stiffening

Pintucked Diamonds Dress

Beyond fabulous describes this double needle pintucked white on white dress. Made of white Swiss batiste, the skirt has diamond shapes and actual lace shaped diamonds all the way around. There are diamonds within the diamonds made of double needle pintucks. The bodice has an overlay of double needle pintucks sometimes called waffle pintucks. Curved lace makes the front so pretty. The sleeves have waffle pintucked diamonds on them like the ones on the skirt. The bottom of the sleeves have gathered lace edging. The back is closed with button and buttonholes. What a gorgeous doll dress!

Fabric Requirements

Fabric Requirements:

	13"	17 1/2", 18" and 19 1/2"
Swiss batiste	3/4 yard	1 yard
Lace insertion (1/4")	4 1/4 yards	4 1/2 yards
Lace edging (1")	4 1/2 yards	4 3/4 yards

Notions

Lightweight sewing thread, Velcro™, snaps or tiny buttons, wash-out marker, twin needle, pintuck foot

Directions

All Seams 1/4" unless otherwise indicated. Finish all seams with a zigzag or serge to finish the fabric edges.

Please read through both the General Directions and the Specific Directions before starting the dress. The General Directions can be found on page 4 and give instructions for neck, sleeves and hem finishes. These Specific Directions give instructions for the special details concerning this particular dress and the sequence of the construction.

The follow pattern pieces found on the pull-outs are needed for this dress: "V" waist bodice front and inner bodice section, waisted bodice back, elbow-length sleeve.
The following templates will also be needed and are found on the pull-outs: skirt front "V" template, diamond template, skirt hem template.

A. Preparing the Dress Pieces

1. From Swiss batiste, cut the following: two "V" waist front bodices from the fold, two back bodices from the selvage, two elbow-length sleeves, one skirt piece 45" wide by the following measurements:
   13" doll   6"
   17 1/2" doll   8 1/4"
   18" doll   9"
   19 1/2" doll   9"
   Also, cut one block of fabric 10" by 22" for the pintucking. This pintucked piece will be used for the bodice, and diamond shapes for the sleeves and skirt.
2. Bring the shorter edge of the block cut above up to meet the top long edge of the block, folding at the corner. Crease the fold into place to create a diagonal line on the block. Unfold and trace the line with a wash-out marker (fig. 1a and b).
3. Bring the same shorter edge of the block to meet the lower long edge of the block, folding at the corner. Crease the fold into place to create a diagonal line on the block (fig. 1c). Unfold and trace the line with a wash-out marker. This X on the block will be the placement lines for the first pintuck to be stitched in each direction (fig. 1d).

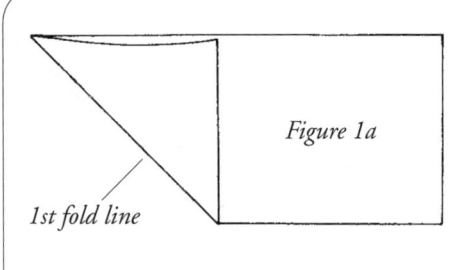

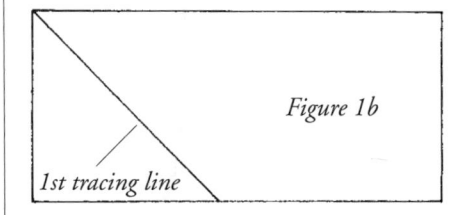

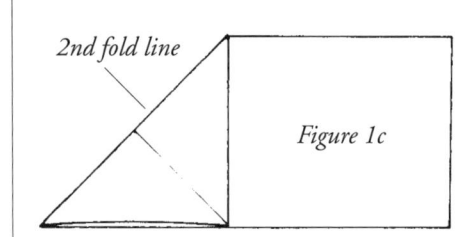

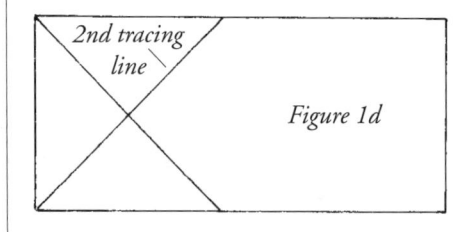

Pintucked Diamonds Dress

Figure 1a — 1st fold line

Figure 1b — 1st tracing line

Figure 1c — 2nd fold line

Figure 1d — 2nd tracing line

Figure 2

Figure 3

trim fabric from behing insertion

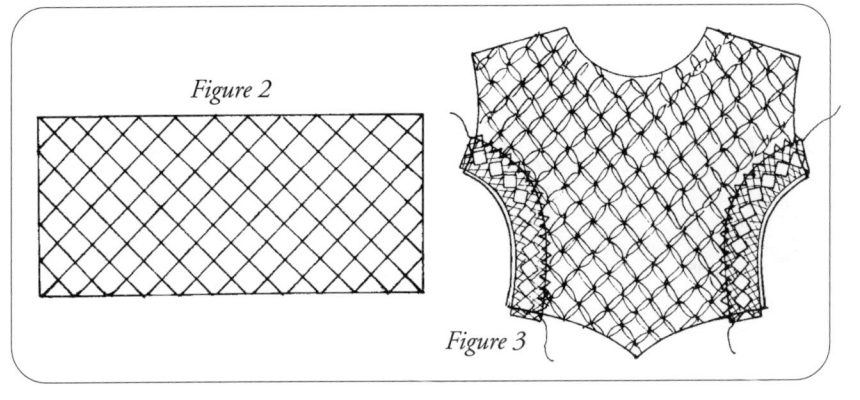

Figure 4a

Figure 4b

4. Refer to the technique for pintucking and tuck the entire block spacing the pintucks approximately 1/4" apart using the pintuck foot as a guide (fig. 2).
5. Trace the inner bodice section on the pintucked fabric and cut out.
6. Cut 10 diamonds from the pintucked block using the diamond template.
7. Refer to the lace shaping techniques and shape the 1/4" lace insertion along the curves of the pintucked inner bodice section. The lace will be placed on top of the bodice section with the outside edge of the lace even with the raw edge of the bodice piece.
8. Stitch the inside edge of the curved lace with a small zigzag (fig. 3) and trim the excess pintucked fabric from behind the lace (fig. 4a).
9. Refer to the lace shaping techniques and shape the 1/4" lace insertion around the diamond shaped pintucked pieces using the markings on the template as the guidelines for mitering (fig. 4b). Trim the excess pintucked fabric from behind the lace on all of the diamonds.

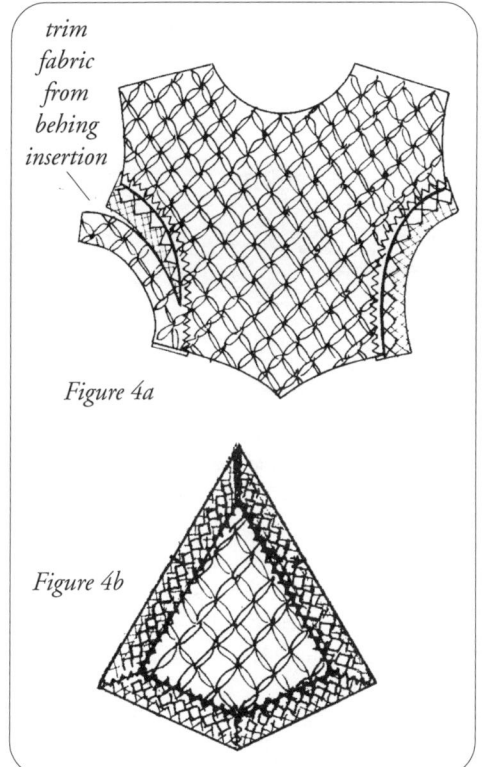

B. Constructing the Dress

1. Place the pintucked inner bodice on top of one of the front bodices matching the shoulders and neck. Stitch with a small zigzag along the outside edge of the lace (fig. 5). Trim away the excess fabric from behind the lace and the pintucked piece (fig. 6).
2. Place the pintucked bodice piece on top of the other fabric bodice. Straight stitch through both layers of the bodices around the outside edge to secure in place. Treat these two layers as one.
3. Place the bodice front to the bodice backs and stitch at the shoulders. Set aside (fig. 7).
4. Fold each sleeve in half and mark the center with a line. Cut two pieces of lace insertion the length given for the elbow-length sleeve in the sleeve band chart in the General Directions found on page 6.
5. Unfold the sleeves and run two rows of gathering stitches at 1/8" and 1/4" from the lower edge of the sleeves. Flatten out the gathering stitches. Pin the piece of insertion at the center to the lower edge of the sleeve matching the centers of both the sleeve and lace.
6. Center the pintucked diamond on top of the sleeve lace so that the side points of the diamond are at the top edge of the lace. Pin (fig. 8).

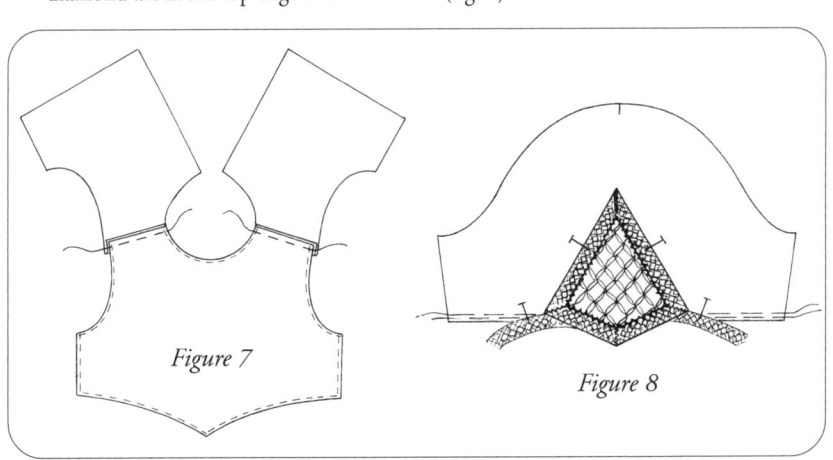

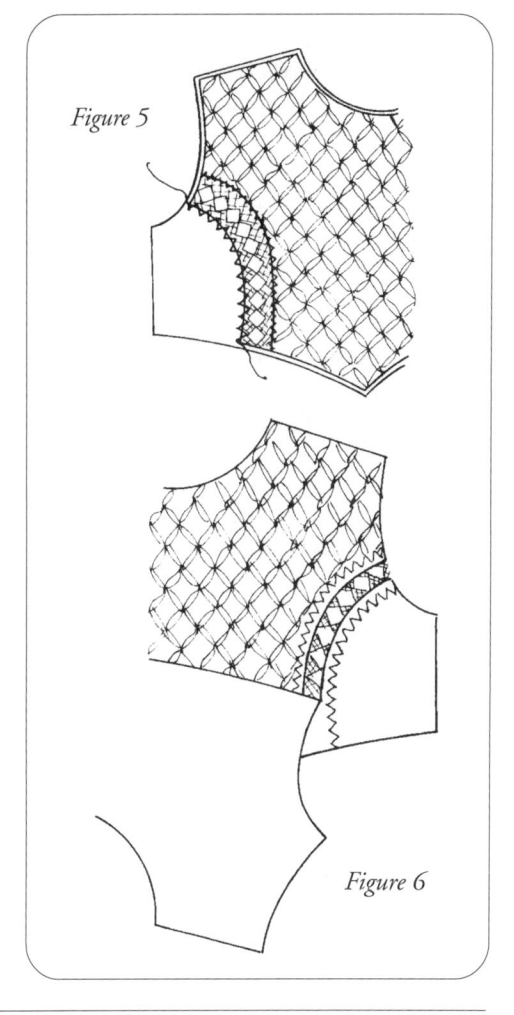

Figure 5

Figure 6

Figure 7

Figure 8

Figure 9

Figure 10

Figure 11

Figure 12

Figure 13

center front

bottom edge of skirt

Figure 14

Figure 15

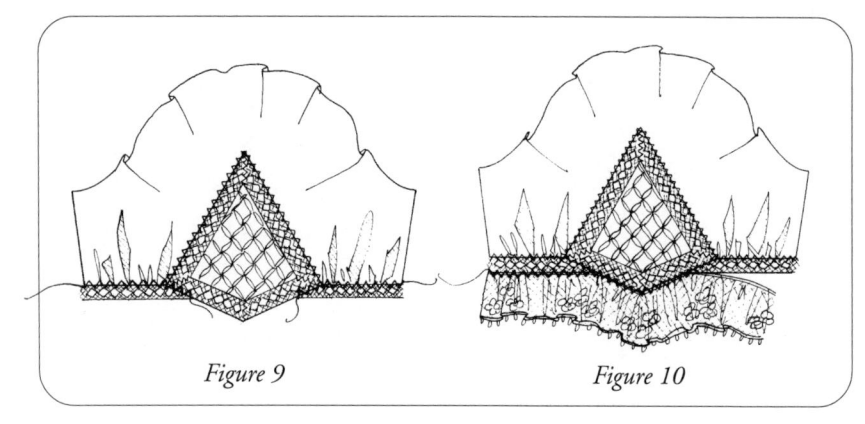

7. Pull the gathers on the sleeves to fit the lace insertion. Stitch across the top of the lace insertion and around the top edge of the diamond with a small zigzag stitch. Trim the excess fabric from behind the lace and from behind the pintucked diamond. Zigzag along the overlaped lace areas of the lace insertion (fig. 9).
8. Cut two pieces of lace edging three times the measurement given in the sleeve band chart. Refer to the technique "lace to lace" and attach the gathered lace to the bottom edge of each sleeve (fig. 10).
9. Refer to the General Directions, C. Neck Finishes, e. Bias Facing and finish the neck edge of the dress.
10. Refer to the General Directions, B. Sleeves and Sleeve Finishes, h. Attaching the Sleeves and attach the sleeves to the bodice (fig. 11).
11. Place the bodice and sleeves right sides together matching the lower edge of the bodice, the underarm seam and the edge of the lace on the sleeves. Stitch the side seams (fig. 12).
12. Fold the skirt piece in half and mark the center front. Place the skit piece onto the skirt front "V" template and trace the cut away line through both layers. Cut away the fabric from above the line.
13. Refer to the lace shaping techniques and shape the lace along the template lines. Let the ends of the lace extend into the diamond shaped area.
14. Place a diamond shape onto the skirt, lining up the center of the diamonds with the center placement line. The points on each side of the diamonds are lined up with the lower edge of the lace.
15. Stitch along the top of the lace and along the top edge of the lace of the diamonds (fig. 13). Trim away the excess fabric from beneath the lace and the diamonds (fig. 14). Zigzag along the overlaped lace areas.
16. Measure along the lower edge of the skirt and gather the lace edging two times this measurement. Attach the gathered lace to the lower edge of the skirt using the technique "lace to lace".
17. Refer to the General Directions, A. Plackets, b. Placket in a Seam and finish the back of the skirt. NOTE: The back seam will need to be stitched so that it lines up with the center miter of the "V" so that the design is continuous. If it is necessary to cut away any excess fabric from the selvages, the seam will need to be finished before putting in the placket.
18. Fold the skirt in half to find the center. Mark at the top edge. Fold the skirt again to find the quarter points. Mark.
19. Place the back bodices to the skirt backs, right sides together with the placket edges to the fold lines of the back bodices. Remember, one side of the placket will be folded to the inside of the skirt and pinned, while the other side will remain extended. Wrap each bodice back around the placket opening in the skirt. Gather the skirt to fit the bodice, matching the center of the skirt to the center front bodice and the quarter markings on the skirt with the side seams of the bodice. Stitch together (fig. 15). Flip the bodice away from the skirt.
20. Close the dress using Velcro, snaps, or tiny buttons and buttonholes along each side of the back bodice.

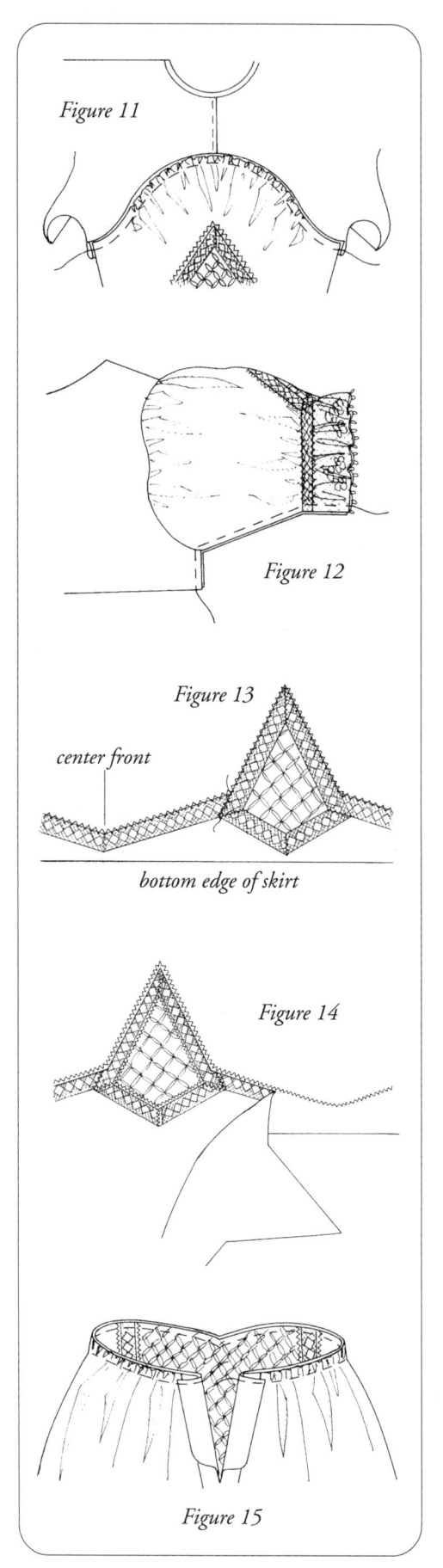

English Flower Girl Dress

White silk dupioni is the base fabric for this very special flower girl dress. English netting covers the skirt, the bodice and the sleeves of this spectacular doll dress. The sleeves are gathered near the lower edge creating a ruffle with the lower edge of the netting and are finished with double pieces of white silk ribbon tied into a bow. The dress is closed with Velcro™ in the back. The Three Best Friends love the way the English netting lends a princess look to the front, right below the waistline. If all of the Three Best Friends get to be flower girls, they would like being dressed like triplets.

Fabric Requirements

Fabric Requirements:

	13"	17 1/2", 18" and 19 1/2"
Fabric - Silk Dupioni	1/2 yard	5/8 yard
Swiss Netting Edging (6" wide)	2 1/8"	------
Swiss Netting Edging (10" wide)	------	2 1/8"
Silk Ribbon	2 yards	2 yards

English Flower Girl Dress

Notions

Lightweight sewing thread, Velcro™, snaps or tiny buttons

Directions

All Seams 1/4" unless otherwise indicated. Finish all seams with a zigzag or serge to finish the fabric edges.

Please read through both the General Directions and the Specific Directions before starting the dress. The General Directions can be found on page 4 and give instructions for neck, sleeves and hem finishes. These Specific Directions give instructions for the special details concerning this particular dress and the sequence of the construction.

The following pattern pieces needed for this dress are found on the pull-outs: waisted front, waisted back and elbow-length sleeve.

Figure 1

A. Preparing the Dress Pieces

1. From the silk dupioni cut the following: one front bodice from the fold, two back bodices from the selvage, two sleeves and one skirt piece 45" wide by the following length:
   13" doll - 6 1/4"   17 1/2" doll - 8 1/2"
   18" doll - 9 1/4"   19 1/2" doll - 9 1/4"
2. Turn one long edge of the skirt piece to the wrong side 1/8" and 1/8" again. Stitch in place (fig. 1).
3. Place a 45" strip of netting edging to the right side of the fabric skirt piece. Allow the scalloped edge to extend past the hemmed edge of the skirt by 3/4". Pin in place. Baste the netting edging to the fabric skirt piece 1/8" from the top edge of the fabric skirt. Trim away the excess netting at the top of the fabric skirt. Set aside (fig. 2).
4. Turn the lower edge of each sleeve to the wrong side 1/8" and 1/8" again. Stitch in place.
5. Place netting edging to the sleeve pieces allowing the scalloped edge of the netting to extend past the hemmed edge of the sleeve by 1". Stitch the netting to each fabric sleeve 1/8" from the edges of the sleeve. Trim the netting even with the sides and top of the sleeve. Set aside (fig. 3).
6. Place a piece of netting edging to the front bodice centering one of the scallops to the center of the bodice. Allow the center scallop to extend beyond the lower edge of the bodice by 1/2". Stitch the netting to fabric bodice 1/8" from the edge of the shoulders, neck and sides. Do not stitch across the lower edge of the bodice. Trim the excess netting from around the bodice. Do not trim the lower edge of the bodice (fig. 4).
7. All netting covered dress pieces, bodice front, skirt and sleeves, will be treated as one layer of fabric.

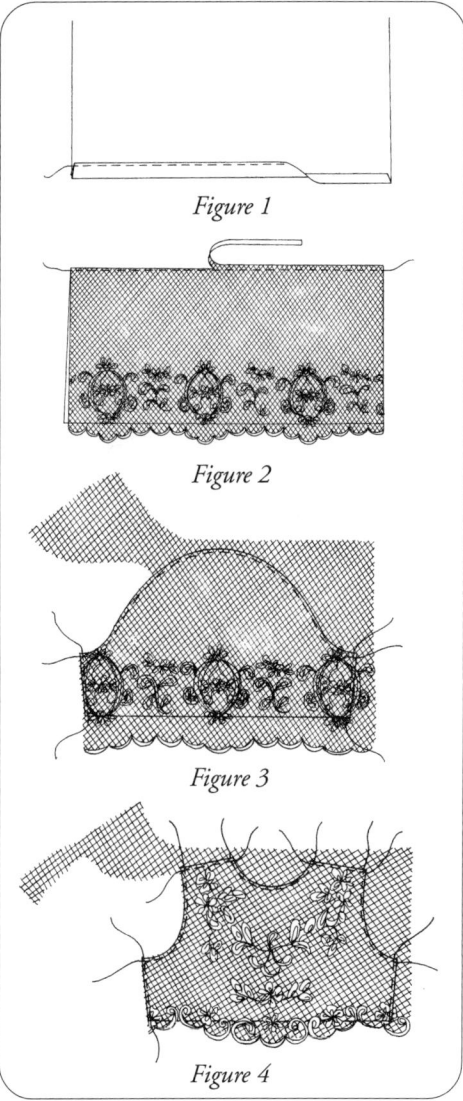

Figure 2

Figure 3

Figure 4

Dresses — Three Best Friends — 35

B. Constructing the Dress

1. Place the front bodice to the back bodices, right sides together. Stitch in place at the shoulders (fig. 5). Finish the neck referring to the General Directions, C. Neck Finishes, e. Bias Facing.
2. Finish each sleeve referring to the General Directions - B. Sleeves and Sleeves Finishes (steps 1 - 2); however, do not run gathering rows along bottom edge of sleeve. Stitch elastic to the wrong side of each sleeve 1" from the edge, referring to the instructions given under e. Gathered Sleeve with Elastic and Lace - steps 2 to 4 (fig. 6).
3. Place the sleeves to the arm openings, right sides together, matching the center of each sleeve to the shoulder seam of the bodice. Gather the sleeves to fit the openings. Stitch in place (fig. 7).
4. Place the sides of the bodice right sides together, matching the ends of the sleeves, the underarm seams and the lower edges of the bodice. Stitch the side seams in place (fig. 8).
5. Fold the skirt in half to find the center. Mark at the top edge. Fold the skirt again to find the quarter points. Mark (fig. 9).
6. Create a placket in the skirt referring to the General Directions, A. Plackets, b. Placket in a Seam.
7. Place the back bodices to the skirt back, right sides together with the placket edges to the fold lines of the back bodices. Remember, one side of the placket will be folded to the inside of the skirt and pinned, while the other side will remain extended. Wrap each bodice back around the placket opening in the skirt. Gather the skirt to fit the bodice, matching the center of the skirt to the center front bodice and the quarter markings on the skirt with the side seams of the bodice (fig. 10). Stitch in place but do not stitch the center netting scallop of the bodice to the skirt (fig. 11). Flip the bodice away from the skirt. The center scallop will overlap the top of the skirt by 1/2".
8. Cut four pieces of 4mm silk ribbon 15" long. Place two pieces of ribbon together and hand stitch the center of the ribbon to the underarm seam of the sleeve at the elastic.
9. Close the dress using Velcro™, snaps, or tiny buttons and buttonholes along each side of the back bodice.
10. After the dress is placed on the doll tie the ribbons over the elastic gathers in the sleeve.

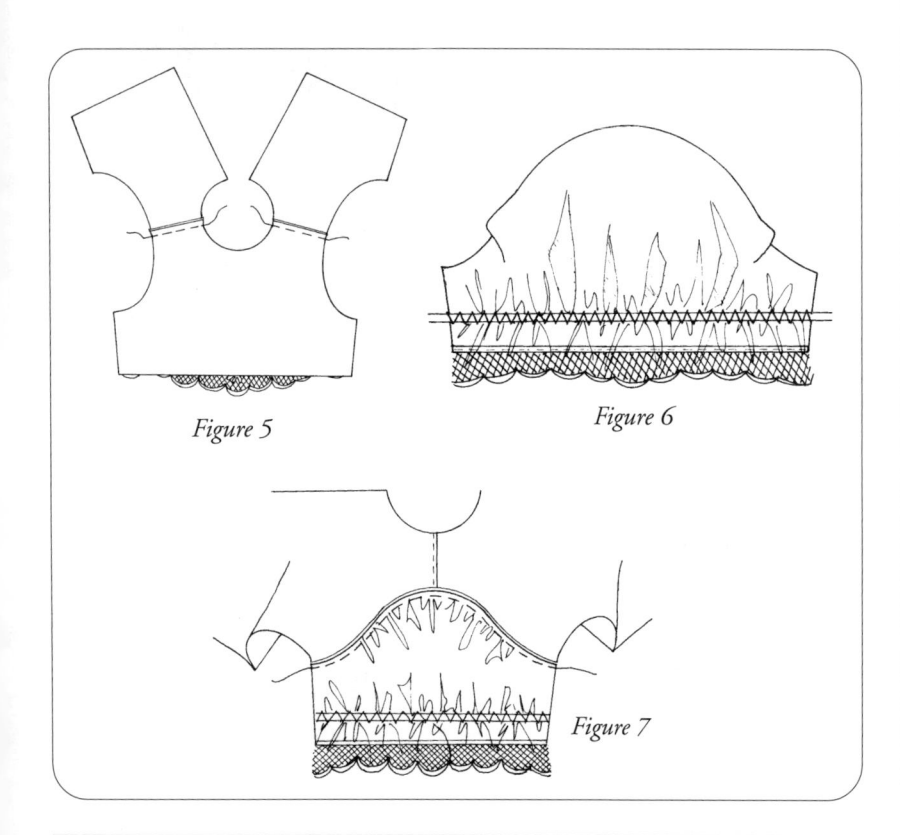

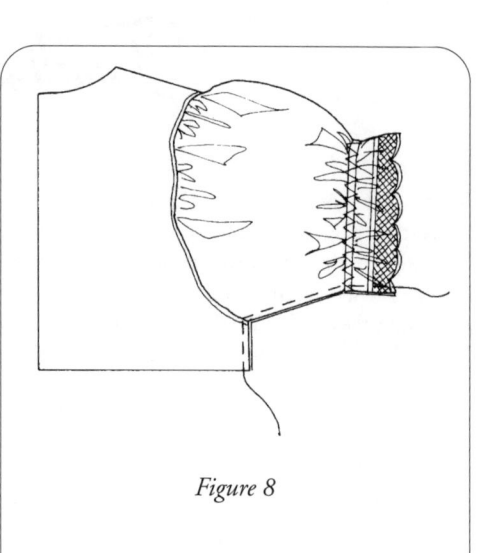

Figure 8

Figure 9

Figure 5

Figure 6

Figure 7

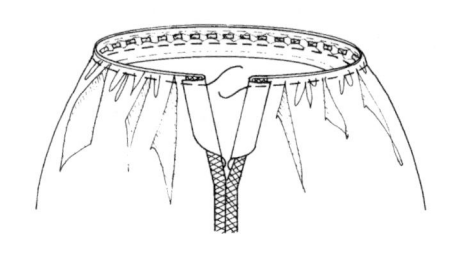

Figure 10

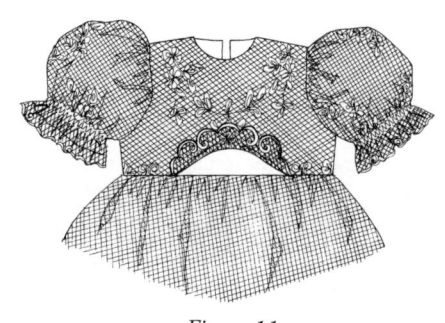

Figure 11

English Netting Blue Bow Dress

Absolutely delicate and gorgeous is this blue Swiss Nelona dress with its complete covering of wide cotton English netting with a bow design. The pale blue dress has puffed sleeves which are finished with entredeux and gathered narrow French edging. An English angel sleeve overlay covers the puffed sleeve. The neckline is finished with entredeux and gathered narrow French edging. Entredeux is used to join the bodice to the skirt at the waistline. The very full, gathered, blue batiste skirt has flat white French edging stitched on flat; the skirt has the wide English cotton netting which completely covers the blue skirt. The dress is closed in the back with Velcro™. This is the perfect party dress for the Three Best Friends.

Fabric Requirements

Fabric Requirements:

	13"	17 1/2", 18" and 19 1/2"
Fabric - Swiss Batiste	1/2 yard	5/8 yard
Swiss Netting Edging (6" wide)	2 1/8 yards	-----
Swiss Netting Edging (10" wide)	-----	2 1/8 yards
Lace Edging (1/2")	2 1/4 yards	2 1/2 yards
Entredeux	3/4 yard	7/8 yard

Notions

Lightweight sewing thread, Velcro™, snaps or tiny buttons

Directions

All Seams 1/4" unless otherwise indicated. Finish all seams with a zigzag or serge to finish the fabric edges.

Please read through both the General Directions and the Specific Directions before starting the dress. The General Directions can be found on page 4 and give instructions for neck, sleeves and hem finishes. These Specific Directions give instructions for the special details concerning this particular dress and the sequence of the construction.

The following pattern pieces needed for this dress are found on the pull-outs: waisted front, waisted back and elbow-length sleeve.

A. Preparing the Dress Pieces

1. From the Swiss batiste cut the following: one front bodice from the fold, two back bodices from the selvage, two sleeves and one skirt piece 45" wide by the following length:

    | 13" doll | 5 1/2" |
    | 17 1/2" doll | 7 3/4" |
    | 18" doll | 8 1/2" |
    | 19 1/2" doll | 8 1/2" |

2. Stitch edging lace to one long side of the skirt using the technique "lace to fabric".
3. Place a 45" strip of netting edgeing to the right side of the fabric skirt piece. Allow the edging lace of the fabric skirt to extend 1/4" from the lower edge of the scalloped netting edge. Pin in place. Baste the netting edging to the fabric skirt piece 1/8" from the top edge of the fabric skirt. Trim away the excess netting at the top of the fabric skirt (fig. 1). Set aside.
4. Place a piece of netting to the front bodice centering the design. Stitch the netting to fabric bodice 1/8" from the edges of the bodice. Trim away the excess netting (fig. 2).
5. Place a piece of netting to each bodice back. Stitch the netting to the fabric bodice pieces 1/8" from the edges of the bodice. Trim away the excess netting (fig 3).

English Netting Blue Bow Dress

Figure 1

Trim away excess netting

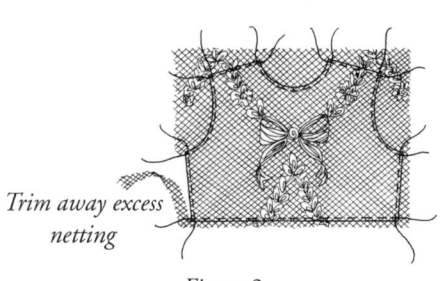

Figure 2

Figure 3

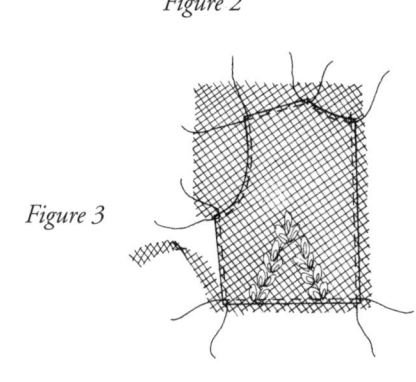

Figure 4

Figure 5

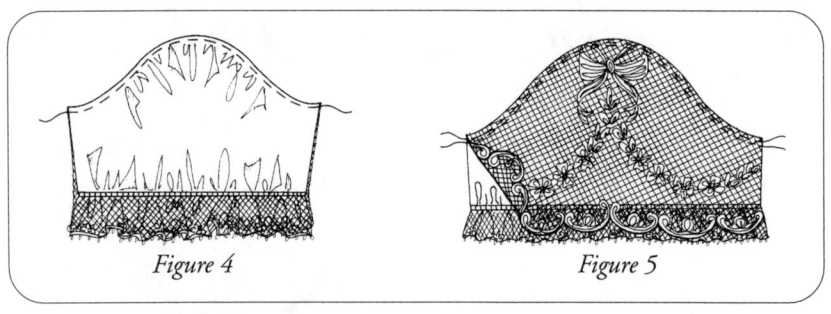

6. Finish each batiste sleeve referring to the General Directions, B. Sleeves and Sleeves Finishes, a. Entredeux to Gathered Edging Lace (fig. 4).
7. Using the elbow-length sleeve pattern, cut two sleeves from the netting edging lining up the lace bottom to the lower sleeve edge.
8. Place the netting sleeve to the fabric sleeve, matching the upper edges and sides.
9. Run two gathering rows in the top of each sleeve through both the netting and the fabric sleeve at $1/8$" and $1/4$" (fig. 5).

B. Constructing the Dress

1. Place the front bodice to the back bodice pieces, right sides together. Stitch the shoulder seams.
2. Finish the neck referring to the General Directions, C. Neck Finishes, a. Entredeux to Gathered Edging Lace.
3. Place the sleeves to the arm openings, right sides together, matching the center of each sleeve to the shoulder seam of the bodice. Gather the sleeves to fit the openings. Stitch in place (fig. 6).
4. Place the sides of the bodice right sides together, matching the ends of the sleeves, the underarm seams and the lower edges of the bodice. Stitch the side seams in place (fig. 7).
5. Attach entredeux to the lower edge of the bodice, back folds extended using the technique "entredeux to fabric" (fig. 8).
6. Fold the skirt in half to find the center. Mark at the top edge. Fold the skirt again to find the quarter points. Mark (fig. 9).
7. Create a placket in the skirt referring to the General Directions, A. Plackets, b. Placket in a Seam, treating the two layers as one.
8. Run two gathering rows, $1/8$" and $1/4$" in the top edge of the skirt (fig 10).
9. Place the back bodices to the skirt back, right sides together with the placket edges to the fold lines of the back bodices. Remember, one side of the placket will be folded to the inside of the skirt and pinned, while the other side will remain extended. Wrap each bodice back around the placket opening in the skirt. Gather the skirt to fit the bodice, matching the center of the skirt to the center front bodice and the quarter markings on the skirt with the side seams of the bodice. Stitch in place using the technique "entredeux to gathered fabric" (fig. 11). Flip the bodice away from the skirt
10. Close the dress using Velcro™, snaps, or tiny buttons and buttonholes along each side of the back bodice.

Figure 6

Figure 7

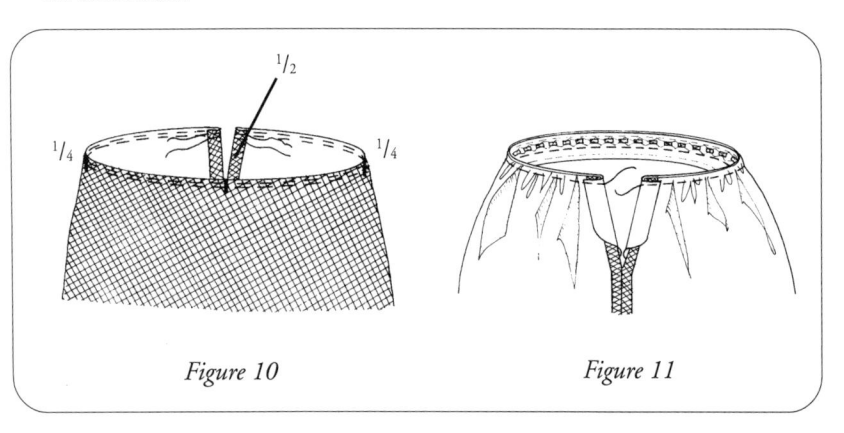

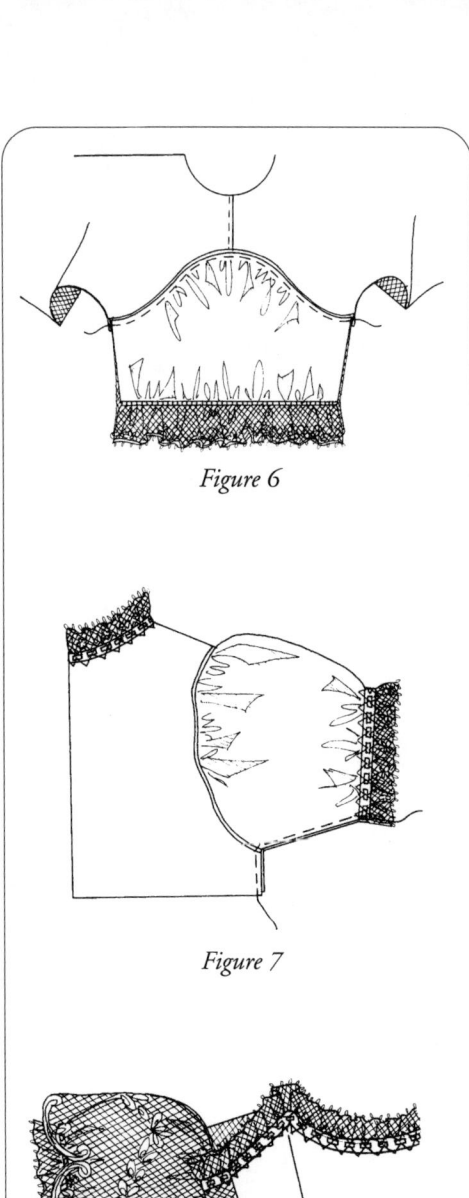

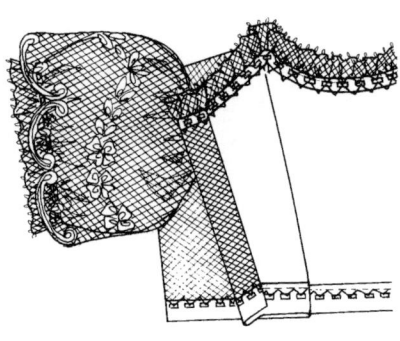

Figure 8

Figure 10

Figure 11

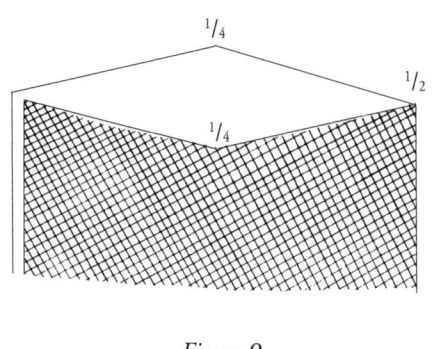

Figure 9

Seaside Garden Dress

Robin's egg blue Swiss Nelona batiste and ecru English netting combine perfectly in this gorgeous dress for the friends. Ecru English cotton netting is used for the dress; the underdress is of Nelona Swiss batiste. On the bottom of the netting skirt there is a row of insertion, a row of beading, another row of ecru insertion, and flat French edging stitched on straight. A tiny row of ecru French edging is found on the bottom of the dress. On the overbodice there is a row of beading, entredeux, and a ruffle of ecru French insertion plus edging. A gathered row of ecru edging travels around the waist of the dress. Tiny little flowers of silk ribbon embroidery are found in shades of pink with green leaves. Pink silk ribbon is run through the beading and through the entredeux on both the neckline and the sleeves of the dress. Entredeux is found on the bottom of the sleeves as well as around the neckline of the dress. The little dress closes with clear, plastic snaps.

Fabric Requirements

Fabric Requirements:

	13"	17 1/2", 18 and 19 1/2"
Green Batiste	1/2 yard	5/8 yard
Ecru Netting	3/8 yard	1/2 yard
1/2" lace insertion	4 1/4 yards	4 3/4 yards
1/2" lace beading	1 3/4 yards	2 yards
1/4" lace edging	1 1/3 yards	1 1/3 yards
1/2" lace edging	1/2 yard	1/2 yard
1" lace edging	3 2/3 yards	4 1/4 yards
Entredeux	1 3/4 yard	2 yards

Notions

Lightweight sewing thread, #007 silk ribbon (2mm), #008 silk ribbon (2mm), #032 silk ribbon (4mm), tiny seed beads for the centers of the flowers, Velcro™, snaps or tiny buttons, wash-out marker

Directions

All Seams 1/4" unless otherwise indicated. Finish all seams with a zigzag or serge to finish the fabric edges.

Please read through both the General Directions and the Specific Directions before starting the dress. The General Directions can be found on page 4 and give instructions for neck, sleeves and hem finishes. These Specific Directions give instructions for the special details concerning this particular dress and the sequence of the construction.

The following pattern pieces needed for this dress are found on the pull-outs: waisted front, waisted back, elbow-length sleeve.

Seaside Garden Dress

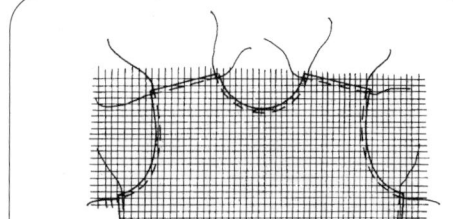

Figure 1

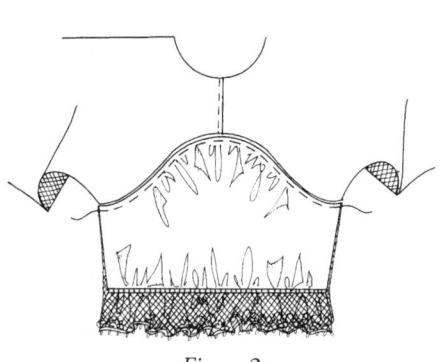

Figure 2

Preparing the Dress

1. Cut one front bodice, two back bodices and two sleeves from both the batiste and the netting. Place the netting piece on top of the batiste piece, stitch together and treat the layers as one. Place a mark at the center front along the lower edge of the front bodice (fig. 1).
2. Cut a piece of batiste 6" by 45" for the 13" doll, 8 1/4" by 45" for the 17 1/2", and 9" by 45" for the 18" and 19 1/2" dolls for the skirt.
3. Cut a piece of netting 6" by 45" for the 13" doll and 8 1/4" by 45" for the 17 1/2", and 9" by 45" for the 18" and 19 1/2" dolls for the overskirt.
4. Place the front bodice and the back bodices right sides together. Stitch at the shoulders.
5. Refer to B. Sleeves and Sleeve Finishes, a. Entredeux to Gathered Edging Lace and finish the lower edge of the sleeves.
6. Refer to B. Sleeves and Sleeve Finishes, h. Attaching the Sleeves and attach the sleeves to the bodice (fig. 2).

Figure 3

Cut ½" past raw edge on each end

Figure 4

Figure 5

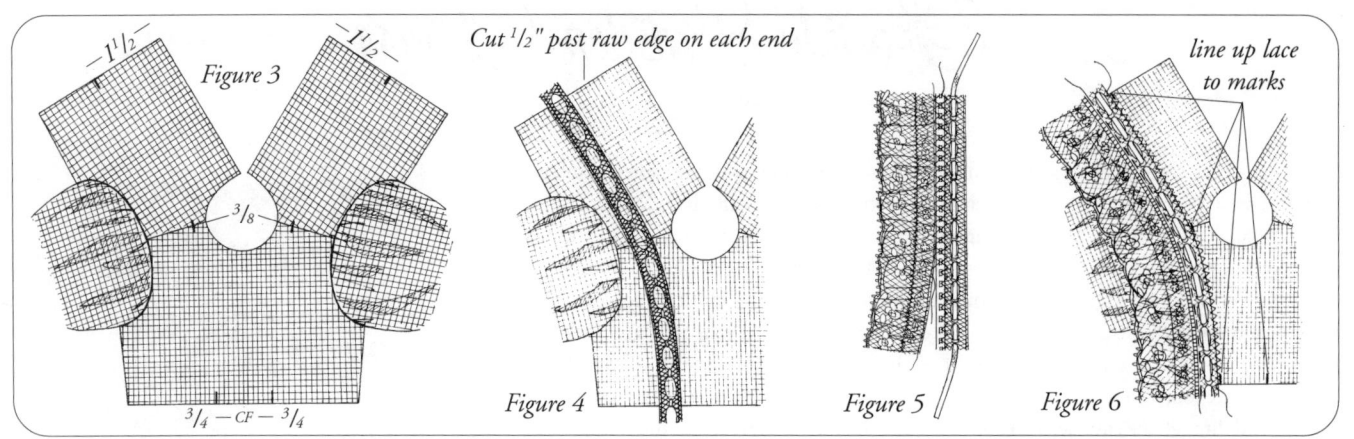

line up lace to marks

Figure 6

7. Place a mark ¾" from the center mark on each side of the bodice front. Place a mark ⅜" from the raw edge of the neck opening at each shoulder seam. Place a mark 1½" from the center back raw edge on each side of the back bodice (fig. 3).
8. Measure from the mark at the lower edge of the back bodice to the dot at the shoulder and to the mark on the lower edge of the bodice front. Cut two pieces of lace beading to this measurement plus 1". Cut two pieces of entredeux the same measurement as the beading (fig. 4).
9. Refer to the technique "lace to entredeux" and attach the entredeux to one side of the lace beading. Repeat this step for the other piece of beading and entredeux.
10. Cut two pieces of both the lace insertion and 1" lace edging twice the measurement of the beading.
11. Refer to the technique "lace to lace" and attach the lace edging to the lace insertion.
12. Pull a thread on the lace insertion and gather the lace strip to fit the entredeux attached to the beading.
13. Refer to the technique "gathered lace to entredeux" and attach the gathered edge of the insertion to the entredeux (fig. 5).
14. Run a piece of the pink silk ribbon through each piece of beading (fig. 5).
15. Place the strip of beading, with the other laces attached, onto the bodice matching the edge of the lace with the marks made in step 7. Pin in place. With a tiny zigzag, stitch along the edge of the beading to attach it to the bodice (fig. 6).
16. Straight stitch on the lace beading right up against the entredeux to attach the other side of the beading (fig. 6).
17. Repeat steps 11 - 16 for the other pieces of lace.
18. Refer to C. Neck Finishes, a. Entredeux to Gathered Edging Lace, using the ½" lace edging.
19. With a tapestry needle lace a piece of silk ribbon through every other hole of the entredeux at the neckline, starting at the center front. Stitch the ribbon at each back edge to secure. Pull up the silk ribbon at the center front and tie into a bow (fig. 7).
20. Place the bodice front and backs right sides together and stitch the side seams (fig. 8). Baste the lace ruffle to the lower front bodice and lower back bodices (fig. 9).
21. Measure around the lower bodice (front and backs) and cut a piece of entredeux to this measurement. Cut a piece of lace insertion and a piece of 1" lace edging twice the measurement of the entredeux.
22. Stitch the laces and entredeux together referring to steps 11 - 13. Note: One side of the entredeux will still have the bias edge attached (fig. 10). Lay this piece aside.
23. Refer to the technique lace to fabric and attach the ¼" lace edging along the lower edge of the batiste skirt piece.
24. Create a 45" long fancy band consisting of lace insertion, lace beading, lace insertion and 1" lace edging. Refer to the technique lace to lace to construct this band.
25. With a tapestry needle or bodkin lace the 2mm pink silk ribbon through the beading in the fancy band. Pull up the silk ribbon and tie a bow that is positioned over the left knee area of the skirt.

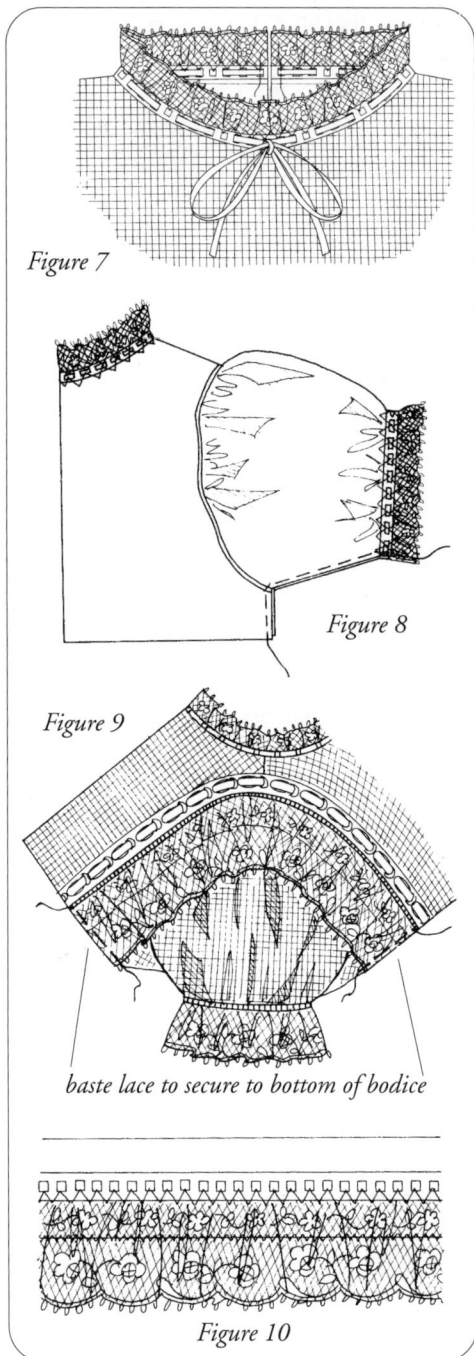

Figure 7

Figure 8

Figure 9

baste lace to secure to bottom of bodice

Figure 10

26. Place the fancy lace band on top of the netting skirt piece having the lower edge of the netting even with the lace edging at the bottom of the band.
27. With a small zigzag stitch, sew the fancy band onto the netting skirt piece along the top edge of the insertion strip and along the seam line which connects the other piece of lace insertion to the 1" lace edging (fig. 11). Trim away any excess netting underneath the 1" lace edging.
28. Place the netting skirt piece on top of the batiste skirt piece positioning them so that the narrow lace edging on the under skirt shows below the wide edging on the top skirt.
29. Stitch along the top edge of the batiste skirt, stitching the two layers together.
30. Refer to A. Placket, b. Placket in a Seam, and finish the back of the dress.
31. Run two rows of gathering stitches along the top edge of the skirt (fig. 12). Pull up the gathers to fit the bodice from back fold line to back fold line. Remember to keep the right side of the placket folded in and the left side extended.
32. Wrap the facings of the bodices around the skirt pieces and pin in place.
33. Stitch the skirt to the bodice. Flip the bodice portion of the dress up so that the facings fold to the wrong side (fig. 13).
34. Run pink silk ribbon through the entredeux on the sleeves beginning and ending at the point opposite the seam and tie a bow with the ends of the ribbon.
35. Trim away the bias edge of the entredeux of the piece created in step 22. Butt the edge of the entredeux up to the seam which joins the bodice to the skirt. Pin in place. Wrap the ends of the entredeux around the back fold lines.
36. With a small zigzag stitch, sew the top edge of the entredeux to the lower edge of the bodice at the seam line (fig. 14).
37. Refer to the section on embroidery techniques and the embroidery template and complete the design on the center bodice of the dress.
38. Close the back of the dress with Velcro™, snaps or tiny buttons and buttonholes.

bottom raw edge of net skirt

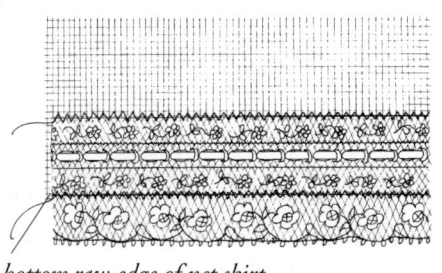

Figure 11

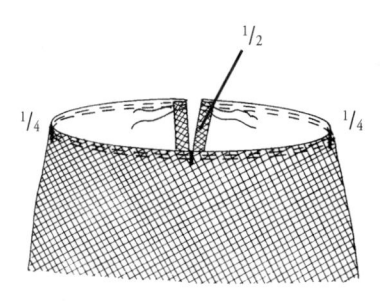

Figure 12

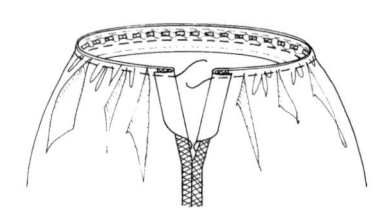

Figure 13

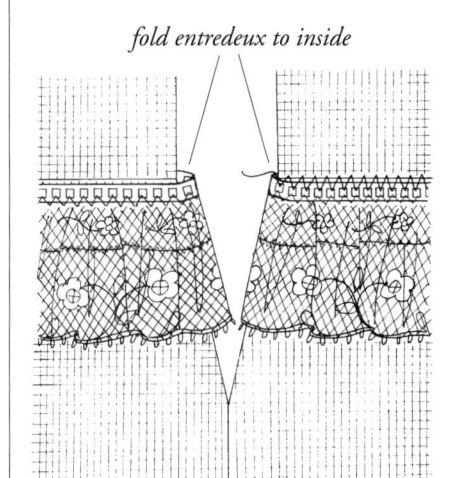

fold entredeux to inside

Figure 14

Embroidery Template

Japanese Ribbon Stitch Leaves

Lazy Daisy Stitch, Lt. Pink

Frech Knot, Medium Pink

Dresses — *Three Best Friends*

English Netting Dress with Pink Rose

The Three Best Friends absolutely love silk ribbon embroidery. This is the perfect dress to wear to church or for a portrait. This magnificent, bridal white silk dupioni dress has cotton English netting in a little curved apron on the front. The English netting is also used for a little bib on the front where the pink and green silk ribbon has been stitched. Gathered ecru French edging is stitched around the V insert in the front of the dress and it travels down the back to the waistline to give a pretty touch to the back also. The neckline is finished with entredeux and gathered French ecru edging. The puffed sleeves are finished with entredeux and slightly gathered French edging. A little pink silk ribbon bow has been tied on each sleeve. This little beauty is closed in the back with Velcro.

English Netting Dress with Pink Rose

Fabric Requirements

Fabric Requirements:

	13"	17 1/2", 18" and 19 1/2"
Fabric -Silk Dupioni	1/2 yard	5/8 yard
Lace Edging (1/2")	2 yards	2 1/2 yards
Lace Netting (6")	7/8 yard	—
Lace Netting (10")	—	7/8 yard
Entredeux	5/8 yard	3/4 yard
Ribbon (1/8")	1/2 yard	1/2 yard

Pink and green silk ribbon for embroidery

Notions

Lightweight sewing thread, Velcro™, snaps or tiny buttons

Directions

All Seams 1/4" unless otherwise indicated. Finish all seams with a zigzag or serge to finish the fabric edges.

Please read through both the General Directions and the Specific Directions before starting the dress. The General Directions can be found on page 4 and give instructions for neck, sleeves and hem finishes. These Specific Directions give instructions for the special details concerning this particular dress and the sequence of the construction.

The following pattern pieces needed for this dress are found on the pull-outs: waisted front bodice, waisted back bodice, and elbow-length sleeve.

A. Preparing the Dress Pieces

1. From the silk dupioni cut the following: two back bodices from the selvage, one front bodice on the fold, two sleeves, and one skirt piece 45" wide by the following length:
   13" doll   7 3/4"
   17 1/2" doll   10"
   18" doll   10 3/4"
   19 1/2" doll   10 3/4"

Figure 1

Figure 2

Figure 3

B. Constructing the Dress

1. Place the front bodice to the back bodice pieces, right sides together. Stitch the shoulder seams (fig. 1).
2. Place a dot on the shoulder seam 1/2" from the neck edge, locate center front of bodice and put a dot 1/2" from the center front on each side of the center at the waist. Place a dot 1 3/8" in from the **back fold line** at waist.
3. Connect the dot on the shoulder with the dots at the waist on both the front and back (fig. 2).
4. Lay a piece of netting so that the edging on the netting is 1/2" from the neck line. Stitch the netting to the front bodice on the line drawn in step 3. Trim away the extra netting outside of the stitching (fig. 3).

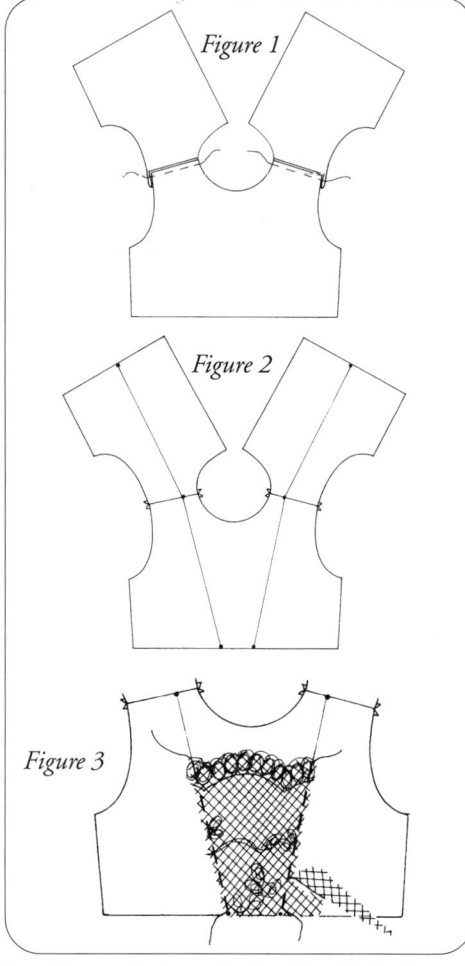

5. Measure the length of the line from bottom front waist over the shoulder to the bottom back waist and cut two pieces of edging lace twice this length. Gather the lace strips to fit the line and zigzag them to bodice following the lines drawn in step 3 (fig. 4).
6. Finish the neck referring to the General Directions, C. Neck Finishes, a. Entredeux to Gathered Edging Lace.
7. Finish each sleeve referring to the General Directions, B. Sleeves and Sleeves Finishes, a. Entredeux to Gathered Edging Lace.
8. Refer to the General Directions, B. Sleeves and Sleeve Finishes, h. Attaching the Sleeves and attach the sleeves to the bodice (fig. 5).
9. Place the sides of the bodice, right sides together, matching the ends of the sleeves, the underarm seams and the lower edges of the bodice. Stitch the side seams in place (fig. 6).
10. Fold the skirt in half to find the center. Mark at the top edge (fig. 7). Fold the skirt again to find the quarter points. Mark.
11. Create a placket in the skirt referring to the General Directions, A. Plackets, b. Placket in a Seam.
12. Fold to the wrong side $1/4$" at the bottom edge of the skirt.
13. Turn up a $1 1/2$" hem and hem bottom of skirt by hand or machine.
14. The netting will be draped across the front of the skirt. Take a 22" piece of netting and fold it in half, place a mark on the center fold the following inches from the bottom (refer to fig. 8).

    13"   5"
    $17 1/2$"   7"
    18" and $19 1/2$"   8"

15. Make another mark 6" on each side of the center the same distance from the bottom as the above measurement. Draw a 12" line connecting the two marks (refer to fig. 8).
16. Connect the mark made in step 15 to the lower corner of the netting (refer to fig. 8).
17. Run two rows of gathering threads, one above and one below the line. Excess netting may be trimmed off (fig. 8).
18. Pull up gathering threads in the netting to fit across the front of the bodice. Pin to the bottom of the front bodice with right sides together and stitch in place (fig. 9).
19. Place the back bodices to the skirt back, right sides together with the placket edges to the fold lines of the back bodices. Remember, one side of the placket will be folded to the inside of the skirt and pinned, while the other side will remain extended. Wrap each bodice back around the placket opening in the skirt. Gather the skirt to fit the bodice, matching the center of the skirt to the center front bodice and the quarter markings on the skirt with the side seams of the bodice. Stitch the waistline seam. Flip the bodice away from the skirt
20. Close the dress using Velcro™, snaps, or tiny buttons and buttonholes along each side of the back bodice.
21. Embroider the roses, stem and leaves referring to the section on Silk Ribbon Embroidery. The leaves and stem are green and worked in a lazy daisy stitch and stem stitch. The flower petals are pink and worked in a lazy daisy stitch (fig 10).
22. Cut the ribbon into three 6" pieces and tie in small bows. Attach the bows at the center of the neck and sleeves (refer to the finished drawing).

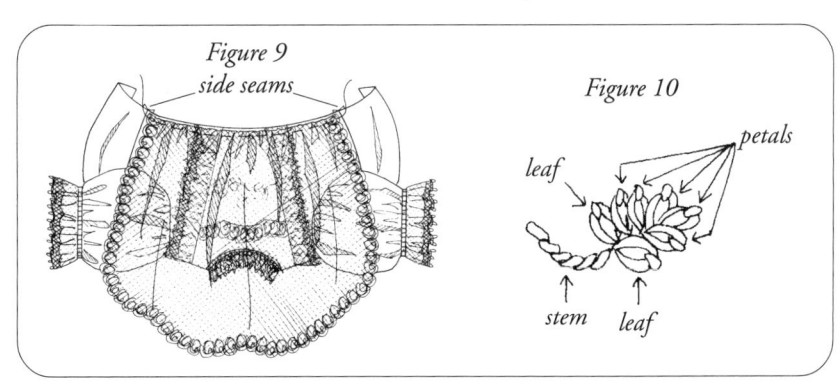

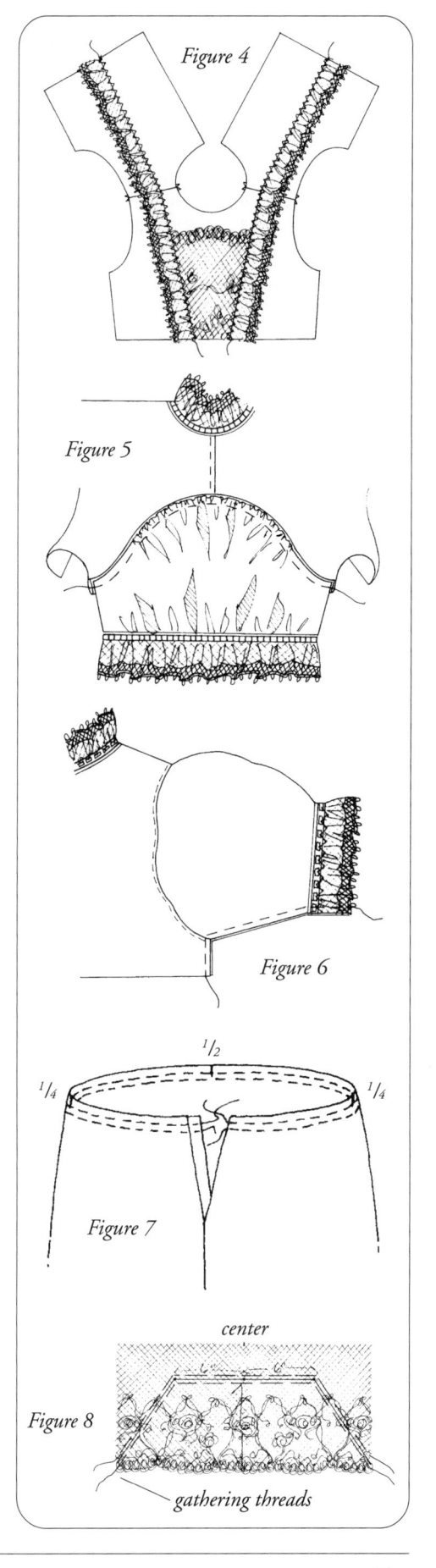

Figure 4

Figure 5

Figure 6

Figure 7

Figure 8
center
gathering threads

Figure 9
side seams

Figure 10
petals
leaf
stem
leaf

Dresses — Three Best Friends

Smocked Bodice Dress

Pink Swiss Nelona batiste is used for this beautiful dress, which is smocked to the shoulders. The dress is back smocked and finished with beautiful heirloom bullion rosebuds, French knots, and lazy daisy stitches. Satin ribbon finishes the neckline, the sleeves, and the skirt of this beautiful dress. The dress is not smocked in the back. There are clear plastic snaps to close the dress; however, little buttons are stitched on the outside giving the appearance of the dress's being buttoned. The sleeves are gathered with elastic.

Fabric Requirements

Fabric Requirements:

	13"	17 1/2", 18" and 19 1/2"
Fabric - Pink bastise	1/2 yard	2/3 yard
Fabric - Pink organdy (sleeves)	1/8 yard	1/4 yard
Pink Satin (neck bias)	1/4 yard	1/4 yard
Pink Satin Ribbon 7/8" (sleeves & hem)	2 yards	2 yards

2 1/2 yards of 1/2" ribbon can be substituted for the sleeve and hem trim.

Notions

Sewing thread, floss for smocking - DMC #963 (light pink), #3716 (medium pink), #955 (green), #800 (light blue), hand sewing needles for smocking, option: wash-away basting tape, Velcro™, snaps or tiny buttons

Directions

All Seams 1/4" unless otherwise indicated.

Please read through both the General Directions and the Specific Directions before starting the dress. The General Directions can be found on page 4 and give instructions for plackets, neck, and sleeve finishes. These Specific Directions give instructions for the special details concerning this particular dress and the sequence of the construction.

The following pattern pieces needed for this dress are found on the pull-outs: waisted front, mid-yoke back, elbow-length sleeve. Tiny roses smocking plate found on page 46.

A. Smocking & Creating the Dress Front

1. Cut a piece of fabric for the dress front 22" wide by the following lengths: 9" for the 13" doll, 14" for the 17 1/2" doll, 14 1/2" for the 18" doll and 15" for the 21 1/2" doll.
2. Fold the fabric in half to measure 11" wide. Mark the top edge of the fold, indicating the center front, using a fabric marker (fig. 1). Pleat the suggested number of rows for the following sizes:

    13" and 17 1/2" dolls   -   10 rows   18" and 19 1/2" dolls   -   11 rows
3. Pull a loop of pleating thread at each pleated row from the center of the pleated fabric. Cut the thread at the top of each loop (fig. 2). Remove one pleat from each side of the center, creating a 1/2" flat space in the center of the pleated fabric. Lay the pleated fabric on top of the waisted bodice and block to fit the width of the lower portion of the pattern below the armholes. Tie off pleating threads (fig. 3).

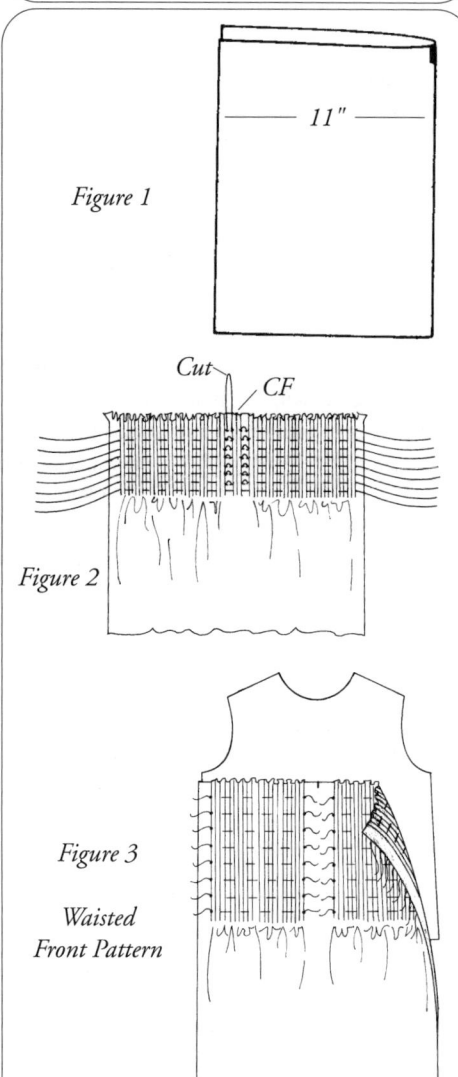

Smocked Bodice Dress

Figure 1

Figure 2

Figure 3

Waisted Front Pattern

Figure 4

Figure 5

Center Front
Dress Embroidery Design

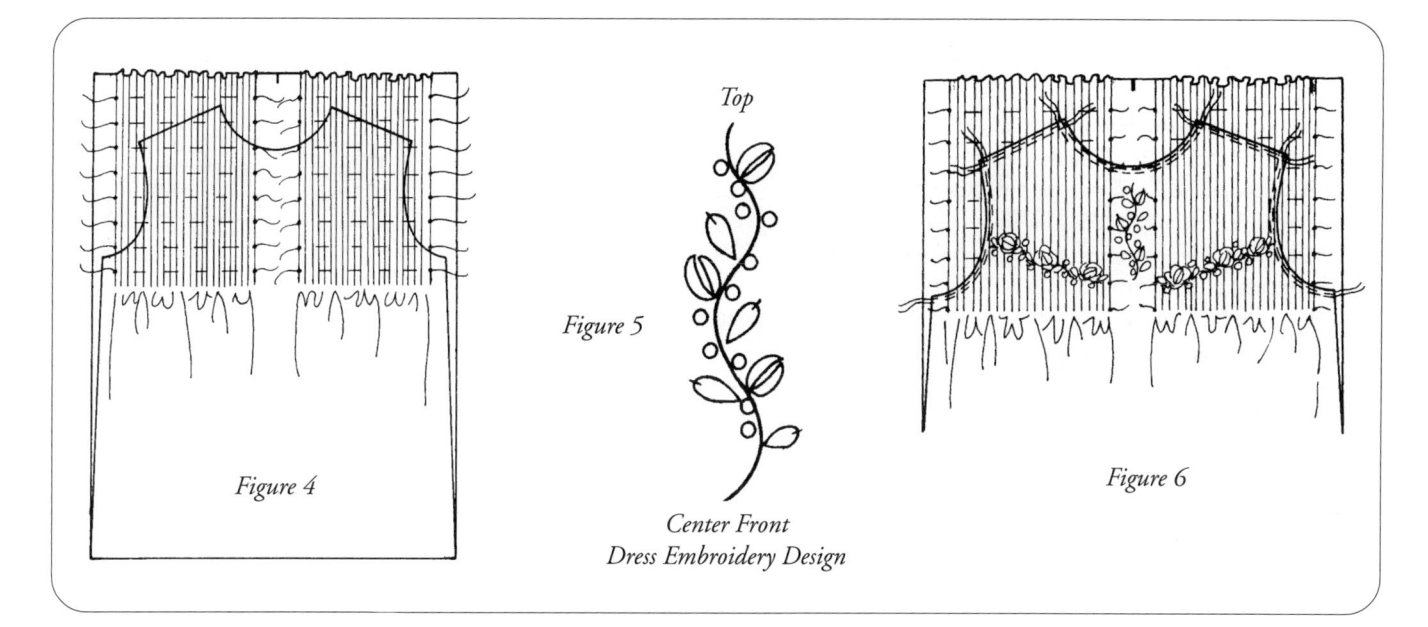

Figure 6

4. Backsmock all rows, except the top row and the bottom three rows, using a cable stitch.
5. When the backsmocking is complete, lay the front pattern piece on the pleated fabric with the top point of the neck/shoulder between the first and second pleating threads. Trace the outline of the pattern on the pleated fabric (fig. 4).
6. Starting at the center on the second pleating row from the bottom, work a *down cable, two steps up, up cable, two cable stitches (down, up), repeat from the * to form a "v". This "v" will cover 3 whole spaces and is worked in light pink floss. Repeat the same stitch combination just above the light pink row, stitching in green.
7. Work bullion roses about $5/8$" apart along "v" smocking. Add green lazy daisy stitches, filling in with French knots of blue and medium pink. Trace the embroidery template along the center space between the pleats. Work the vine in green using a stem stitch. Add bullion buds in medium pink, lazy daisy leaves in green and French knots in blue and medium pink.
8. Straight stitch several times just inside the drawn lines of the neck, armhole curve and shoulder lines (fig. 6). If this stitching stretches the bodice lines, use one of the stitching lines as a gathering line, pull the bobbin thread to shape the bodice to it's original meaurement. Trim the fabric along the drawn lines and trim any excess fabric from the sides.

B. Constructing the Dress

1. Cut out two mid-waist back bodices from the selvage, two sleeves (extend the length of the sleeve $5/8$") from organdy and one skirt back to the following measurement: 22" wide by the following length:
   13" $6 \, 1/2$"
   $17 \, 1/2$" $9 \, 3/4$"
   18" $10 \, 3/4$"
   $19 \, 1/2$" $10 \, 3/4$"
2. Place a placket in the center back of the skirt piece referring to the General Directions, A. Plackets, a. Continous Lap Placket.
3. Place the back bodices to the skirt backs, right sides together with the placket edges to the fold lines of the back bodices. Remember, one side of the placket will be folded to the inside of the skirt and pinned, while the other side will remain extended. Wrap each yoke back around the placket opening in the skirt (fig. 7a). Gather the skirt to fit the back yoke pieces. Stitch in place. Flip the yokes away from the skirt (fig. 7b).

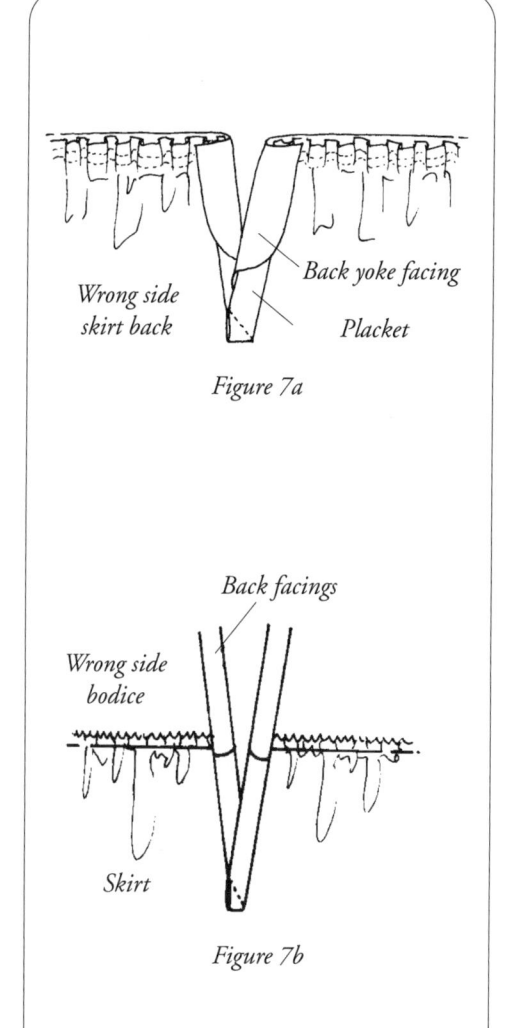

Figure 7a — Wrong side skirt back, Back yoke facing, Placket

Figure 7b — Wrong side bodice, Back facings, Skirt

Dresses   Three Best Friends   45

4. Stitch the dress front to the dress back at the shoulders. Match the arm openings and trim the lower front skirt piece even with the back skirt piece. Remove all pleating threads (fig. 8)
5. Finish the neck of the dress using a satin bias strip referring to the General Directions, C. Neck Finishes, c. Bias Binding. Before turning the bias binding to the wrong side of the dress and hemming, use the Tiny Roses Neck Embroidery Template (fig. 9) and work the embroidery along the front of the neck binding (fig. 10).
6. Finish the ends of the sleeves referring to the General Directions, B. Sleeves and Sleeve Finishes, f. Gathered Sleeves with Elastic and Ribbon.
7. Refer to the General Directions, B. Sleeves and Sleeve Finishes, h. Attaching the Sleeves and attach the sleeves to the dress.
8. Place the sides of the dress, right sides together, matching the ends of the sleeves, the underarm seams and the lower edges of the skirt. Stitch the side seams in place.
9. Finish the lower edge of the dress. If instructions are needed to attach the ribbon to the lower edge of the skirt, refer to the General Directions, B. Sleeves and Sleeve Finishes), f. Gathered Sleeves with Elastic and Ribbon, steps 2 - 4.
10. Close the dress using Velcro™, snaps, or tiny buttons and buttonholes along each side of the back bodice.

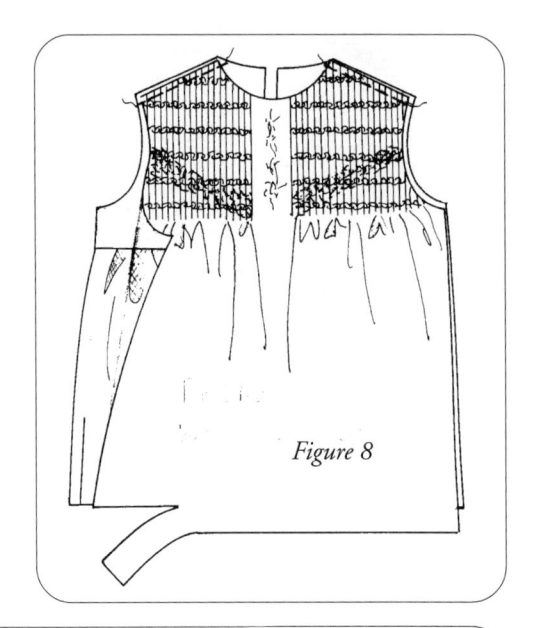

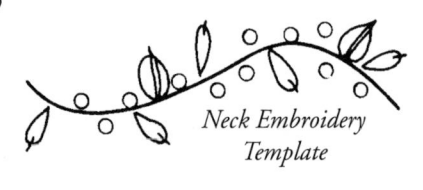

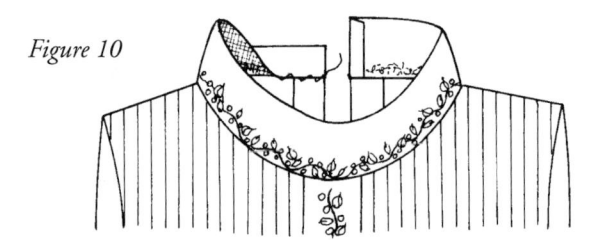

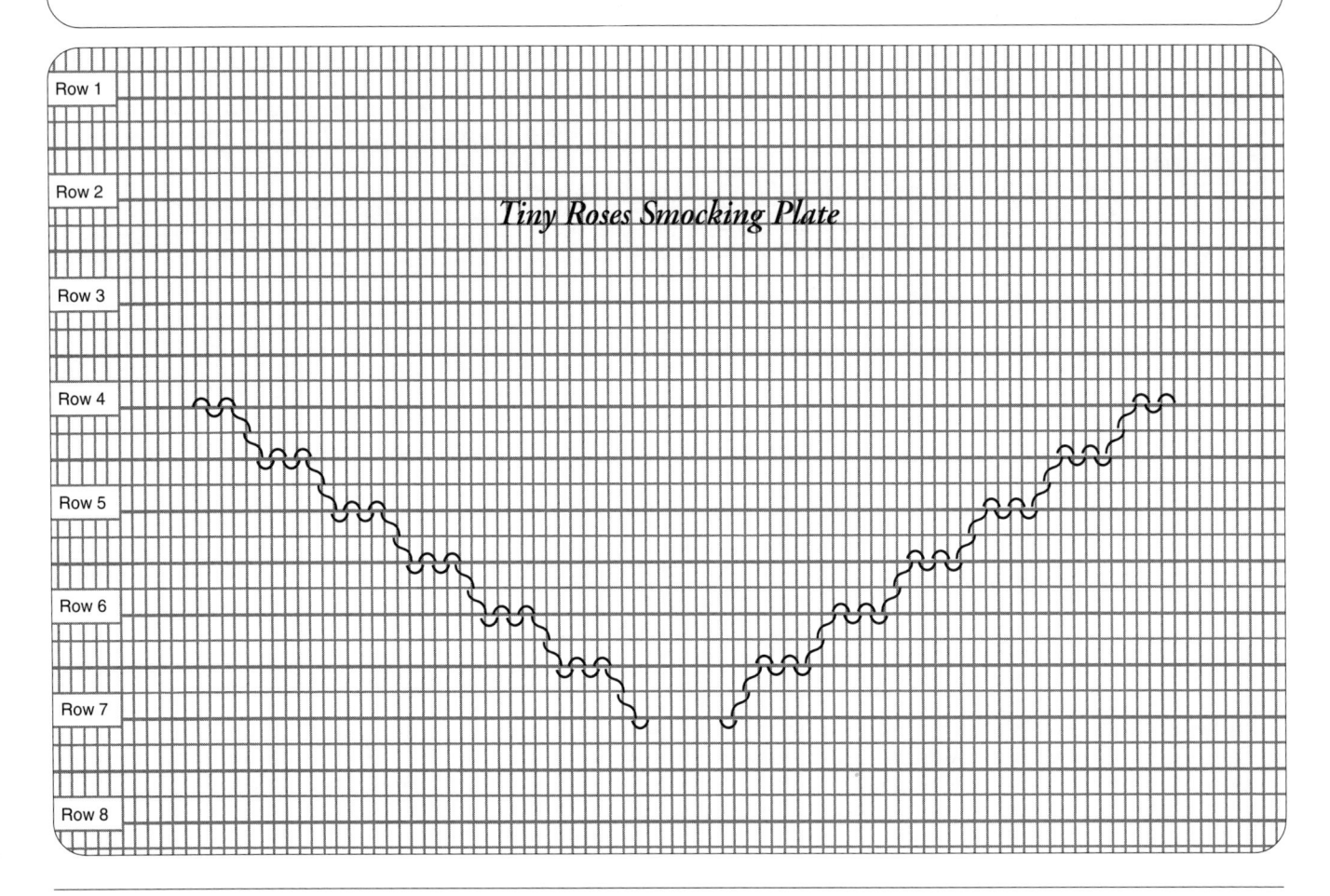

Figure 8

Figure 9

Neck Embroidery Template

Figure 10

Tiny Roses Smocking Plate

Row 1
Row 2
Row 3
Row 4
Row 5
Row 6
Row 7
Row 8

Three Best Friends *Dressses*

White Smocked Yoke Dress

Smocking done in shades of blue and pink shows the delicate side of doll dressing for the friends. The neckline is finished with entredeux and gathered narrow white edging on the top and two rows of white French insertion with edging for the collar. The sleeves are gathered and pink silk ribbon is threaded through the zigzag which holds the elastic. Narrow white French edging is found on the bottom of the sleeves. The skirt is finished with two rows of white French insertion and one row of French edging stitched on without any fullness. There is a beautiful sash which ties in the back of the dress. The back closes with Velcro™.

Fabric Requirements

Fabric Requirements:

	13"	17 1/2", 18" and 19 1/2"
Fabric - Swiss Batiste	1/2 yard	5/8 yards
Lace Insertion (1/2")	4 yards	4 1/4 yards
Lace Edging (3/8")	1/3 yard	1/3 yard
Lace Edging (1/2")	1 1/4 yards	1 1/2 yards
Lace Edging (1")	1 1/3 yards	1 1/3 yards
Entredeux	1/4 yard	1/4 yard
Silk Ribbon (2mm)	2/3 yard	2/3 yard
Elastic (1/8")	1/4 yard	1/4 yard
Baby Piping (white)	1/4 yard	1/4 yard

NOTE: You may make your own piping using tiny cord or gimp cord and a strip of bias fabric. Refer to the technique "Piping".

White Smocked Yoke Dress

Notions

Lightweight sewing thread, wash-out marker, Velcro™, snaps or tiny buttons (3).

Directions

Please read through both the General Directions and the Specific Directions before starting the dress. The General Directions can be found on page 4 and give instructions for the neck, sleeves and hem finishes. These Specific Directions give instructions for the special details concerning this particular dress and the sequence of the construction. The following pattern pieces are needed for this dress: High-yoke front, waisted-back, elbow-length sleeve and armhole guide. Smocking graph found on the pull-outs.

Figure 1

Figure 2

A. Creating the Lace Fancy Band and Lace Collar

1. Using the technique "lace to lace", create a strip of lace band 45" long. This band will have two strips of insertion and a strip of 1" lace edging (fig. 1). Lay this piece aside to attach to the skirt bottom.
2. Using the technique "lace to lace", create a strip of lace band 18" long for the 13" doll and 20" long for the 17 1/2", 18", and 19 1/2" dolls. This band will have two strips of insertion and a strip of 1/2" lace edging. Lay this piece aside to attach to the neck edge (fig. 2).

Figure 3

B. Embellishing the Sleeves

1. Cut two sleeves from the sleeve pattern. With a wash-out marker draw a line along the fold line down the center of each sleeve. Center a piece of lace insertion over the drawn line on each sleeve (fig. 3). Refer to the technique "Extra-stable Lace Finish" and attach the lace to the sleeves. Cut fabric from behind the lace insertion (fig. 4).
2. Refer to the General Directions, B. Sleeves and Sleeve Finishes, e. Gathered Sleeve with Elastic and Lace to finish the sleeve edges.

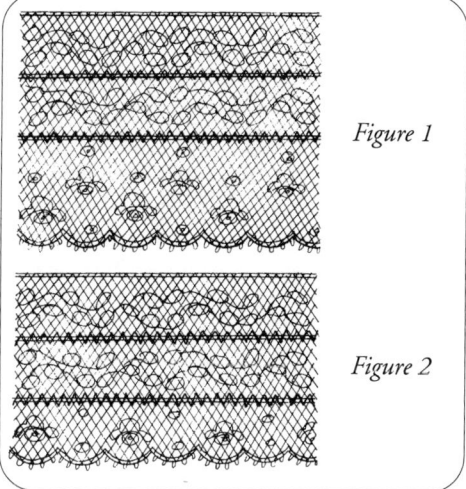

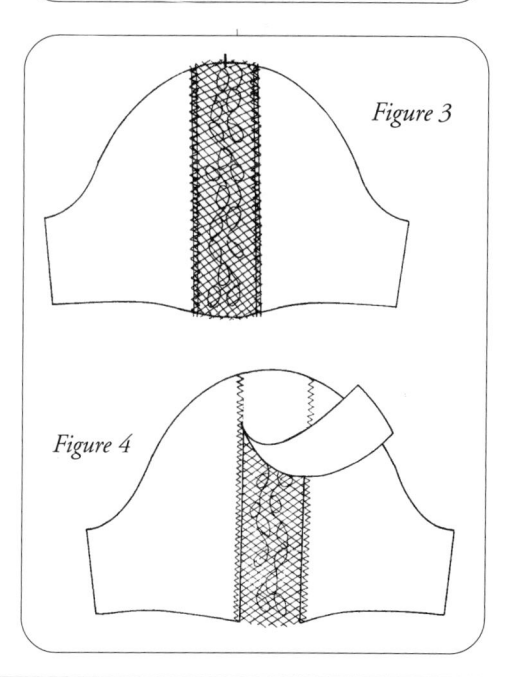

Figure 4

C. Yokes and Neckline

1. Cut one high-yoke front and two waisted backs on the selvage.
2. Place the pieces right sides together and stitch at the shoulder seams (fig. 5).
3. Finish the neck of the dress using the 3/8" edging lace and referring to the General Directions, C. Neck Finishes, A. Entredeux to Gathered Edging Lace.
4. The lace collar will be attached after the sleeves and skirts are attached to the yokes.

Figure 5

D. Skirts

1. Cut or tear a piece of fabric 5 1/4" by 22" for the 13" doll, 8 1/2" by 22" for the 17 1/2" doll, 9 1/4" by 22" for the 18" doll and 9 3/4" by 22" for the 19 1/2" doll. This piece is for the smocked skirt front.
2. Pleat 8 rows of 1/2 spaces. Rows 1 and 8 will not be smocked. Refer to the Smocking Plate found on the pull-outs and smock the skirt according to the directions below. All cables and waves are smocked in blue and the "dots" in the centers of the diamond shapes are stitched in pink.
   a. On row 2 smock a cable row beginning with a down cable.
   b. On row 3 begin with an up cable. *Step down one step to row 4, down cable, one step up to row 3, up cable. Repeat from * across the row.
   c. On row 5 begin with a down cable. *Step up one step to row 4, up cable, one step down to row 5, down cable. Repeat from * across the row.
   d. On row 5 begin with an up cable. *Step down one step to row 6, down cable, one step up to row 5, up cable. Repeat from * across the row.
   e. On row 7 begin with a down cable. *Step up one step to row 6, up cable, one step down to row 7, down cable. Repeat from * across the row.
   f. In the center of each diamond shape, stitch two cables butted up against each other to create the "dots". Note: You do not have to tie off between each "dot" if you go to the next diamond at an angle from the one you just stitched.
3. Trace the armhole curve onto each side of the smocked piece. Straight stitch with short stitches on the drawn line catching the smocking. Trim away the smocking inside the curve (fig. 6).
4. Block the smocked skirt piece to fit the front yoke (fig. 7).

Stitching line — Cut out armhole curves

Figure 6

Figure 7

E. Constructing the Dress

1. Attach the piping along the smocked skirt piece on the unsmocked row 1. Stitch very close to the piping (fig. 8).
2. Pin the yoke right sides together with the skirt front, sandwiching the piping in between. Stitch using the previous piping stitching line as a guide. Trim the seam to 1/8" and finish (fig. 9).
3. Cut or tear a skirt back piece 4" by 22" for the 13" doll, 6 1/4" by 22" for the 17 1/2" doll, 7" by 22" for the 18" and 19 1/2" doll.
4. Refer back to the General Directions, A. Placket, a. Continuous Lap Placket, to complete the back of the skirt.
5. Pull up the gathers in the skirt backs to fit the back bodice. Pin the bodice backs to the top gathered edges of the skirt with the right sides together, wrapping the back facings of the bodice around the skirt pieces (fig. 10). Stitch seams.

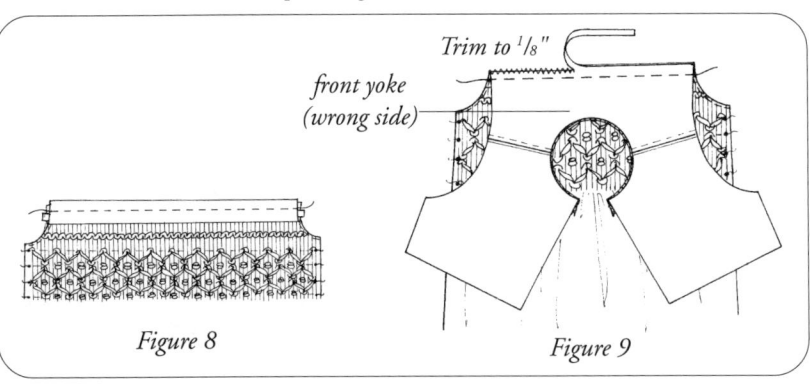

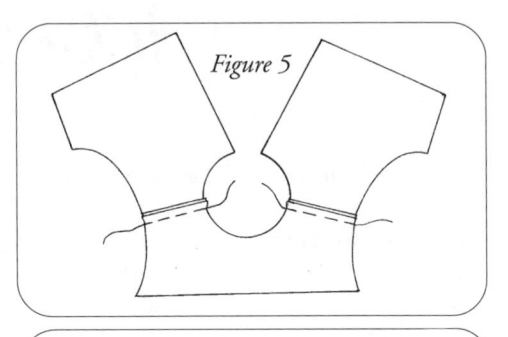

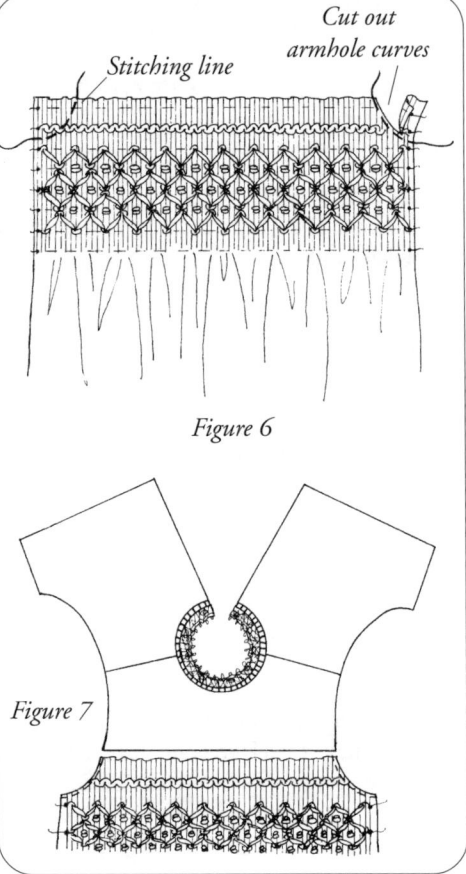

Trim to 1/8"
front yoke (wrong side)

Figure 8

Figure 9

back yoke (wrong side)
skirt back — skirt back

Figure 10

6. Place the sleeves to the arm openings, right sides together, matching the center of each sleeve to the shoulder seam of the bodice. Gather the sleeves to fit the openings with the gathers falling $3/4$" to $1 1/2$" on each side of the shoulder seam (fig. 11). Stitch in place.
7. Cut two pieces of fabric for the sashes $2 3/4$ by $14 1/2$". Fold each piece, right sides together and stitch. You may wish to angle the ends of the sashes to create a point approximately 1" from the end of each sash (fig. 12). Trim.
8. Turn the sashes and press well.
9. Pleat the sash at the unfinished end and pin to the back bodices on each side even with the raw edges of the bodice backs and having the lower edge of each sash even with the waist seam (fig. 13).
10. On the collar lace band you created in A., step 2, fold under $1/8$" once and then again along the raw edge of each end. Stitch in place to finish the edges (fig.14).
11. Pull a thread in the top edge of the collar fancy band and pull up the gathers to fit the neckline. The fancy band will be stitched from the fold of the facing on the right back bodice to $1/4$" from the fold of the facing on the left back bodice. Place the band onto the right side of the bodice and zigzag into place, catching the lace and hitting the holes of the entredeux (fig. 15).
12. Stitch one side seam of the dress from the lace edging on the sleeve to the lower skirt edge (fig. 16). Leave the other side seam open.
13. Attach the skirt fancy lace band to the lower edge of the skirt front and back using the technique "lace to fabric".
14. Stitch the remaining side seam of the skirt from the edge of the lace on the sleeve to the lower edge of the skirt lace band (fig. 17).
15. Cut the silk ribbon into two equal pieces. With a large tapestry needle or bodkin, lace through the zigzag stitch every $1/4$" beginning and ending on the outside center of the sleeve. Tie into a bow.
16. Close the back of the dress using Velcro™, snaps, or tiny buttons and buttonholes along each side of the back bodice.

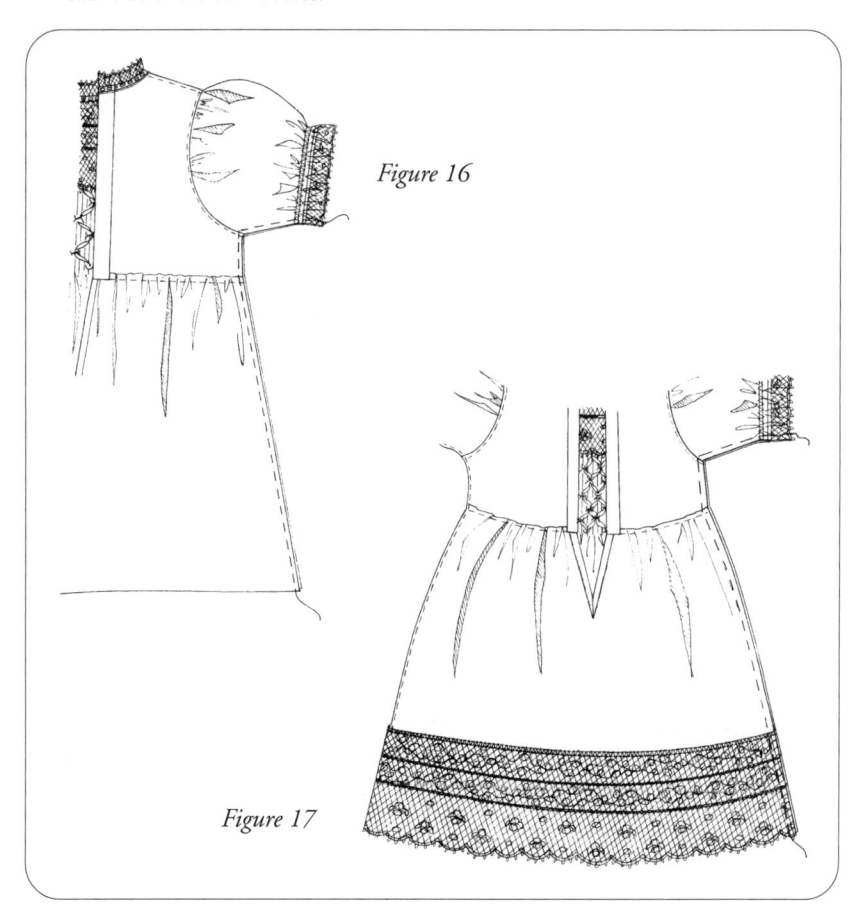

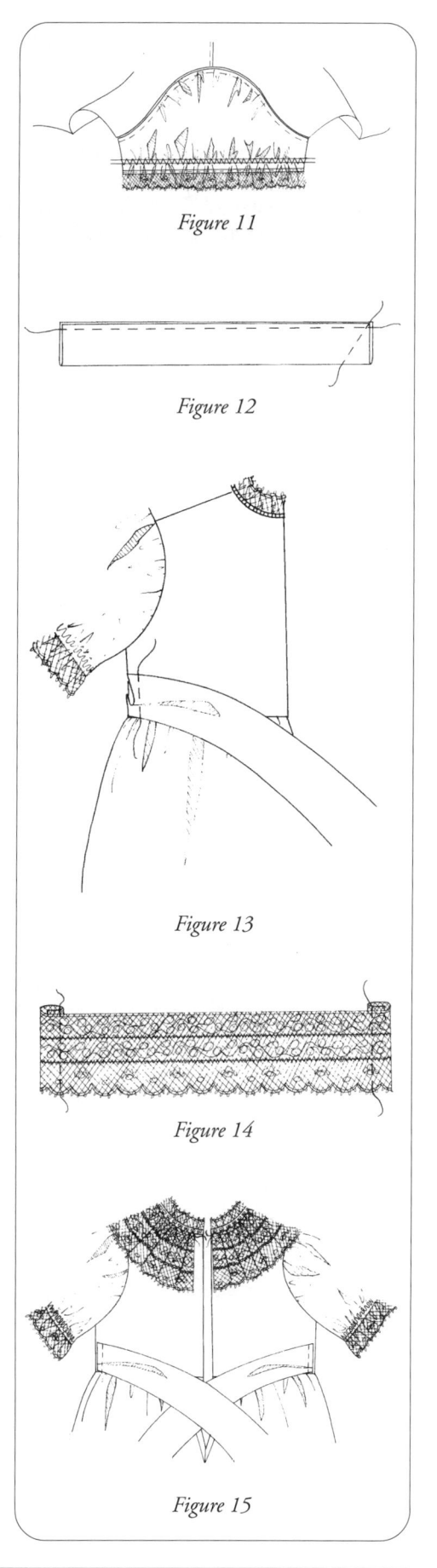

Figure 11

Figure 12

Figure 13

Figure 14

Figure 15

Figure 16

Figure 17

Lady Bugs Smocked Yoke Dress

Perfect for summer picnics or for back to school is this red baby gingham dress smocked with little ladybugs. The details on this dress are simply wonderful. The smocked inset is on ecru broadcloth and it is inserted into the dress with navy piping on both the top and the bottom. The little ruffle around the bias finished neckline has tiny navy blue piping at the bottom of the red gingham ruffle. The puffed sleeves have the sweetest little cuff with navy piping at the top of the cuff. The back of the dress is closed with snaps; however, little navy buttons are stitched on top to look like it is buttoned rather than snapped.

Fabric Requirements

Fabric Requirements:

	13"	17 1/2", 18" and 19 1/2"
Fabric - Micro check (red-white)	1/2 yard	5/8 yard
Fabric - Ecru for smocking	3" by 36"	3" by 36"
Fabric - Fabric (blue for piping) (purchased baby piping can be used)	1/4 yard	1/4 yard

Notions

Sewing thread, hand sewing needles for smocking, tiny cord or yarn for piping, option: wash-away basting tape, Velcro™, snaps or tiny buttons, wash-out marker, Floss for smocking - DMC #820 (royal blue), #321 (red), #890 (forest green), #310 (black), Ecru

Directions

All Seams 1/4" unless otherwise indicated. Finish all seams with a serger or zigzag stitch.

Please read through both the General Directions and the Specific Directions before starting the dress. The General Directions can be found on page 4 and give instructions for neck, sleeves and hem finishes. These Specific Directions give instructions for the special details concerning this particular dress and the sequence of the construction.

The following pattern pieces needed for this dress are found on the pull-outs: High yoke front, waisted back, armhole guide, elbow-length sleeve. Lady bugs smocking plate found on page 52.

Lady Bugs Smocked Yoke Dress

Figure 1

A. Smocking

1. Cut a piece of ecru fabric 2 1/2" by 36" for the 13" doll and 2 1/2" by 40" for the 17 1/2", 18" and 19 1/2" dolls.
2. Pleat 10 **half-space rows** in the center of the ecru fabric strip. Flatten the ends of the pleated piece and place the armhole guide along each side in the following manner: top edge of the armhole guide even with the first pleating row and the side of the armhole guide even with the side of the fabric. Trace the curve using a fabric marker or fabric pencil. Remove the pleating rows from the armhole. Block the top pleating row, from armhole line to armhole line to fit the lower edge of the front yoke. Tie off the pleating threads (fig. 1).
3. Smock using the following directions:
   (Note: The numbered rows indicate half-space rows.)
   a. Rows 1 and 10 are not smocked. These rows will be used for construction.
   b. Backsmock Rows 4 and 6 using one strand of ecru floss and a cable stitch.
   c. Cable across Row 2 in royal blue.
   d. Between Rows 8 and 9, work a five cable baby wave combination using ecru in the following manner: five cables are worked on row 9, beginning and ending with a down cable and the baby wave is worked up to Row 8 and down to Row 9. Continue across the row.
   e. Work a vine between Rows 4 and 6 in green using the following directions: beginning on Row 4 * work four stem stitches and one up cable, work eight steps down to Row 6 and continue across Row 6 with five stem stitches, work up to Row 4 with seven steps and an up cable. Continue the vine between Rows 4 and 6 from the *. Add leaves to the vine using lazy daisy stitches.

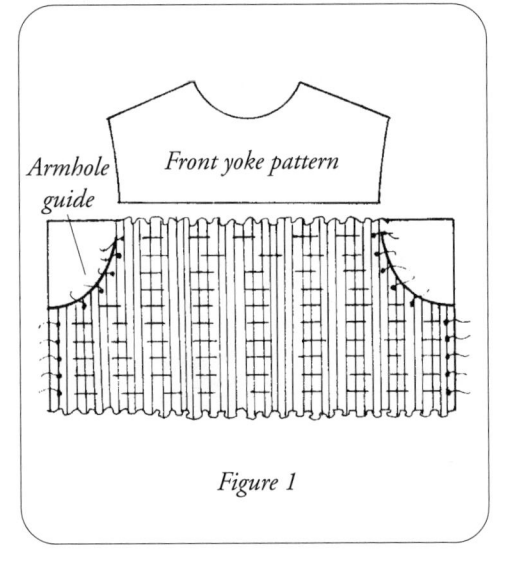

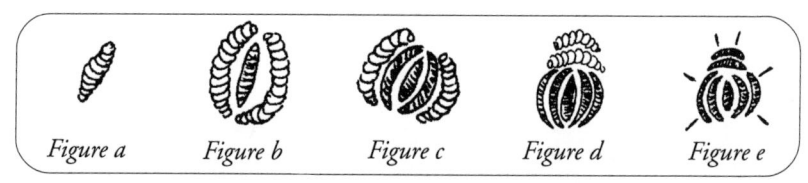

Figure a   Figure b   Figure c   Figure d   Figure e

f. Add lady bugs to the vine in the desired locations (Refer to Lady Bug diagram above). The lady bugs are made with bullion stitches using the following colors: body center - black (12 wraps)(fig. a); each side of center - red (14 wraps)(fig. b); outer body each side - red (10 wraps)(fig. c); head - black (10 wraps)(fig. d), black (8 wraps)(fig. d). Add straight stitches for legs and antenna (fig. e).

B. Dress and Sleeve Construction

1. Cut one front yoke from the fold, cut two back bodices from the selvage and cut two sleeves. Also cut skirt, collar and cuff pieces to the following measurements:

	one skirt piece (allows for 2" hem)	two collar pieces	two cuff pieces
13" doll	8 1/2" by 45"	1" by 12"	1" by 3 3/4"
17 1/2" doll	10 3/4" by 45"	1" by 13"	1" by 5"
18" doll	11 1/2" by 45"	1" by 14"	1" by 5 1/4"
19 1/2" doll	11 1/2" by 45"	1" by 15"	1" by 5 1/2"

2. Cut 4 to 5 bias strips, 3/4" wide from blue fabric for the piping. For the larger dresses, join two of the strips together to form a strip long enough for the collar strip. Construct the piping pieces using the directions for Making Piping (pg. 118) or you may use purchased piping.

3. Place one of the piping strips above the blue smocked cable row and one strip below the smocking on row 9. Baste the strips in place by machine or stick in place using wash-away basting tape. Machine baste around the armhole markings and cut out the armhole (fig. 2).

4. Place the front yoke to the top of the pleated strip, right sides together and stitch in place close to the piping (fig. 3).

5. Place the front bodice to the back bodice at the shoulders and stitch in place.

6. Match the underarm seams (front to back) and trim the lower edges of the back bodices even with the lower piped edge of the smocked front bodice (fig. 4).

7. To create the collar, baste the long piping strip to the right side of one long side of one collar piece. The piping should extend past the ends of the collar (fig. 5). Place the second collar piece to the first, right sides together. Stitch along the short sides and very close to the piping. One long side is left open (fig. 6).

8. Turn the collar piece to the right side and press.

9. Run two gathering rows, 1/8" and 1/4" from the cut edge of the collar piece (fig. 7).

10. Gather the collar to fit the neck of the dress, from back fold line to back fold line. Stitch in place (fig. 8).

11. Finish the neck of the dress referring to the General Directions - C. Neck Finishes - c. Bias Binding (fig. 9).

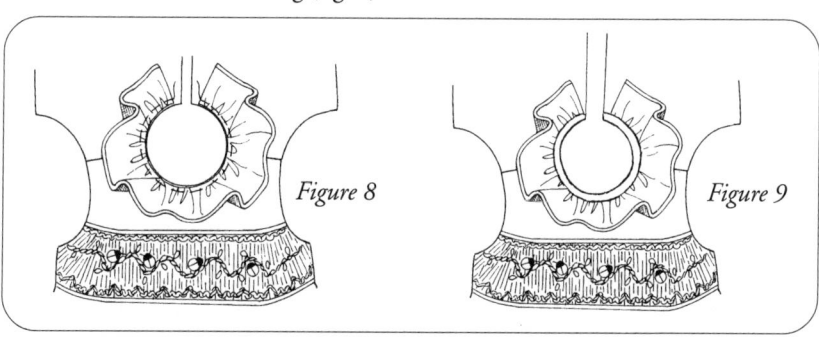

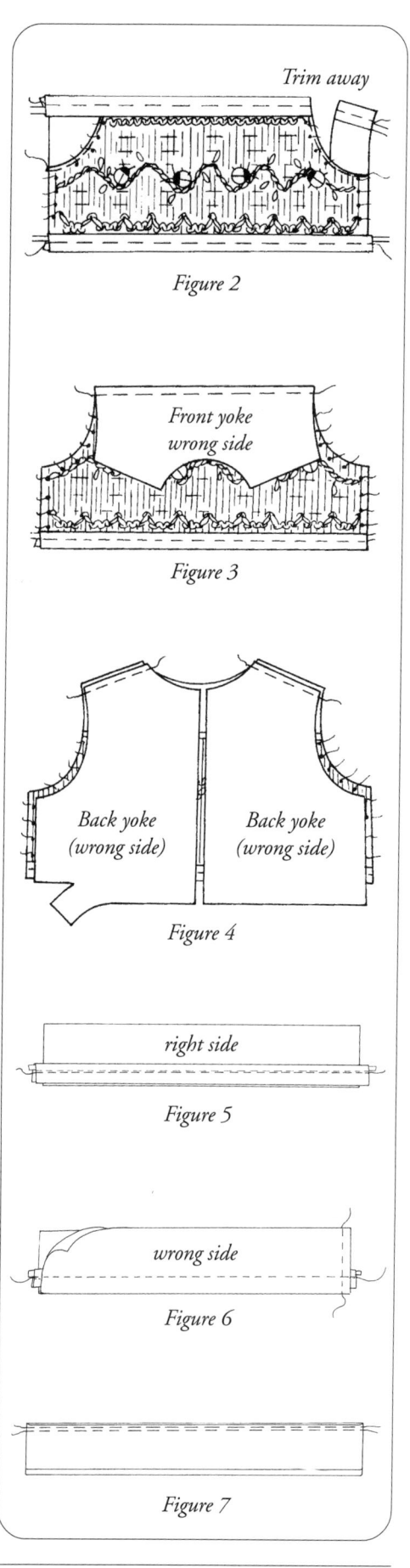

Trim away

Figure 2

Front yoke wrong side

Figure 3

Back yoke (wrong side)   Back yoke (wrong side)

Figure 4

right side

Figure 5

wrong side

Figure 6

Figure 7

Figure 8

Figure 9

Dresses   Three Best Friends

12. Finish the ends of the sleeves referring to the General Directions, B. Sleeves and Sleeve Finishes, d. Bias Sleeve Bindings adding piping between the sleeve and the sleeve binding.
13. Refer to the General Directions, B. Sleeves and Sleeve Finishes. Complete steps 1 - 3. Gather the sleeves to fit the openings with the gathers falling $3/4$" to $1 1/2$" on each side of the shoulder seam. Place the sleeves to the arm openings, right sides together, matching the center of each sleeve to the shoulder seam of the bodice. Stitch in place (fig. 10).
14. Place the sides of the dress, right sides together, matching the ends of the sleeves, the underarm seams and the lower edges of the bodice. Stitch the side seams in place (fig. 11).
15. Create a placket in the skirt referring to the General Directions, A. Plackets, b. Placket in a Seam. Fold the skirt in half to find the center. Mark at the top edge. Fold the skirt again to find the quarter points. Mark at the top edge.
16. Run two gathering rows, $1/8$" and $1/4$" in the top edge of the skirt Place the back bodices to the skirt back, right sides together with the placket edges to the fold lines of the back bodices. Remember, one side of the placket will be folded to the inside of the skirt and pinned, while the other side will remain extended (fig. 12). Wrap each bodice back around the placket opening in the skirt. Gather the skirt to fit the bodice matching the center of the skirt to the center front bodice and the quarter markings on the skirt with the side seams of the bodice. Stitch in place (fig. 13). Remember to stitch very close to the piping along the front bodice. Flip the bodice away from the skirt.
17. Measure the length of the dress from the neck edge down the center back. Hem to a finished length of 9" for the 13" doll, 13 $1/4$" for the 17 $1/2$" doll, 14 $1/4$" for the 18" doll and 15" for the 19 $1/2$" doll. (fig. 14).
18. Close the dress using Velcro™, snaps, or tiny buttons and buttonholes along each side of the back bodice.

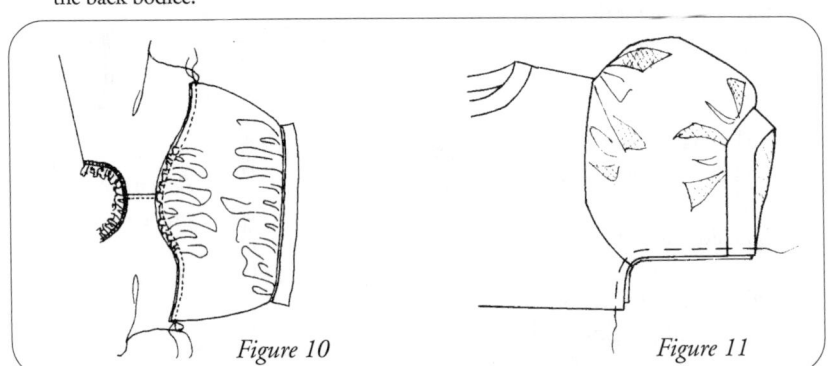

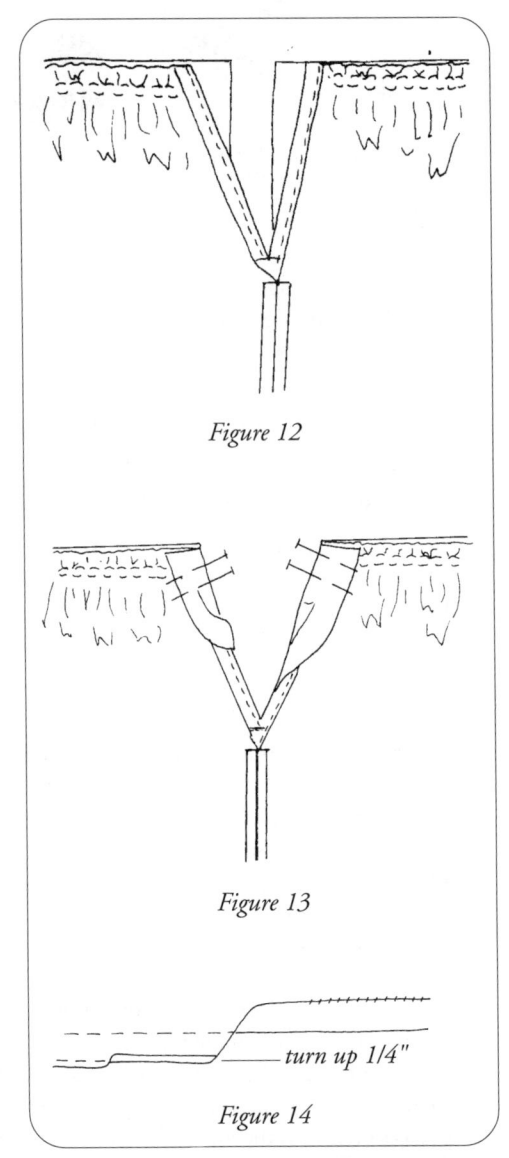

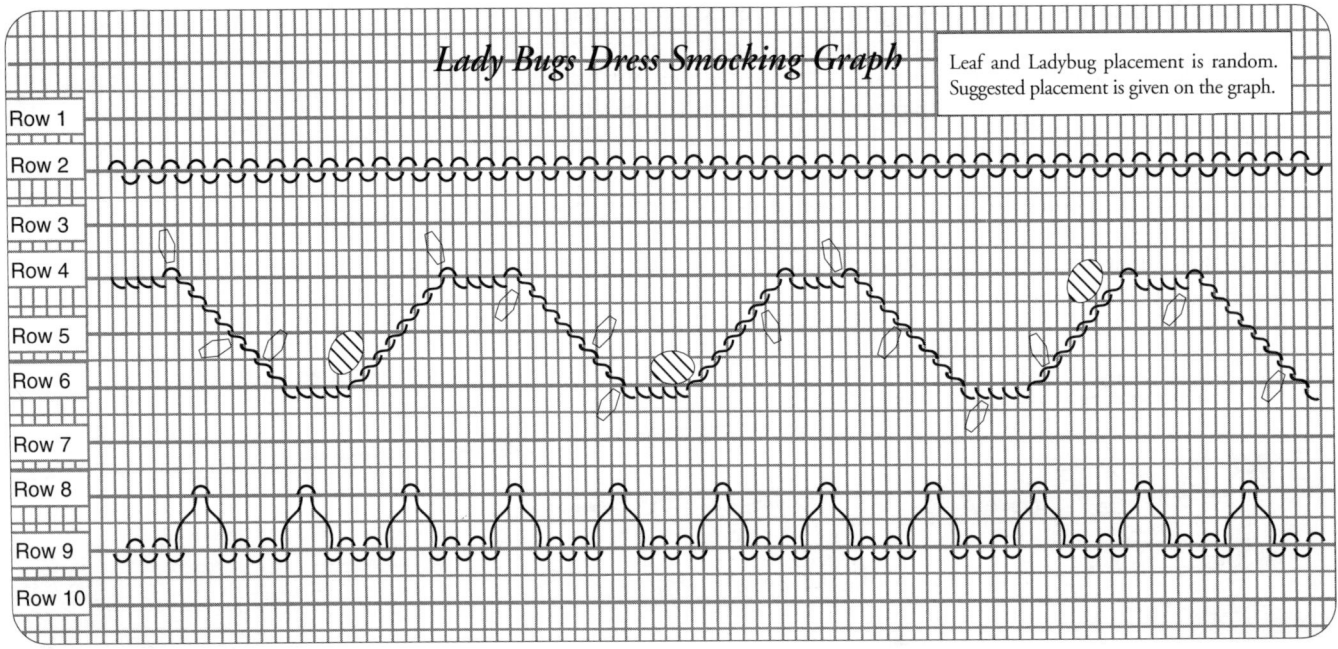

Figure 10

Figure 11

Figure 12

Figure 13

turn up 1/4"

Figure 14

Lady Bugs Dress Smocking Graph

Leaf and Ladybug placement is random. Suggested placement is given on the graph.

Row 1
Row 2
Row 3
Row 4
Row 5
Row 6
Row 7
Row 8
Row 9
Row 10

Dusty Pink Antique Middy

This doll dress is an exact copy of an antique dress from my vintage doll dress collection. Finding antique doll dresses is quite a task as I am sure you can imagine. This dress is made of dusty pink Swiss batiste. The reason this dress is called a French Middy is because around 1890-1910, this style was referred to as "French style" in the turn-of-the-century pattern books. This dress is made very beautifully with a little camisole underneath the top which holds the puffy middy in place so it won't droop. The trims are absolutely gorgeous, and the Swiss white and pink entredeux bordered trim is found on the sleeves, on the V on the front of the dress, and on the fancy band around the bottom. Gathered white French lace has been placed on the bottom side of this Swiss trim on the V in the front, the square shape on the back and on the sleeves. The neckline is finished with entredeux and gathered French edging trim. The fancy band is French insertion, Swiss trim, French insertion, and flat French edging. The dress skirt is lined with the dusty pink Nelona. The dress closes in the back with Velcro™. If you are entering a dress competition where historically correct clothing is necessary, this dress pattern is the one for you. It is historically correct even to the upper camisole lining which holds the fullness in the French middy. The Three Best Friends will enjoy wearing this dress for a portrait or for Sunday School.

Dusty Pink Antique Middy

Fabric Requirements

Fabric Requirements:

	13"	17 1/2", 18" and 19 1/2"
Dusty Pink Nelona	2/3 yard	1 yard
1/2" lace insertion	2 3/4 yards	2 3/4 yards
3/4" lace edging	4 1/2 yards	5 yards
1/2" Swiss insertion with entredeux	2 1/4 yards	2 1/2 yards
Entredeux	1/4 yard	1/4 yard

Notions

Lightweight sewing thread, Velcro™, snaps or tiny buttons, wash-out marker

Directions

All Seams 1/4" unless otherwise indicated. Finish all seams with a zigzag or serge to finish the fabric edges.

Please read through both the General Directions and the Specific Directions before starting the dress. The General Directions can be found on page 4 and give instructions for neck, sleeves and hem finishes. These Specific Directions give instructions for the special details concerning this particular dress and the sequence of the construction.

The following pattern pieces, found on the pull-outs, are needed for this dress: Over-bodice front, over-bodice back, inner-bodice front, inner-bodice back and long sleeve.

Clip to stitching

Figure 1

Press to inside

Figure 2 *Zigzag folded edge*

Construction

1. Cut out the over-bodice front from the fold.
2. Cut out two over-bodice backs from the selvage. Mark the placket fold lines along the backs.
3. Cut out the inner-front bodice from the fold. Cut out the inner-back bodice from the selvage. Mark the placket fold lines along the backs.
4. Cut out two sleeves.
5. Cut one skirt lining piece 45" wide by the following lengths: 4 3/4" for the 13" doll, 6 1/4" for the 17 1/2" doll, 6 3/4" for the 18" doll and 7 3/4" for the 19 1/2" doll.
6. Cut one skirt piece 45" wide by the following lengths: 3 1/4" for the 13" doll, 4 3/4" for the 17 1/2" doll, 5 1/4" for the 18" doll and 6 1/4" for the 19 1/2" doll.
7. Place the shoulders of the inner bodice front and the inner bodice back right sides together and stitch.
8. Finish the edge of the neck and armholes of the inner bodice using the following directions:
   a. Stitch 1/4" from the raw edge of the neck and armhole.
   b. Clip the curve to the stitching line (fig. 1).
   c. Press the seam allowance to the wrong side along the stitching line.
   d. From the right side stitch over the folded edge using a small zigzag (fig. 2).

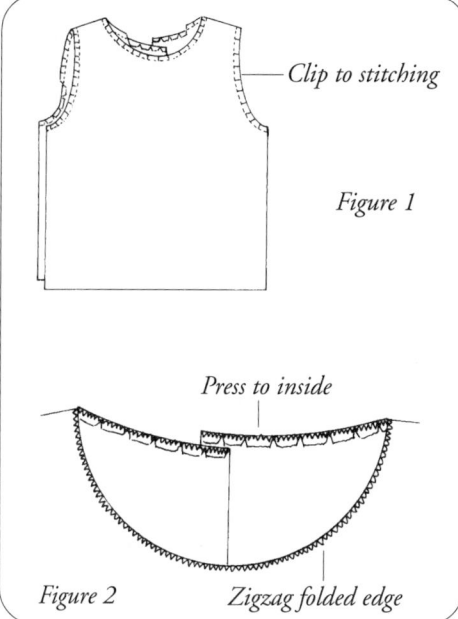

Dresses *Three Best Friends*

Figure 3

Figure 4

Clip to zigzag

Inner Bodice

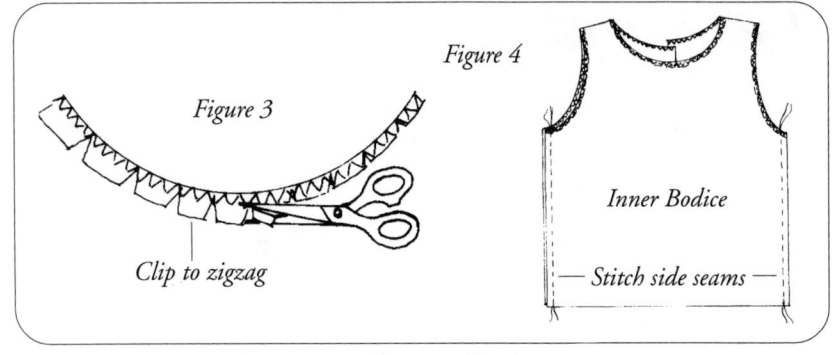

Stitch side seams

   e. Trim the excess fabric close to the zigzag (fig. 3).
9. Place the sides of the inner bodice, right sides together. Pin and stitch (fig. 4).
10. Set aside.
11. Place the shoulders of the over-bodice front and over-bodice backs, right sides together and stitch.
12. Referring to General Directions, B. Sleeves and Sleeve Finishes, a. Entredeux to Gathered Edging Lace finish the sleeves using the Swiss insertion with entredeux in place of the entredeux.
13. Refer to General Directions, B. Sleeves and Sleeve Finishes, h. Attaching the Sleeves and attach the sleeves to the bodice (fig. 5).
14. Place a mark measuring from the raw neck edge at each shoulder seam 1" for the 13" doll and $1 \frac{1}{4}$" for the $17 \frac{1}{2}$", 18" and $19 \frac{1}{2}$" dolls (fig. 6 - point A).
15. Place a mark measuring from the raw neck edge at the center front $2 \frac{1}{4}$" for the 13" doll and $2 \frac{3}{4}$" for the $17 \frac{1}{2}$", 18" and $19 \frac{1}{2}$" dolls (fig. 6 - point B).
16. Place a mark measuring down the selvage from the raw neck edge 2" for the 13" doll and $2 \frac{1}{2}$" for the $17 \frac{1}{2}$", 18" and $19 \frac{1}{2}$" dolls (fig. 6 - point C).
17. Place a mark on each side of the over-bodice back straight across from the dot made in step 16. Measure over 2" for the 13" doll and $2 \frac{1}{4}$" for the $17 \frac{1}{2}$", 18" and $19 \frac{1}{2}$" dolls (fig. 6 - point D).
18. On the over-bodice front draw a line from the shoulders to the mark at the center front creating a "V". On the over-bodice back draw a line from the shoulders to the mark made in step 17 and across to the selvage at the dot made in step 16.
19. Place the Swiss insertion with the outside edge along the drawn line mitering the insertion at the center front and the corner on the over-bodice backs. Press the miters well.
20. Remove the insertion from the bodice, zigzag the folds of the miter with the miters still folded in place. Trim away the excess insertion from behind the miters if needed (fig. 7).
21. Reposition the insertion on the over-bodice and straight stitch in place in the "ditch" between the entredeux edge and the fabric portion of the insertion. Stitch both edges of the insertion in place on the bodice (fig. 8).
22. Measure around the outside edge of the insertion and cut a piece of lace edging twice this measurement. Gather the lace edging by pulling a thread and stitch the gathered lace edging in place with a small zigzag attaching it to the outside entredeux edge of the insertion (this will be similar to the technique "gathered lace to entredeux") (fig. 9).
23. Refer to C. Neck Finishes, a. Entredeux to Gathered Edging Lace and finish the neckline of the dress.
24. Place the over-bodice front to the over-bodice back, right sides together and stitch the side seams (fig. 10).

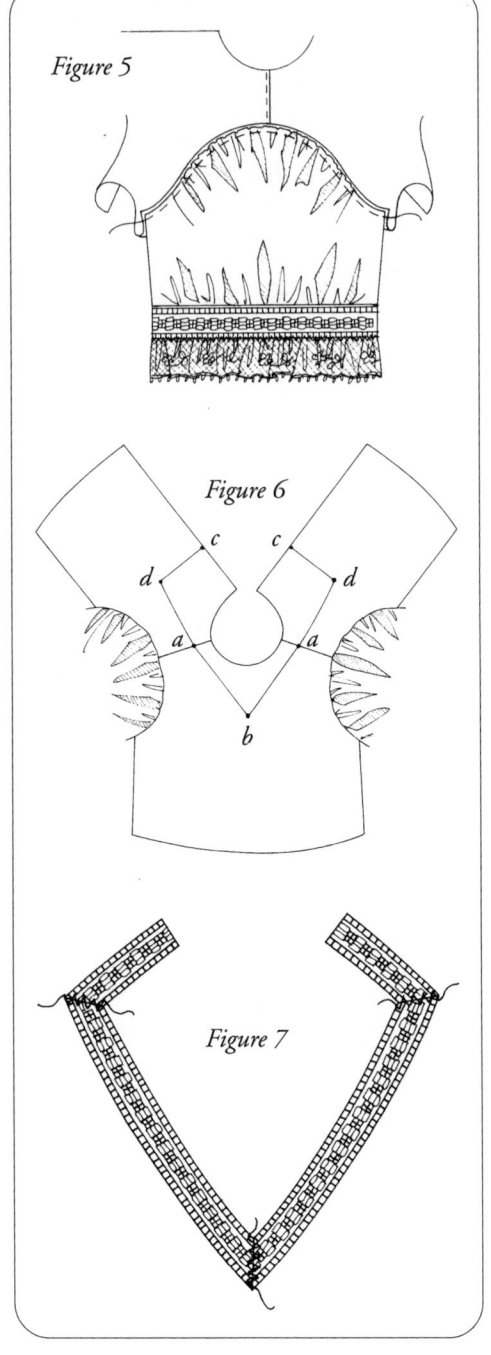

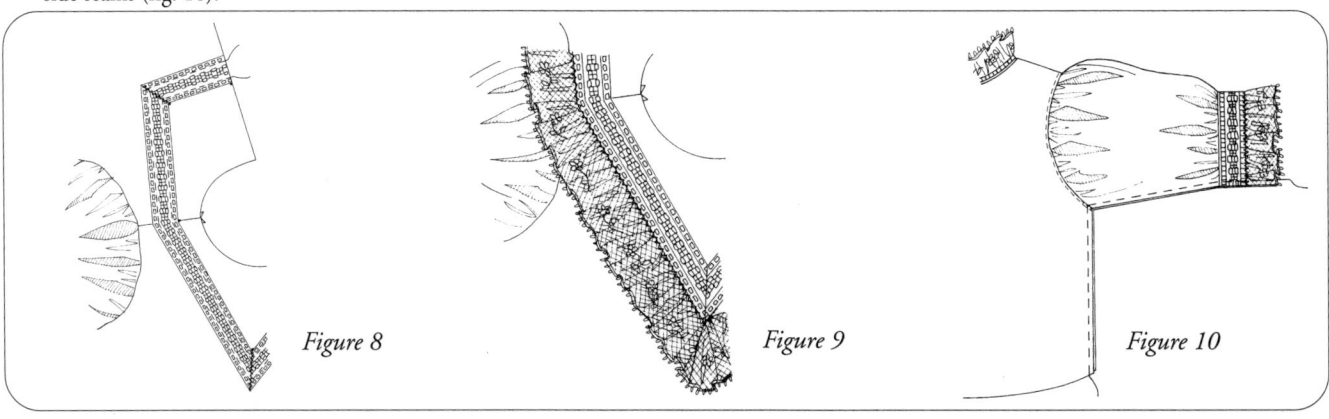

Figure 5

Figure 6

Figure 7

Figure 8

Figure 9

Figure 10

54 Three Best Friends Dresses

25. Press the back facings to the inside of the over bodice along the fold lines.
26. Run two gathering rows along the bottom of the over bodice at $1/4$" and $1/8$" from the raw edge.
27. Place the wrong side of the over bodice to the right side of the inner bodice with the folded edge of the outer to the fold line of the inner bodice. The inner bodice will extend beyond the folded edge of the over bodice. Gather the bottom of the over-bodice to fit the bottom of the inner bodice. Baste the two bodices together along the lower edge using a $1/4$" seam. Lay the bodice of the dress aside.
28. Refer to the technique "lace to fabric" and attach the lace edging flat to the lower edge of the skirt lining.
29. Create a 45" fancy band of laces and insertion using the techniques "lace to lace" and "lace to entredeux". The order of the laces are: lace insertion, Swiss insertion, lace insertion and lace edging.
30. Attach the fancy band to the lower edge of the skirt using the technique "lace to fabric"
31. Place the right side of the skirt lining to the wrong side of the skirt having the top edges even. Baste the two layers together and treat them as one layer (fig. 11).
32. Refer to A. Placket, b. Placket in a Seam, and place a placket in the back of the double layered skirt. Remember to treat the layers as one when stitching the back seam and inserting the placket.
33. Mark the center and quarter points of the skirt. Place the skirt to the outer/inner bodice, right sides together matching the quarter points of the skirt to the side seams and the center front of the skirt to the center of the bodice. Gather the top edge of the skirt to fit the outer/inner bodices (fig. 12).
34. Place the left side of the skirt opening $3/8$" from the left edge of the inner bodice. The fold of the skirt will be even with the fold of the outer bodice. Wrap the inner bodice over the edge of the skirt (fig. 13).
35. Place the right folded edge of the skirt opening even with the folded edge of the outer bodice (see fig. 13). Wrap the inner bodice over the edge of the skirt. Stitch in place using a $1/4$" seam. Overcast or serge. Pull the bodice away from the skirt allowing the back placket to flip to the inside of the bodice. Note: the plackets will be flipped to the right side of the inner bodice (fig. 14).
36. Turn the dress to the right side. Holding the shoulder of the outer bodice and the shoulder of the inner bodice together, match the back folded edges of the inner and outer bodices. The neck edge of the inner bodice will fall about $1/4$" below the seam line edge of the neck. At the skirt seam pull the excess fabric of the outer bodice over the skirt to form a fold. Place buttonholes, snaps or Velcro™ along the back openings through both layers of the inner and outer bodices. (fig. 15).
37. A ribbon sash can be added at the dropped waist line if desired.

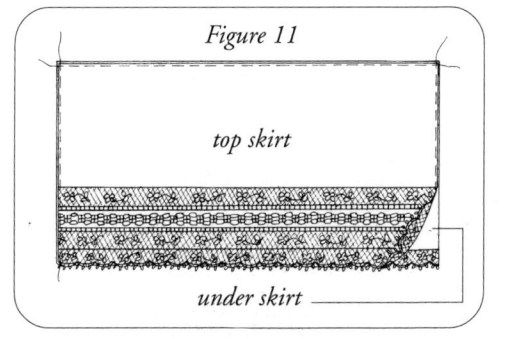

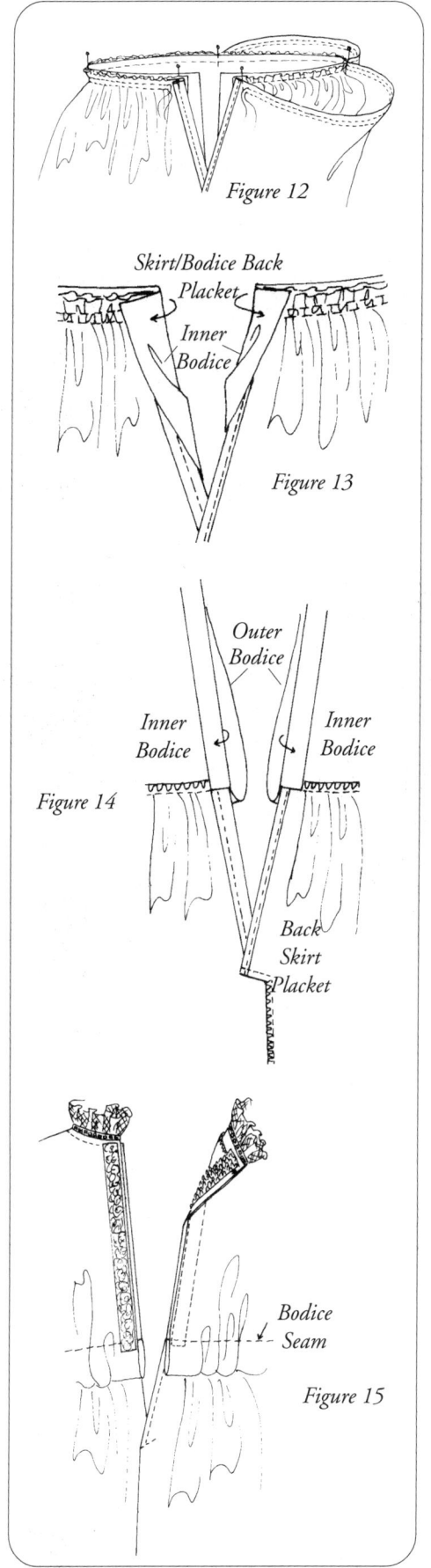

Figure 11

top skirt

under skirt

Figure 12

Skirt/Bodice Back Placket
Inner Bodice

Figure 13

Outer Bodice
Inner Bodice
Inner Bodice
Figure 14
Back Skirt Placket

Bodice Seam
Figure 15

Middy Bow Dress

White is such a special color and the Three Best Friends feel special when they wear white. This little middy made of white Victorian batiste has so many wonderful details. The middy front has double needle pintucks as well as a French insertion lace diamond on the front. The bottom of the diamond is trimmed with gathered white French edging. There is a tiny embroidered bow in the center of the diamond. The puffed sleeves have an entredeux, white French insertion, and white French edging on the bottom of the entredeux. The neckline is trimmed with entredeux and gathered white French edging. The skirt is fabulous with its three double needle pintucks and the fancy band below that. The fancy band consists of white French insertion, embroidered white bow insertion on batiste, two rows of white French insertion, and a row of white French edging stitched on flat. The back of the dress is closed with Velcro™. This would be a perfect First Communion dress for the Three Best Friends.

Middy Bow Dress

Fabric Requirements

Fabric Requirements:

	13"	17 1/2", 18 and 19 1/2"
White Batiste	1/2 yd	5/8 yd
Lace insertion (3/8")	5 yds	5 1/4 yds
Lace edging (3/8")	2 1/2 yds	2 5/8 yds
Lace edging (1/2")	1/3 yd	1/2 yd
2" Swiss insertion	1 1/2 yds	1 1/2 yds
Entredeux	5/8 yd	3/4 yd

Notions

Lightweight sewing, paper, Velcro™, snaps or tiny buttons, wash-out marker

Directions

All Seams 1/4" unless otherwise indicated. Finish all seams with a zigzag or serge to finish the fabric edges.

Please read through both the General Directions and the Specific Directions before starting the dress. The General Directions can be found on page 4 and give instructions for neck, sleeves and hem finishes. These Specific Directions give instructions for the special details concerning this particular dress and the sequence of the construction.

The follow pattern pieces found on the pull-outs are needed for this dress: dropped-waist front, dropped-waist back, elbow-length sleeve. Bodice Template found on the pull-outs.

Figure 1

Figure 2

Construction

1. Cut the following pieces for the given sizes of dolls:

	13"	17 1/2", 18", 19 1/2"
One rectangle of batiste	5" by 8"	6" by 9"
One rectangle of batiste	5" by 7"	6" by 8"

2. Cut one skirt piece 45" wide by the following lengths for the dolls: 13" = 2 7/8", 17 1/2" = 4 3/8", 18" = 4 7/8" and 19 1/2" = 5 7/8".
3. Cut two back bodices and two sleeves from the pattern pieces.
4. Fold the smaller rectangle of batiste in half to find the center front, draw a line down the center front and trace the front bodice. Place the bodice template underneath the fabric, line up the center front line and place the lower drawn edge of the dropped-waist bodice at the placement line on the template for the particular size you are making and trace the lace shaping lines for lace A (fig. 1). Cut out the bodice around the traced lines.
5. Refer to lace shaping techniques and place a piece of the 3/8" insertion along the placement lines for lace A mitering the lace at the center front. Cut off the excess lace according to the lace placement template. Note that lace A will extend underneath lace B so be sure not to cut it too short. Pin the lace in place. With a narrow zigzag, stitch the lace along the lower edge of the lace from the point where the lace will be under lace B to the same point on the other side of the "V" (fig. 2). Cut a piece of the lace edging 7" long.

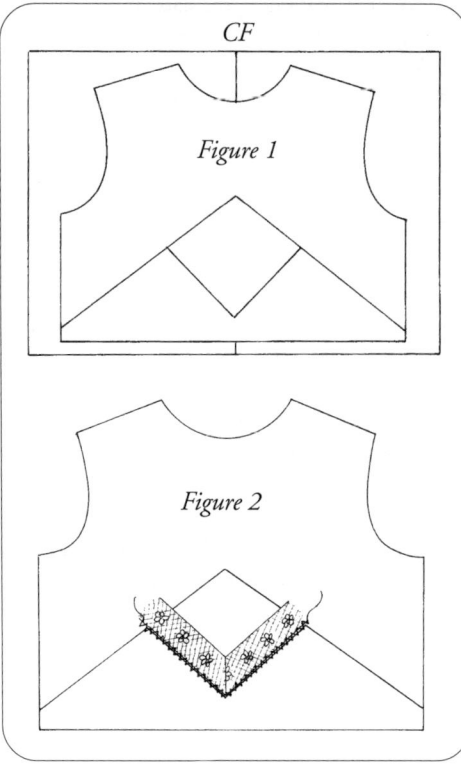

Figure 3

Figure 4

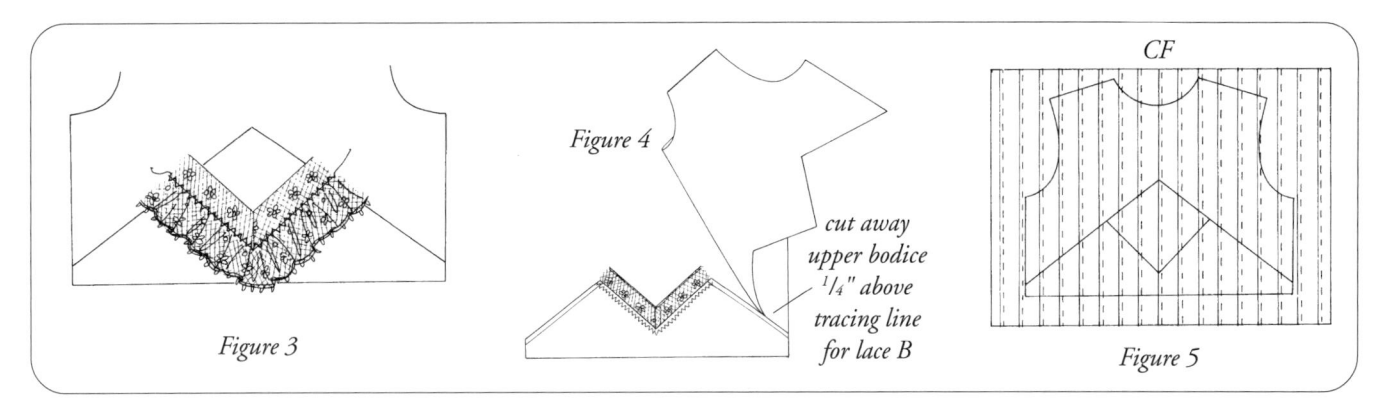

cut away upper bodice ¼" above tracing line for lace B

Figure 5 CF

Pull a thread to gather the ½" lace edging and place the gathered edge of the lace along the lower edge of the insertion lace A. Stitch the gathered lace in place with a narrow zigzag (fig. 3).

6. Cut away the upper bodice ¼" above the traced line for lace B as well as the fabric behind the insertion lace A (fig. 4).
7. On the larger of the two rectangles, stitch double needle pintucks spaced approximately ⅜" apart using the pintuck foot as a guide. The pintucks will be stitched vertically and fill the entire rectangle. Press the pintucked piece. Fold the pintucked piece in half to find the center front, draw a line down the center front and trace the front bodice onto the piece. Place the bodice template underneath the pintucked piece, line up the center front line and place the lower drawn ledge of the drpped-waist bodice athe placement line on the template for the particular size you are making. Trace the lace shaping lines for lace B (fig. 5). Cut out the bodice around the drawn lines.
8. Refer to lace shaping techniques and place a piece of the ⅜" insertion along the placement lines for lace B mitering the lace at the center front. Pin the lace in place. With a narrow zigzag, stitch the top edge of the lace to the pintucked fabric (fig. 6). Cut away the pintucked fabric from beneath the lace. This will at the same time remove the pintucked piece from the lower portion of the bodice (fig. 7).
9. Place the lower portion of the bodice onto the lace shaping template.
10. Place the upper portion of the bodice onto the lace shaping template so that lace B overlaps lace A and the gathered lace. Pin the upper portion of the bodice to the lower portion of the bodice (fig. 8).
11. Place a small square of the Swiss insertion with the embroidered shape centered in the center of the diamond-shaped opening underneath the laces. Pin or baste the insertion piece in place.
12. Stitch the top edge of lace A (inside the V) with a narrow zigzag (fig. 9).
13. Stitch the lower edge of lace B with a narrow zigzag. Trim away the excess fabric from behind the laces (fig. 10).
14. Place the shoulders of the front bodice and back bodices, right sides together and stitch.
15. Cut a piece of lace insertion and ⅜" lace edging four times the measurement given on the sleeve band chart for the elbow-length sleeve. Refer to the technique "lace to lace' and attach the insertion to the edging. Cut this strip in half (one piece for each sleeve). These strips will be used as the edging to be attached to the entredeux.

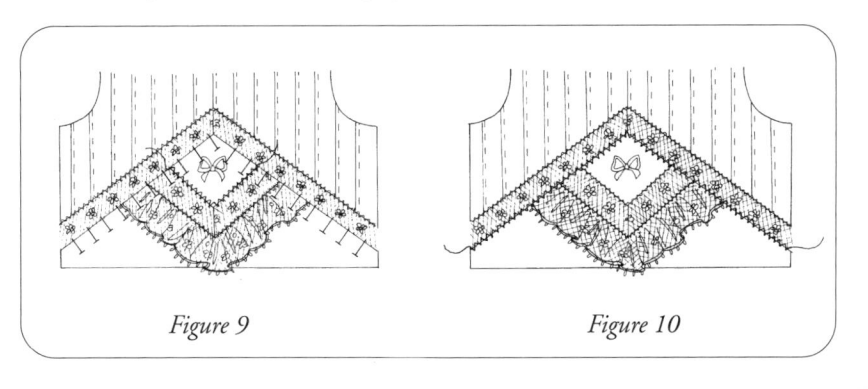

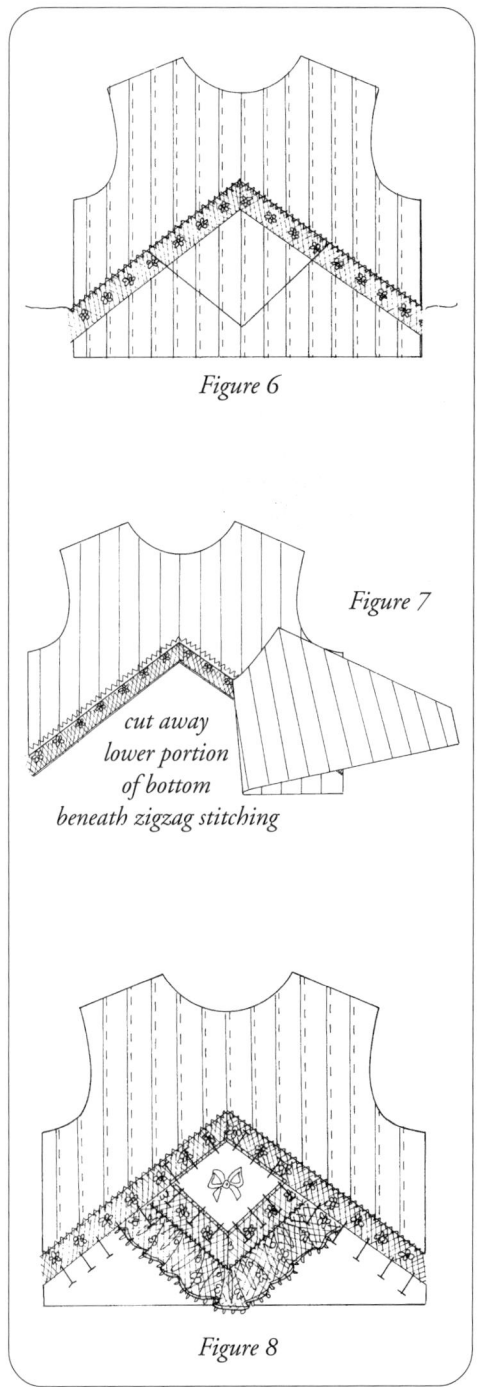

Figure 6

Figure 7

cut away lower portion of bottom beneath zigzag stitching

Figure 9

Figure 10

Figure 8

Dresses   Three Best Friends   57

16. Refer to the General Directions, B. Sleeves and Sleeve Finishes, a. Entredeux to Gathered Edging Lace and finish the lower edge of the sleeve.
17. Refer to the General Directions, B. Sleeves and Sleeve Finishes, h. Attaching the Sleeves, and attach the sleeves to the bodice (fig. 11).
18. Refer to the General Directions, C. Neck Finishes, a. Entredeux to Gathered Edging Lace, and finish the neckline of the dress using the entredeux and $3/8$" lace edging.
19. Place the front bodice to the back bodice, right sides together and stitch the side seams (fig. 12).
20. Press the back facings to the inside of the bodice along the fold lines.
21. Create a 45" fancy band of laces and insertion using the techniques "lace to lace" and "lace to fabric". The order of the laces are: lace insertion, Swiss insertion (trimmed down to measure $1 1/2$" wide), lace insertion, lace insertion, and $3/8$" lace edging (fig. 13).
22. Stitch a double-needle pintuck $1/2$" from the bottom edge of the skirt piece. Stitch a second pintuck $3/8$" above the first and a third pintuck $3/8$" above from the second.
23. Attach the fancy band to the lower edge of the skirt using the technique "lace to fabric" (fig. 14).
24. Refer to the General Directions, A. Placket, b. Placket in a Seam, and complete the back of the skirt.
25. Fold the skirt in half to find the center. Mark at the top edge. Fold the skirt again to find the quarter points (fig. 15). Mark.
26. Place the back bodice to the skirt back, right sides together with the placket edges to the fold lines of the back bodices. Remember, the right side of the placket will be folded to the inside of the skirt and pinned, while the left side will remain extended. Wrap each bodice back around the placket opening in the skirt. Gather the skirt to fit the bodice, matching the center of the skirt to the center front bodice and the quarter markings on the skirt with the side seams of the bodice (fig. 16). Stitch in place. Finish the seam. Flip the bodice portion of the dress up so that the facings fold to the wrong side (fig. 17).
27. Close the dress using Velcro™, snaps, or tiny buttons and buttonholes along each side of the back bodice.

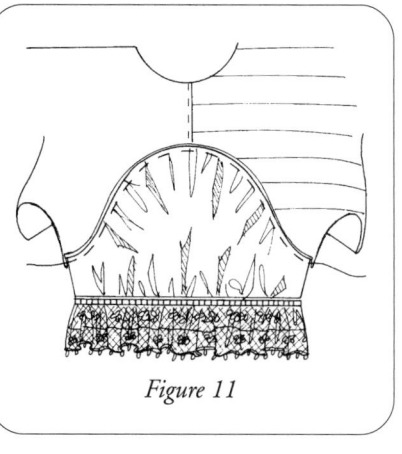

Figure 11

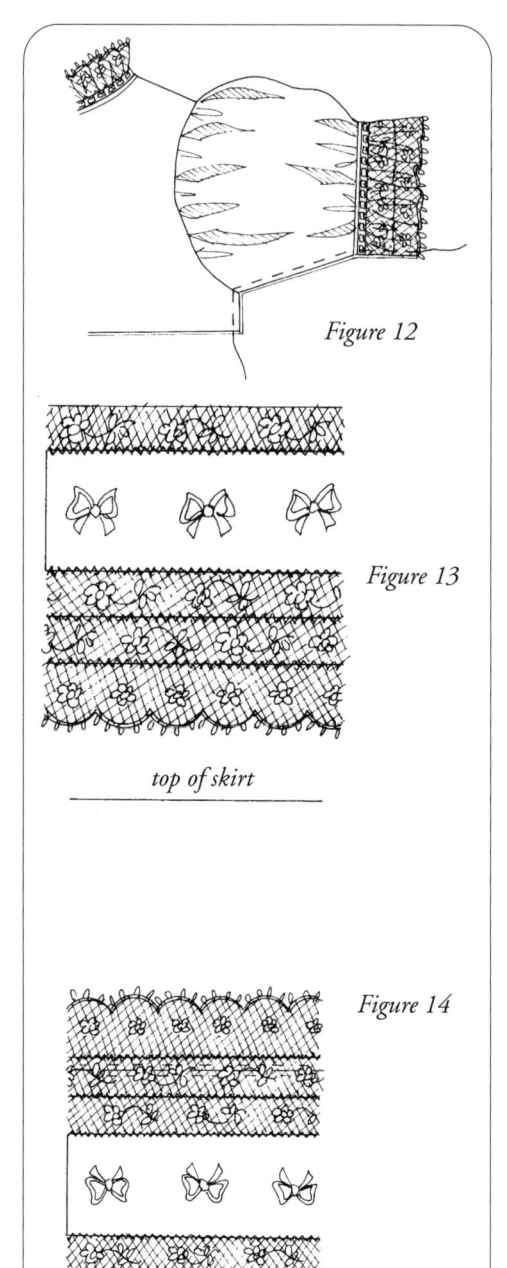

Figure 12

Figure 13

top of skirt

Figure 14

placket folded back   placket extended
$1/4$ $1/4$
$1/2$

Figure 15

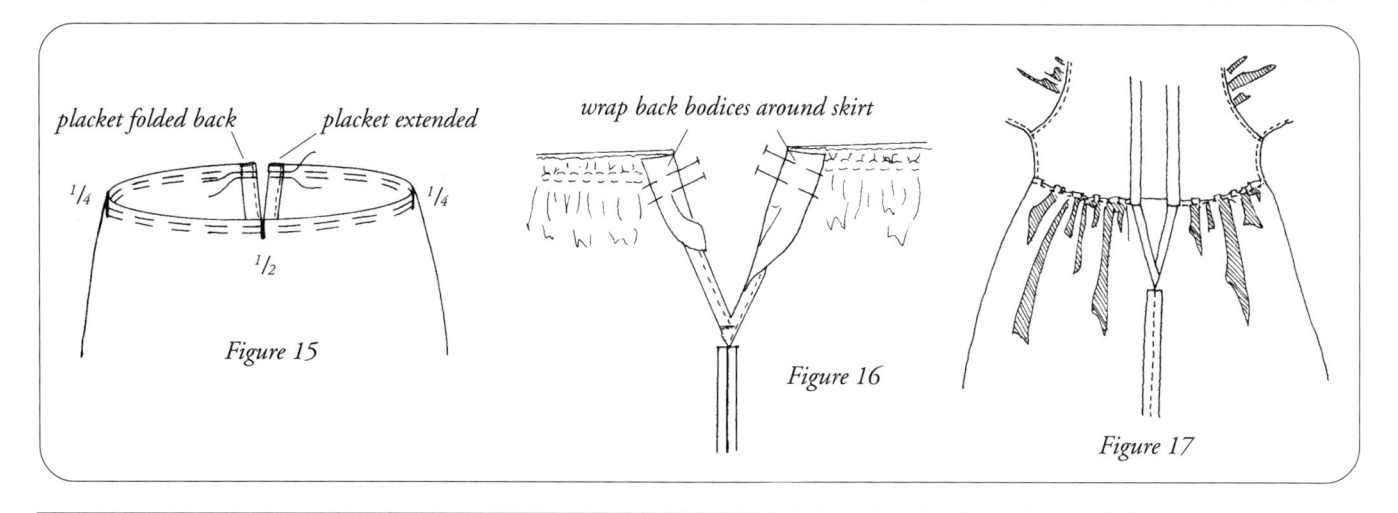

wrap back bodices around skirt

Figure 16

Figure 17

Peach and Pink Linen Middy

What an elegant dress for the Three Best Friends to wear for any dress up occasion! Linen has always been one of my favorite classic fabrics for children and dolls. This dress has so many special details. The middy bodice has a Swiss embroidered insertion with pink and peach flowers and green leaves; entredeux is on either side of this trim. Two sets of three double needle pintucks are on either side of this trim. Next comes French insertion with entredeux on either side of the insertion. The sleeves have this same treatment in the center: entredeux, French white insertion, entredeux, three sets of pintucks on pink linen, entredeux, white French insertion, entredeux, and more linen. The bottom of the sleeves are gathered and finished with faggoting and gathered white French edging. Peach ribbons are run through this faggoting. The same faggoting is found at the bottom of the middy waist. Peach ribbon is run through this faggoting also. The back of the dress closes with snaps; however, three tiny buttons are stitched to the back so it looks like buttons and buttonholes. A tiny bias trim finishes the neckline. The very full skirt is so special with its scallops. Slightly gathered French edging is attached to the scallops with a beautiful machine entredeux.

Peach and Pink Linen Middy

Fabric Requirements

Fabric Requirements:

	13"	17 1/2", 18" and 19 1/2"
Pink Linen Fabric	1/2 yard	5/8 yard
1/2" lace insertion	1 yard	1 1/4 yards
1" lace edging	3 yards	3 1/4 yards
1 1/4" Swiss insertion	1/4 yard	1/4 yard
Entredeux	4 1/4 yards	5 1/2 yards
3/8" Swiss faggoting (with bias fabric attached)	1 yard	1 1/3 yards
3/8" satin ribbon	2 1/4 yards	2 3/4 yards

Notions

Lightweight sewing thread, paper, Velcro™, snaps or tiny buttons, wash-out marker

Directions

All Seams 1/4" unless otherwise indicated. Finish all seams with a zigzag or serge to finish the fabric edges.

Please read through both the General Directions and the Specific Directions before starting the dress. The General Directions can be found on page 4 and give instructions for neck, sleeves and hem finishes. These Specific Directions give instructions for the special details concerning this particular dress and the sequence of the construction.

The following pattern pieces found on the pull-outs are needed for this dress: dropped-waist front bodice, dropped-waist back bodice, elbow-length sleeve. The scallop border template is found on page 61.

Figure 1

drawing line 1/2"

Figure 2

Construction

1. Cut two rectangles of fabric 5 1/4" by 3 1/4" for the 13" doll and 7 1/2" by 4 1/2" for the 17 1/2", 18" and 19 1/2" doll. These pieces will be used to create the bodice.
2. Cut two rectangles of fabric 5" by 11" for the 13" doll and 8" by 11" for the 17 1/2", 18" and 19 1/2" doll. These pieces will be used to create the sleeves.
3. Cut one skirt 45" wide by the following length: 5" for the 13" dolls, 6 1/2" for the 17 1/2" dolls, 7" for the 18" dolls and 8" for the 19 1/2" dolls.
4. Refer to the technique "entredeux to fabric" and attach the entredeux to each side of the Swiss insertion using a 1/4" seam allowance. Press well (fig. 1).
5. Refer to the technique "entredeux to fabric" and attach the long side of the bodice pieces to each side of the insertion/entredeux strip. Press well (fig. 2).
6. Refer to the technique "pintucks" and stitch 3 pintucks on each side of the center insertion placing the first tuck 1/4" from the entredeux (fig. 2).

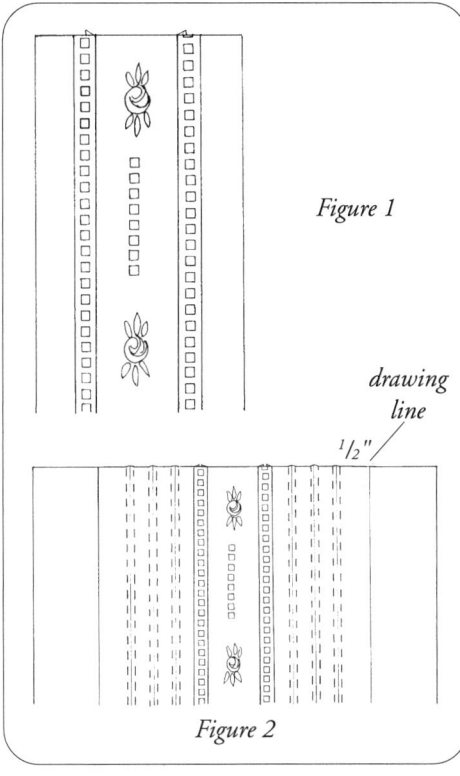

Figure 3

cut fabric away at drawn line

Figure 4

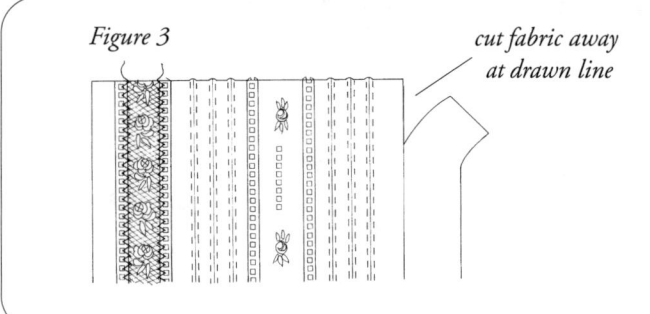

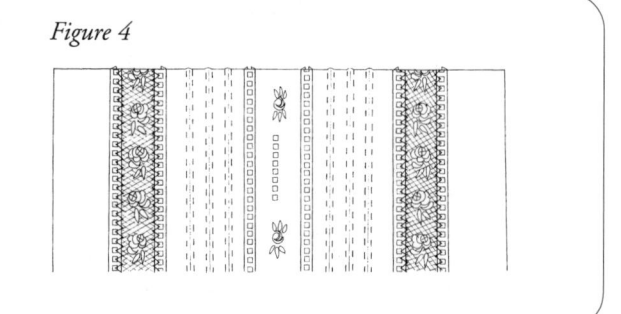

7. Draw a line ½" from the third pintuck on each side of the bodice rectangle (fig. 2).
8. Measure the insertion piece down the center of the rectangle. Cut a piece of lace insertion twice this measurement plus 1". Cut two pieces of entredeux the same measurement as the insertion.
9. Attach the entredeux along each side of the lace insertion referring to the technique "lace to entredeux".
10. Cut the strip of lace/entredeux in half. Cut the bodice rectangle along the lines drawn in step 8 and lay the cut away pieces of fabric aside. Refer to the technique "entredeux to fabric" and attach the insertion/entredeux strip to the center portion of the bodice with a ¼" seam (fig. 3).
11. Attach the cut away pieces of fabric from step 10 to each side of the entredeux using the technique "entredeux to fabric". Press the entire rectangle well (fig. 4).
12. On the bodice front and bodice back patterns, cut away ⅜" from the bottom edge. This will allow for the addition of the ⅜" faggoting.
13. Place the front bodice pattern onto the rectangle created having the center front of the pattern along the center of the Swiss insertion. Trace the bodice pattern onto the rectangle.
14. With a tiny straight stitch, stitch around the outline of the bodice on the rectangle. Trim away the excess fabric just outside the stitching line around the bodice. Lay this bodice piece aside (fig. 5).
15. On one of the rectangles for the sleeves, mark the center of the sleeve by folding it in half. Stitch 3 pintucks with the center one placed at the center fold of the rectangle.
16. Measure ½" from the first and third pintuck and draw a line. Cut along the drawn lines and lay the cut away pieces of fabric aside (fig. 6).
17. Cut a piece of lace insertion 2 times the measurement of the pintucks plus 1".
18. Refer to the technique "entredeux to lace" and attach the entredeux to each side of the lace insertion.
19. Cut the lace/entredeux strip in half and attach each piece on each side of the pintucks with a ¼" seam referring to the technique "entredeux to fabric". The fabric which you cut away will be attached to each side of the entredeux with a ¼" seam. Press the piece well.
20. Repeat steps 15 through 19 for the other sleeve.
21. Trace the outline of each sleeve onto the rectangles created above placing the center of the sleeve along the center tuck.
22. Stitch around the drawn line with tiny stitches and trim away the excess fabric from outside the stitching line (fig. 7).
23. Cut two back bodices from the pattern.
24. Place the front bodice and the back bodices right sides together and stitch along the shoulders (fig. 8).

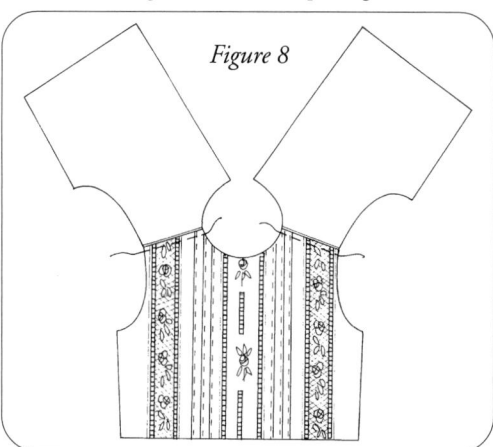

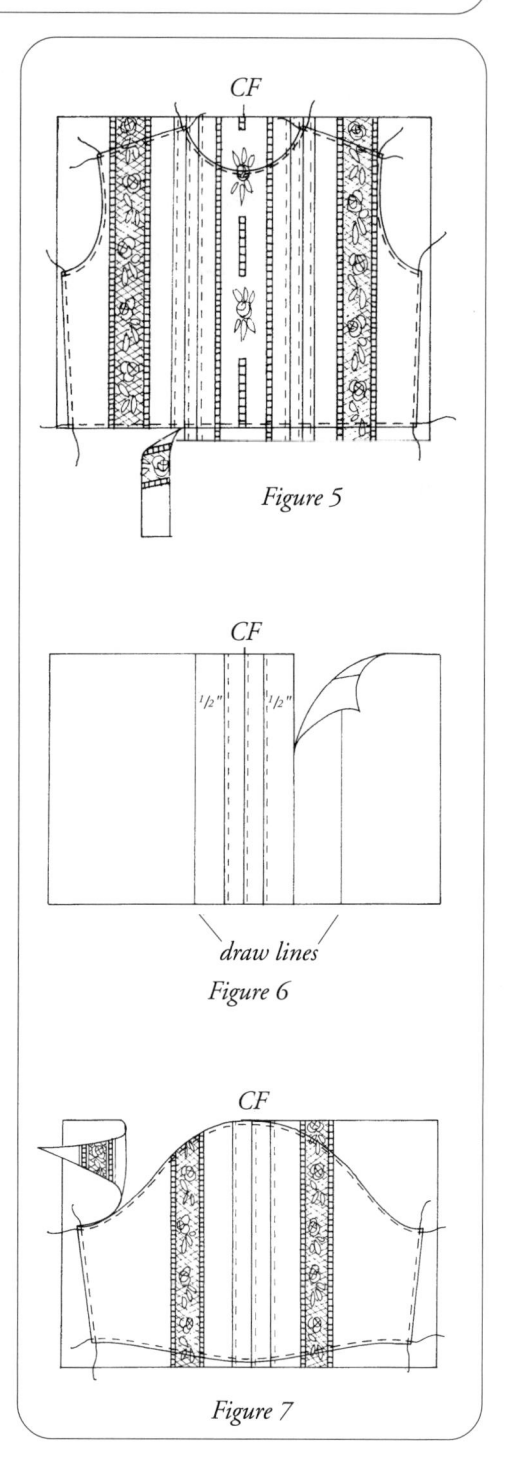

Figure 5

Figure 6

draw lines

Figure 8

Figure 7

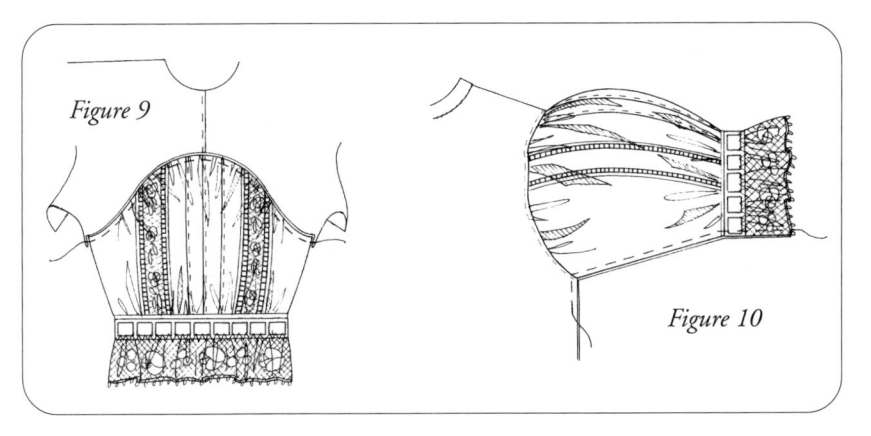

Figure 9

Figure 10

Figure 11

Figure 12

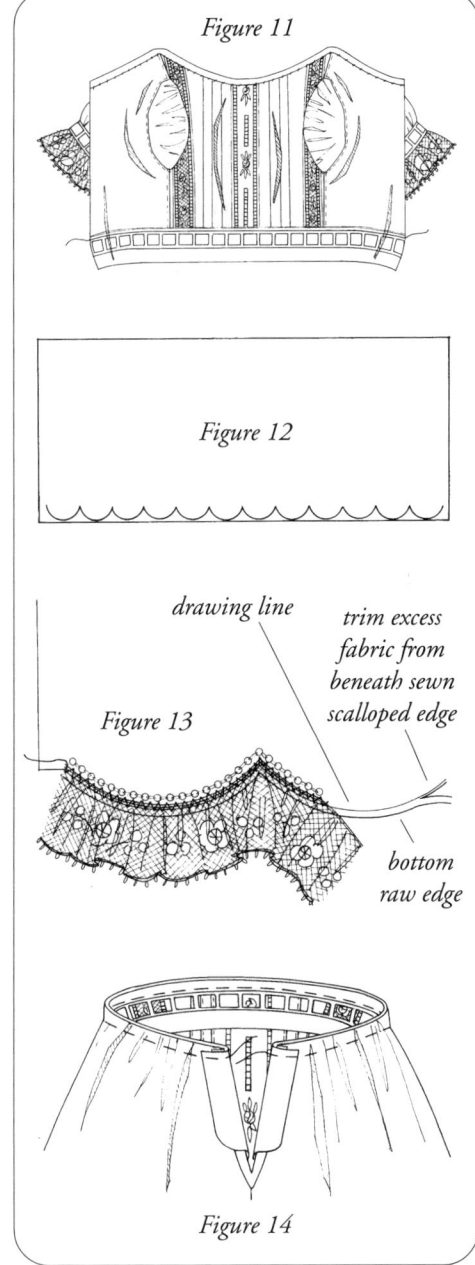

Figure 13

drawing line

trim excess fabric from beneath sewn scalloped edge

bottom raw edge

Figure 14

25. Refer to B. Sleeves and Sleeve Finishes, a. Entredeux to Gathered Edging Lace and attach the faggoting and lace to the sleeves in the same manner.
26. Refer to B. Sleeves and Sleeve Finishes, h. Attaching the Sleeves and attach the sleeves to the bodice (fig. 9).
27. Refer to C. Neck Finishes, c. Bias Binding and finish the neck edge.
28. Place the bodice front and back right sides together lining up the underarm seam and lace edging. Stitch the side seams of the bodice (fig. 10).
29. Referring to the technique "entredeux to fabric", attach a strip of faggoting to the lower edge of the bodice (fig. 11).
30. Place the skirt template along the lower edge of the skirt piece and trace the scallop (fig. 12).
31. Gather the remaining lace edging and pin in place along the curve of the scallops. Attach the lace with a zigzag stitch. Trim away the excess fabric from beneath the lace. Pinstitch just above the zigzag line on the upper edge of lace (fig. 13).
32. Trim away any partial scallops ¼" from a top point at each end of the skirt piece so that the back seam of the skirt will meet at a point of the scallop.
33. Refer to A. Placket, b. Placket in a Seam and finish the center back of the skirt.
34. Pull up the gathers on the top edge of the skirt to fit the bodice from back fold line to back fold line. Remember to keep the right side of the placket folded in and the left side extended.
35. Wrap the facings of the bodices around the skirt pieces and pin in place.
36. Stitch the skirt to the bodice stitching in the ditch between the edge of the faggoting and the bias edge. Flip the bodice portion of the dress up so that the facings fold to the wrong side (fig. 14).
37. Run ribbon through the faggoting and tie into a bow at the center back and on each sleeve.
38. Close the back of the dress with Velcro™, snaps or tiny buttons and buttonholes.

Scallop Border Template

3" repeat

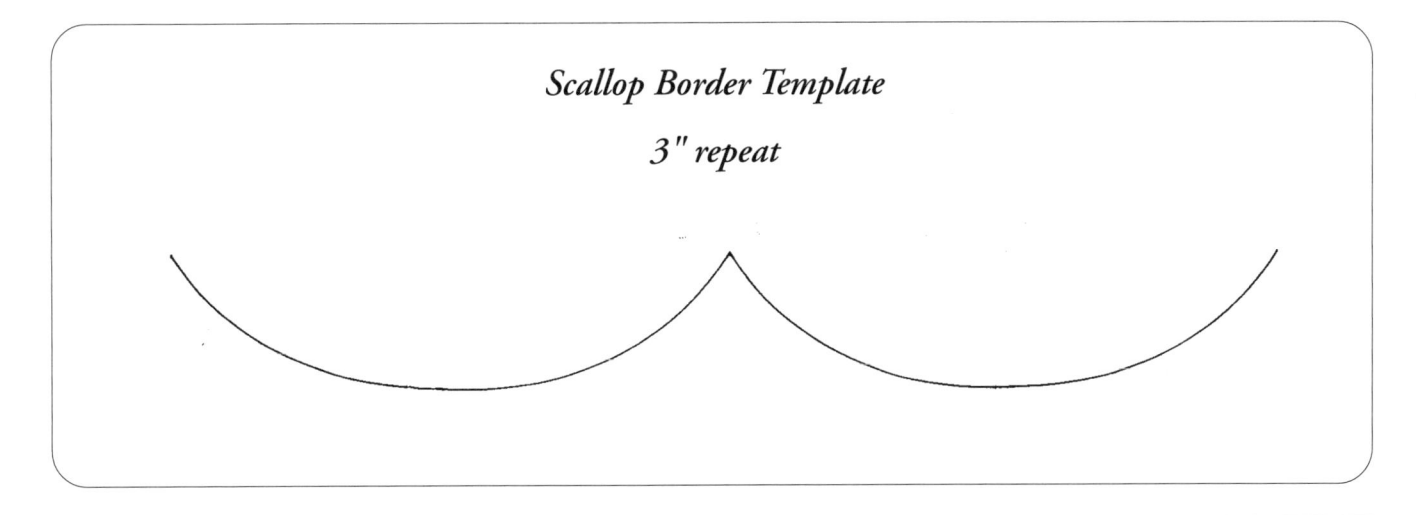

Red, White and Blue Sailor Middy

Ready for the Fourth of July picnic is this red, white and blue sailor middy. The tiny blue and white striped fabric is the perfect background for this long sleeved dress. The front V white broadcloth panel is an overlay which features narrow piping. The sleeves have a bias binding and the hem has this piping and is hemmed at the front. A red broadcloth bow and a cute little anchor button finish the front of this beauty. The back is closed with Velcro™. The Three Best Friends will enjoy wearing this dress to school or for a patriotic occasion.

Fabric Requirements

Fabric Requirements:

	13"	17 1/2", 18" and 19 1/2"
Light blue baby wale	1/2 yard	5/8 yard
White broadcloth	1/4 yard	1/4 yard
Navy piping*	2 1/3 yard	2 1/3 yard

Scrap of red broadcloth (5" x 2 1/2")

*You may make your own piping using 2 1/3 yard tiny cord or gimp and 2 1/3 yard of 1" navy bias tape unfolded and pressed. Or you may cut bias from 1/4 yard of navy fabric.

Notions

Lightweight sewing thread, red thread or floss to match the red fabric for the bow, Velcro™ or snaps or tiny buttons, one decorative sailor button, wash-out marker, wash-away basting tape.

Directions

All Seams 1/4" unless otherwise indicated. Finish all seams with a zigzag or serge to finish the fabric edges.

Please read through both the General Directions and the Specific Directions before starting the dress. The General Directions can be found on page 4 and give instructions for the special details concerning this particular dress and the sequence of the construction.

The following pattern pieces found on the pull-outs are needed for this dress: Dropped-waist front, dropped-waist back, long sleeve, sailor dress V-bodice template.

Construction

1. From the light blue fabric, cut out one front bodice and two back bodices, two sleeves and cut or tear one skirt piece 45" by the following length: 6 3/4" for the 13" doll or 8 1/4" for the 17 1/2" doll, 8 3/4" for the 18" doll and 9 3/4" for the 19 1/2" doll.
2. From navy fabric, cut two arm bands 5/8" be the length given for the long sleeve in the sleeve band chart found in the General Directions, B. Sleeve and Sleeve Finishes.
3. From the white fabric, cut one piece from the sailor dress V-bodice template. From the red fabric, cut a piece 5" by 2 1/2".
4. Press under 1/4" along the two long sides of the V-shaped piece for the bodice.
5. Cut 5/8" wide by 14" long bias from the navy fabric, fold in half lengthwise and press well.
6. Place the folded bias underneath the white bodice piece having 1/16" of the navy extending from beneath the white. Pin or use wash-away basting tape to secure until sewn (fig. 1).
7. Place the bib onto the bodice, lining up the shoulder seams, neckline and waist. Pin in place.
8. Stitch the V-shaped fabric very close to the fold line on each side. The lower edge will be sewn into the waistline (fig. 2).
9. Place the back bodices and the front bodice right sides together and stitch at the shoulders (fig. 3).

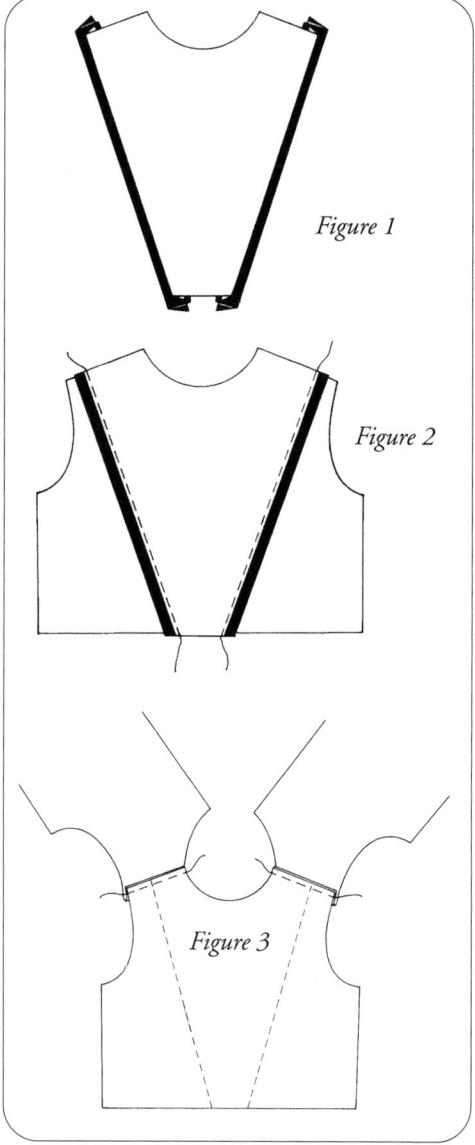

Red, White and Blue Sailor Middy

Figure 1

Figure 2

Figure 3

10. Refer to the General Directions, C. Neck Finishes, c. Bias Binding and add a bias binding using the navy fabric. When turning under the bias, do not turn it under even with the seam, but allow a small edge of the navy fabric to extend above the seam line.
11. Refer to the General Directions, B. Sleeves and Sleeve Finishes, g. Sleeve Band, to complete the sleeve.
12. Refer to the General Directions, B. Sleeve and Sleeve Finishes, h. Attaching the Sleeves and attach the sleeves to the bodice (fig. 4).
13. Place the front and back bodices, right sides together, matching the underarm seam and the arm band and stitch the side seam of the bodice and the sleeve seam (fig. 5).
14. Fold the skirt $1/2$" towards the right side (fig. 6). Turn up another $1\ 1/4$" and press well (fig. 7). Note: the hem will be turned to the right side.
15. Cut bias strips $5/8$" wide from the navy fabric to equal at least 45". Fold the bias in half and press well.
16. Insert the folded bias underneath the turned up hem of the skirt allowing approximately $1/16$" to extending above the fold.
17. Straight stitch very close to the fold line of skirt hem to secure both the hem and the bias strip (fig. 8).
18. Refer to the General Directions, A. Placket, b. Placket in a Seam to complete the back of the skirt.
19. Pull up the gathers to fit the bodice from back fold line to back fold line. Remember to keep the right side of the skirt placket folded to the inside of the skirt. Wrap the facings of the bodices around the skirt opening and pin in place (fig. 9).
20. Stitch the skirt to the bodice. Flip the bodice away from the skirt so that the bodice facings fold to the wrong side (fig. 10).
21. Fold the red fabric piece in half to measure $2\ 1/2$" by $2\ 1/2$". Stitch the one end together to form a tube leaving $3/4$" open in the center for turning (fig. 11). Reposition the seam in the center of the tube. Stitch each end of the tube closed (fig. 12). Turn the tube through the opening. Press well.
22. Thread a needle with several strands of the matching thread or floss, pinch the bow in the center and secure the thread at the back of the bow with a few whip stitches. Wrap the thread around the center of the bow several times and secure at the back with a few whip stitches (fig. 13).
23. Hand stitch the bow to the center front bodice at the waistline.
24. Attach the button at the center front on the white bodice piece.
25. Close the back of the dress with Velcro™, snaps or tiny button and buttonholes.

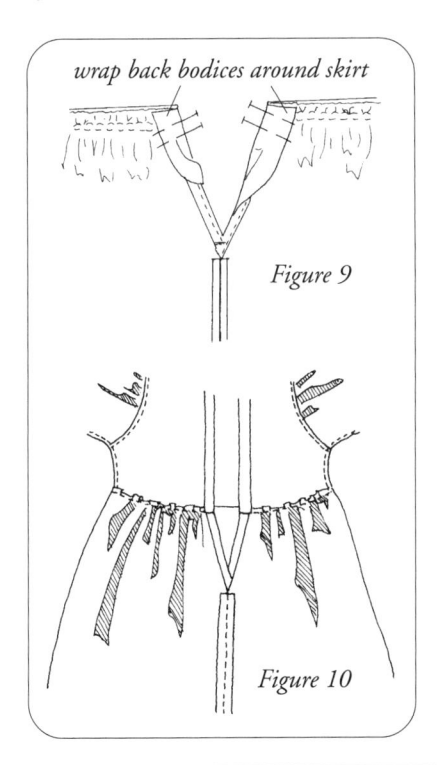

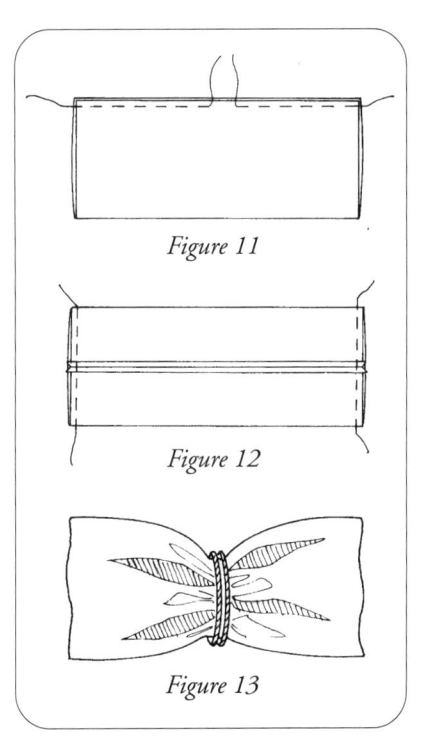

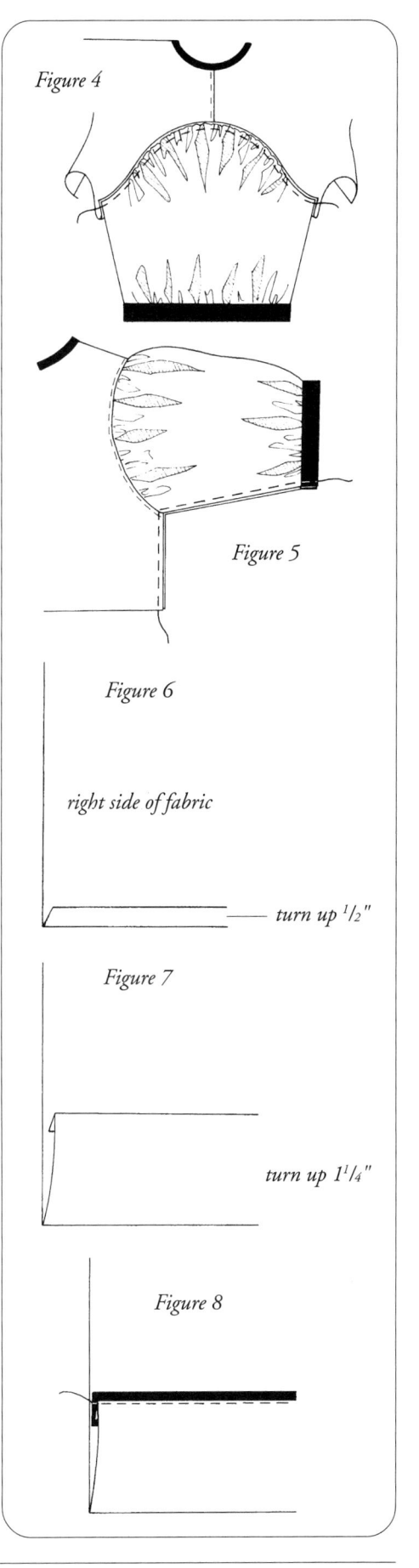

Figure 4

Figure 5

Figure 6

right side of fabric

turn up $1/2$"

Figure 7

turn up $1\ 1/4$"

Figure 8

wrap back bodices around skirt

Figure 9

Figure 10

Figure 11

Figure 12

Figure 13

Dresses — Three Best Friends

Blue Plaid School Dress

The Three Best Friends love to look pretty when they go to school, and they are especially fond of helping their mothers do machine embroidery on their clothing. This dress is made of blue broadcloth and has the cutest plaid trims. The sleeves, hem, and front "V" are in the pretty pink, blue, yellow, green and white plaid. The little machine embroidered flowers are found on the sleeve cuff, the front of the dress, and around the skirt. A little perky bow finishes the front of the dress at the waistline. The back of the dress is closed with Velcro™.

Fabric Requirements

Fabric Requirements:

	13"	17 1/2", 18" and 19 1/2"
Blue fabric	3/8 yard	1/2 yard
Plaid fabric	1/3 yard	3/8 yard

Notions

Lightweight sewing thread for construction, contrasting lightweight sewing thread for decorative stitching, Velcro™, snaps or tiny buttons, wash-out marker

Directions

All Seams 1/4" unless otherwise indicated. Finish all seams with a zigzag or serge to finish the fabric edges.

Please read through both the General Directions and the Specific Directions before starting the dress. The General Directions can be found on page 4 and give instructions for the special details concerning this particular dress and the sequence of the construction.

The following pattern pieces needed for this dress are found on the pull-outs: waisted front, waisted back, elbow-length sleeve, "V"-front overlay

Construction

1. From the blue fabric, cut out one front bodice and two back bodices, tear or cut one skirt piece 45" wide by the following measurement: 5" for the 13" doll, 7 1/4" for the 17 1/2" doll, and 8" for the 18" or 19 1/2" doll, also cut two arm bands 5/8" wide by 3 1/2" for the 13" doll, 5/8" wide by 4" for the 17 1/2" doll and 5/8" by 4 3/4" for the 18" or 19 1/2" doll.
2. From the plaid fabric cut two sleeves, one "V"-front overlay for the bodice, one strip of fabric 4" by 45" for the band around the skirt, one piece 1 3/4" by 3 1/4" for the bow and a piece for the knot in the bow 1/2" by approximately 4".
3. Press under 1/4" along the two long sides of the "V"-front overlay.
4. Place the "V"-shaped plaid fabric onto the bodice, lining up the shoulder seams and neckline. Pin in place and stitch to the front bodice very close to the fold line. Baste around the neck and shoulders (fig. 1).
5. Place the back bodices and the front bodice right sides together and stitch at the shoulders. Lay the bodice piece aside.
6. Fold 1/2" to the wrong side along each long side of the 4" by 45" plaid piece. Fold the piece in half lengthwise, wrong sides together (fig. 2).
7. Unfold the plaid strip. Place the strip to the skirt bottom, right sides. Stitch using a 1/2" seam (in the crease) (fig. 3).
8. Refold the plaid piece along the creases to enclose the lower edge of the skirt. Line up the 1/2" fold even with the stitching line on the wrong side of the skirt. Pin in place. Topstitch

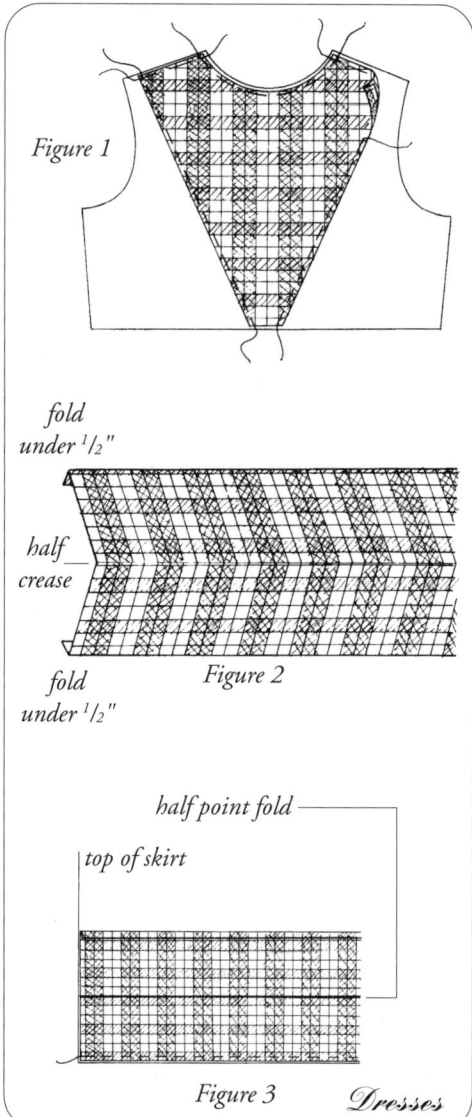

Blue Plaid School Dress

Figure 1

fold under 1/2"

half crease

fold under 1/2"

Figure 2

half point fold

top of skirt

Figure 3

Dresses

Floral Dress with a Detachable Collar

Pointed Collar Dress

Red, White & Blue Sailor Middy

School Days Pinafore

Lady Bug Smocked Yoke Dress

(above, l-r) Seaside Garden Dress, Dusty Pink Antique Middy, Two Tone Pink Scallop Dress

(right) Paris Bonnet

(right, l-r) Robin's Egg Blue Tiered Dress, Smocked Bodice Dress, White and Ecru Dress

(below, l-r) Peach & Pink Linen Middy, White Smocked Yoke Dress & Bonnet, English Netting Blue Bow Dress

(above, l-r) Blue Batiste Dress, English Flower Girl Dress, Fancy Collar Bib Dress

(l-r) Flip-flop Border Dress, Pintucked Diamond Dress, English Netting Dress with Pink Rose

Figure 4

Figure 5

Figure 6

Figure 7

Figure 8

Figure 9

Figure 10

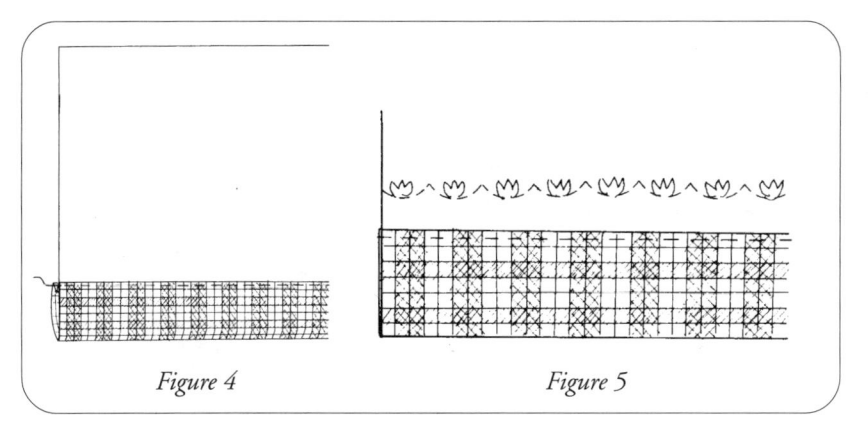

on the right side of the skirt $1/16$" from the seam line. This will "hem" the dress (fig. 4).
9. Fold the arm band strips in half lengthwise.
10. With the contrasting thread, stitch a decorative stitch of your choice on the blue fabric $1/4$" from the border on the skirt (fig. 5), and $1/4$" from the edges of the "V"-front overlay on the bodice (fig. 6) and just above the folded edge of each arm band (fig. 7).
11. Refer to the General Directions, C. Neck Finishes, c. Bias Binding and add a bias binding using the plaid material. When turning under the bias, do not turn it under even with the seam, but allow a small edge of the plaid fabric to extend above the seam line (as seen in finished drawing).
12. Refer to the General Directions, B. Sleeves and Sleeve Finishes, g. Sleeve Band to finish the sleeves.
13. Refer to the General Directions, B. Sleeve and Sleeve Finishes, h. Attaching the Sleeves and attach the sleeves to the bodice (fig. 8).
14. Place the front and back bodices right sides together matching the underarm seam and the arm band and stitch the side seam of the bodice and the sleeve seam (fig. 9).
15. Refer to the General Directions, A. Placket, b. Placket in a Seam to complete the back of the skirt.
16. Run two rows of gathering stitches $1/8$" and $1/4$" from the top edge of the skirt and pull up the gathers to fit the bodice from back fold line to back fold line. Remember to keep the right side of the placket folded in and the left side extended.
17. Wrap the facings of the bodices around the skirt pieces and pin in place.
18. Stitch the skirt to the bodice. Flip the bodice up so that the facings fold to the wrong side (fig. 10).
19. For the bow, fold the plaid piece in half lengthwise and stitch leaving about 1" in the center for turning (fig. 11). This will create a tube. Reposition the seam so that it is in the center of the tube. Stitch a seam at each end of the tube (fig. 12). Turn the tube through the opening you left. Press well.
20. On the strip for the knot of the bow, turn under $1/8$" along each long side and press well (fig. 13).
21. Pinch the bow piece in the middle and tie the strip around the center holding the bow to its shape (fig. 14). Hand stitch the back of the "knot" to secure it. Trim off the excess fabric from the back of the "knot".
22. Hand stitch the bow to the center front of the bodice at the point of the overlay.
23. Close the back of the dress with Velcro™, snaps or tiny buttons and buttonholes.

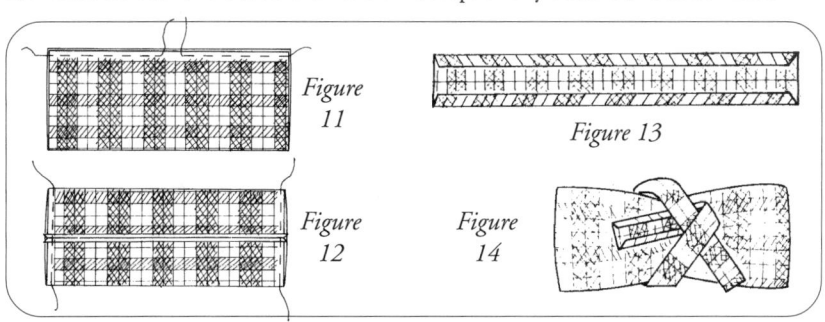

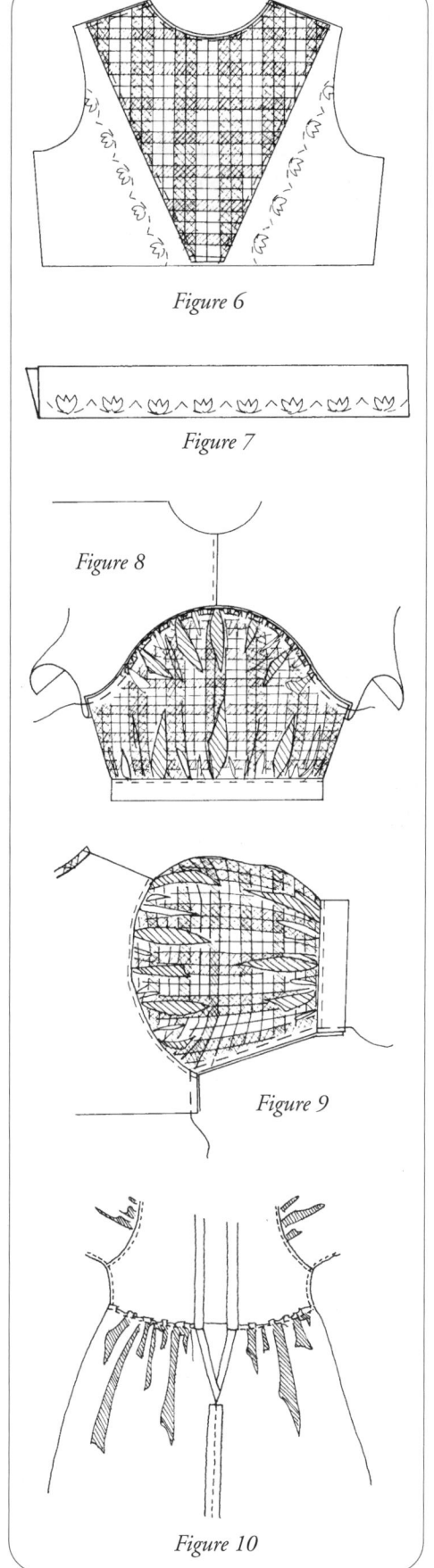

Figure 11

Figure 12

Figure 13

Figure 14

School Days Pinafore

Plaid just says "back to school" to our friends. The dark green and red plaid pinafore is really stitched into the dress. The underdress is ecru muslin and the sleeve bindings are plaid. The underdress has a decorative green machine trim around the bottom. The dress closes in the back with Velcro™. It is so much fun to use your decorative machine trims on doll clothes; you don't need a fancy machine to have beautiful stitches to decorate the hem of a doll dress.

Fabric Requirements

Fabric Requirements:

	13"	17 1/2", 18" and 19 1/2"
Plaid Fabric	3/8 yard	1/2 yard
Ecru or White batiste	1/2 yard	5/8 yard

Notions

Lightweight sewing thread to match garment, thread to coordinate with a color in the plaid fabric to do the decorative stitching, Velcro™, snaps or tiny buttons, wash-out marker

Directions

All Seams 1/4" unless otherwise indicated. Finish all seams with a zigzag or serge to finish the fabric edges.

Please read through both the General Directions and the Specific Directions before starting the dress. The General Directions can be found on page 4 and give instructions for neck, sleeves and hem finishes. These Specific Directions give instructions for the special details concerning this particular dress and the sequence of the construction.

The following pattern pieces are needed for this dress: waisted front, waisted back, elbow-length sleeve, pinafore front, pinafore back.

Construction

1. From the ecru or white fabric cut one front bodice, two back bodices, two sleeves and tear a skirt piece the following measurements:

	13"	17 1/2"	18", 19 1/2"
Skirt piece	8" by 45"	10 1/4" by 45"	11" by 45"

2. From the plaid fabric cut one pinafore front, two pinafore backs, two sleeve band pieces by the measurements on the sleeve band chart, and pieces by the following measurements:

	13"	17 1/2"	18", 19 1/2"
Pinafore ruffle (Cut two)	1 3/4" by 15"	2" by 25"	2" by 25"
Pinafore skirt	6" by 45"	8 1/4" by 45"	9" by 45"

3. Place the bodice front to the bodice backs matching the shoulder seams and stitch at the shoulders (fig. 1).
4. Refer to B. Sleeves and Sleeve Finishes, g. Sleeve Band and attach the sleeve bands to the sleeves.
5. Refer to B. Sleeves and Sleeve Finishes, h. Attaching the Sleeves and attach the sleeves to the bodice (fig. 2).

School Days Pinafore

Figure 1

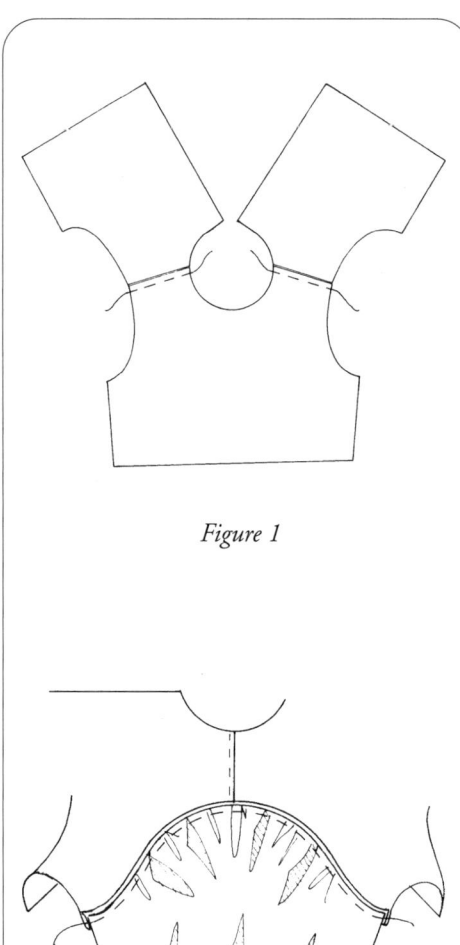

Figure 2

Figure 3

Figure 4

Figure 5

wrong side

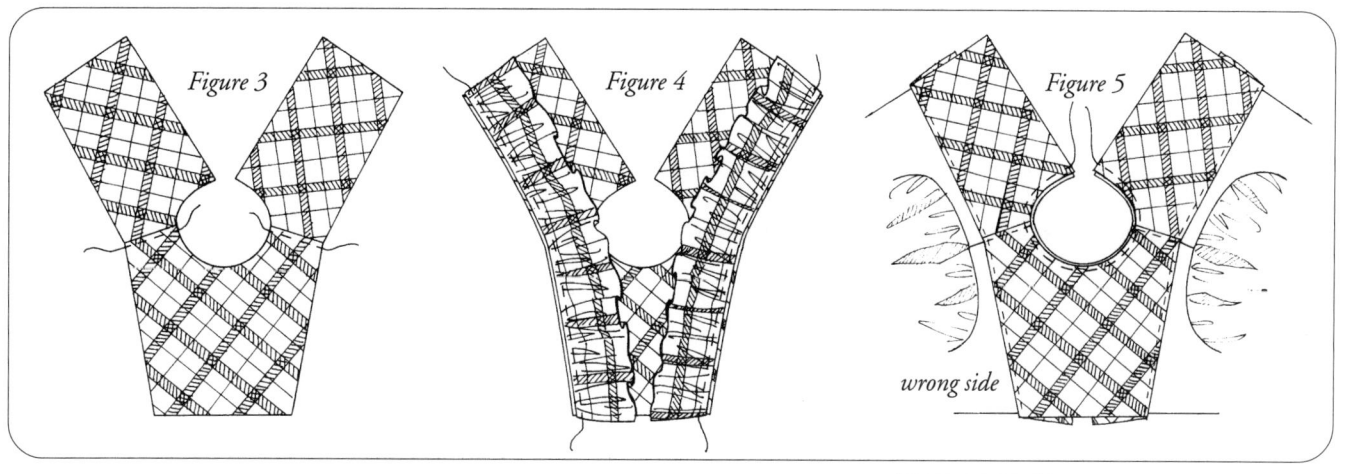

6. Place the pinafore front to the pinafore backs matching the shoulder seams and stitch at the shoulders (fig.3).
7. Hem one long edge of each pinafore ruffle with a tiny 1/8" hem.
8. Run two rows of gathering stitches at 1/8" and 1/4" from the other long edge and pull up the gathers to fit the sides of the pinafore front and back.
9. Stitch the ruffle to the pinafore (fig. 4). Top stitch the pinafore piece 1/4" away from the seam line of the ruffle.
10. Place the pinafore piece to the bodice piece with the right side of the pinafore to the wrong side of the bodice.
11. Stitch the neckline seam and turn the pinafore to the outside of the bodice (fig. 5).
12. Baste the pinafore piece to the bodice piece along the waistline of the front and back lining up the back raw edges and matching the center fronts (fig. 6).
13. Turn the bodice front and backs right sides together and stitch the side seams (fig. 7).
14. On the ecru or white skirt piece, turn up 1/2" and press. Turn up 1 1/2" and stitch the hem in place by hand or machine.
15. With a contrasting thread stitch a decorative stitch of your choice 1" from the lower edge of the skirt.
16. On the plaid skirt piece, turn up 1/4" and press. Turn up 1/4" again and stitch the hem in place by hand or machine.
17. Place the plaid skirt piece on top of the plain skirt piece lining up the top edges. The skirt underneath will extend below the plaid skirt. Baste the layers together and baste along the sides and top treating the two layers as one (fig. 8).
18. Refer to A. Placket, b. Placket in a Seam and complete the back of the skirt.
19. Run two rows of gathering stitches along the top edge of the skirt and pull up the gathers to fit the bodice from back fold line to back fold line. Remember to keep the right side of the placket folded in and the left side extended (fig. 9).
20. Wrap the facings of the bodices around the skirt pieces and pin in place (fig. 10).
21. Stitch the skirt to the bodice. Flip the bodice portion of the dress up so that the facings fold to the wrong side (fig. 11).
22. Close the back of the dress with Velcro™, snaps or tiny buttons and buttonholes.

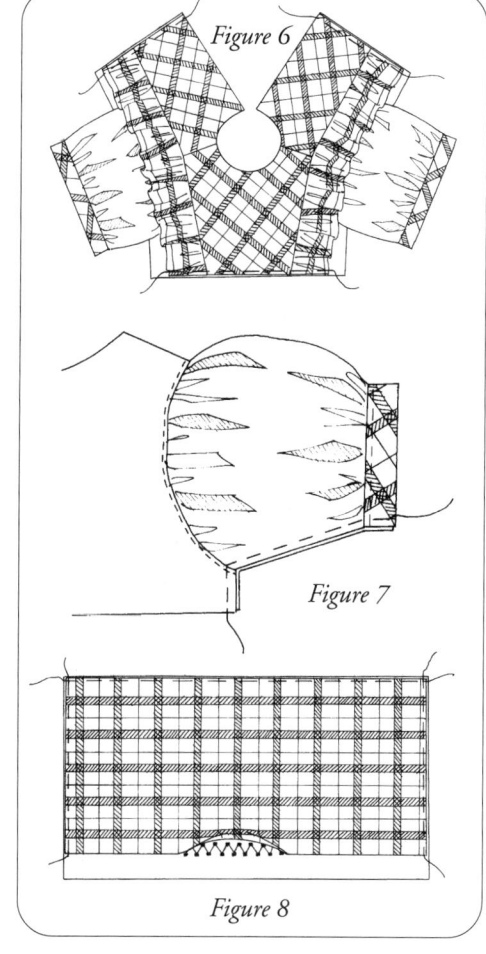

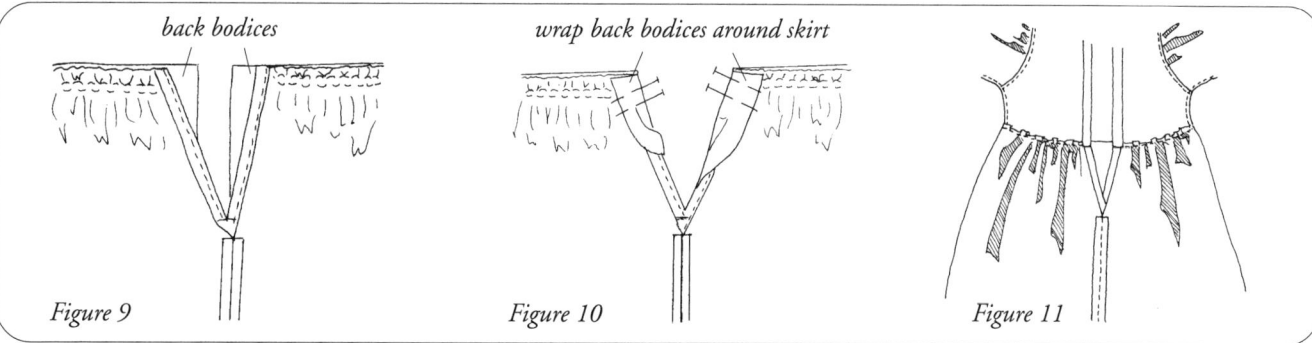

Figure 6

Figure 7

Figure 8

back bodices

wrap back bodices around skirt

Figure 9

Figure 10

Figure 11

Dresses — Three Best Friends

Pointed Collar Dress

Dolls love little printed dresses, especially when they have a white batiste collar with silk ribbon embroidery on it. The pointed collar is finished with entredeux and tiny tatting. The edges of the sleeves are finished with entredeux and tatting also. The dress closes in the back with Velcro™. The friends would love this dress in any print to match any season. This dress would be so pretty with a dress for the friend's "mommy" in a matching print.

Fabric Requirements

Fabric Requirements:

	13"	17 1/2", 18" and 19 1/2"
Fabric - Floral Print	1/2 yard	5/8 yard
Collar fabric - White batiste	1/4 yard	1/4 yard
Tatted Edging Lace (1/4")	3/4 yard	1 yard
Entredeux	3/4 yard	1 yard

Silk Ribbon (4mm) - lavendar, pink and moss green
Small bead or small pearl

Notions

Lightweight sewing thread, paper, Velcro™, snaps or tiny buttons for back closure

Directions

All Seams 1/4" unless otherwise indicated. Finish all seams with a zigzag or serge to finish the fabric edges.

Please read through both the General Directions and the Specific Directions before starting the dress. The General Directions can be found on page 4 and give instructions for plackets, neck and sleeve finishes. These Specific Directions give instructions for the special details concerning this particular dress and the sequence of the construction.

The following pattern pieces needed for this dress are found on the pull-outs: waisted front, waisted back, elbow-length sleeve and pointed collar.

Construction

1. Cut two pointed collars (one collar, one lining) from the white batiste. Using the floral print fabric, cut two back bodices from the selvege, one front bodice from the fold and two elbow-length sleeves. Cut one skirt piece 45"wide by the following length:
13"	7"
17 1/2"	9 1/4"
18"	10"
19 1/2"	10"

2. Place the front bodice to the back bodice pieces, right sides together. Stitch the shoulder seams in place (fig. 1).
3. Finish the ends of each sleeve using sleeve bands of entredeux and flat tatting. Refer to the General Directions - B. Sleeves and Sleeves Finishes (steps 2 - 3)- b. Entredeux to Flat Lace (fig. 2).
4. Refer to B. Sleeves and Sleeve Finishes, h. Attaching the Sleeves and attach the sleeves to the bodice (fig. 3).
5. Place the collar pieces together and stitch along the outer edge using a 1/4" seam allowance. Trim the seam to 1/8" (fig. 4). Turn the collar to the right side through the neck opening. Press.

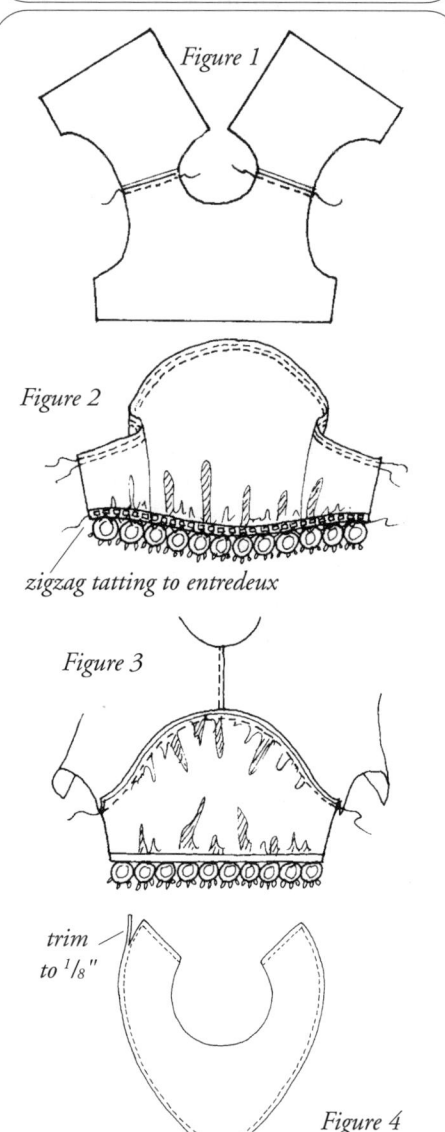

Pointed Collar Dress

Figure 1

Figure 2

zigzag tatting to entredeux

Figure 3

trim to 1/8"

Figure 4

Figure 5 — enlarged detail of corner overlap — zigzag

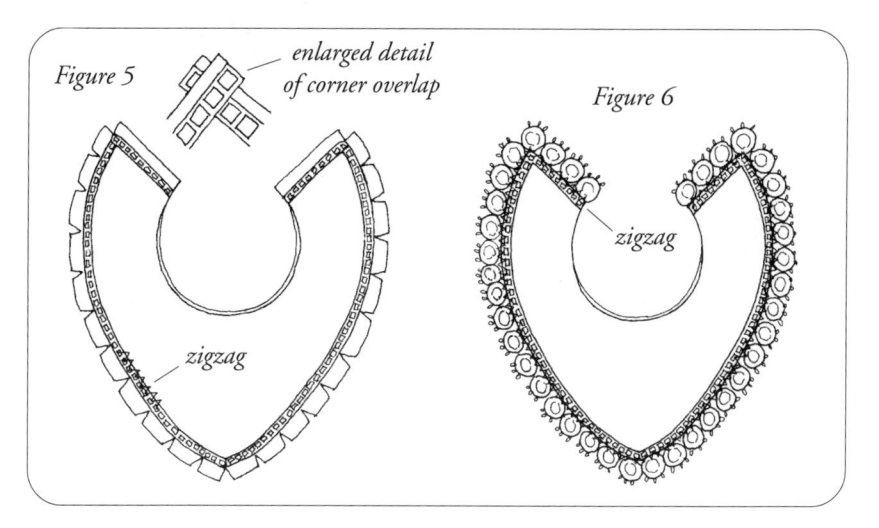

Figure 6 — zigzag

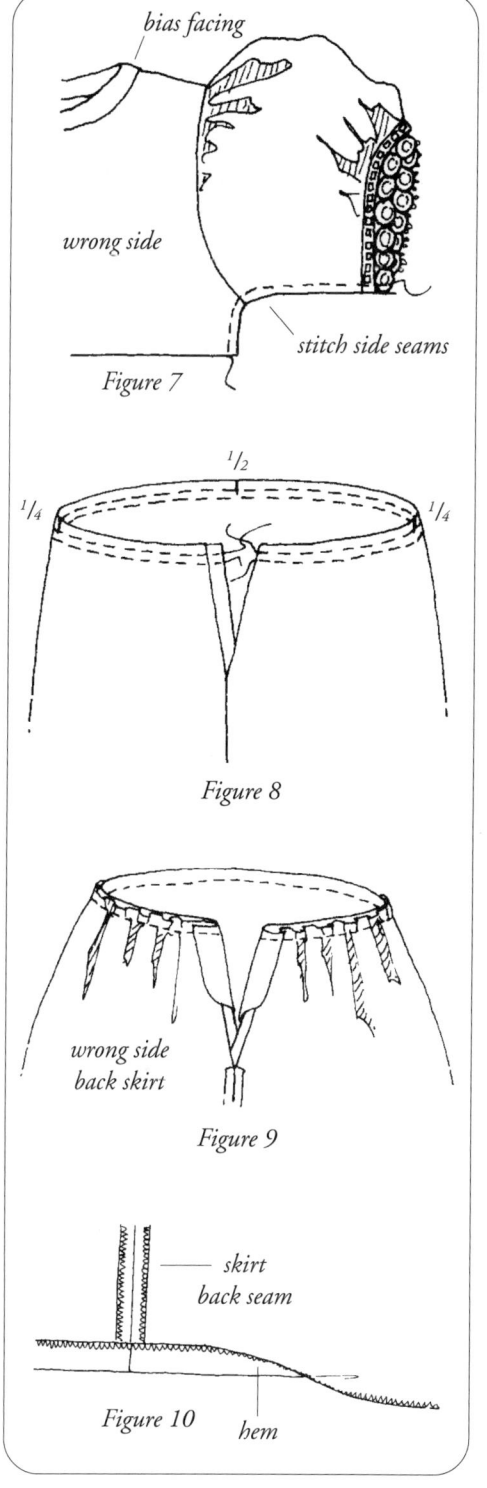

6. Cut a piece of entredeux 1" longer then the outer edge of the collar. Trim one side of the entredeux fabric away. Place clips in the remaining fabric side in order for the entredeux to curve. Butt the entredeux to the outer edge of the collar and zigzag in place (fig. 5). To make pretty corners, cut the entredeux 1 hole past the corner of the collar. Place another piece of entredeux along the other side of the collar overlapping one hole of the entredeux with the last hole from the first piece of entredeux (see enlarged detail of corner overlap).
7. Trim the remaining fabric edge from the entredeux. Butt the tatting to the entredeux and zigzag the tatting in place (fig. 6).
8. Place the collar to the dress bodice. Finish the neck of the bodice referring to the General Directions - C. Neck Finishes - f. Attaching A Collar with a Bias Facing.
9. Place the sides of the bodice together and stitch in place (fig. 7).
10. Create a placket in the skirt referring to the General Directions - A. Plackets - b. Placket in a Seam.
11. Fold the skirt in half to find the center. Mark at the top edge. Fold the skirt again to find the quarter points. Mark (fig. 8).
12. Place the back bodices to the skirt back, right sides together with the placket edges to the fold lines of the back bodices. Remember, one side of the placket will be folded to the inside of the skirt and pinned, while the other side will remain extended. Wrap each bodice back around the placket opening in the skirt. Gather the skirt to fit the bodice, matching the center of the skirt to the center front bodice and the quarter markings on the skirt with the side seams of the bodice. Stitch in place (fig. 9). Flip the bodice away from the skirt.
13. Serge or zigzag around the lower edge of the skirt. Turn the finished edge of the skirt to the inside of the dress 1" and hem by hand or machine (fig. 10).
14. Close the dress using Velcro™, snaps, or tiny buttons and buttonholes along each side of the back bodice.
15. Stitch the silk ribbon embroidery in the center of the collar using the template (fig. 11) and referring to the embroidery techniques.

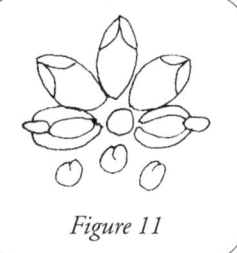

Figure 7 — bias facing, wrong side, stitch side seams

Figure 8

Figure 9 — wrong side back skirt

Figure 10 — skirt back seam, hem

Figure 11

Dresses — Three Best Friends

Floral Dress with Detachable Collar

Made of beautiful imported cotton, this dress features a square collar edged with insertion and gathered ecru French edging. The collar has magnificent silk ribbon embroidered flowers almost covering the front. The sleeves have a bias binding for their finish. There is a pretty little bias band on the collar which is made of pink batiste. The back is closed with buttons and buttonholes. This dress is a real treasure.

Fabric Requirements

Fabric Requirements:

	13"	17 1/2", 18" and 19 1/2"
Fabric	1/2 yd	5/8 yd
Organdy	1/8 yd	1/4 yd
Lace Edging (5/8")	1 yd	1 1/2 yd
Lace Insertions (1/4")	1/2 yd	3/4 yd

Notions

Lightweight sewing thread, Silk ribbon for embroidery in light pink, dark pink, light blue, dark blue, yellow, light green, and dark green, Velcro™, snaps or tiny buttons, one hook and eye set

Directions

All Seams 1/4" unless otherwise indicated. Finish all seams with a zigzag or serge to finish the fabric edges.

Please read through both the General Directions and the Specific Directions before starting the dress. The General Directions can be found on page 4 and give instructions for neck, sleeves and hem finishes. These Specific Directions give instructions for the special details concerning this particular dress and the sequence of the construction.

The following pattern pieces needed for this dress are found on the pull-outs: waisted front, waisted back, detachable collar, and elbow-length sleeve.

A. Preparing the Dress Pieces

1. From the floral fabric cut the following: two waisted back bodices from the selvage, one waisted front bodice on the fold, two sleeves, and one skirt piece 45" wide by the following length:
   - 13" doll — 7 5/8"
   - 17 1/2" doll — 9 7/8"
   - 18" doll — 10 5/8"
   - 19 1/2" doll — 10 5/8"
2. From the organdy trace one collar. Do not cut out the collar until the embroidery is complete.

B. Constructing the Dress

1. Place the front bodice to the back bodice pieces, right sides together. Stitch the shoulder seams (fig. 1).
2. Finish the neck referring to the General Directions, C. Neck Finishes, e. Bias Facing.
3. Finish each sleeve referring to the General Directions, B. Sleeves and Sleeves Finishes, d. Bias Sleeve Bindings.
4. Refer to the General Directions, B. Sleeves and Sleeve Finishes, h. Attaching the Sleeves and attach the sleeves to the bodice (fig. 2).
5. Place the sides of the bodice, right sides together, matching the ends of the sleeves, the underarm seams and the lower edges of the bodice. Stitch the side seams in place (fig. 3).

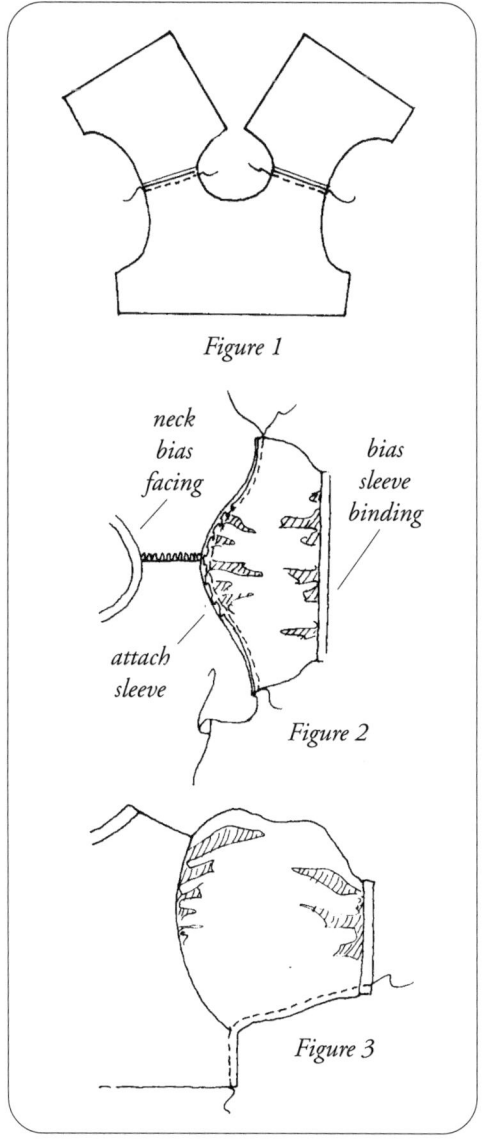

Floral Dress with Detachable Collar

Figure 1

Figure 2 — neck bias facing, bias sleeve binding, attach sleeve

Figure 3

Figure 4

Figure 5

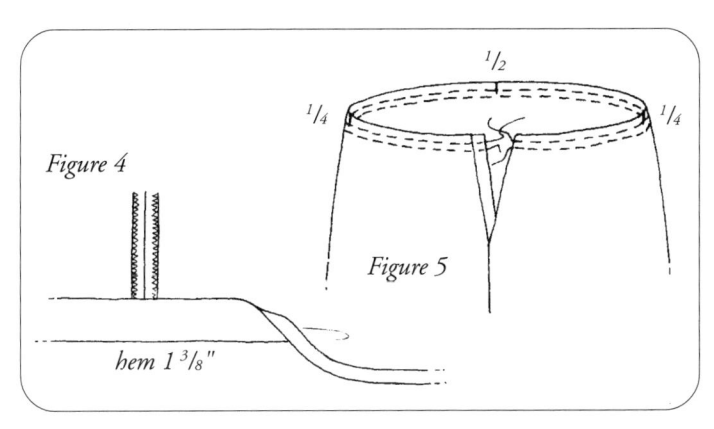

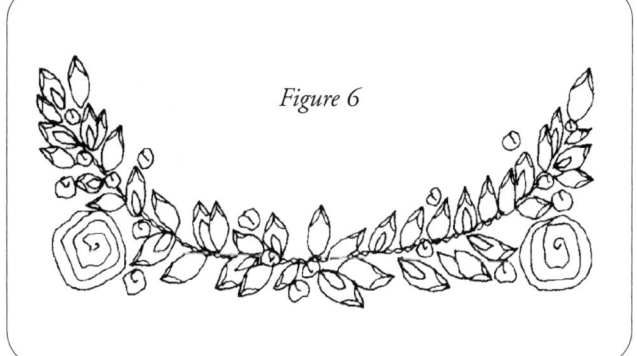

hem 1 3/8"

Figure 6

6. Create a placket in the skirt referring to the General Directions, A. Plackets, b. Placket in a Seam.
7. Fold to the wrong side 1/4" at the bottom edge of the skirt.
8. Turn up a 1 3/8" hem and hem bottom of skirt by hand or machine (fig. 4).
9. Fold the skirt in half to find the center. Mark at the top edge. Fold the skirt again to find the quarter points. Mark (fig. 5).
10. Place the back bodices to the skirt back, right sides together with the placket edges to the fold lines of the back bodices. Remember, one side of the placket will be folded to the inside of the skirt and pinned, while the other side will remain extended. Wrap each bodice back around the placket opening in the skirt. Pull up the gathers at the top edge of the skirt to fit the bodice, matching the center of the skirt to the center front bodice and the quarter markings on the skirt with the side seams of the bodice. Stitch the waistline seam (fig. 5). Flip the bodice away from the skirt
11. Close the dress using Velcro™, snaps, or tiny buttons and buttonholes along each side of the back bodice.

C. Collar

1. Trace the embroidery design (fig. 6) onto the traced collar.
2. Stitch the embroidery design refering to the Embroidery Instructions found on page 119 (fig. 7).
3. Shape the insertion lace around the outside line of the collar, refer to the technique "lace shaping" (fig. 8).
4. Zigzag the inner edge of the lace to the collar fabric. Cut the fabric from behind the lace (fig. 8).
5. Measure the outer edge of the lace insertion. Cut a strip of lace edging twice this length and gather to fit around the outer edge of the collar (fig. 8).
6. Make a small hem in the back edge of the collar by folding under 1/8" once then 1/8" again and whip in place by hand or machine (fig. 9).
7. Refer to the General Directions C. Neck Finishes, c. Bias Binding and finish the neck edge with a bias band.
8. Close the back of the collar with a hook and eye.

organdy

traced collar

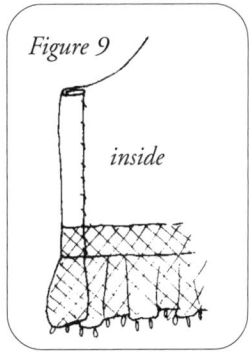

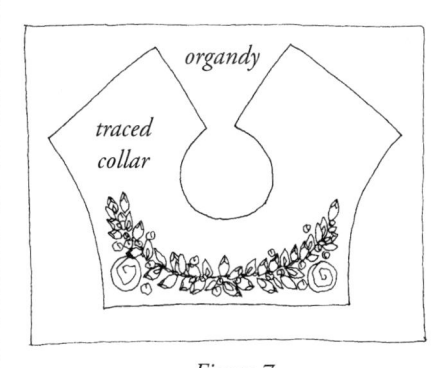

Figure 7

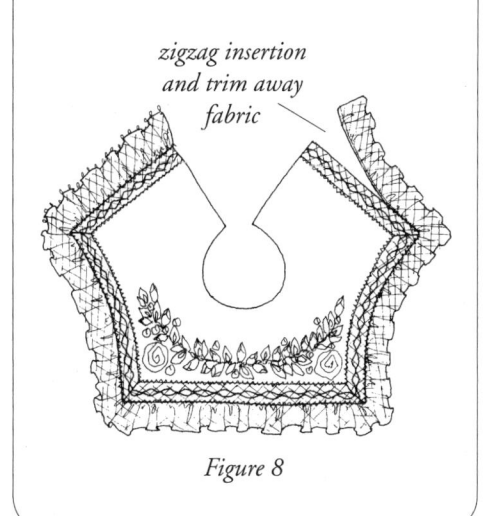

Figure 9

inside

zigzag insertion and trim away fabric

Figure 8

Dresses — Three Best Friends

Robin's Egg Blue Tiered Dress

All three girls have always loved to wear robin's egg blue. It just seems to go with everybody's hair color. This very special party dress has a pink and green silk ribbon embroidery design in the center front. The puffed sleeves have a row of white French insertion lace in the center; the bottom is finished with entredeux, French insertion and French edging stitched on flat. The upper bodice has white French insertion stitched on in a V; the upper bodice has entredeux at the bottom. The center tier has a row of white French insertion at the bottom, which is attached to the bottom gathered tier with white entredeux. The very full bottom tier has a row of white French lace insertion and white French lace edging stitched on straight on the bottom The dress is closed with Velcro™. Since this dress is very full, the Three Best Friends call this their swish dress. They feel so special dressed in this color.

Robin's Egg Blue Tiered Dress

Fabric Requirements

Fabric Requirements:

	13"	17 1/2", 18" and 19 1/2"
Robin's Egg Blue Batiste	1/2 yard	5/8 yard
Lace insertion (3/8")	3 yards	3 1/4 yards
Lace insertion (1/2")	1/2 yard	5/8 yard
Lace edging (3/8")	1/2 yard	5/8 yard
Lace edging (1/2")	2 1/4 yards	2 3/8 yards
Entredeux	1 1/2 yards	1 3/4 yards

Notions

Lightweight sewing, Velcro™, snaps or tiny buttons, wash-out marker, 4mm pink silk ribbon and 4mm green silk ribbon for the embroidery.

Figure 1

Directions

All Seams 1/4" unless otherwise indicated. Finish all seams with a zigzag or serge to finish the fabric edges.

Please read through both the General Directions and the Specific Directions before starting the dress. The General Directions can be found on page 4 and give instructions for neck, sleeves and hem finishes. These Specific Directions give instructions for the special details concerning this particular dress and the sequence of the construction.

The follow pattern pieces found on the pull-outs are needed for this dress: mid-yoke front, mid-yoke back, elbow-length sleeve.

Figure 2

A. Preparing the Dress Pieces

1. From the Swiss batiste, cut the following: one front yoke from the fold, two back yokes from the selvage, two short sleeves, two skirt pieces 45" wide by the following measurements:

13" doll	2 3/4"
17 1/2" doll	4 3/8"
18" & 19 1/2" doll	4 7/8"

   Cut one of the strips in half to create two pieces approximately 22" long. One 22" strip will be used for the top tier and the other one will be sewn to the end of the remaining 45" strip to create a strip approximately 67" long for the bottom tier.

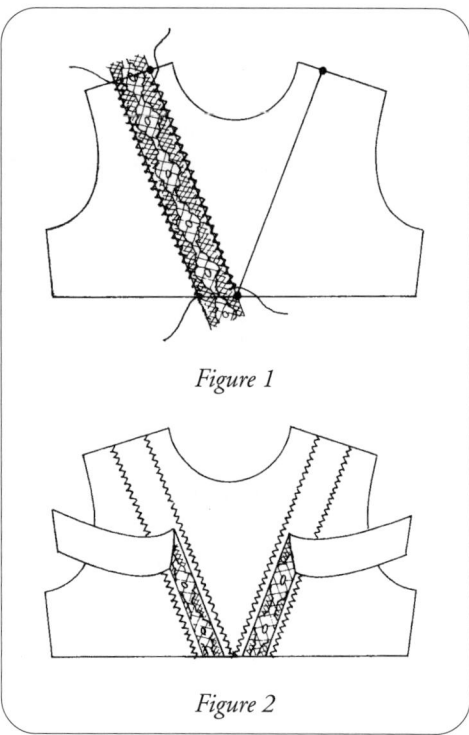

Constructing the Dress

1. Using a fabric marker, place a dot 3/8" from the neck edge on each shoulder and at the center front on the lower edge of the front bodice. Draw a line from each shoulder dot down to the center front dot.

2. Cut two pieces of 3/8" lace insertion, each piece being the length of one line. Position each lace piece along a line and zigzag both sides of the insertion into place (fig. 1). Trim the ends even with the bodice edges and then trim the fabric from behind each piece of lace (fig. 2).

72   *Three Best Friends*   *Dresses*

Figure 3

Figure 4 — Center drawn line

Figure 5

Figure 6

Figure 7

Figure 8

Figure 9

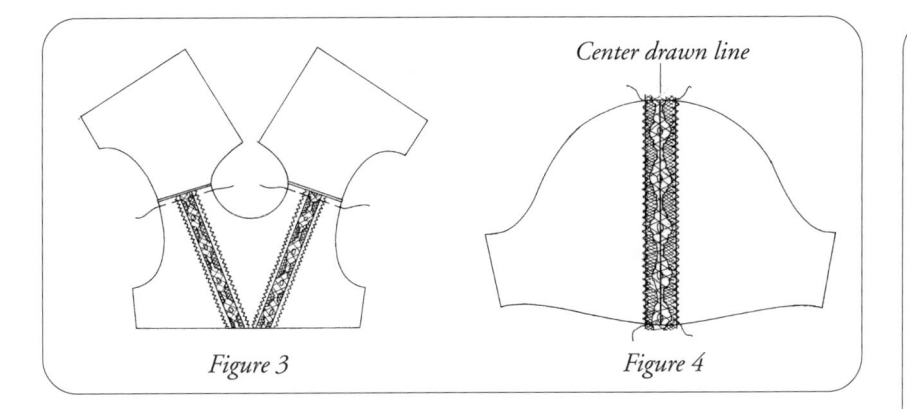

3. Place the front bodice to the back bodice pieces, right sides together. Stitch the shoulder seams in place (fig. 3).
4. Finish the neck of the dress, using entredeux and ½" edging lace and referring to the General Directions, C. Neck Finishes, a. Entredeux to Gathered Edging Lace.
5. Fold each sleeve in half and draw a line down the middle of each sleeve.
6. Cut two pieces of ⅜" insertion lace, each one the length of the drawn line. Center the lace over the drawn line and zigzag both sides into place (fig. 4). Cut the lace even with the sleeve edges and trim the fabric from behind the lace (fig. 5).
7. Cut two pieces of ½" lace insertion and ⅜" edging two times the length of the bottom sleeve edge. Zigzag the laces together (fig. 6). Finish each sleeve referring to the General Directions, B. Sleeves and Sleeve finishes, a. Entredeux to Gathered Edging Lace using the lace strip created above.
8. Place the sleeves to the arm openings, right sides together, matching the center of each seam to the shoulder seam of the yokes. Gather the sleeves to fit the openings. Stitch in place (fig. 7).
9. Place the sides of the bodice, right sides together, matching the ends of the sleeves, the underarm seams and the lower edges of the bodice. Stitch the side seams in place (fig. 8).
10. Attach the entredeux to the lower edge of the bodice, back folds extended using the technique "entredeux to fabric" (fig. 9).
11. To make the top tier of the skirt, cut a strip of ⅜" insertion lace 22" long and attach the lace to one long side of the 22" fabric strip, using the technique "lace to fabric".
12. Cut a piece of entredeux the same length as the 22" top tier skirt piece and attach the entredeux to the bottom of the lace insertion using the technique "lace to entredeux" (fig. 10).
13. To make the bottom tier of the skirt, place the 45" strip and the remaining 22" strip right sides together and stitch a seam along the short side.
14. Stitch the ⅜" insertion lace to one long side of the long fabric strip using the technique "lace to fabric". Then, stitch the edging lace to the insertion using the technique "lace to lace" to complete the bottom tier.
15. Run two gathering rows, ⅛" and ¼" in the top edge of the bottom tier skirt piece. Pull up the gathering threads to fit the entredeux on the bottom of the top tier skirt piece and stitch the top tier to the bottom tier in place using the technique "entredeux to gathered fabric" (fig. 11).

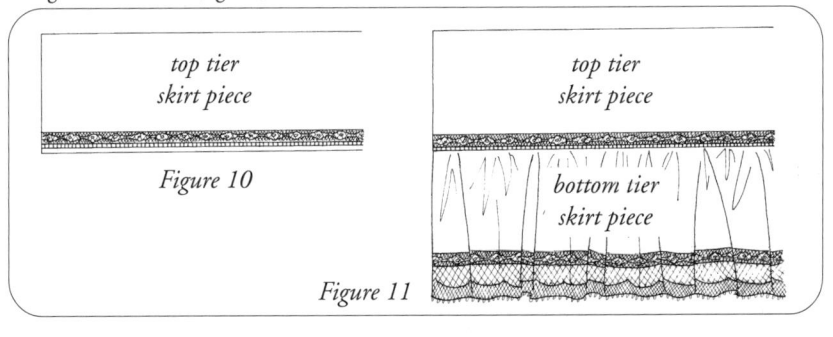

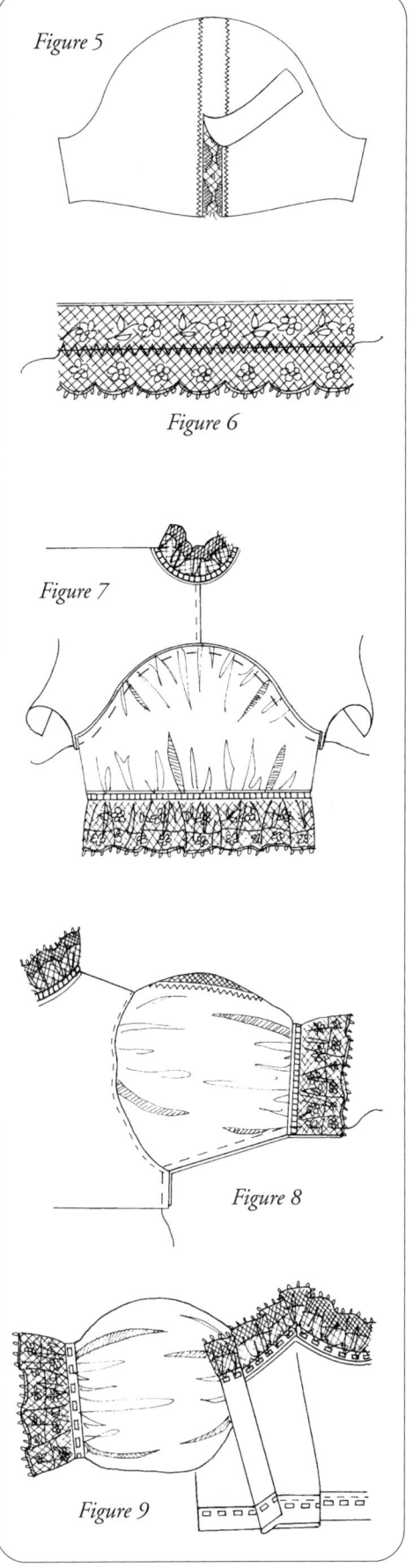

Figure 10 — top tier skirt piece

Figure 11 — top tier skirt piece / bottom tier skirt piece

Dresses — Three Best Friends — 73

16. Create a placket in the skirt referring to the General Directions, A. Plackets, b. Placket in a Seam.
17. Fold the skirt in half to find the center. Mark at the top edge. Fold the skirt again to find the quarter points. Mark (fig. 12).
18. Place the back yokes to the skirt back, right sides together with the placket edges to the fold lines of the back bodices. Remember, one side of the placket will be folded to the inside of the skirt and pinned, while the other side will remain extended. Wrap each yoke back around the placket opening in the skirt. Gather the skirt to fit the bodice, matching the center of the skirt to the center front yoke and the quarter markings on the skirt with the side seams of the yoke. Stitch in place using the technique "entredeux to gathered fabric". Flip the yokes away from the skirt (fig. 13).
19. Close the dress using Velcro™, snaps or tiny buttons and buttonholes along each side of the back yoke.
20. Using the silk ribbon, work three lazy daisy stitches in pink for the flower and two lazy daisy stitches in green for the leaves. Work one French knot in green for the center of the leaves (fig. 14). Refer to Embroidery Techniques.

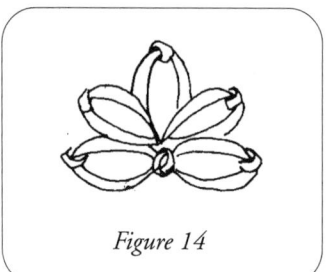

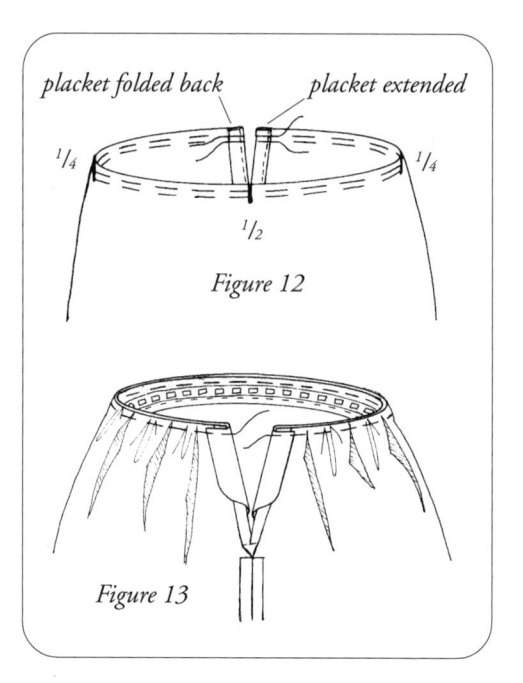

Figure 12

Figure 13

Figure 14

Pink Silk Dress

Pink silk dupioni is the perfect fabric for this little dress. The fabric has just the right amount of body to allow the skirt to stand out beautifully. A tiny vine stitch edges the bodice overlay and dances across the lower edge of the skirt. Delicate edging lace peeks out from beneath both the overlay and the skirt hem. Tiny beads are sewn along the vine stitch to give the dress just the right amount of sparkle. Any one of the three best friends would love this dress.

Fabric Requirements

Fabric Requirements:

	13"	17 1/2", 18" and 19 1/2"
Fabric -Silk Dupioni	1/2 yard	5/8 yard
Lace Edging (1/2")	2 1/8 yards	2 1/3 yards
Lace Edging (3/8")	1/2 yard	1/2 yard
Entredeux	5/8 yard	3/4 yard
Ribbon (1/8")	1/2 yard	1/2 yard

Notions

Lightweight sewing thread, Decorative sewing thread, Tiny pearls or beads, Velcro™, snaps or tiny buttons

Directions

All Seams 1/4" unless otherwise indicated. Finish all seams with a zigzag or serge to finish the fabric edges.

Please read through both the General Directions and the Specific Directions before starting the dress. The General Directions can be found on page 4 and give instructions for neck, sleeves and hem finishes. These Specific Directions give instructions for the special details concerning this particular dress and the sequence of the construction.

Pink Silk Dress

The following pattern pieces are needed for this dress: waisted front bodice, waisted back bodice, front "V" overlay, and elbow-length sleeve.

A. Preparing the Dress Pieces

1. From the Silk Dupioni cut the following: two back bodices from the selvage, one front bodice on the fold, two sleeves, one front "V" overlay on the fold, and one skirt piece 45" wide by the following length:

13" doll	7"
17 1/2" doll	9 1/4"
18" doll	10"
19 1/2"	10"

B. Embellishing the Bodice and Skirt

1. Create a placket in the skirt referring to the General Directions, A. Plackets, b. Placket in a Seam.
2. Fold to the wrong side ¼" at the bottom edge of the skirt.
3. Decorative stitching will be centered 1" above the folded edge. Select a decorative stitch and sew all around the bottom of the skirt (fig. 1). Add decorative pearls or beads.
4. Sew ½" lace around the bottom edge of the skirt. Place the right side of the lace to the right side of the skirt with the scalloped edge toward the top of the skirt and the straight edge of the lace placed ¼" from the folded edge of the skirt. Stitch the lace to the skirt with a straight stitch (fig. 2).
5. Turn up a ½" hem and hem bottom of skirt by hand or machine.
6. Stitch the decorative stitch ½" from outer edges of the overlay (fig. 3). Add decorative pearls or beads.
7. Lay ½" lace edging on the right side of the overlay with the right side of the lace to the right side of fabric with the scalloped edge toward the decorative stitching and the straight edge even with the edge of the fabric. Sew the lace to the edge of the fabric with a straight stitch (fig. 4).
8. Fold the edges of the overlay under ¼" and press. The lace will extend out pass the folded edge.
9. Lay the overlay on the front bodice and secure in place at the shoulder, neck and waist with a ⅛" seam. The overlay and the front bodice will now be treated as one piece (fig. 5).

C. Constructing the Dress

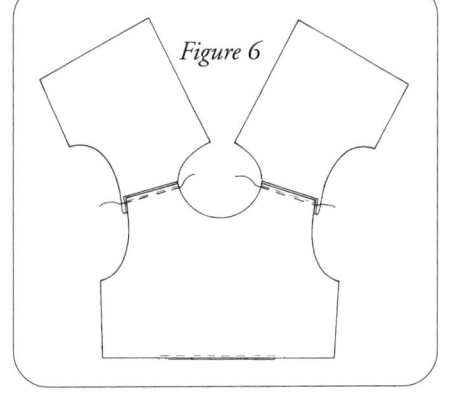

1. Place the front bodice to the back bodice pieces, right sides together. Stitch the shoulder seams (fig. 6).
2. Finish the neck referring to the General Directions, C. Neck Finishes, a. Entredeux to Gathered Edging Lace.
3. Finish each sleeve referring to the General Directions, B. Sleeves and Sleeves Finishes, a. Entredeux to Gathered Edging Lace.
4. Refer to the General Directions, B. Sleeves and Sleeve Finishes, h. Attaching the Sleeves and attach the sleeves to the bodice.
5. Place the sides of the bodice, right sides together, matching the ends of the sleeves, the underarm seams and the lower edges of the bodice. Stitch the side seams in place.
6. Fold the skirt in half to find the center. Mark at the top edge. Fold the skirt again to find the quarter points. Mark.
7. Place the back bodices to the skirt back, right sides together with the placket edges to the fold lines of the back bodices. Remember, one side of the placket will be folded to the inside of the skirt and pinned, while the other side will remain extended. Wrap each bodice back around the placket opening in the skirt. Pull up the gathers at the top edge of the skirt to fit the bodice, matching the center of the skirt to the center front bodice and the quarter markings on the skirt with the side seams of the bodice. Stitch the waistline seam. Flip the bodice away from the skirt
8. Close the dress using Velcro™, snaps, or tiny buttons and buttonholes along each side of the back bodice.
9. Cut the ribbon into three 6" pieces and tie in small bows and attach at center of neck and sleeves.

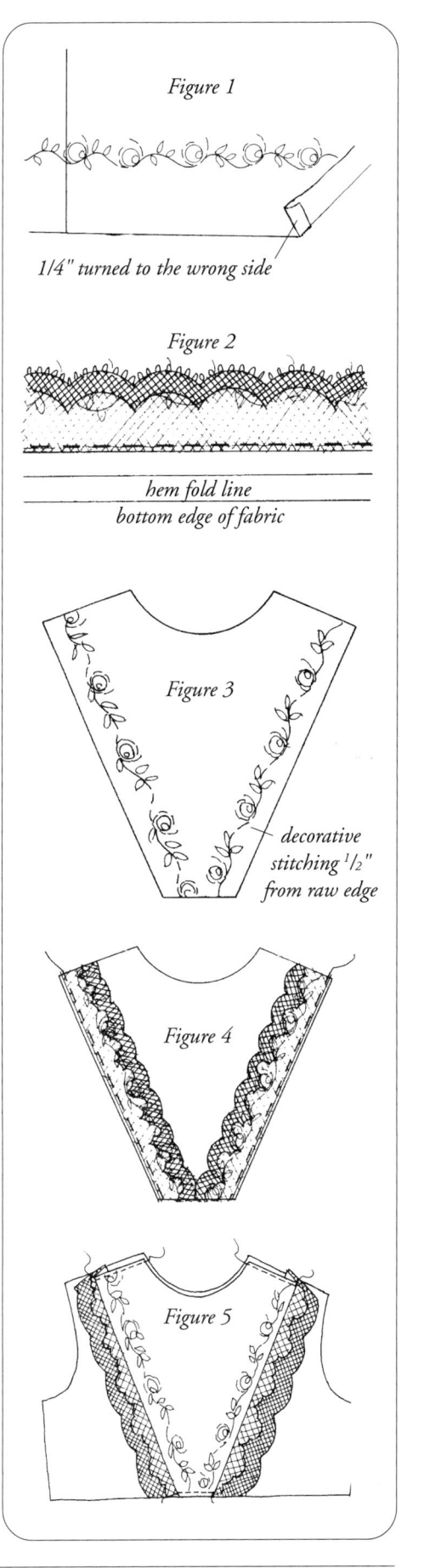

Figure 1

¼" turned to the wrong side

Figure 2

hem fold line
bottom edge of fabric

Figure 3

decorative stitching ½" from raw edge

Figure 4

Figure 5

Figure 6

Bonnet

This bonnet is so easy to make and so pretty! The back casing gathers the back; the front is gathered onto entredeux, white French insertion, and baby white French edging. The bonnet is fastened with two ribbon ties.

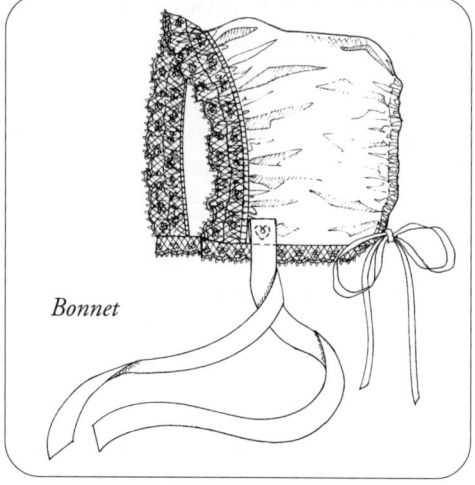

Fabric Requirements

Fabric Requirements:

	All sizes
Fabric - Swiss Batiste	1/8 yard
Lace Insertion (1/2")	2/3 yard
Lace Edging (3/8")	1 yard
Entredeux	1/3 yard
Satin Ribbon (3/8")	3/4 yard
Satin Ribbon (1/8")	1 yard

Cut the following pieces for the given sizes:

	13"	17 1/2", 18" and 19 1/2"
Fabric	3 1/2 x 23"	4 1/2 x 24"
Lace Insertion (1/2")	18"	20"
Lace Edging (3/8")	20"	22"
Entredeux	8 1/2"	9 1/2"

Notions

Lightweight sewing thread

Directions

All Seams 1/4" unless otherwise indicated. Finish all seams with a serger or zigzag stitch.

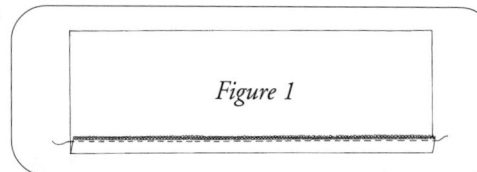

1. On the piece of batiste, overcast one long side. Fold over 1/2" and straight stitch 3/8" from the folded edge to form the casing (fig. 1).
2. Stitch the lace edging to the lace insertion using the technique "lace to lace".
3. Trim one side of the entredeux.
4. Gather the lace insertion along the long side and attach it to the entredeux using the technique "gathered lace to entredeux" (fig. 2).
5. Run two rows of gathering stitches at 1/8" and 1/4" from the long unfinished edge of the batiste piece. Pull up the gathers to fit the entredeux (fig.3).
6. Trim the fabric edge of the entredeux strip 1/4" from the entredeux.
7. Attach the batiste piece to the entredeux strip using the technique "gathered fabric to entredeux" (fig. 4).
8. Hem one end of the lace by turning under 1/8" and 1/8" again. Attach a piece of lace edging on each end of the bonnet piece using the technique "lace to fabric". Begin the lace at the stitching line of the casing and stop the lace at the edge of the edging on the front of the bonnet. Finish the lace with a narrow hem even with the lace edging on the front of the bonnet. (fig. 5). Zigzag in place.
9. Cut the piece of 3/8" satin ribbon into two equal pieces and fold under 1/2" on one end of each piece. Press well.
10. Place the folded end of the ribbon just beside the entrudeux on the batiste part of the bonnet. Secure with a decorative machine stitch or tiny hand stitches (see finished drawing of bonnet for ribbon placement).
11. With a large tapestry needle or bodkin, run the 1/8" ribbon through the opening in the casing.
12. Pull both ends of the ribbon to gather the back of the bonnet and tie into a bow.

Bonnet

Figure 1

Figure 2

Figure 3

Figure 4

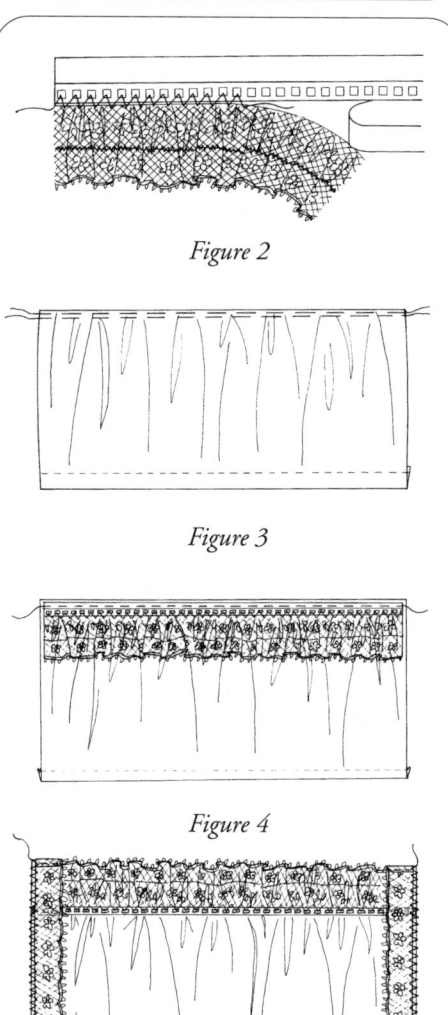

Figure 5

Paris Bonnet

On my travels I always shop antique clothing stores and doll shops. The original of this bonnet was purchased at a very exclusive doll shop in Paris, France. The bonnet is composed of ecru laces, beading and insertions, zigzagged together to form the fabric from which the bonnet is cut. A circular crown in the back is encircled by gathered ecru French edging. Two rows of ecru French edging are slightly gathered to one row of ecru insertion for the ruffle around the bonnet. A beautiful scalloped treatment of gathered French ecru lace insertion and edging trims the top of the bonnet and four robin's egg blue silk ribbon rosettes add such a pretty touch. Blue silk ribbons are used for running through the beading areas on the bonnet, and the same ribbon is used for tying the bonnet under the chin. What lucky little girls to have a bonnet like this.

Paris Bonnet

Fabric Requirements

Fabric Requirements:

	13"	17 $1/2$", 18" & 19 $1/2$"
Edging Lace ($5/8$")	4 $5/8$ yards	5 yards
Lace Insertion ($3/4$")	2 $1/2$ yards	2 $1/2$ yards
Lace Beading ($1/2$")	3 yards	3 $1/2$ yards
Lace Insertion ($1/2$")	3 yards	3 $1/2$ yards
Satin Ribbon (4mm)	6 yards	6 yards
Medium Wt. Interfacing	$1/8$ yard	$1/8$ yard

Notions

Lightweight sewing thread, wing needle (optional), Velcro™, snaps or tiny buttons

Directions

All Seams $1/4$" unless otherwise indicated. Finish all seams with a serger or zigzag stitch.

The following pattern pieces are needed for this bonnet: Paris bonnet, Paris bonnet back circle, Paris bonnet facing. These patterns are found on the pull-outs.

Constructing the Bonnet

1. Cut 9" of beading and 9" of $1/2$" insertion. (fig. 1). Stitch the two pieces together using the technique "lace to lace". Weave ribbon through the beading. Cut the lace strip into 3" pieces. Zigzag the lace pieces together with the beading attached to the lace. Starch and press. Trace the bonnet back circle onto this lace piece. Stitch with a tiny zigzag along the outline of the circle. Cut the bonnet back circle along the outside edge of zigzag stitching (fig. 1).

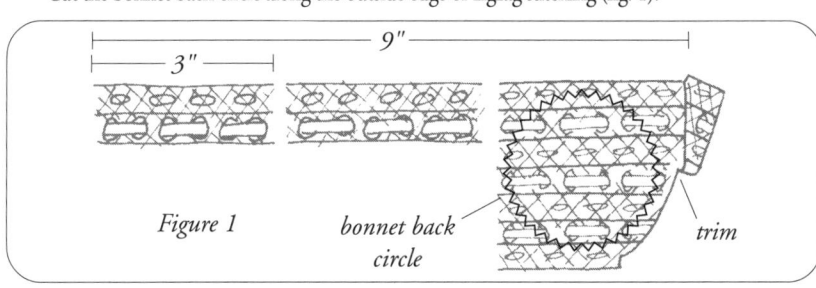

Figure 1 — bonnet back circle — trim

Figure 2

Figure 3 — facing

Figure 4 — trim

Trace dotted lines onto bonnet from bonnet side. You can see lines through lace and facing.

2. Attach the remaining beading to the $1/2$" lace insertion. Cut the piece in half and zigzag the lace pieces together with the beading attached to the lace. Continue cutting and stitching until the following measurement is achieved: 13" dolls - 16" long by 5" wide, 17 $1/2$", 18" & 19 $1/2$" dolls - 17" long by 6" wide. Starch and press. Trace the bonnet onto this created lace piece. Weave ribbon through the beading (fig. 2).
3. Cut the bonnet facing from the interfacing and zigzag along the back edge. Trace the dotted lines onto the facing piece (fig. 3). Place the right side of the facing to the wrong side of the bonnet, lining up the lines on the bonnet with the front edge of the facing.

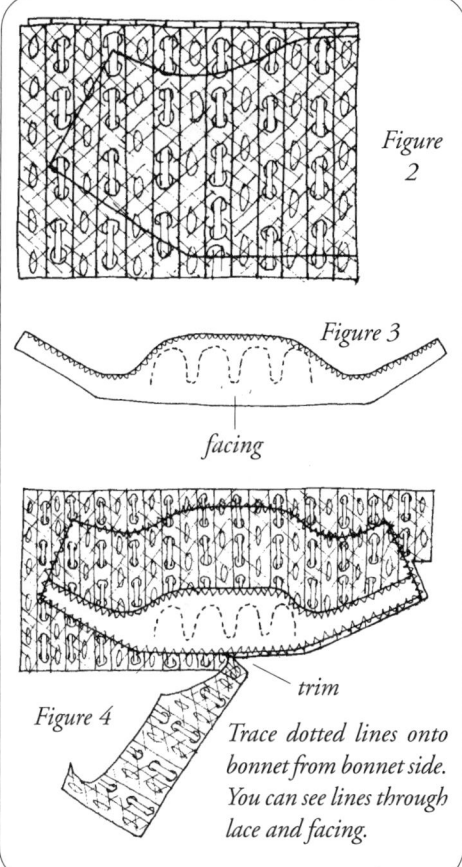

Place a tuck at the tuck line so that the center back edges line up. Using a zigzag (1.0 length and 2.0 width) stitch the facing to the bonnet. Zigzag along the other drawn lines. Cut just outside the zigzags. Trace the dotted lines of the facing on the bonnet using a fabric marker or pencil. Run two gathering rows in the back of the bonnet at $1/8$" and $1/4$", starting and stopping $3/8$" from the ends (fig. 4).

Figure 5 — edging / insertion

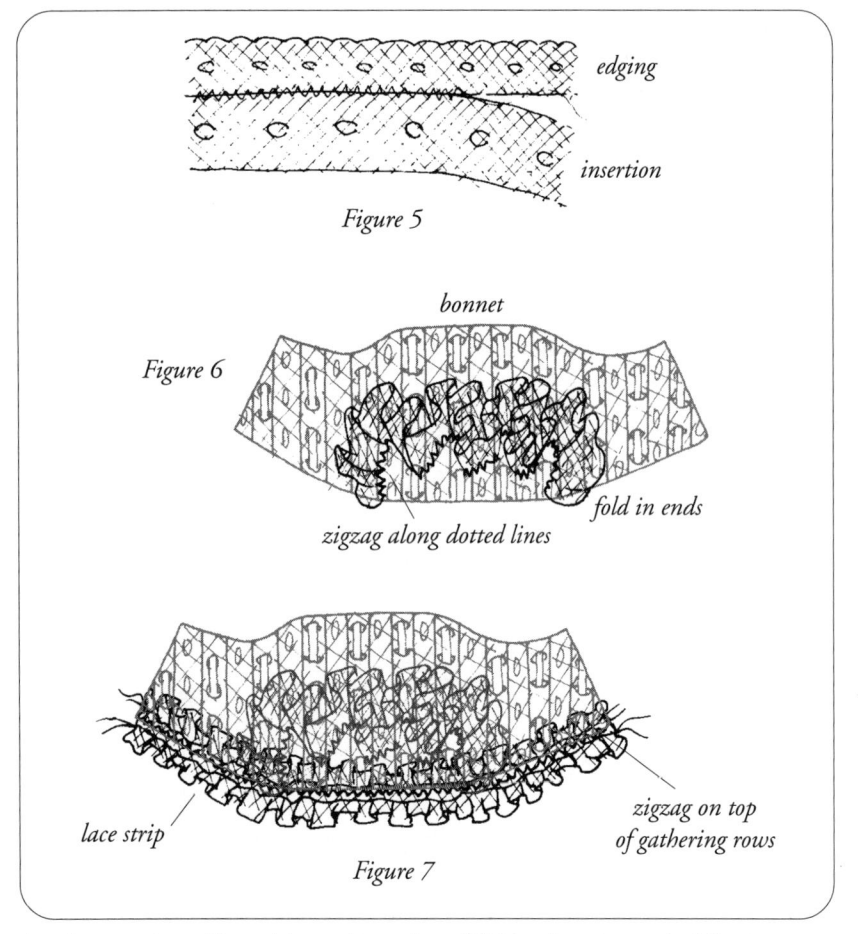

Figure 6 — bonnet / zigzag along dotted lines / fold in ends

Figure 7 — lace strip / zigzag on top of gathering rows

Figure 8 — bonnet / silk ribbon with decorative stitch

Figure 9 — (wrong side) bonnet / stitch center back edges

Figure 10 — stitch back of bonnet to circle / facing / back seam / (wrong side) bonnet

Figure 11 — stitch edging to circle by hand / back of bonnet

4. Cut one piece of lace edging and one piece of ³/₄" lace insertion to the following measurement: 35" for 13" dolls, and 38" for the 17 ¹/₂", 18" and 19 ¹/₂" dolls. Stitch the laces together using the technique "lace to lace" (fig. 5).

5. Gather the insertion side of the lace strip to fit the dotted lines of the bonnet. Fold the ends of the lace to the inside ¹/₈" and ¹/₈" again. Stitch the gathered lace in place along the dotted lines using a zigzag. Curl and tack each folded end of the lace to the bonnet by hand or with a zigzag (fig. 6).

6. Cut two pieces of lace edging and one piece of ³/₄" lace insertion to 52". Stitch edging lace to each side of the insertion using the technique "lace to lace". Run two gathering rows about ¹/₁₆" apart down the center of the insertion lace (fig. 7). Pull up the gathers and place the piece on the top of the bonnet with the gathering rows ¹/₄" from the front edge of the bonnet.

7. Place silk ribbon along the gathering lines and stitch in place with a feather stitch or other decorative stitch (fig. 8).

8. Make four 12 loop ribbon rosettes each from 26" of ribbon placing the dots about 2" apart. (Refer to Ribbon Rosette Technique found on page 119.) Tack a ribbon rosette in place at each X along the front of the bonnet (see finished drawing).

9. Create two more ribbon rosettes with streamers, using 18" of ribbon for each. Place dots in ribbons 1" apart, starting 12" from the end. This will create a rosette with a long ribbon streamer for the bonnet tie. Tack the ties to the silk ribbon at each front corner of the bonnet (see finished drawing).

10. Place the center back edges right sides together and stitch using a ¹/₄" seam (fig. 9).

11. Tie a bow using about 6" of silk ribbon. Tack at the center back seam (see finished drawing).

12. Gather the back of the bonnet to fit the back bonnet circle. Place the circle to the bonnet, right sides together and stitch in place using a ¹/₄" seam (fig. 10).

13. Gather 24" of edging lace to fit the seam line of the bonnet circle. Stitch in place on the right side by hand (fig. 11).

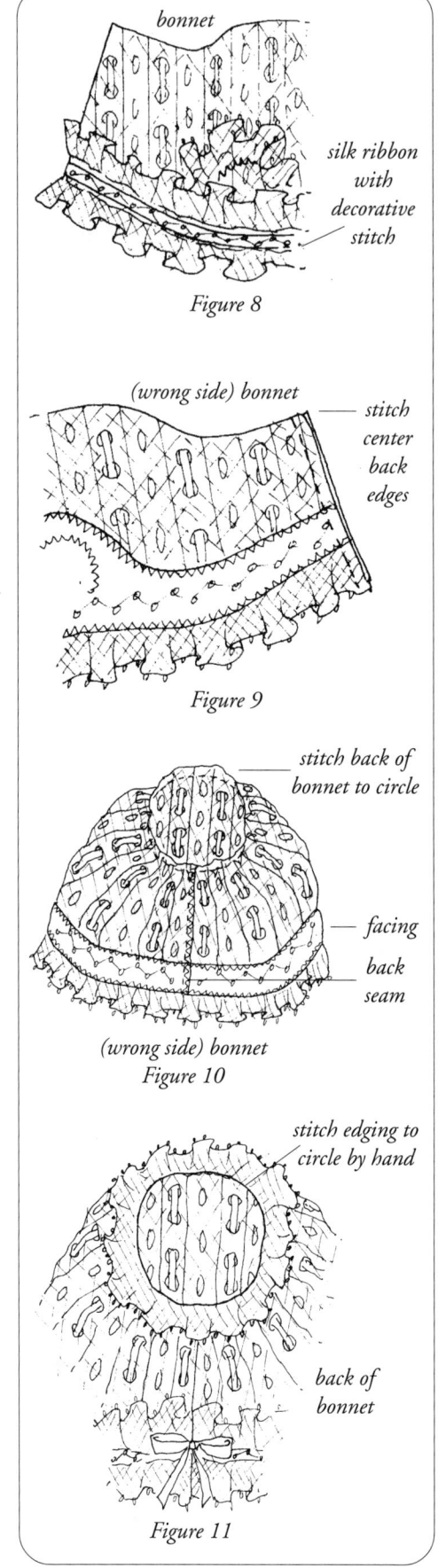

Nightgown

What doll wouldn't love this pink satin nightgown with entredeux and gathered French white edging around the neckline? Gathered French edging is stitched down both the front and the back. Long sleeves end with entredeux and gathered French edging. Tiny silk ribbon is woven through the entredeux around the neckline and the sleeves. The hem is put in with a wonderful machine decorative stitch. The back closes with Velcro™.

Fabric Requirements

Fabric Requirements:

	13"	17 1/2", 18" and 19 1/2"
Fabric	1/2 yard	5/8 yard
Edging Lace (1/2")	1 1/2 yards	1 3/4 yards
Entredeux	1/2 yard	3/4 yard

Silk Ribbon (2mm): pink and green

Notions

Lightweight sewing thread, Velcro™, Snaps or tiny buttons

Directions

All seams 1/4" unless otherwise indicated. Finish all seams with a zigzag or serge to finish the fabric edges.

Please read through both the General Directions and the Specific Directions before starting the dress. The General Directions can be found on page 4 and give instructions for plackets, neck and sleeve finishes. These Specific Directions give instructions for the special details concerning this particular dress and the sequence of the construction.

The following pattern pieces needed for this dress are found on the pull-outs: mid-yoke front, mid-yoke back, and long sleeve.

A. Cutting & Constructing the Gown

1. Cut two back bodices from the selvege, one front bodice from the fold and two long sleeves. Cut one skirt piece 45" wide by the following measurement:
13"	8 1/4"
17 1/2"	11 1/2"
18", 19 1/2"	12 1/2"
2. Place the front bodice to the back bodice pieces, right sides together. Stitch the shoulder seams in place (fig. 1).
3. Using a fabric marker, place dots in the center of each shoulder seam. Place dots along the lower edge of the bodice front 3/8" from the center front. Place dots along the lower edge of the bodice backs 1" from the fold lines (fig. 2).
4. Join the front dot, shoulder dot and back dot on each side of the bodice (fig. 2). Measure one of the drawn lines. Cut two pieces of edging lace twice the length of the line. Gather each piece to fit the lines. Pin the lace along the lines. Zigzag the lace in place (fig. 2).
5. Finish each sleeve referring to the General Directions, B. Sleeves and Sleeves Finishes (steps 2 - 3), a. Entredeux to Gathered Lace.
6. Finish the neck, referring to the General Directions, C. Neck Finishes, a. Entredeux to Gathered Edging Lace.
7. Refer back to the General Directions, B. Sleeves and Sleeve and Sleeve Finishes, h. Attaching the Sleeves and attach the sleeves to the bodice (fig. 3).

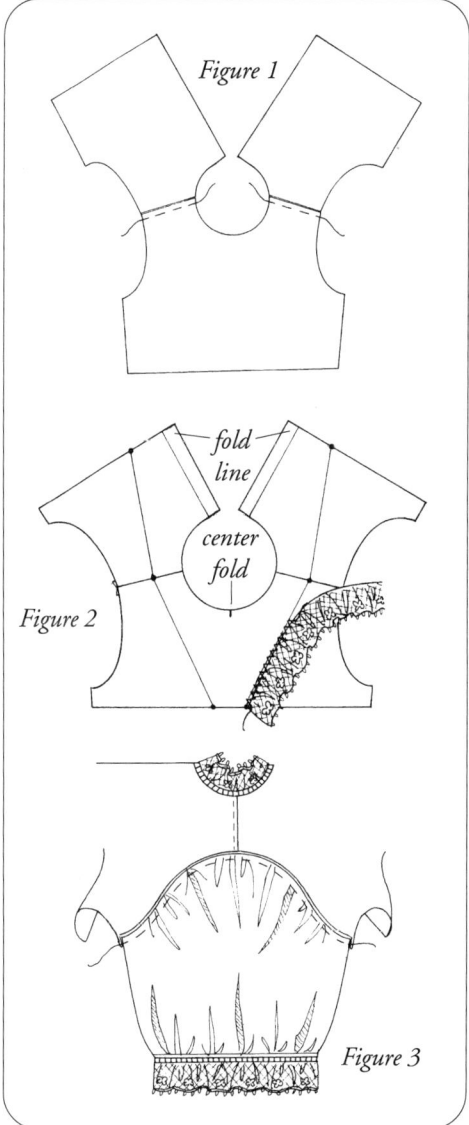

Nightgown

Figure 1

Figure 2

Figure 3

8. Place the sides of the bodice together and stitch the sleeve and underarm seam (fig. 4).
9. Fold the skirt in half to find the center. Mark at the top edge. Fold the skirt again to find the quarter points. Mark (fig. 5).
10. Create a placket in the skirt referring to the General Directions, A. Plackets, b. Placket in a Seam.
11. Place the back bodices to the skirt back, right sides together with the placket edges to the fold lines of the back bodice (fig 6). Remember, one side of the placket will be folded to the inside of the skirt and pinned, while the other side will remain extended. Wrap each bodice back around the placket opening in the skirt. Gather the skirt to fit the bodice, matching the center of the skirt to the center front bodice and the quarter markings on the skirt with the side seams of the bodice. Stitch in place. Flip the bodice away from the skirt (fig. 7).
12. Serge or zigzag around the lower edge of the skirt. Turn the finished edge of the skirt to the inside of the dress 1". Stitch the hem in place using a decorative stitch.

B. Finishing the Nightgown

1. Close the dress using Velcro™, snaps, or tiny buttons and buttonholes along each side of the back bodice.
2. Cut two pieces of silk ribbon the length of the entredeux at the neck. Weave each piece of silk ribbon through the neck entredeux starting at the back and ending at the center front. Tie the excess ribbon into a bow in the center front.
3. Cut two pieces of silk ribbon the length of the sleeve entredeux plus 8". Weave silk ribbon through the entredeux of the sleeves beginning and ending in the center of the sleeve. Tie the excess ribbon into a bow.
4. Stitch a pink five petal lazy daisy flower with green lazy daisy leaves in the center of the bodice front. Add a pearl to the center of the flower to complete the embroidery (fig. 8).

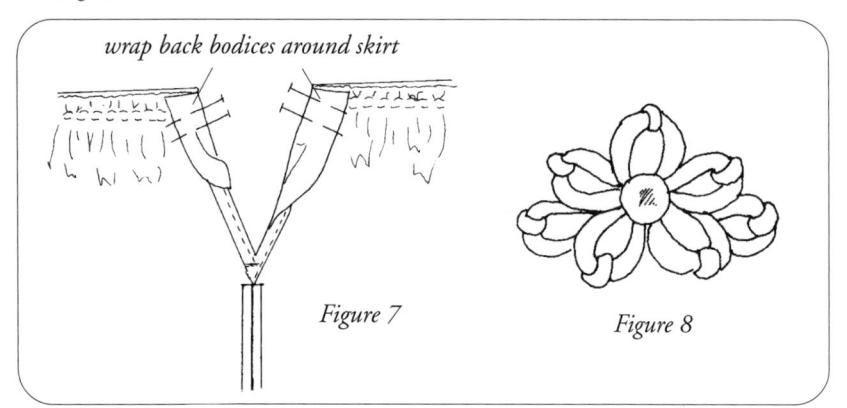

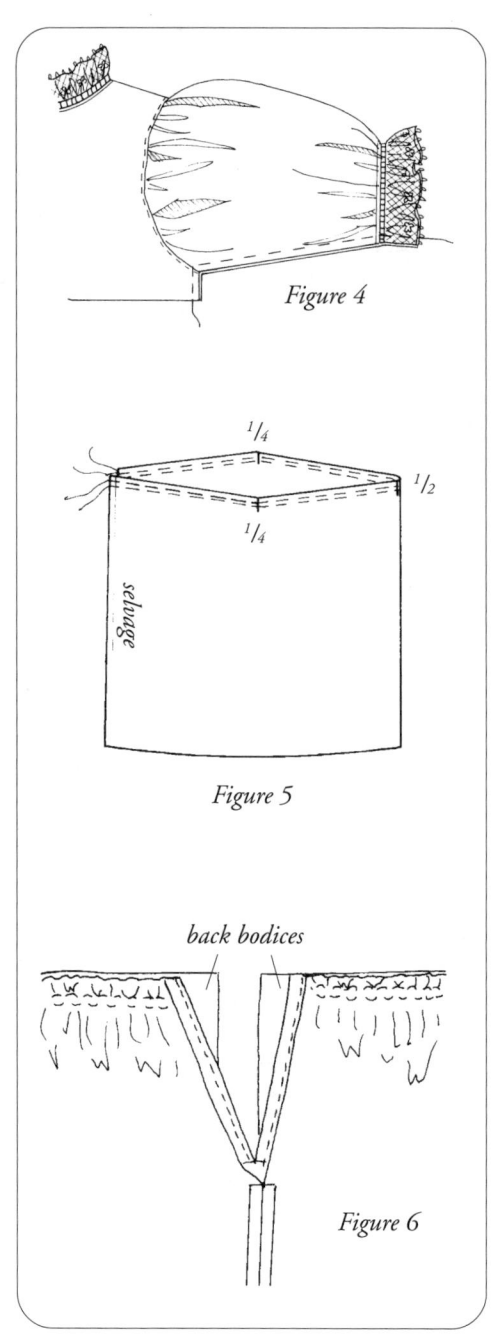

Figure 4

Figure 5

Figure 6

Figure 7

Figure 8

Intimate Apparel

Made of white batiste and beautifully embellished, the friend's lingerie ensemble is sure to delight you (and your dolls)! The ensemble includes a wasited slip, short bloomers, long bloomers, straight legged pantaloons, camisole, half slip, and dropped-waist slip; French lace, beading, and pink ribbon adorn these precious "undergarments". You will have so much fun selecting the appropriate "undergarment" for each dress, and the friends will enjoy playing "dress up".

Half Slip

Fabric Requirements

Fabric Requirements:

	13"	17 1/2"	18"	19 1/2"
Batiste	1/4 yard	1/4 yard	1/4 yard	1/4 yard
Lace insertion (3/8")	1 1/3 yards	1 1/3 yards	1 1/3 yards	1 1/3 yards
Lace beading (1/2")	1 1/3 yards	1 1/3 yards	1 1/3 yards	1 1/3 yards
Lace edging (5/8")	1 1/3 yards	1 1/3 yards	1 1/3 yards	1 1/3 yards
Elastic (1/8")	1/4 yard	1/4 yard	1/3 yard	1/3 yard

7 mm silk ribbon or 1/4" satin ribbon - 1 2/3 yds, all sizes

Notions

Lightweight sewing thread, bodkin or large tapestry needle

Directions

All Seams 1/4" unless otherwise indicated. Finish all seams with a zigzag or serge to finish the fabric edges. Please read through the directions before beginning the slip.

Construction

1. Tear or cut a piece of fabric for the slip 45" wide by the following: 5" for 13" dolls, 7" for the 17 1/2" dolls and 8" for 18" and 19 1/2" dolls.
2. Create a fancy band by stitching the three laces together with the lace beading in the middle. Refer to the technique "lace to lace".
3. Refer to the technique "lace to fabric" and attach the fancy band to the fabric along one side of the 45" strip.
4. Trim the edges of the fancy band even with the edge of the fabric.
5. Place the slip right sides together and sew the back seam (fig. 1).
6. To create an elastic casing at the top of the slip, turn the unfinished edge turn under 1/4" and 1/4" again. Stitch the casing very close to the lower fold leaving a 1" opening in the stitching (fig. 2).
7. Cut a piece of elastic the following lengths: 8" for the 13" doll, 9" for the 17 1/2" dolls and 10" for the 18" and 19 1/2" dolls.
8. Insert the elastic into the casing, overlap the ends of the elastic about 1/4" and stitch to secure (fig. 3). Let the elastic slip into the casing and stitch the opening closed.
9. Weave the ribbon through the beading, beginning and ending 6 1/2" to the left of the center front of the slip. Tie the ends into a bow and trim the excess ribbon at an angle.

Half Slip

Figure 1

Figure 2

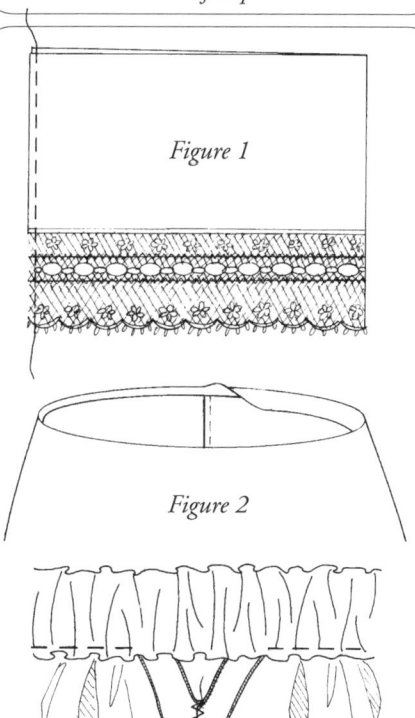

Figure 3

Waisted Slip

Fabric Requirements

Fabric Requirements:

	13"	17 1/2", 18" and 19 1/2"
Fabric - batiste	1/2 yard	5/8 yard
Lace edging (7/8")	2 1/2 yards	2 1/2 yards

Notions

Sewing thread, Velcro™, snaps or tiny buttons

Directions

All Seams 1/4" unless otherwise indicated. Finish all seams with a zigzag or serge to finish the fabric edges.

The following pattern pieces needed for this slip are found on the pull-outs: waisted front, waisted back

Construction

1. Cut out two bodice backs from the selvage and one front bodice from the fold. Also, cut two fabric strips 1 1/4" by 45". Cut one skirt 45" wide by the following lengths:

13"	4 1/4"
17 1/2"	6 1/2"
18" and 19 1/2"	7 1/4"

2. Place the shoulders of the slip bodice right sides together and stitch.
3. Finish the neck and the arm openings using the following finishing technique:
   a. Stitch 3/8" from the raw edge of the neck and arm opening.
   b. Clip the curve to the stitching line (fig. 1).
   c. Press the seam allowance to the wrong side along the stitching line.
   d. From the right side stitch over the folded edge using a small zigzag (fig. 2).
   e. Trim the excess fabric close to the zigzag (fig. 3) (fig. 4).
4. Place the right sides of the bodice together and stitch the side seams (fig. 5). Set aside.

Waisted Slip

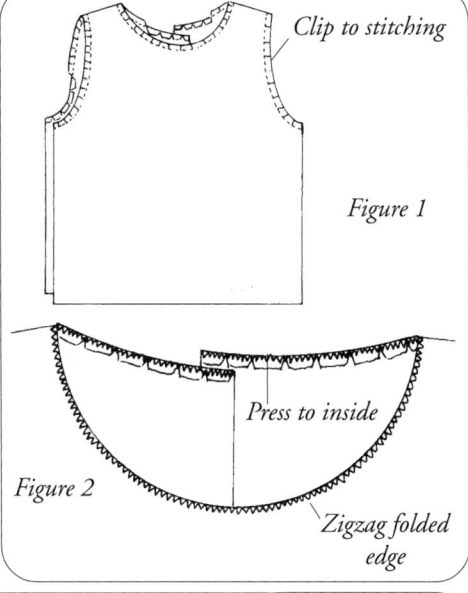

Clip to stitching

Figure 1

Press to inside

Figure 2

Zigzag folded edge

Clip to zigzag

Figure 3

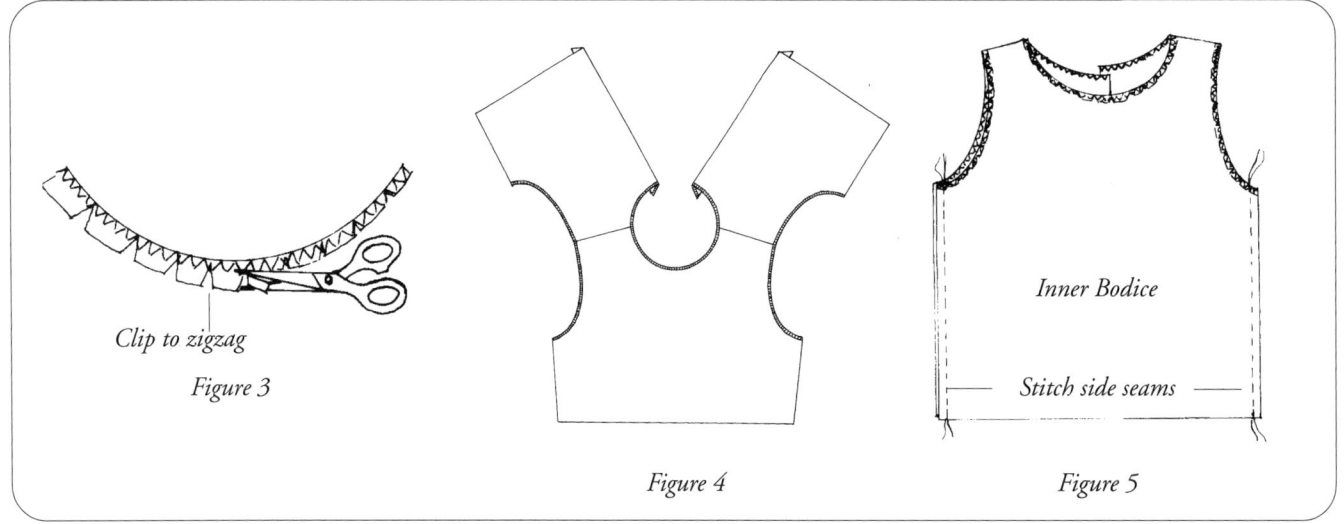

Figure 4

Inner Bodice

Stitch side seams

Figure 5

5. Cut one of the 45" ruffle strips in half. Stitch each half strip to each side of the remaining 45" strip (fig. 6).
6. Place the edging lace along one long edge of the ruffle strip using the technique "lace to fabric". Stitch two gathering rows at $1/8$" and $1/4$" on the top edge of the ruffle (fig. 6). Gather the ruffle piece to fit the bottom edge of the slip skirt.
7. Stitch the ruffle to the skirt piece, right sides together.
8. Refer to the General Directions, A. Placket, b. Placket in a Seam and complete the placket in the skirt back.
9. Fold the skirt in half to find the center. Mark at the top edge. Fold the skirt again to find the quarter points. Mark.
10. Place the back bodices to the skirt back, right sides together with the placket edges to the fold lines of the back bodices. Remember, one side of the placket will be folded to the inside of the skirt and pinned, while the other side will remain extended. Wrap each bodice back around the placket opening in the skirt. Pull up the gathers at the top edge of the skirt to fit the bodice, matching the center of the skirt to the center front bodice and the quarter markings on the skirt with the side seams of the bodice. Stitch the waistline seam. Flip the bodice away from the skirt.
11. Close the slip with Velcro™, snaps, or small buttons and buttonholes along each side of the back bodice.

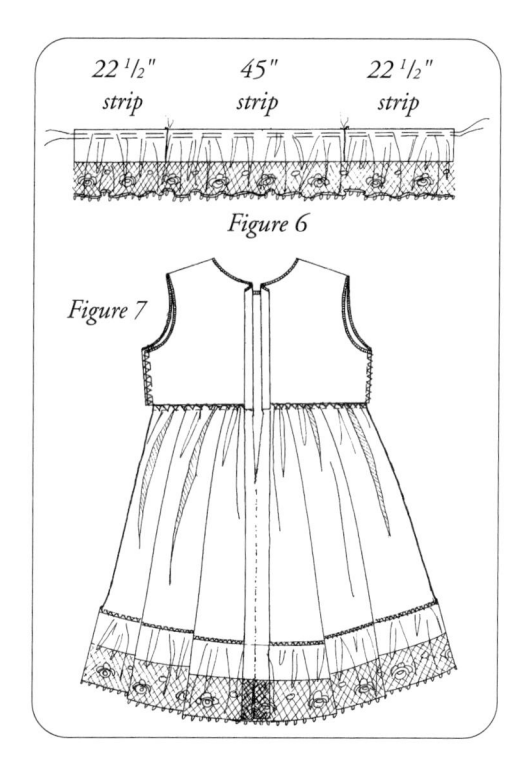

Figure 6

Figure 7

Dropped - waist Slip

Fabric Requirements

Fabric Requirements:

	13"	17 $1/2$", 18 and 19 $1/2$"
White batiste	$1/3$ yd	$1/2$ yd
Lace insertion ($3/8$")	$1 1/3$ yds	$1 1/3$ yds
Lace edging ($3/8$")	2 yds	$2 1/4$ yds
Entredeux	$1/3$ yd	$1/2$ yd

Notions

Lightweight sewing thread, rayon thread for the decorative stitching (optional), twin needle, pintuck foot, Velcro™ or snaps, wash-out marker, 7mm white silk ribbon, small tapestry needle

Directions

All seams are $1/4$" unless otherwise noted. Finish seams with a zigzag stitch or serger. Please read through the directions before beginning the slip.

The following pattern pieces are needed for the dropped-waist slip and are found on the pull-outs: dropped-waist front, dropped waist back

Construction

1. Cut two back slip pieces from the selvage. Cut a square of fabric 1" larger than the slip bodice front (fig. 1).
2. Fold the square for the front bodice in half to find the center front. Choose a decorative stitch from your machine and stitch the design down the center front with the rayon thread. Any vine stitch or stitch with leaves will work well for the stitching.

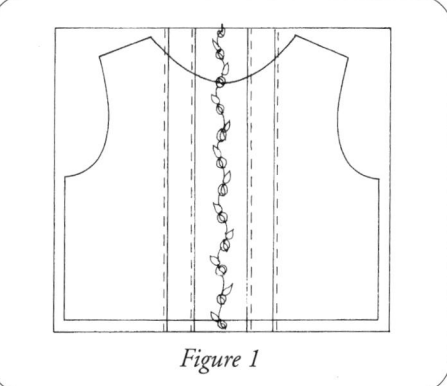

Dropped-waist Slip

Figure 1

Figure 2

Figure 3

right side of fabric

Figure 4

Figure 5

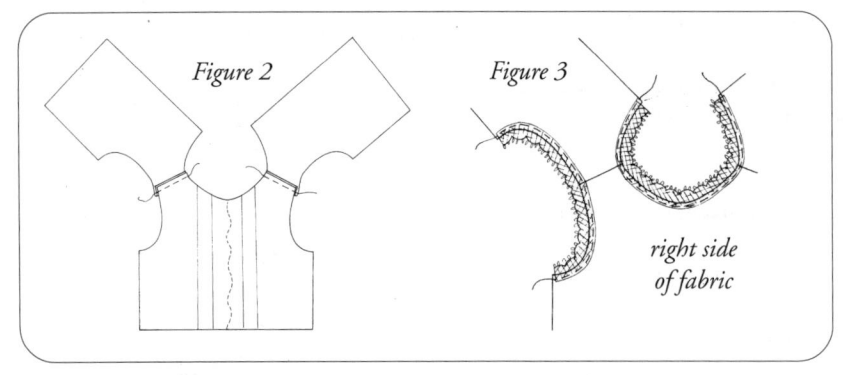

Figure 6

3. Stitch a pintuck ³/₈" from the decorative stitching. Add other pintucks ³/₈" from the first two (refer to fig. 1). Cut out the slip front.
4. Place the slip backs and slip front right sides together matching the shoulder. Stitch together with a ¹/₄" seam (fig. 2).
5. Refer to the technique for "extra-stable lace finish" and attach the lace edging ¹/₄" from the cut edge at the armholes and neckline (fig. 3).
6. Place the slip backs and front right sides together and stitch the side seams (fig. 4).
7. Trim both sides of the entredeux so that the bias fabric edge measures ¹/₄". Attach one side of the entredeux to the lower edge of the slip bodice referring to the technique "entredeux to fabric" (fig. 5).
8. Place the ³/₈" lace edging with the scallop along the raw edge of the lower edge of the skirt. Refer to the technique "extra-stable lace finish" and attach the lace to the fabric.
9. Stitch a double-needle pintuck ³/₈" from the top edge of the lace edging. Stitch a second pintuck ³/₈" from the first tuck.
10. Draw a line ³/₈" from the last pintuck you stitched and place the lower edge of the lace insertion along this line. Stitch both sides of the lace insertion with a small zigzag stitch and trim the fabric away from behind the lace (fig. 6).
12. Refer to the General Directions, A. Placket, b. Placket in a Seam, and complete the back of the skirt.
13. Pull up the gathers on the top edge of the skirt to fit the bodice from back fold line to back fold line. (Remember to keep the right side of the placket folded in and the left side extended).
14. Wrap the facings of the bodices around the skirt pieces and pin in place.
15. Stitch the skirt to the bodice stitching in the ditch between the edge of the entredeux and the bias edge. Finish the seam. Flip the bodice portion of the dress up so that the facings fold to the wrong side.
16. Randomly place colonial knots along the decorative stitching down the center front referring to silk ribbon stitches, colonial knots.
17. Tie a small bow with a piece of the silk ribbon and attach it at the center front at the neck edge (see finished drawing).
18. Close the back of the camisole with snaps or Velcro™.

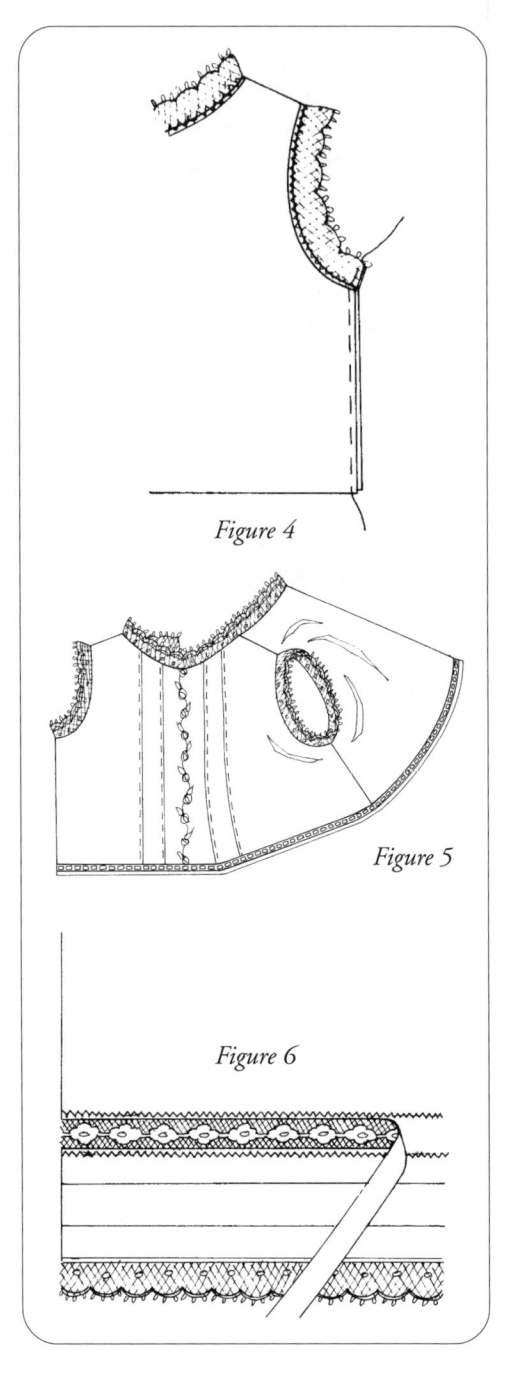

Short Bloomers and Long Bloomers

Fabric Requirements

Short Bloomers

Fabric Requirements:

	13"	17 ¹/₂", 18 and 19 ¹/₂"
Fabric - Swiss Batiste	¹/₄ yard	¹/₃ yard
Lace Edging (⁵/₈")	⁵/₈ yard	²/₃ yard
Elastic (¹/₈")	1 yard	1 ¹/₄ yards
Silk Ribbon (2mm) (optional)	²/₃ yard	³/₄ yard

Notions

Lightweight sewing thread

Directions

Please read through the directions before beginning the pantaloons/bloomers/short bloomers. All seams are $1/4$" unless otherwise noted. Finish seams with a zigzag stitch or serger.

The pattern pieces for the bloomers are found on the pull-outs.

Construction

1. Cut out two bloomer pieces using the desired length.
2. Cut two pieces of lace edging to fit along the lower leg edge of each bloomer piece. Attach the lace to the lower edge of each piece using the technique "lace to fabric".
3. Draw a line on the wrong side of each piece with a wash-out marker $3/8$" above this seam on each leg.
4. Place the bloomers right sides together matching the center fronts and stitch the center front seam (fig. 1).
5. Cut the elastic for the pantaloons/bloomers to the following measurement(s):

	Waist (one piece)	Legs (two pieces)
13" doll	6 $1/2$"	5 $1/2$"
17 $1/2$" doll	8 $1/2$"	7"
18" doll	10"	7"
19 $1/2$" doll	9 $1/2$"	7"

6. Mark each piece of the elastic for the legs 1" from each end. Place the elastic over the drawn line with the mark even with the edge of the bloomers. Take several straight stitches in the elastic tacking the end in place. Continue stitching with a zigzag wide enough to cover the elastic without piercing it. Stop about $1/4$" from the other side, pull the elastic so that the mark is even with the side of the pantaloons/bloomers and take several straight stitches to secure the elastic. Trim the elastic even with the sides of the fabric (fig. 2). Complete this step on both legs.
7. Fold $3/8$", to the wrong side, along the top edge of the bloomers and press in place. Place the elastic over the raw edge of the fabric which was turned down and follow the directions in step 6 to attach the elastic to the waist. (fig. 3).
8. Place the bloomers right sides together and stitch the center back seam (fig. 4).
9. Place the inner legs right sides together matching the crotch seam and the elastic at the lower legs. Stitch in place (fig. 5).
10. Optional: Cut the silk ribbon into two equal pieces. Along the lower legs, thread the silk ribbon with a large tapestry needle or bodkin beneath a zigzag stitch every $1/4$". Begin and end at the sides of the bloomers and tie a bow with the ends of the ribbon (fig. 6).

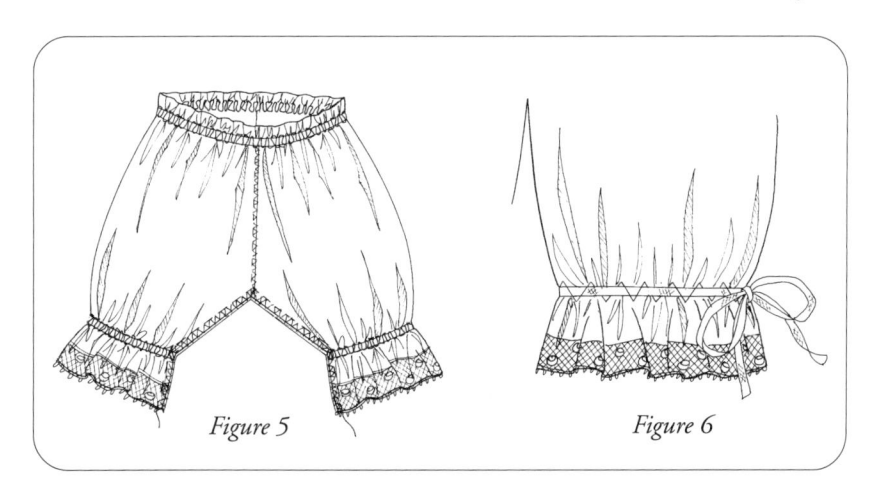

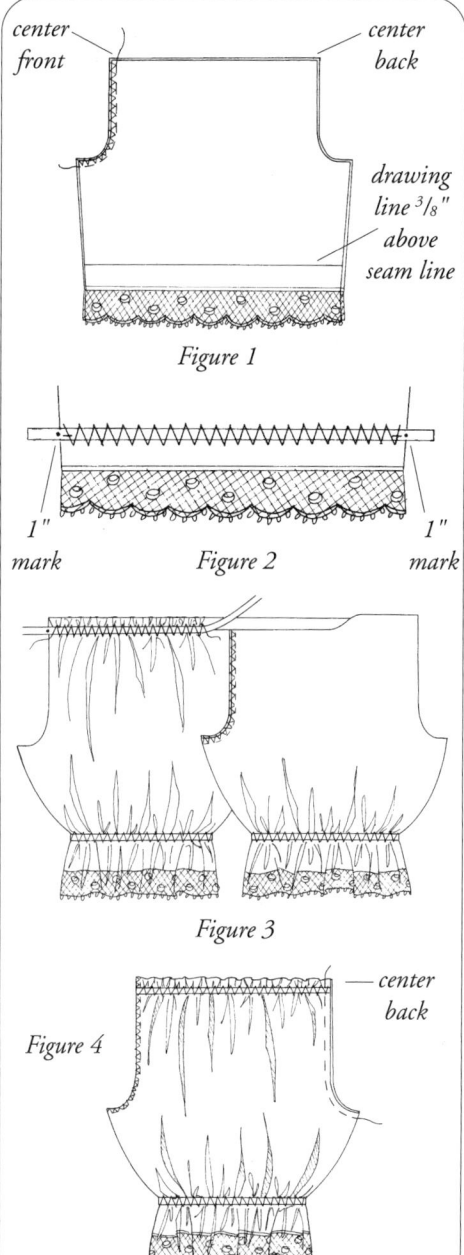

Long Bloomers

Figure 1

Figure 2

Figure 3

Figure 4

Figure 5

Figure 6

Intimate Apparel — *Three Best Friends*

Straight Legged Pantaloons

Fabric Requirements

Fabric Requirements:

	13"	17 1/2"	18"	19 1/2"
Batiste	1/4 yard	1/3 yard	1/3 yard	1/3 yard
Lace insertion (3/8")	1/2 yard	1/2 yard	1/2 yard	1/2 yard
Lace beading (1/2")	1/2 yard	1/2 yard	1/2 yard	1/2 yard
Lace edging (1/2 yard)	1/2 yard	1/2 yard	1/2 yard	1/2 yard
Elastic (1/8")	1/4 yard	1/4 yard	1/3 yard	1/3 yard

7 mm silk ribbon or 1/4" satin ribbon - 1 yard, all sizes

Notions

Lightweight sewing thread, bodkin or large tapestry needle

Directions

All Seams 1/4" unless otherwise indicated. Finish all seams with a zigzag or serge to finish the fabric edges.

Please read through the directions before beginning the pantaloons. The pattern piece for the pantaloons is found on the pull-outs.

Construction

1. Cut two pieces from the pantaloon pattern.
2. Refer to the technique "lace to lace" and stitch the three laces together with the lace beading in the middle (fig. 1). Cut the strip in half.
3. Refer to the technique "lace to fabric" and attach the lace band to the lower edge of each leg of the pantaloons (fig. 2).
4. Place the pantaloons right sides together, stitch the center front and center back seams (fig. 2).
5. Place the pantaloons right sides together matching up the crotch seam and the laces on each leg. Stitch the inside leg seam (fig. 3).
6. Turn under 1/4" along the waistline of the pantaloons and press well. Turn under 1/4" again and press. Stitch the casing very close to the lower fold leaving a 1" opening in the stitching (fig. 4).
7. Cut a piece of elastic the following lengths: 8" for the 13" doll, 9" for the 17 1/2" dolls and 10" for the 18" and 19 1/2" dolls.
8. Insert the elastic into the casing, overlap the ends of the elastic about 1/4" and stitch to secure. Let the elastic slip into the casing and stitch the opening closed (fig. 5).
9. Cut the ribbon in half. Weave through the beading on each leg, beginning and ending on the side of the leg. Tie the ribbon into a bow and trim the ends of the ribbon at an angle (see finished drawing).

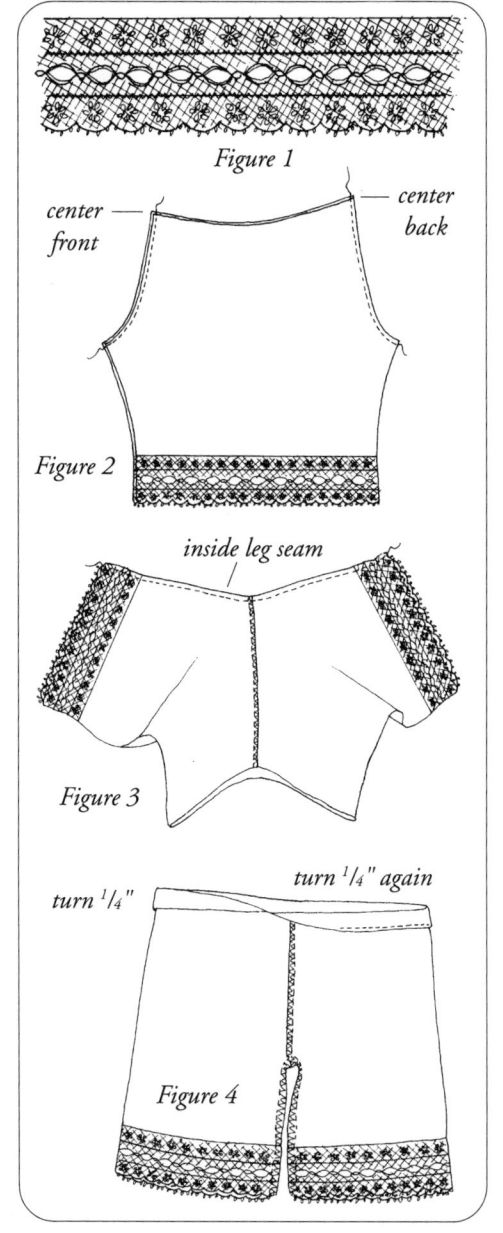

Straight Legged Pantaloons

Figure 1

center front — center back

Figure 2

inside leg seam

Figure 3

turn 1/4" — turn 1/4" again

Figure 4

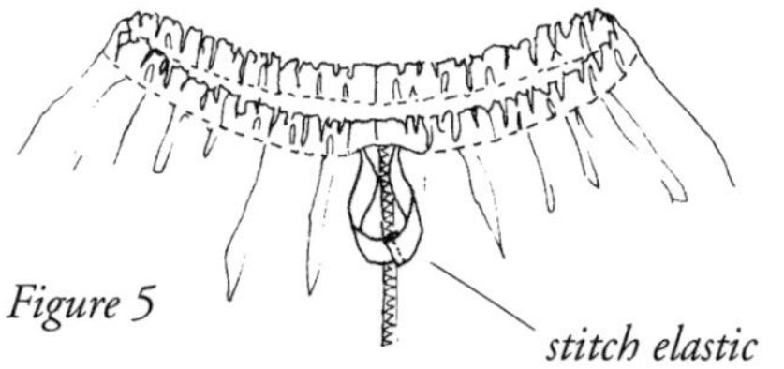

Figure 5 — stitch elastic

Camisole

Fabric Requirements

Fabric Requirements:

	13"	17 1/2"	18"	19 1/2"
Batiste	1/4 yard	1/4 yard	1/4 yard	1/4 yard
Lace insertion (3/8")	1/4 yard	1/4 yard	1/4 yard	1/4 yard
Lace beading (1/2")	1/4 yard	1/4 yard	1/4 yard	1/4 yard
Lace edging (1/2")	1 yard	1 yard	1 yard	1 yard

7 mm silk ribbon or 1/4" satin ribbon - 1/2 yard, all sizes

Notions

Lightweight sewing thread, bodkin or large tapestry needle, Velcro™, wash-out marker

Directions

Please read through the directions before beginning the camisole. The pattern pieces for the camisole are found on the pull-outs.

Construction

1. Cut two camisole backs from the selvage. Cut one camisole front from the fold. Transfer the lace shaping lines and center marking onto the camisole front (fig. 1).
2. Refer to the technique "lace to lace" and stitch the lace insertion and the lace beading together creating a band of lace (fig. 2).
3. Shape the lace band along the template lines. Miter the corner and stitch in place referring to the directions for lace shaping (fig. 3).
4. Cut the ribbon in half and weave each piece from the side to the miter. Tie a bow at the miter (fig. 4).
5. Place the camisole backs and camisole front right sides together at the shoulders. Stitch.
6. Attach the edging lace to the neck and arm openings using the technique "extra stable lace finish" (fig. 5).
7. Place the camisole backs and front right sides together and stitch the side seams (fig. 6).
8. Attach the edging lace along the lower edge of the camisole referring to the technique "lace to fabric" (see finished drawing).
9. Fold under the back facings of the camisole and press well (fig. 7).
10. Close the back of the camisole with snaps or Velcro™.

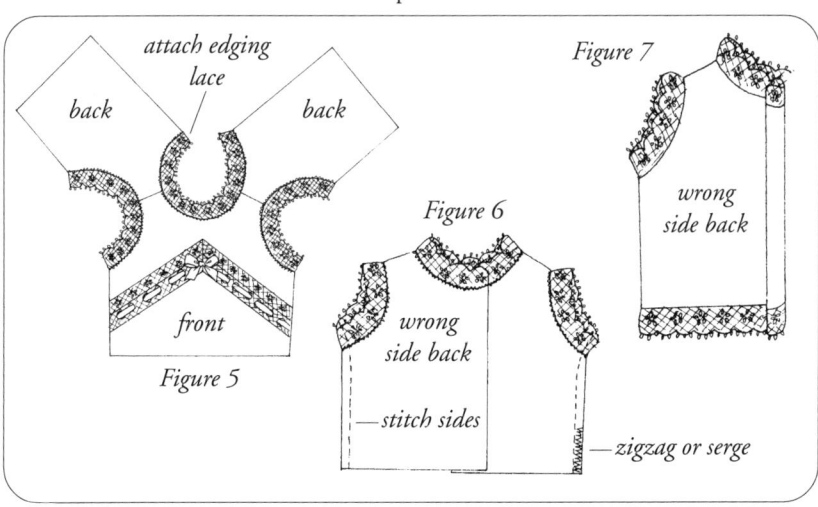

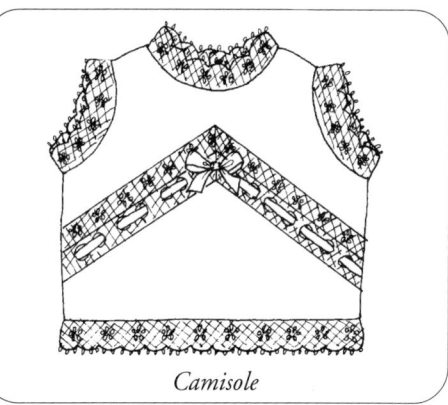

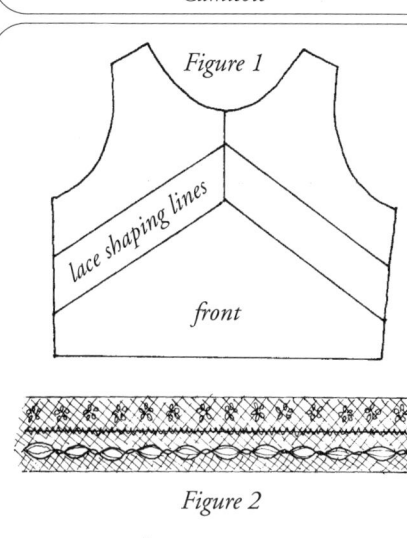

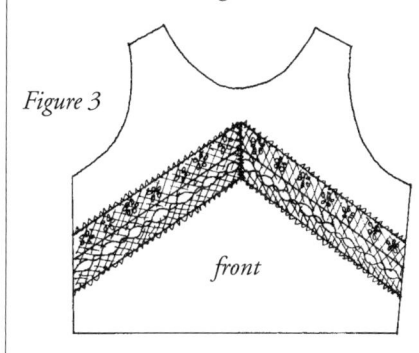

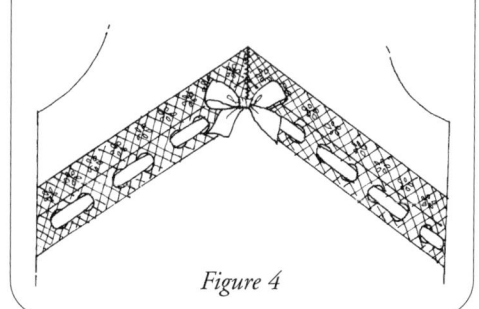

Intimate Apparel   *Three Best Friends*

Padded Doll Hangers

Having wonderful clothing and a roomy trunk are necessary for the Three Best Friends. They also have spectacular hand-made hangers to hang their dresses on. The pink one with pink ribbons has French insertion and French beading on either side of the insertion. Entredeux and gathered lace trim the bottom, and pink ribbon runs through the beading. The back is a pink batiste. The ladybug hanger has red piping on the bottom and lady bugs embroidered on both sides of the hanger. These ladybugs were embroidered in Switzerland; however, if you have an embroidery machine you can embroider your own. The white and blue hanger has one strip of blue satin ribbon with white French edging on the top. On each little flower is a pearl stitched in the center of the flower. White Gathered French edging finishes each side of this lace/ribbon/pearl center treatment. The peach and white hanger has a peach underlining with yellow and peach bullion roses and green bullion leaves. Gathered white French edging finishes the bottom. The fabric on top of the peach lining is white dotted Swiss. A peach bow is tied at the top of the hanger. Have fun making your hangers. The Three Best Friends suggested that they would really like a hanger to match each dress, if anyone has the time to make them. That would be very special.

General Hanger Directions

General Requirements

Fabric - $1/8$ yard, Ribbon ($1/16$") - $1/4$ yard, Batting - $1/8$ yard, Cup Hook, Dowel ($1/2$" diameter by $4\ 1/2$" long)

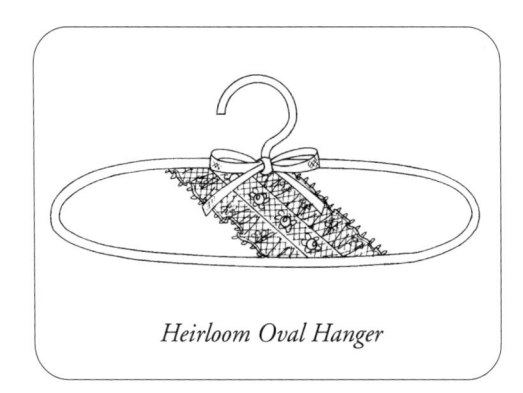

Directions

All seams $1/4$".

1. Create the hanger cover using the specific directions below.
2. Find the center of the dowel and screw the cup hook into the dowel creating a hole. Remove the cup hook from the dowel (fig. 1) and place the dowel into the created hanger cover.
3. Slip the dowel into the end opening of the hanger cover.
4. Center the hole in the dowel over the center opening of the hanger cover. Place the cup hook through the opening and screw into the hole in the dowel.
5. Fold under the seam allowance, tuck in the batting and stitch the openings closed by hand.
6. Tie a bow with ribbon around the cup hook where it enters the fabric. You may wish to tack the ribbon in place with a few hand stitches.

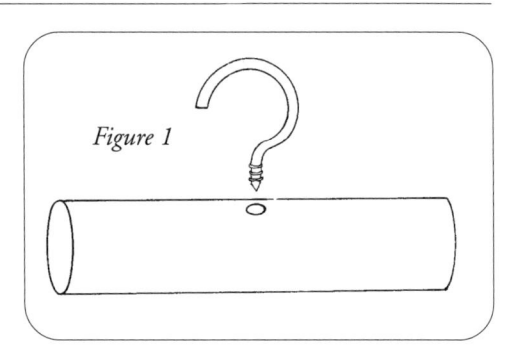

Figure 1

Heirloom Oval Hanger

Specific Requirements

Fabric	$1/8$ yard
Lace insertion ($3/8$")	$3\ 1/2$"
Ribbon ($1/4$")	$3\ 1/2$"
Ribbon ($1/16$")	$1/4$ yard
Edging lace ($1/2$")	$1/4$ yard
Baby piping	$3/8$ yard
Batting	$1/8$ yard
Small pearls (4)	
Cup Hook	
Dowel ($1/2$" diameter by $4\ 1/2$" long)	

Heirloom Oval Hanger

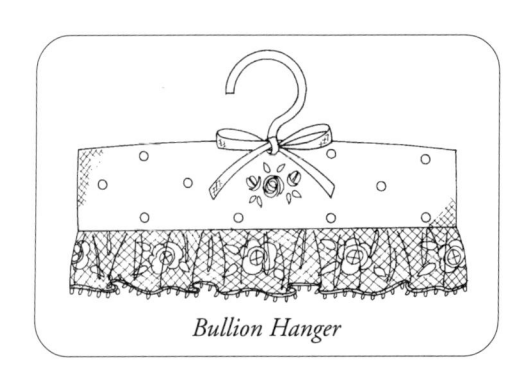

Directions

1. Cut two rectangles of fabric 5 1/2" by 2". Draw curved lines across the corners of the rectangle creating an oval. Cut along these lines. Cut two pieces of batting to fit the fabric ovals (fig. 2).
2. To create the embellishment for the hanger, cut the lace edging in half and gather each piece to fit each side of the lace insertion. Stitch the insertion to the gathered edging using the technique "lace to lace". Pin a piece of 1/4" ribbon underneath the lace insertion portion of the embellishment (fig. 3). Place the laces with the ribbon underneath at an angle across the center of one of the oval fabric pieces. Stitch in place with a straight stitch along each side of the insertion lace. Trim the excess lace away that extends beyond the fabric (fig. 4).
3. Place the batting pieces to the wrong side of each fabric oval. Pin in place.
4. If necessary, trim the piping seam allowance to 1/4". Clip the edges of the piping so that it will curve smoothly around the oval. Place the piping around one of the fabric ovals, beginning at the center of one long side. The beginning and end of the piping should overlap and extend into the seam allowance. Stitch the piping in place through both the fabric and the batting, almost to the cord of the piping (fig. 5).
5. Place the remaining fabric oval to the piped oval, right sides together. The batting will be on the outside of the fabric pieces.
6. Restitch just inside the stitching line of the piping, stitching very close to the cord. Begin the stitching leaving a 1/4" opening at the overlapped piping. Also leave an opening in one small end of the fabric/batting cover. Clip the curve of the seam and turn the piece right side out through the open end (fig. 6).
7. Tiny sew-on pearls may be sewn down the center of the lace embellishment.
8. Complete the hanger using the General Hanger Directions.

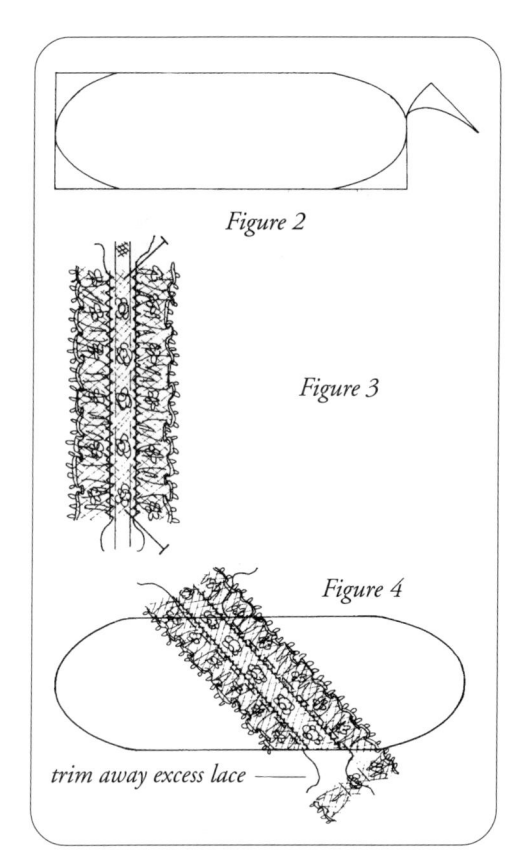

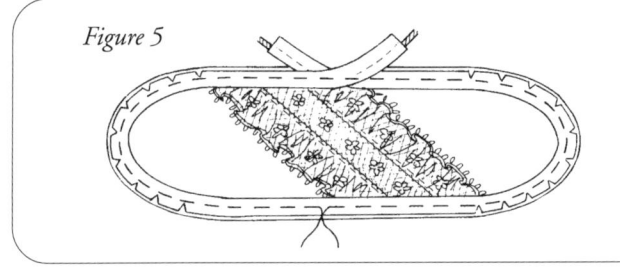

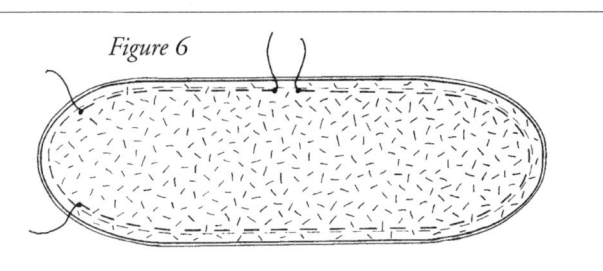

Figure 2

Figure 3

Figure 4

trim away excess lace

Figure 5

Figure 6

Bullion Hanger

Specific Requirements

Batiste	1/8 yard
Fabric-Dotted Swiss	1/8 yard
Batting	1/8 yard
Edging lace (1/2")	1/4 yard
Ribbon (1/4")	1/4 yard
Cup Hook	
Dowel (1/2" diameter by 4 1/2" long)	
Variegated peach floss	
Green Floss	

Bullion Hanger

Directions

1. Cut two fabric rectangles from the Swiss batiste and the dotted-swiss and two batting rectangles 5 1/2" by 2". Stitch three bullion roses in the center of one dotted-swiss fabric piece using the bullion template (fig. 7).
2. Place the dotted-swiss on top of batiste layer and treat as one layer.
3. Place the two fabric pieces right sides together with the batting pieces on the outsides.
4. Stitch around the rectangle leaving 1/4" open at the center of one long side of the rectangle, also leave one short side open. Turn the hanger cover to the right side out through the open end (fig. 8).
5. Finish the hanger using the General Hanger Directions.
6. Fold the cut edges of the edging lace to the wrong side 1/8" and 1/8" again. Stitch the folds in place.
7. Gather the edging to fit the lower edge of the hanger.
8. Zigzag or hand stitch the lace edging to the lower edge of the hanger (fig. 9).

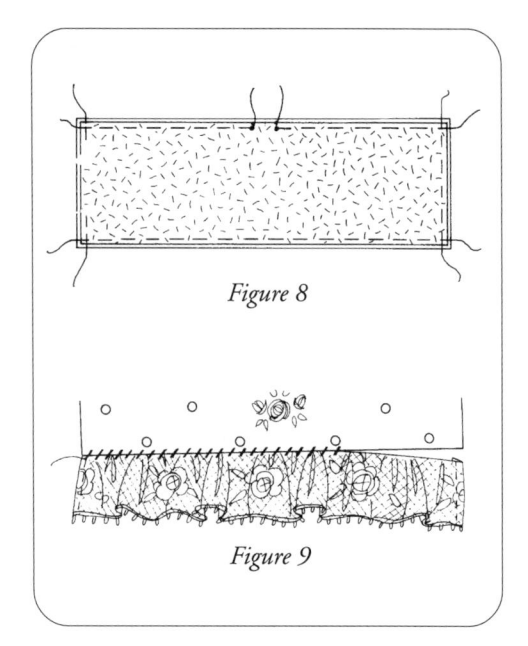

Figure 7

leaves
8 wraps each side

6 wraps
8 wraps
12 wraps

6 wraps center
8 wraps each side
14 wraps x 4

Figure 8

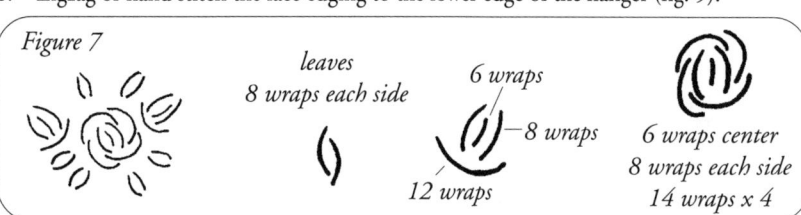

Figure 9

Pink Heirloom Hanger

Specific Requirements

Fabric-Pink Swiss Batiste	1/8 yard
Batting	1/8 yard
Edging lace (1/2")	1/4 yard
Lace beading	1/3 yard
Lace insertion (5/8")	1/6 yard
Entredeux	1/3 yard
Ribbon (to fit beading)	1/2 yard
Cup Hook	
Dowel (1/2" diameter by 4 1/2" long)	

Directions

1. Cut two fabric rectangles and two batting rectangles 5 1/2" by 2".
2. Cut the lace beading in half and attach to each side of the lace insertion using the technique "lace to lace".
3. Cut the entredeux in half. Set one piece aside. Attach one piece of the entredeux to the beading using the technique "lace to entredeux". Trim the fabric edge of the attached entredeux to 1/4". Weave ribbon through the beading.
4. Place the created lace band on one of the fabric pieces with the fabric edge of the entredeux even with the edge of the fabric. Baste in place creating an embellished rectangle (fig. 10).
5. Place the embellished rectangle to the remaining fabric rectangle, right sides together with the batting pieces on the outsides.
6. Stitch around the rectangle leaving 1/4" open at the center of one long side of the rectangle, also leave one short side open (see fig. 8). Turn the hanger cover to the right side out through the open end.
7. Finish the hanger using the General Hanger Directions.
8. Trim one fabric edge from the remaining entredeux piece. Cut the entredeux to fit the lower edge of the hanger cover.
9. Fold the cut edges of the edging lace to the wrong side 1/8" and 1/8" again. Stitch the folds in place (fig. 11).
10. Gather the edging lace to fit the entredeux. Stitch the lace to the entredeux using the technique "gathered lace to entredeux".
11. Trim the remaining fabric edge of the entredeux. Butt the entredeux to the lower edge of the hanger and zigzag or hand stitch in place.

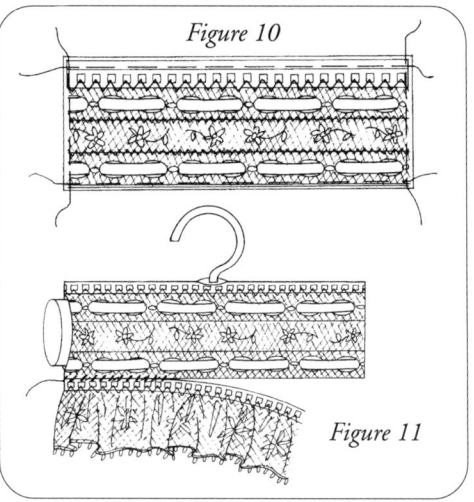

Pink Heirloom Hanger

Figure 10

Figure 11

Ladybug Hanger Cover

Specific Requirements

Embroidered Insertion	1/3 yard
Batting	1/8 yard
Baby piping	1/4 yard
Ribbon (1/4")	1/4 yard
Cup Hook	
Dowel (1/2" diameter by 4 1/2" long)	

Ladybug Hanger Cover

Figure 12

Directions

1. Cut two pieces of embroidered insertion 5 1/2" long by 2". Note: center the design before cutting. Cut two pieces of batting 5 1/2" by 2".
2. If the seam allowance of the piping is not already 1/4", trim to 1/4". Place the piping along the lower edge of one embroidered insertion piece having the cut edges even.
3. Stitch the piping to the fabric 1/16" away from the cord of the piping (fig. 12).
4. Place a batting piece to the wrong side of the piped embroidered insertion. Stitch one piece of batting to the wrong side of the piped embroidered insertion piece, restitching along the piping seam.
5. Place a piece of batting to the wrong side of the remaining piece of embroidered insertion. Sandwich the batting/embroidered insertion pieces together, with the embroidered insertion pieces in the middle. Pin all layers together.
6. Stitch around the rectangle leaving 1/4" open at the center of the top side of the rectangle, also leave one short side open. Turn the hanger cover to the right side out through the open end (see fig. 8).
7. Finish the hanger using the General Hanger Directions.

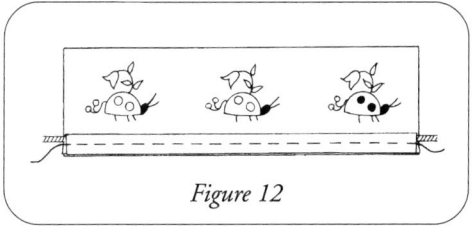

Silk Ribbon Bed Ensemble

Silk Ribbon Quilt

fig. 1 - Silk Ribbon Bed Ensemble Layout

Supplies

2 yards pink silk dupioni, 1 yard lining fabric, 2 yards of ¾" ecru lace insertion, 3 ¾ yards of ½" ecru lace edging, 20" of 1¾" wide ecru lace edging, 20" entredeux, 4 mm Y.L.I. silk ribbon: Pink, #7 - 2 ½ yards, Green, #60 - 3 yards, Red, # 93 - ¼ yard, Dark pink, #128 - 1 yard, Blue/Lavender #101 - 3 ½ yards (a variegated color can be used), Beige, #162 - 6 ½ yards, Dusty pink, #163 - 1 yard, 2 mm Y.L.I. silk ribbon: Soft green, #31 - 2 ½ yards, DMC flower thread: Beige, #2842, Green, #2471, Black for ladybugs, Quilt batting/fleece for quilt , Polyfil for pillow and bolster
1 ½ yards of ½" elastic, 100 to 120 wing needle, Graphite pencil for marking on silk dupioni, 5" to 7" embroidery hoop

NOTE: This ensemble fits a bed that measures 13 ½" wide, 22 ½" long and 7 ½" high (not including the matress). The matress measures 12" wide, 21" long and 2" high. Items to fit different size beds can be adjusted as necessary. Using the layout diagram, cut out the pieces from the silk dupioni. Label each piece (fig. 1). All templates for the bed ensemble can be found on the pull-outs.

Silk Ribbon Quilt

Supplies

25" x 28" rectangle silk dupioni, 25" x 28" lining fabric, 25" x 28" lightweight batting or fleece, ¾" wide ecru lace insertion, 1¼" wide bias binding , thread to match fabric, silk ribbon for the embroidery, Lightweight ecru heirloom sewing thread

Directions

1. Trace the design for the quilt outline, embroidery and lace insertion on the silk dupioni with the graphite pencil. Mark very lightly (fig. 2).
2. Complete the silk ribbon embroidery following the quilt template.
3. Shape the lace on the template line around the silk ribbon embroidery in the center and the corners following the directions for lace shaping.
4. Using the wing needle, ecru lightweight heirloom sewing thread and the pinstitch, stitch both sides of the lace to the silk dupioni. The "fingers" of the pinstitch should go into

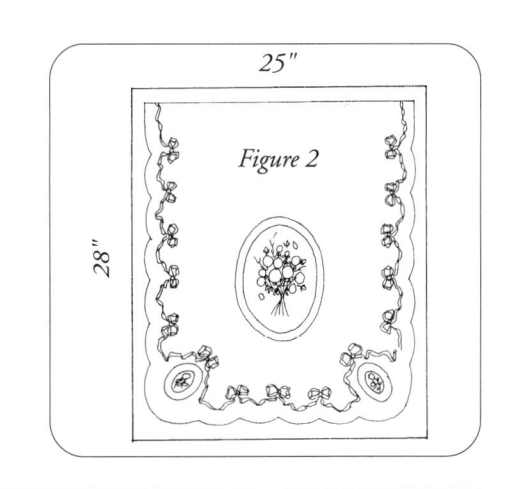

the lace with the straight part of the stitch next to the heading (fig. 3).
5. Place the lining rectangle on a flat surface, wrong side up. Tape the lining to the surface, keeping the fabric taut and free of wrinkles.
6. Place the fleece or batting on top of the lining.
7. Place the embroidered quilt top on the batting rectangle, right side up, matching the edges and keeping it free of wrinkles.
8. Pin or hand baste all of the layers together (fig. 4).
9. Quilt all of the layers together by hand or machine. Straight stitch on the lines indicated on the pattern. For the center motif, there are three lines on the inside and outside of the lace insertion. There are two rows of stitching on the outside of the lace in the corners and two rows are stitched above the binding stitching line (fig. 5).
10. Using a narrow open zigzag, stitch just inside of the cutting line at the outer edge of the quilt top.
11. Cut away the excess quilt top next to the zigzag stitches on the cutting line (fig. 6).
12. Fold the bias strip in half lengthwise and press.
13. Attach the binding to the top of the quilt first by matching the raw edges of the binding to the raw edge of the quilt top. Stitch using an $1/8$" seam allowance (fig. 7).
14. Fold the binding to the wrong side enclosing the raw edges. Hand or machine stitch in place (fig. 8).

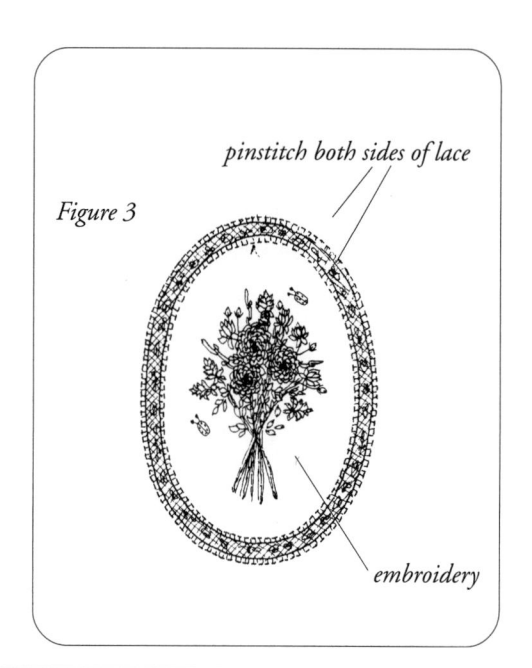

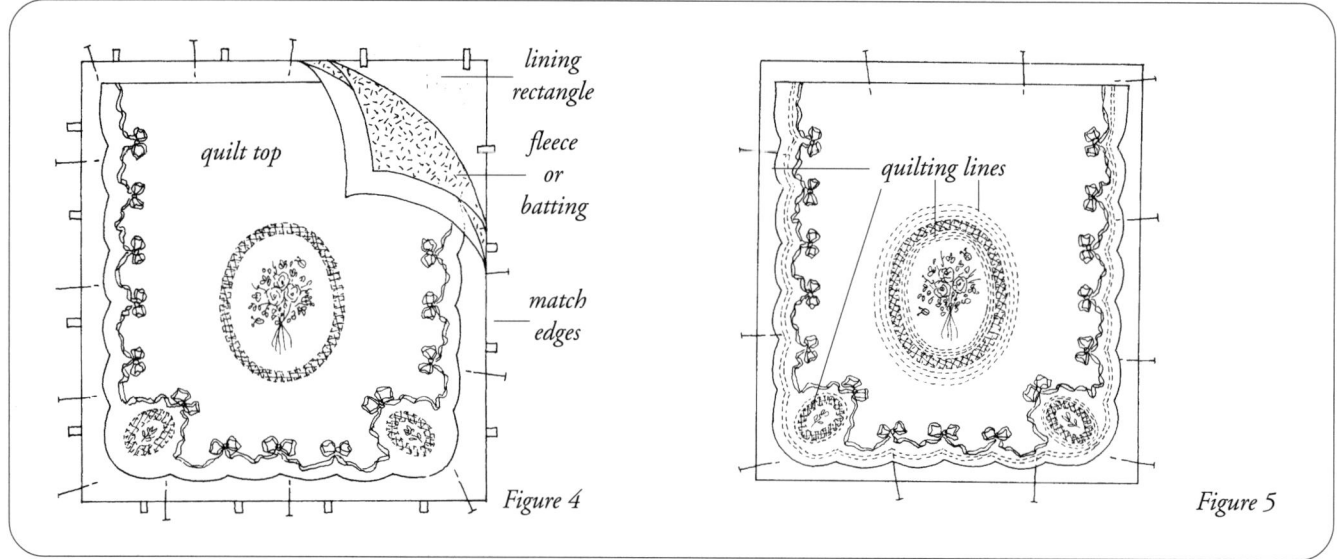

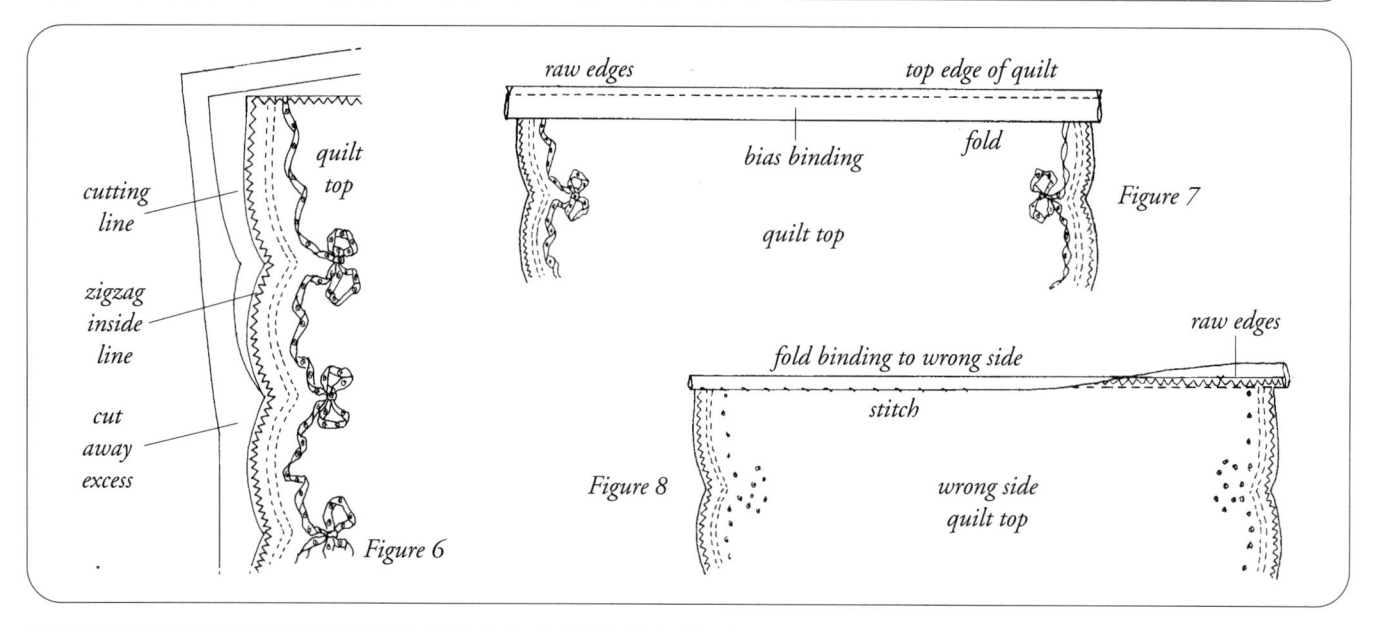

15. Attach the binding to the remaining three sides in the same manner (figs. 9a, 9b and 9c).

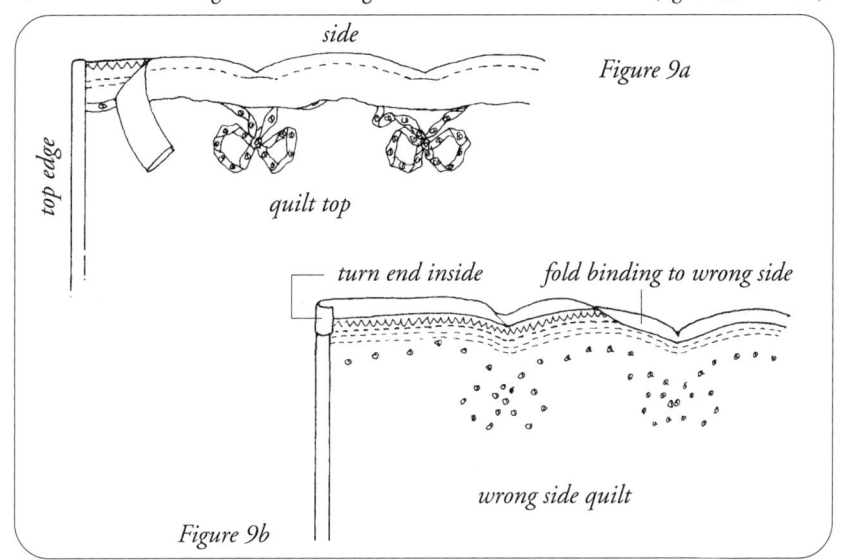

Figure 9a

Figure 9b

Figure 9c

Dust Ruffle

Supplies

Three strips of pink silk duponi, 8½" x 45", 3¾ yards of ½" ecru lace edging, 1.6/70 twin needle, 7 groove pintuck foot, Lightweight ecru heirloom sewing thread, 1½ yards of ½" elastic

Directions

1. Stitch the selvage edges of the dupioni together to form a circle. Press the seams open (fig. 1).
2. Attach the edging lace to one long side of the fabric using the technique "lace to fabric" (fig. 2).
3. Using the 1.6/70 double needle and the 7 groove pintuck foot, stitch one tuck with the edge of the foot against the heading of the lace (fig. 3).
4. Place the finished pintuck in the last groove of the pintuck foot and stitch another pintuck (fig. 4). Repeat to have a total of 5 pintucks (fig. 5).
5. On the upper edge, turn ¼" to the wrong side and ⅝" again to form a casing, or serge the top edge and turn under ⅝". Press (fig. 6).
6. Stitch close to the finished edge, leaving an opening to insert the elastic (fig. 7).
7. Insert the elastic and stitch the ends together (fig. 8). Stitch the opening closed (fig. 9).

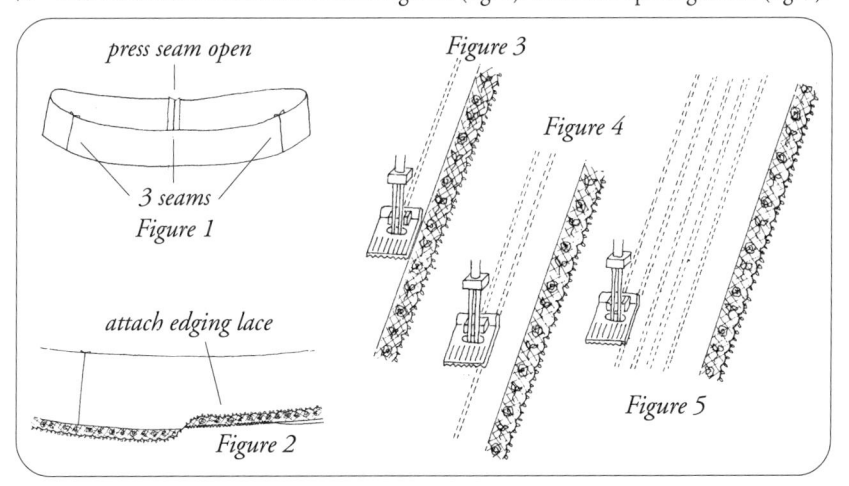

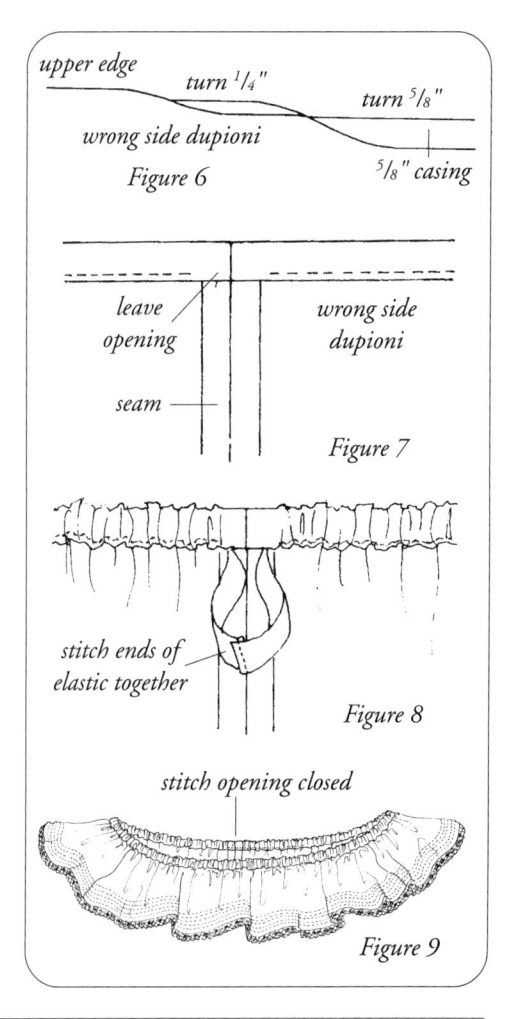

Pillow and Pillow Case

Supplies

12" x 11½" lining fabric, Polyfil, Two pieces of pink silk dupioni, 12" x 6" (pillowcase front and back), Two pieces of pink silk dupioni, 2" x 45" (ruffle), 2" x 6" piece of pink silk dupioni, 14" of the ¾" ecru lace insertion, 12" x 6" batting or fleece, Silk ribbon for design

Directions

1. Fold the lining fabric in half with the 11½" sides together to create the pillow form.
2. Stitch one short side and the long sides together with an ⅛" seam allowance (fig. 1).
3. Turn to the right side and stuff.
4. Hand or machine stitch the remaining side closed (fig. 2).
5. Center and trace the design on the right side of one of the 12" x 6" pieces of silk dupioni. The outer edge of the lace should be 1" from the edge (fig. 3).
6. Shape the lace around the oval.
7. Pinstitch both edges of the lace to the silk dupioni as above (see quilt directions) (fig. 4).
8. Complete the silk ribbon embroidery following the template (fig. 4).
9. Stitch the short ends of the 2" x 45" pieces of silk dupioni together to form a circle. Press the seams open.
10. Fold the circle in half, matching the long cut edges and press.
11. Place a gathering row ⅛" and ⅜" from the raw edges (fig. 5).
12. Pin the seams of the ruffle to the center of the short ends. Pull up the gathers to fit the ruffle to the pillow top. Allow plenty of gathers at the corners to prevent cupping of the ruffle at the corners.
13. Stitch the ruffle to the pillow top using a ¼" seam allowance (fig. 6).
14. Finish one 6" edge of the 2" x 6" piece of silk dupioni and the remaining 12" x 6" piece by turning under ¼" twice and stitching (fig. 7).
15. Place the unfinished 6" edge of the smaller piece to one short end of the pillowcase, sandwiching the ruffle between the pillowcase and this piece. Pin the remaining 12" x 6" piece to the pillowcase matching the unfinished 6" edge to the opposite short end of the pillowcase (fig. 8).
16. Stitch the backs to the pillowcase along the ¼" seam allowance (fig. 8).
17. Turn to the right side and press. Insert pillow form (fig. 9)

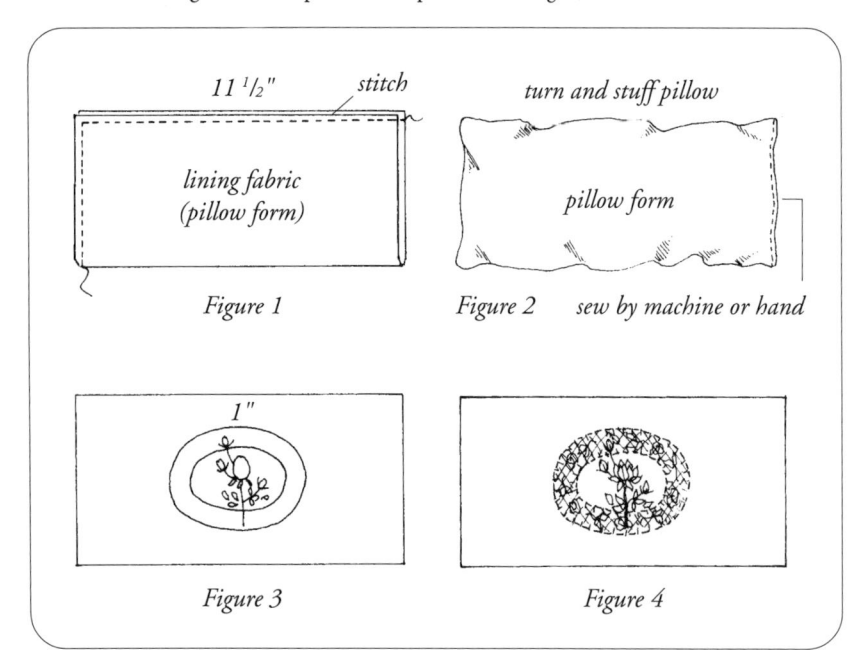

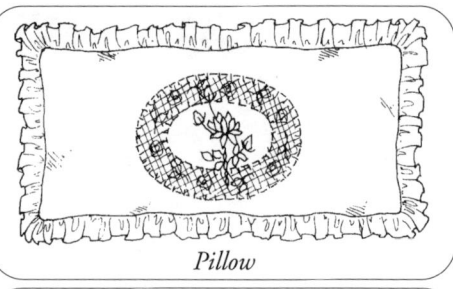

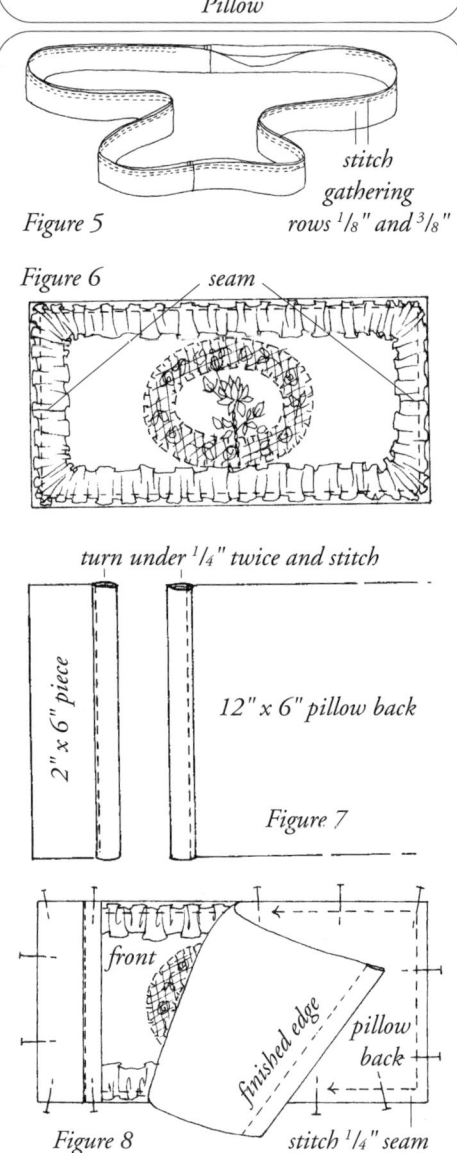

Pillow

Figure 5 — stitch gathering rows ⅛" and ⅜"

Figure 6 — seam

turn under ¼" twice and stitch

2" x 6" piece

12" x 6" pillow back

Figure 7

Figure 8 — front, finished edge, pillow back, stitch ¼" seam

Figure 9 — pillow back, insert pillow form

Figure 1 — 11½", stitch, lining fabric (pillow form)

Figure 2 — turn and stuff pillow, pillow form, sew by machine or hand

Figure 3 — 1"

Figure 4

96 — Three Best Friends — Bed Ensemble

Bolster

Supplies

9 1/2" x 12" rectangle of lining fabric, 10" x 17 1/2" rectangle pink silk dupioni, 20" entredeux 20" of 1 3/4" ecru lace edging, 1.6/70 twin needle, 7 groove pintuck foot, Ecru lightweight heirloom sewing thread, Polyfil

Directions

1. Fold the lining, right sides together, forming a rectangle 4 3/4" x 12"
2. Stitch one short end and one of the long ends using an 1/8" seam allowance (fig. 1).
3. Turn to the right side and stuff lightly with polyfil. Stitch the remaining end closed (fig. 2).
4. Cut the rectangle of pink silk dupioni into two pieces that measure 10" x 6 1/2" and one piece that measures 10" x 4 1/2" (fig. 3).
5. Cut the 1 3/4" lace edging into two equal pieces. Stitch a piece to one 10" side of both of the 10" x 6 1/2" rectangles using the technique "fabric to lace" (fig. 4).
6. Cut the entredeux in half. Stitch entredeux to both 10" sides of the 10" x 4 1/2" rectangle of pink silk dupioni using the technique "fabric to entredeux" (fig. 5). Add the larger 10" rectangles to each side of the entredeux using the technique "fabric to entredeux" (see fig. 6).
7. Using the twin needle, pintuck foot and ecru thread in both needles, stitch a pintuck a foot's width away from the lace edging on each end of the large rectangle (refer to Dust Ruffle drawing #3).
8. Place the completed pintuck in the last groove of the foot and stitch another pintuck. Repeat for the other end (refer to Dust Ruffle drawing #4).
9. Repeat step 8, to complete 5 pintucks (refer to Dust Ruffle drawing #5) (fig. 6).
10. Fold right sides together matching the long edges. Stitch using a 1/4" seam allowance (fig. 7).
11. Turn to the right side and press. Insert the finished pillow (fig. 8).

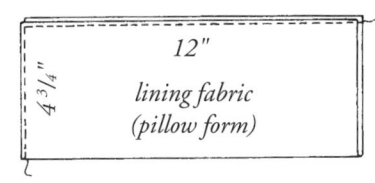

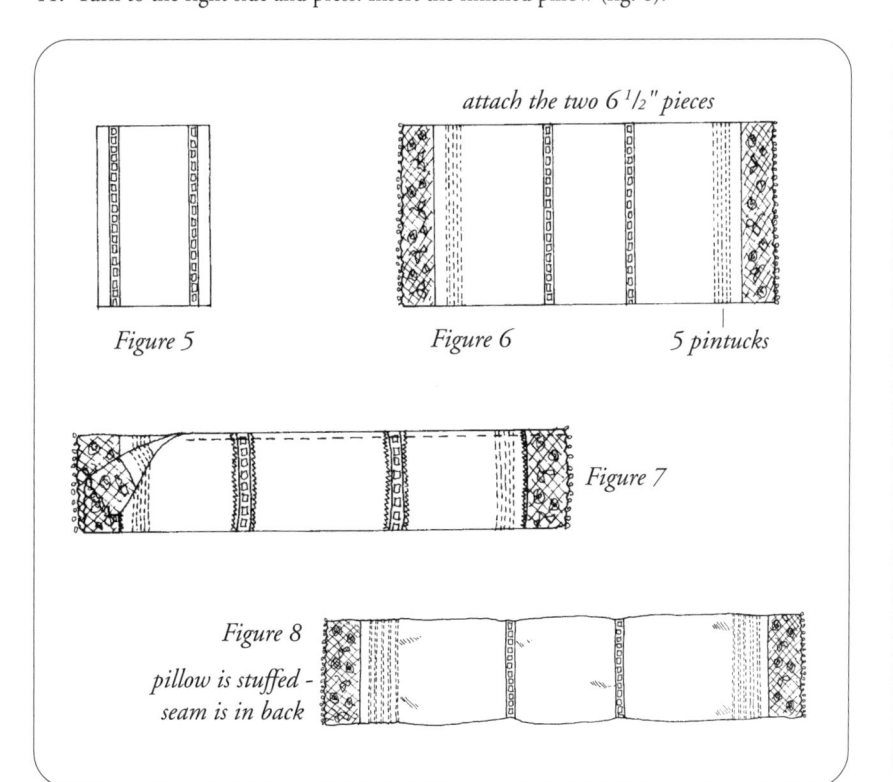

Figure 1 — 12" x 4 3/4" lining fabric (pillow form)

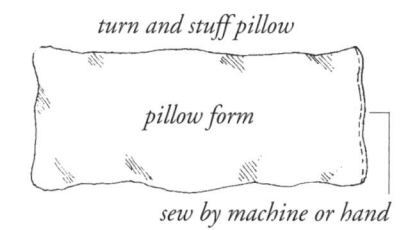

Figure 2 — turn and stuff pillow / pillow form / sew by machine or hand

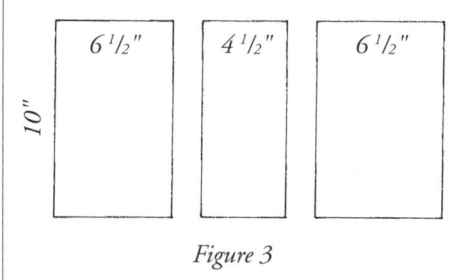

Figure 3 — 10" x 6 1/2", 4 1/2", 6 1/2"

Figure 4 — stitch lace to fabric

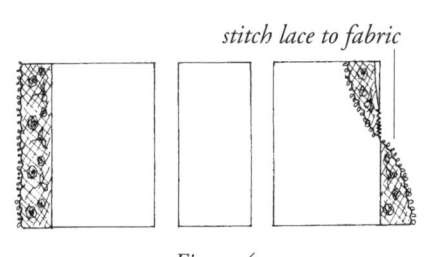

Figure 5

Figure 6 — attach the two 6 1/2" pieces / 5 pintucks

Figure 7

Figure 8 — pillow is stuffed - seam is in back

Bed Ensemble — Three Best Friends

Sheet

Supplies

23" x 28" white fabric, 23" Swiss edging, 3/4" to 1" wide, White and pink lightweight sewing thread, 7 groove pintuck foot, 1.6/70 twin needle, 70 needle

Directions

1. Attach the Swiss insertion to one 23" side of the fabric rectangle. Place right sides together and stitch. Finish the seam with a serger or zigzag (fig. 1).
2. Press the seam allowance toward the body of the sheet (fig. 2).
3. Using the 1.6/70 twin needle and pintuck foot, place one pintuck 1/2" from the seam between the edging and sheet (fig. 3).
4. Place the completed pintuck in the last groove of the pintuck foot and stitch another pintuck (fig. 4). Repeat step to complete 5 equally spaced pintucks (fig. 5).
5. Place a pintuck 3/4" away from the last pintuck. Repeat step 4 to complete another group of 5 equally spaced pintucks (fig. 6).
6. Place the pink thread in the size 70 needle. Stitch a row of narrowed feather stitching in the space between the sets of pintucks and on both sides of each set of pintucks (fig. 6).
7. Clean finish the remaining 3 sides with a 3 thread serged edge or fold under 1/8" twice and straight stitch (fig. 7).
8. Fold the top edge of the sheet down 3/4" from the last row of feather stitching and press (fig. 8).

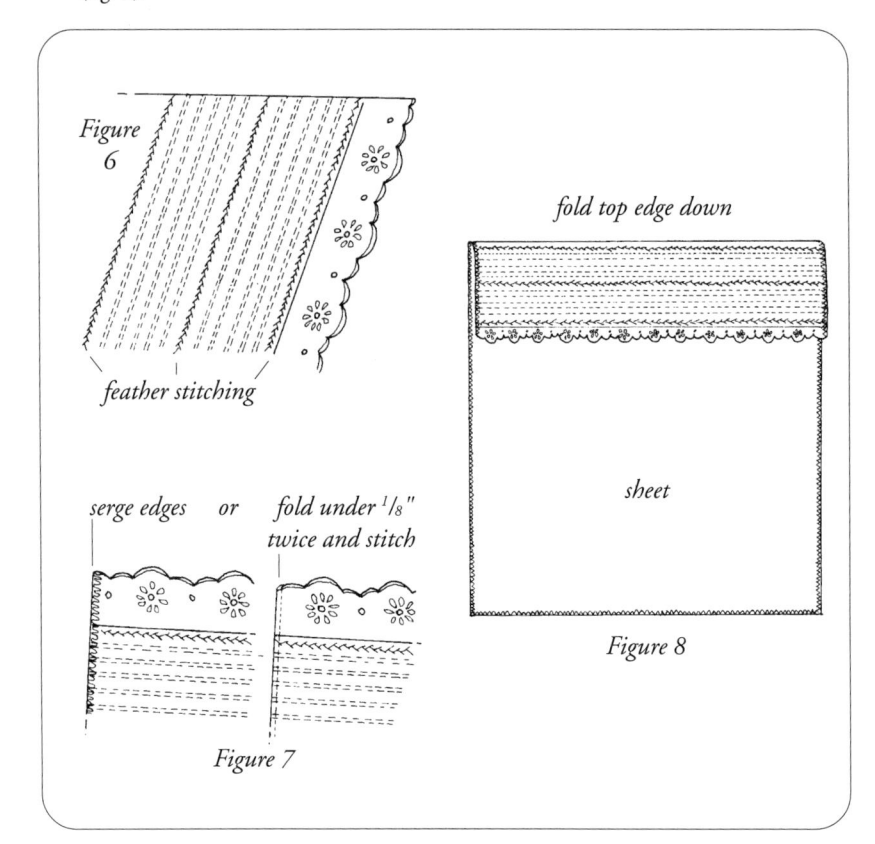

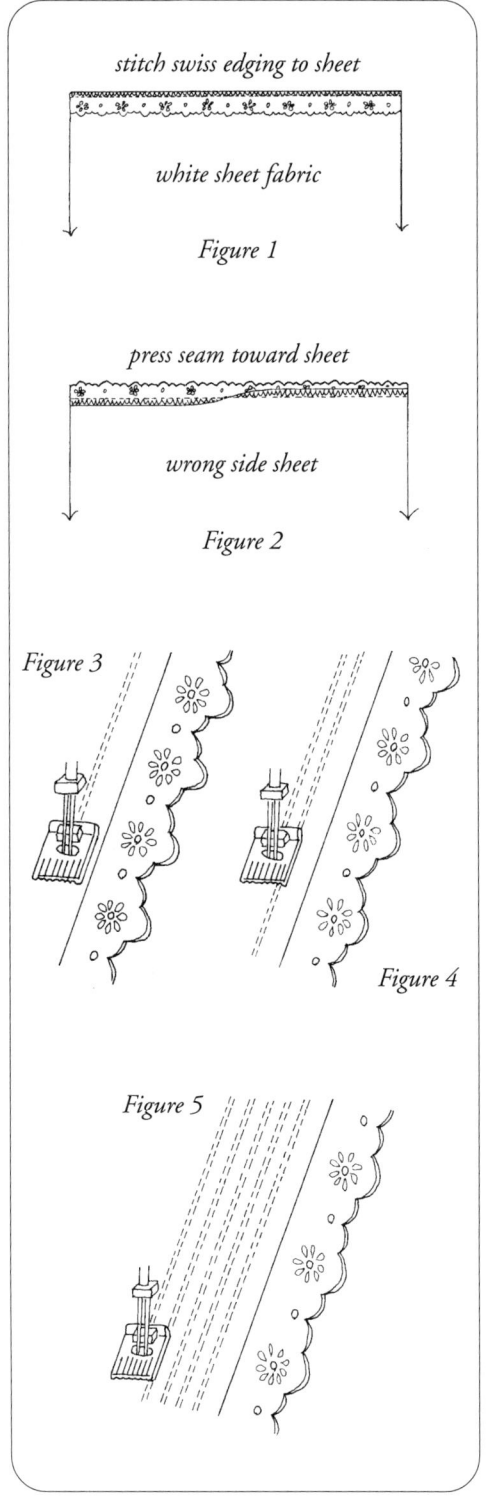

Beginning French Sewing Techniques

Lace to Lace
Butt together and zigzag.
Suggested machine settings: Width 2½, length 1.

Lace to Fabric
Place right sides together.
Fabric extends ⅛" from lace.
Zigzag off the edge and over the heading of the lace.
Suggested Machine Settings: Width 3½, Length ½ to 1 (almost a satin stitch).

Lace to Entredeux
Trim batiste from one side of the entredeux.
Butt lace to entredeux and zigzag.
Suggested Machine Settings: Width 2½, Length 1½.

Gathered Lace to Entredeux
Trim one side of the entredeux.
Gather lace by pulling heading thread.
Butt together and zigzag.
Suggested Machine Settings: Width 2½, Length 1½.

Entredeux to Flat Fabric
Place fabric to entredeux, right sides together.
Stitch in the ditch with a regular straight stitch.
Trim seam allowance to ⅛".
Zigzag over the seam allowance.
Suggested Machine Settings: Width 2½, Length 1½.

Entredeux to Gathered Fabric
Gather fabric using two gathering rows.
Place gathered fabric to entredeux, right sides together.
Stitch in the ditch with a regular straight stitch.
Stitch again 1/16" away from the first stitching.
Trim seam allowance to ⅛".
Zigzag over the seam allowance.
Suggested Machine Settings: Width 2½, Length 1½.

Top Stitch
Turn seam down, away from the lace, entredeux, etc.
Tack in place using a zigzag.
Suggested Machine Settings: Width 1½, Length 1½.

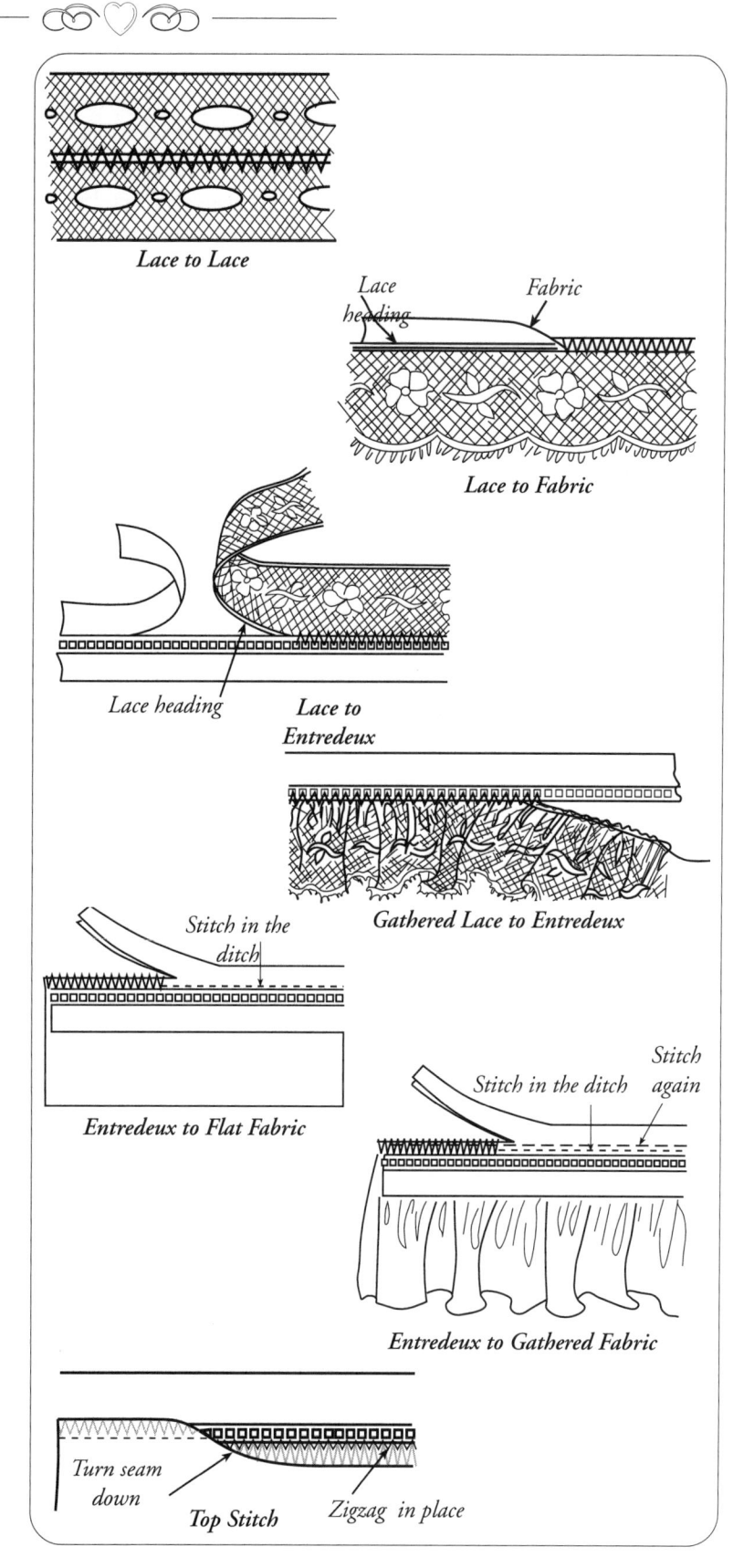

Cutting Fabric From Behind Lace That Has Been Shaped and Zigzagged

I absolutely love two pairs of Fiskars Scissors for the tricky job of cutting fabric from behind lace that has been shaped and stitched on. The first is Fiskars 9491, blunt tip 5" scissors. They look much like kindergarten scissors because of the blunt tips; however, they are very sharp. They cut fabric away from behind laces with ease. By the way, both of the scissors mentioned in this section are made for either right handed or left handed people.

The second pair that I really love for this task are the Fiskars 9808 curved blade craft scissors. The curved blades are very easy to use when working in tricky, small areas of lace shaping. Fiskars are crafted of permanent stainless steel and are precision ground and hardened for a sharp, long lasting edge.

Repairing Lace Holes Which You Didn't Mean To Cut!

Trimming fabric away from behind stitched-down lace can be difficult. It is not uncommon to slip, thus cutting a hole in your lace work. How do you repair this lace with the least visible repair? It is really quite simple.

1. Look at the pattern in the lace where you have cut the hole. Is it in a flower, in a dot series, or in the netting part of the lace (**fig. 1**)?
2. After you identify the pattern where the hole was cut, cut another piece of lace 1/4" longer than each side of the hole in the lace.
3. On the bottom side of the lace in the garment, place the lace patch (**fig. 2**).
4. Match the design of the patch with the design of the lace around the hole where it was cut.
5. Zigzag around the cut edges of the lace hole, trying to catch the edges of the hole in your zigzag (**fig 3**).
6. Now, you have a patched and zigzagged pattern.
7. Trim away the leftover ends underneath the lace you have just patched (**fig. 3**).
8. And don't worry about a piece of patched lace. My grandmother used to say, "Don't worry about that. You'll never notice it on a galloping horse."

Piecing Lace Not Long Enough For Your Needs

From my sewing experience, sometimes you will need a longer piece of lace than you have. Perhaps you cut the lace incorrectly or bought less than you needed and had to go back for more. Whatever the reason, if you need to make a lace strip longer, it is easy to do.

1. Match your pattern with two strips that will be joined later (**figs. 1 and 3**).
2. Is your pattern a definite flower? Is it a definite diamond or some other pattern that is relatively large?
3. If you have a definite design in the pattern, you can join pieces by zigzagging around that design and then down through the heading of the lace (**fig. 2**).
4. If your pattern is tiny, you can zigzag at an angle joining the two pieces (**fig. 2**). Trim away excess laces close to the zigzagged seam (**fig. 4**).
5. Forget that you have patched laces and complete the dress. If you discover that the lace is too short before you begin stitching, you can plan to place the pieced section in an inconspicuous place.
6. If you were already into making the garment when you discovered the short lace, simply join the laces and continue stitching as if nothing had happened.

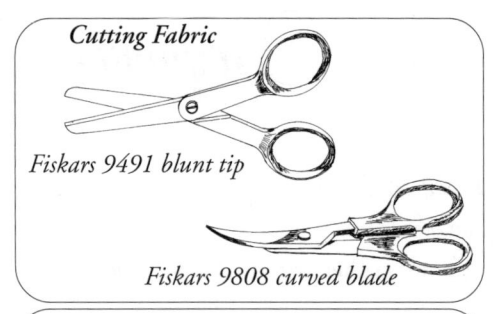

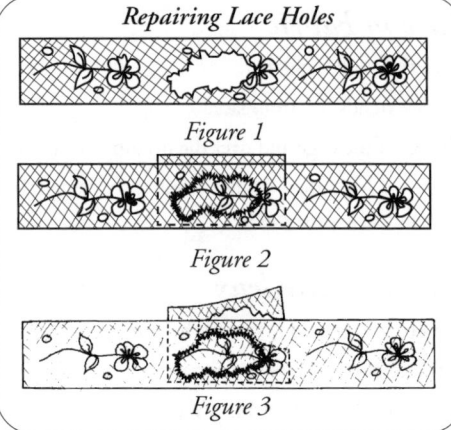

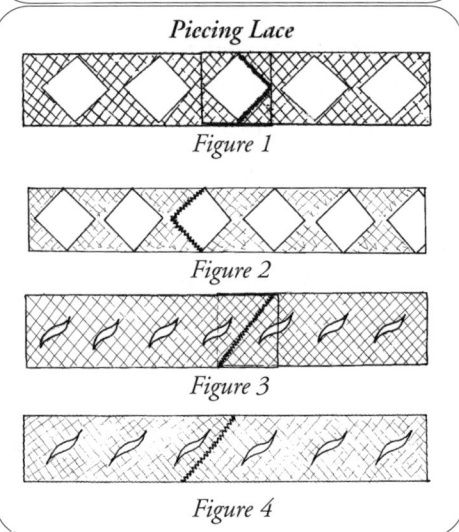

Cutting Fabric

Fiskars 9491 blunt tip

Fiskars 9808 curved blade

Repairing Lace Holes

Figure 1

Figure 2

Figure 3

Piecing Lace

Figure 1

Figure 2

Figure 3

Figure 4

If Your Fancy Band Is Too Short

Not to worry; cut down the width of your skirt. Always make your skirt adapt to your lace shapes, not the lace shapes to your skirt.

Making Diamonds, Hearts, Tear-Drops, Or Circles Fit Skirt Bottom

How do you make sure that you engineer your diamonds, hearts, teardrops, or circles to exactly fit the width skirt that you are planning? The good news is that you don't. Make your shapes any size that you want. Stitch them onto your skirt, front and back, and cut away the excess skirt width. Or, you can stitch up one side seam, and zigzag your shapes onto the skirt, and cut away the excess on the other side before you make your other side seam.

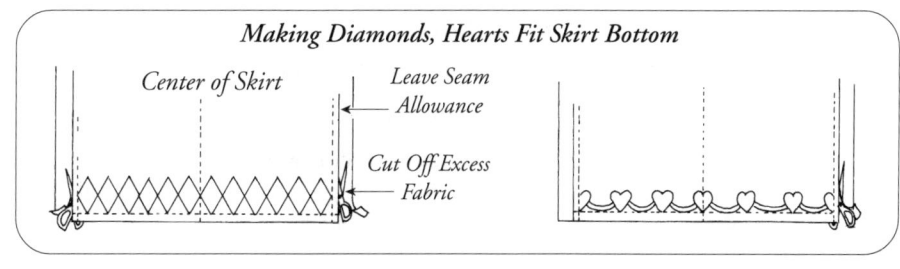

Making Diamonds, Hearts Fit Skirt Bottom

Center of Skirt — Leave Seam Allowance — Cut Off Excess Fabric

Machine Entredeux

Making Entredeux (Or Hemstitching) On Today's Computer Sewing Machines

About eight years ago I was conned into purchasing a 1905 hemstitching machine for $1500. I was told that it had a perfect stitch and that stitch (about 2 inches) was demonstrated to me by the traveling salesman. I was very happy to finally have one of those wonderful machines. Guess how long that wonderful machine lasted before it broke down? I stitched about 10 inches more which looked great; at that point, the stitching was awful. I called several repairmen. It never made a decent hemstitch again.

The good news to follow this sad story is that today's new computer machines do an excellent job of making hemstitching and they work! I am going to give our favorite settings for our favorite sewing machines. Before you buy a new sewing machine, if you love heirloom sewing, please go try out each of these machines and see if you love these stitches as much as we do.

Using A Stabilizer With Wing Needle Hemstitching Or Pinstitching

Before you do any hemstitching or any decorative work with a wing needle which involves lots of stitching on these wonderful machines, first let me tell you that **you must use a stabilizer**! You can use stitch-n-tear, computer paper, tissue paper (not quite strong enough but o.k. in certain situations), wax paper, physician's examining table paper, typing paper, adding machine paper or almost any other type of paper. When you are doing heavy stitching such as a feather stitch, I recommend that type of paper which physicians spread out over their examining tables. You can get a roll of it at any medical supply place. If you use stitch-n-tear or adding machine paper in feather stitch type stitches, it is difficult to pull away all of the little pieces which remain when you take the paper from the back of the garment. This physician's paper seems to tear away pretty easily.

Preparing Fabric Before Beginning Hemstitching or Pinstitching

Stiffen fabric with spray starch before lace shaping or decorative stitching with the hemstitches and wing needles. Use a hair dryer to dry the lace before you iron it if you have spray starched it too much. Also, if you wet your fabrics and laces too much with spray starch, place a piece of tissue paper on top of your work, and dry iron it dry. Hemstitching works best on natural fibers such as linen, cotton, cotton batiste, silk or cotton organdy. I don't advise hemstitching a fabric with a high polyester content. Polyester has a memory. If you punch a hole in polyester, it remembers the original positioning of the fibers, and the hole wants to close up.

Threads To Use For Pinstitching Or Hemstitching

Use all cotton thread, 50, 60, 70, 80 weight. If you have a thread breaking problem, you can also use a high quality polyester thread or a cotton covered polyester thread, like the Coats and Clark for machine lingerie and embroidery. Personally, I like to press needle down on all of the entredeux and pin stitch settings.

Pinstitching Or Point de Paris Stitch With A Sewing Machine

The pin stitch is another lovely "entredeux look" on my favorite machines. It is a little more delicate. Pin stitch looks similar to a ladder with **one of the long sides of the ladder missing**. Imagine the steps being fingers which reach over into the actual lace piece to grab the lace. The side of the ladder, the long side, will be stitched on the fabric right along side of the outside of the heading of the lace. The fingers reach into the lace to grab it. You need to look on all of the pinstitch settings given below and realize that you have to use reverse image on one of the sides of lace so that the fingers will grab into the lace while the straight side goes on the outside of the lace heading.

Attaching Shaped Lace To The Garment With Machine Entredeux Or Pinstitching And A Wing Needle

Probably my favorite place to use the machine entredeux/wing needle hemstitching is to attach shaped laces to a garment. Simply shape your laces in the desired shapes such as hearts, diamonds, ovals, loops, circles, or bows, and stitch the stitch. In addition to stitching this gorgeous decorative stitch, it also attaches the shaped lace to the garment (**fig. 1**). Always use stabilizer when using this type of heavy hemstitching.

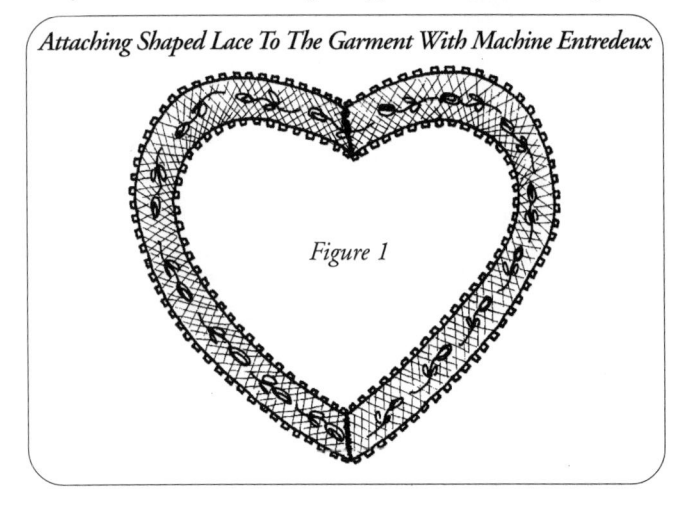

Attaching Shaped Lace To The Garment With Machine Entredeux

Figure 1

Settings For Entredeux (Hemstitch) And Pinstitch

Pfaff 7570

Pinstitch
- 100 wing needle, A - 2 Foot, Needle Down
- Stitch 112, tension 3, twin needle button, 4.0 width, 3.0 length

Entredeux
- 100 wing needle, A - 2 Foot, Needle Down

	width	length
Stitch #132	3.5	5.0
Stitch #113	4.0	2.0
Stitch #114	3.5	2.5
Stitch #115	3.5	3.0

Bernina 1630

Pinstitch
- 100 wing needle
- 1630 menu G, Pattern #10, SW - 2.5, SL - 2

Entredeux
- 100 wing needle
- 1630 menu G, pattern #5, SW - 3.5, SL - 3

Viking #1+

Pinstitch
- 100 wing needle
- Stitch D6, width 2.5-3; length 2.5-3

Entredeux
- 100 wing needle
- Stitch D7 (width and length are already set in)

Elna 9000 and DIVA

Pinstitch
- 100 wing needle
- Stitch #120 (length and width are already set in)

Entredeux
- 100 wing needle
- Stitch #121 (length and width are already set)

Singer XL - 100

Pinstitch
- 100 Wing Needle
- Screen #3
- Stitch #7
- Width 4 (length changes with width)

Entredeux
- 100 Wing needle
- Screen #3
- Stitch #8

Width 5 (Medium) or 4 (small)

New Home 9000

Pinstitch
- 100 Wing Needle
- Stitch #26 (width 2.5; length 2.5)

Hemstitch
- 100 wing needle
- Stitch #39 (width 4.0; length 1.5)

Esanté

Choose Decorative Stitch-Heirloom

Pinstitch
- 100 wing needle
- Stitch #4

Hemstitch
- 100 wing needle
- Stitch #5

Puffing

Gathering The Puffing Using The Gathering Foot On Your Machine

Two years ago, I wouldn't have told you that this was the easiest method of applying puffing into a round portrait collar. The reason being I didn't know how to make perfect puffing using the gathering foot for the sewing machine. I thought you used the edge of the gathering foot to guide the fabric underneath the gathering foot. This left about a ¼" seam allowance. It also made the gathers not perfect in some places with little "humps" and unevenness on some portions. Therefore, I wasn't happy with puffing made on the gathering foot. When I asked my friend, Sue Hausman, what might be wrong, she explained to me that to make perfect gathering, you had to move the fabric over so that you would have at least a ½" seam allowance. She further explained that there are two sides to the feed dogs; when you use the side of the gathering foot, then the fabric only catches on one side of the feed dogs. It works like magic to move your fabric over and guide it along one of the guide lines on the sewing machine. If your machine doesn't have these lines, simply put a piece of tape down to make a proper guide line.

Making Gathering Foot Puffing

1. The speed of the sewing needs to be consistent. Sew either fast or slow but do not sew fast then slow then fast again. For the beginner, touch the "sew slow" button (if available on your machine). This will help to keep a constant speed.

2. The puffing strip should be gathered with a ½ seam allowance, with an approximate straight stitch length of 4, right side up (**fig. 1**). Remember that you can adjust your stitch length to make your puffing looser or fuller. Do not let the strings of the fabric wrap around the foot of the machine. This will cause to fabric to back up behind the foot causing an uneven seam allowance, as well as uneven gathers. Leave the thread tails long in case adjustments are needed. One side of the gathering is now complete (**fig. 2**).

3. Begin gathering the second side of the strip, right side up. This row of gathering will be made from the bottom of the strip to the top of the strip. In other words, bi-directional sewing (first side sewn from the top to the bottom, second side sewn from the bottom to the top) is allowed. Gently unfold the ruffle with the left hand allowing flat fabric to feed under the foot. **Do not** apply any pressure to the fabric (**fig. 3**). The feeding must remain constant. Leave the thread tails long in case adjustments are needed. The puffing strip in now complete.

Placing Machine Gathered Puffing Into A Collar

1. Cut your strips of fabric.
2. Gather both sides of the puffing, running the fabric under the gathering foot. Be sure you have at least a ½" seam allowance. When you use a gathering foot, the moveability of the puffing isn't as great as when you gather it the other way.
3. You, of course, have two raw edges when you gather puffing with the gathering foot (**fig. 1**).
4. Shape the puffing around the fabric board below the row of lace (or rows of lace) that you have already shaped into the rounded shape. Place the pins into the board through the outside edge of the puffing. Place the pins right into the place where the gathering row runs in the fabric (**fig. 2**).

Puffing

Figure 1

Figure 2

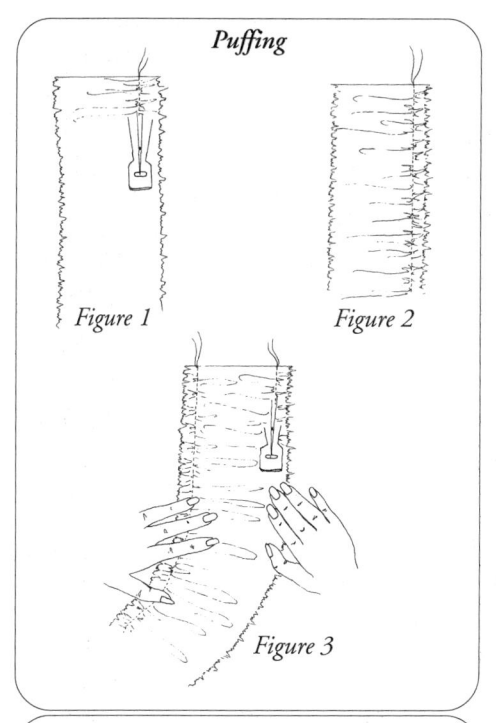

Figure 3

Placing Machine Gathered Puffing Into A Collar

Figure 1

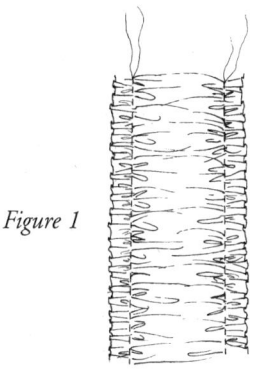

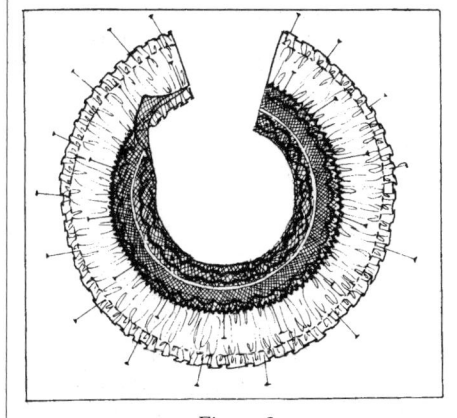

Figure 2

5. Pull the raw edge of the machine puffed strip up **underneath the finished edge of the curved lace**, so that your zigzagging to attach the puffing will be on the machine gathering line. Put the rounded lace edge on top of the puffing. Pin the bottom edge of the puffing first so you can "arrange" the top fullness underneath the curved lace edge which is already in place (the top piece of lace) (**see fig. 2**).

6. It will be necessary to "sort of" arrange the machine gathered puffing, especially on the top edge which will be gathered the fullest on your collar, and pin it where you want it since the machine gathering thread doesn't give too much. After you have pinned and poked the gathering into place where it looks pretty on the top and the bottom, flat pin it to the tissue paper and zigzag the puffing strip to the lace, stitching right on top of the lace.

NOTE: **You will have an unfinished fabric edge underneath the place where you stitched the lace to the puffing.** That is okay. After you have zigzagged the puffing to the lace, then trim away the excess fabric underneath the lace edge. Be careful, of course, when you trim this excess fabric, not to accidentally cut the lace.

7. If you have a machine entredeux/wing needle option on your sewing machine, you can stitch this beautiful stitch in place of the zigzagging. Since the fabric is gathered underneath the lace, you will have to be very careful stitching to get a pretty stitch.

8. Shape another piece of lace around the bottom of this puffing, bringing the inside piece of curved lace exactly to fit on top of the gathering line in the puffing. Once again, you will have unfinished fabric underneath the place where you will zigzag the lace to the puffing collar. After zigzagging the lace to the puffing collar, trim the excess fabric away.

9. Continue curving the rest of the laces to make the collar as wide as you want it to be.

Basic Pintucking

Double Needles

Double needles come in different sizes. The first number on the double needle is the distance between the needles. The second number on the needle is the actual size of the needle. The chart below shows some of the double needle sizes. The size needle that you choose will depend on the weight of the fabric that you are pintucking (**fig. 1**).

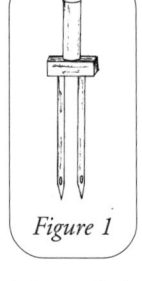

Let me relate a little more information for any of you who haven't used the double needles yet. Some people have said to me, "Martha, I only have a place for one needle in my sewing machine." That is correct and on most sewing machines, you probably still can use a double needle. The double needle has only one stem which goes into the needle slot; the double needles join on a little bar below the needle slot. You use two spools of thread when you thread the double needles. If you don't have two spools of thread of the fine thread which you use for pintucking, then run an extra bobbin and use it as another spool of thread. For most shaped pintucking on heirloom garments, I prefer either the 1.6/70, the 1.6/80 or the 2.0/80 size needle.

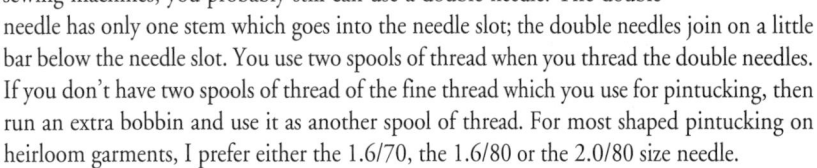

a. 1.6/70 - Light Weight
b. 1.6/80 - Light Weight
c. 2.0/80 - Light Weight
d. 2.5/80 - Light Weight
e. 3.0/90 - Medium Weight
f. 4.0/100 - Heavy Weight

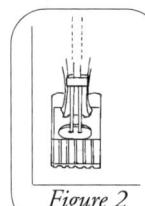

Figure 1

Figure 2

Pintuck Feet

Pintuck feet are easy to use and they shave hours off pintucking time when you are making straight pintucks. They enable you to space straight pintucks perfectly. I might add here that some people also prefer a pintuck foot when making curved and angled pintucks. I prefer a regular zigzag sewing foot for curved pintucks. Pintuck feet correspond to the needle used with that pintuck foot; the needle used corresponds to the weight of fabric. The bottom of these feet have a certain number of grooves 3, 5, 7, or 9. The width of the groove matches the width between the two needles. When making straight pintucks, use a pintuck foot of your choice. The grooves enable one to make those pintucks as close or as far away as the distance on the foot allows (**fig. 2**).

Preparing Fabric For Pintucking

Do I spray starch the fabric before I pintuck it? I usually do not spray starch fabric before pintucking it. Always press all-cotton fabric. A polyester/cotton blend won't need to be pressed unless it is very wrinkled. Tucks tend to lay flatter if you stiffen fabric with spray starch first; that is why I don't advise spray starching the fabric first in most cases. Pintuck a small piece of your chosen fabric with starch and one without starch, then make your own decision.

Straight Pintucking With A Pintuck Foot

Some of my favorite places for straight pintucks are on high yoke bodices of a dress and along the sleeves. On ladies blouses, straight pintucks are lovely running vertically on the front and back of the blouse, and so slenderizing! One of the prettiest treatments of straight pintucks on ladies blouses is stitching about three to five pintucks right down the center back of the blouse. Tuck a little shaped bow or heart on the center back of the blouse; stitch several tiny pintucks and top them off with a lace shape in the center back. Horizontally placed straight pintucks are lovely running across the back yoke of a tailored blouse. Tucks are always pretty running around the cuff of a blouse. I love pintucks just about anywhere.

1. Put in your double needle. Thread machine with two spools of thread. Thread one spool at a time (including the needle). This will help keep the threads from becoming twisted while stitching the tucks. This would be a good time to look in the guide book, which came with your sewing machine, for directions on using pintuck feet and double needles. Some sewing machines have a special way of threading for use with double needles.
2. The first tuck must be straight. To make this first tuck straight, do one of three things: (**a.**) Pull a thread all the way across the fabric and follow along that pulled line. (**b.**) Using a measuring stick, mark a straight line along the fabric. Stitch on that line. (**c.**) Fold the fabric in half and press that fold. Stitch along that folded line.
3. Place the fabric under the foot for the first tuck and straight stitch the desired length of pintuck. (Length=1 to $2^{1}/_{2}$; Needle position is center) (**fig. 1**).
4. Place your first tuck into one of the grooves in your pintuck foot. The space between each pintuck depends on the placement of the first pintuck (**fig. 2**).
5. Continue pintucking by placing the last pintuck made into a groove in the foot.

Straight Pintucking Without A Pintuck Foot

1. Use a double needle. Use your regular zigzag foot.
2. Thread your double needles.
3. Draw the first line of pintucking. Pintuck along that line. At this point you can use the edge of your presser foot as a guide (**fig. 3**).

NOTE: You might find a "generic" pintuck foot for your particular brand of machine.

Corded Pintucks

Cords make pintucks more prominent. Use Mettler gimp or #8 pearl cotton. Cording comes in handy when pintucks are being shaped. When pintucking across a bias with a double needle, you may get some distortion. The cord acts as a filler and will keep the fabric from distorting. Sometimes you might choose to use cording in order to add color to your pintucks. If you asked me, "Martha, do you usually cord pintucks? my answer would be no." However, just because I don't usually cord pintucks, doesn't mean that you won't prefer to cord them.

Some machines have a little device which sits in the base of the machine and sticks up just a little bit. That device tends to make the pintucks stand up a little more for a higher raised effect. Some people really like this feature.

1. If your machine has a hole in the throat plate, run the cord up through that hole and it will be properly placed without another thought (**fig. 2**).
2. If your machine does not have a hole in the throat plate, put the gimp or pearl cotton underneath the fabric, lining it up with the pintuck groove. Once you get the cording lined up under the proper groove, it will follow along for the whole pintuck.
3. You can stitch pintucks without a pintuck foot at all. Some sewing machines have a foot with a little hole right in the middle of the foot underneath the foot. That is a perfectly proper place to place the cord for shadow pintucks. Remember, if you use a regular foot for pintucking, you must use the side of the foot for guiding your next pintuck.

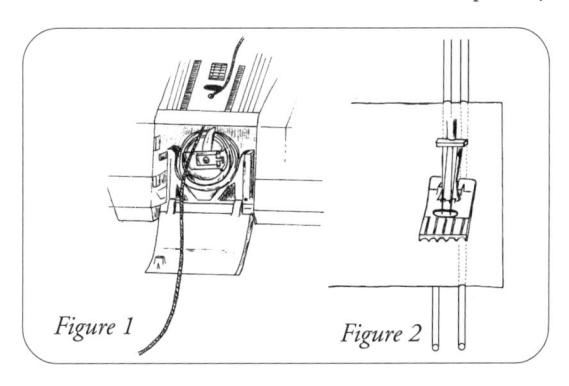

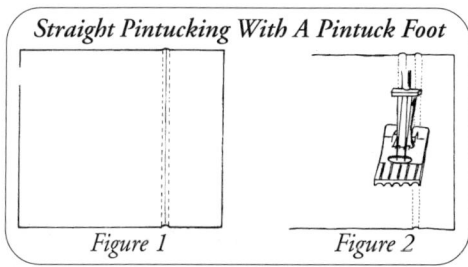

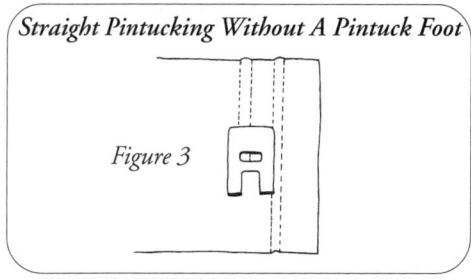

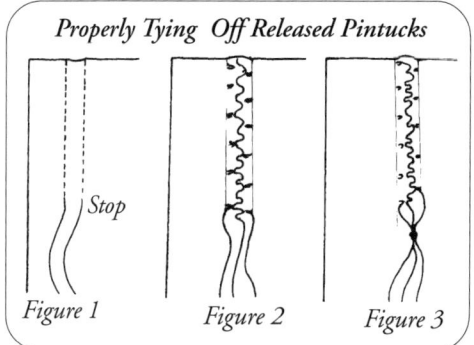

Straight Pintucking With A Pintuck Foot

Figure 1   *Figure 2*

Straight Pintucking Without A Pintuck Foot

Figure 3

Properly Tying Off Released Pintucks

Stop

Figure 1   *Figure 2*   *Figure 3*

Shaping Curves And Angles With Pintucks

Pintucks are inexpensive to make. They add texture and dimension without adding cost to the dress. They're rarely found on store-bought clothing. One of my favorite things in the whole world to do is to follow lace shapes with pintucks or decorative stitches on your machine for an enchanting finish. Or you may simply use your template and pintuck the shape instead of using lace. For threads, use white-on-white, ecru-on-ecru, or any pastel color on white or ecru.

The effect of shaped pintucks is so fabulous and so interesting. Virtually everybody is afraid that she doesn't know how to make those fabulous pintucks thus making a garment into a pintuck fantasy. It is so easy that I just can't wait to share with you the tricks. I promise, nobody in my schools all over the world ever believes me when I tell them this easiest way. Then, everybody, virtually everybody, has done these curved and angled pintucks with absolute perfection. They usually say, "This is really magic!"

The big question here is, "What foot do I use for scalloped pintucks?" For straight pintucks, I use a pintuck foot with the grooves. That foot is fine for

Figure 1   *Figure 2*

curved or scalloped pintucks also, but I prefer either the regular zigzag foot or the clear applique foot, which is plastic and allows easy "see through" of the turning points. Try your pintuck foot, your regular sewing foot, and your clear applique foot to see which one you like the best. Like all aspects of heirloom sewing, the "best" foot is really your personal preference. Listed below are my absolute recommendations for curved and angled pintucks.

Martha's General Rules Of Curving And Angling Pintucks

1. Use a regular zigzag foot, or a pintuck foot (**fig. 1**).

2. Either draw on your pintuck shape, or zigzag your lace insertion to the garment. You can either draw on pintuck shapes or follow your lace shaping. My favorite way to make lots of pintucks is to follow lace shaping which has already been stitched to the garment.

3. Using a ruler, draw straight lines with a fabric marker or washable pencil, bisecting each point where you will have to turn around with your pintuck. In other words, draw a line at all angles where you will have to turn your pintuck in order to keep stitching. This is the most important point to make with curved and angled pintucks. When you are going around curves, this bi-secting line is not necessary since you don't stop and pivot when you are turning curves. Everywhere you have to stop and pivot, these straight lines must be drawn (**fig. 2**).

4. Use a 1.6 or a 2.0 double needle. Any wider doesn't curve or turn well!

5. Set your machine for straight sewing, L=1.5. Notice this is **a very short stitch**. When you turn angles, this short stitch is necessary for pretty turns.

6. Press "Needle Down" on your sewing machine if your machine has this feature. This means that when you stop sewing at any time, your needle will remain in the fabric.

7. Stitch, using either the first line you drew or following around the lace shaping which you have already stitched to your garment. The edge of your presser foot will guide along the outside of the lace shape. When you go around curves, turn your fabric and keep stitching. Do not pick up your foot and pivot, this makes the curves jumpy, not smooth (**fig. 3**).

8. When you come to a pivot point, let your foot continue to travel until you can look into the hole of the foot, and see that your double needles have **straddled the line you drew on the fabric.** Remember your needles are **in the fabric** (**fig. 4**).

9. Sometimes, the needles won't exactly straddle the line exactly the way they straddled the line on the last turn around. Lift the presser foot. (Remember, you needles are still in the fabric.) Turn your fabric where the edge of the presser foot properly begins in a new direction following your lace insertion lace shaping or your drawn line, lower the presser foot, and begin sewing again (**fig. 5**).

10. Wait A Minute! Most of you are now thinking, "Martha, You Are Crazy. There are two major problems with what you just said. You said to leave the double needles in the fabric, lift the presser foot, turn the fabric, lower the presser foot and begin sewing again. If I do that I will probably break my double needles, and there will be a big wad or hump of fabric where I twisted the fabric to turn around to go in a new direction. That will never work!" I know you are thinking these two things because everybody does. Neither one of these things will happen! It is really just like MAGIC. TRY THIS TECHNIQUE AND SEE WHAT I AM SAYING. Ladies all over the world absolutely adore this method and nobody believes how easy it is.

11. After you get your first row of double needle pintucks, then you can use the edge of your regular zigzag sewing machine foot, guiding along the just stitched pintuck row as the guide point for more rows. The only thing you have to remember, is to have made long enough lines to bisect each angle that you are going to turn. You must have these turn around lines drawn so you can know where to stop sewing, leave the needles in the fabric, turn around, and begin stitching again. These lines are the real key.

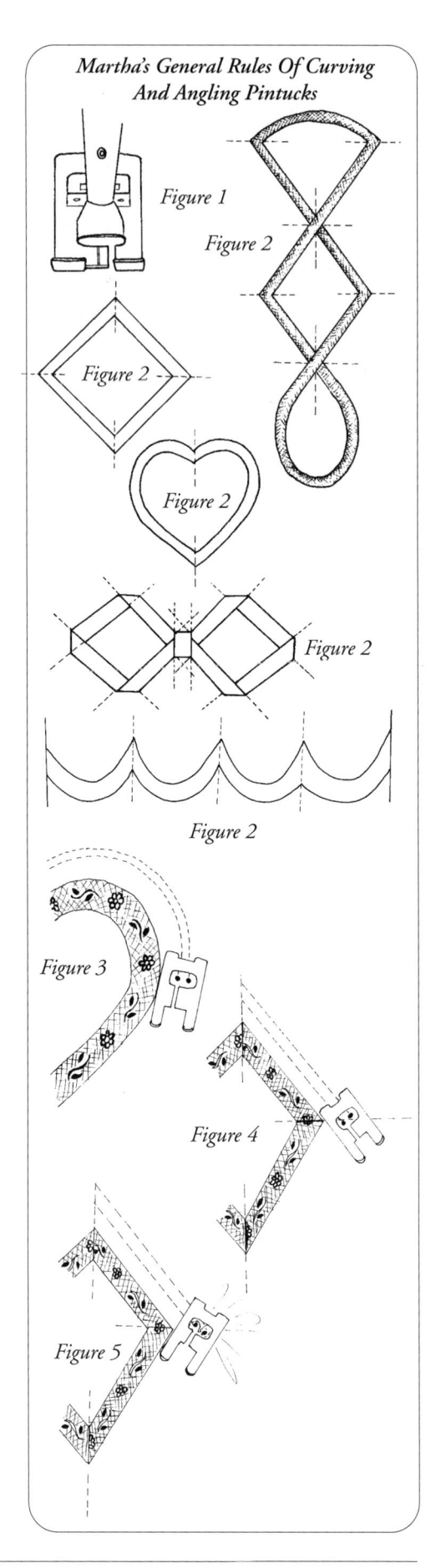

Martha's General Rules Of Curving And Angling Pintucks

Figure 1

Figure 2

Figure 2

Figure 2

Figure 2

Figure 2

Figure 3

Figure 4

Figure 5

Lace Shaping Techniques

General Lace Shaping Supplies

- Fabric to apply lace shape
- Lace (usually insertion lace)
- Glass head pins
- Spray starch
- Lightweight sewing thread
- Lace shaping board or covered cardboard
- Washout marker or washout pencil
- Wing needle (optional)
- Stabilizer (If a wing needle stitch is used)

Using Glass Head Pins

Purchasing GLASS HEAD PINS is one of the first and most critical steps to lace shaping. All types of lace shaping must be pinned in place, starched lightly and pressed. The iron is placed directly on top of the pins. Since plastic head pins melt onto your fabric and ruin your project, obviously they won't do. Metal pins such as the iris pins with the skinny little metal heads won't melt; however, when you pin hundreds of these little pins into the lace shaping board, your finger will have one heck of a hole poked into it. Please purchase glass head pins and throw away your plastic head pins. Glass head pins can be purchased by the box or by the card. For dress projects, as many 100 pins might be needed for each section of lace shaping. So, make sure to purchase enough.

Shape 'N Press (Lace Shaping Board)

I used fabric boards (covered cardboard) until the June Taylor's Shape 'N Press board became available. It is truly wonderful. This board measures 24" by 18" and has permanent lace shaping templates drawn right on the board. I never have to hunt for another lace shaping template again. Here is how I use it. I place my skirt, collar, pillow top or other project on top of the board with the desired template positioned correctly (I can see the template through the fabric), shape the lace along the template lines pinning into the board, spray starch lightly, re-pin the lace just to the fabric. Now I can move the fabric, correctly positioning the template, and start the process again. Did you notice, I never mentioned tracing the design on the fabric? With the Shape 'N Press, drawing on the fabric can be omitted so you never have to worry about removing fabric marker lines. I also use the flip side of the board. It has a blocking guide for bishops and round collars (sizes newborn to adult).

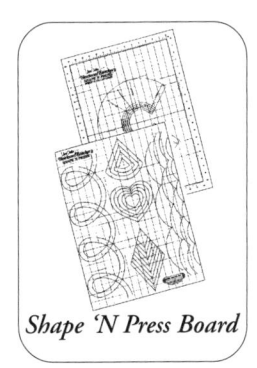

Shape 'N Press Board

Making A Lace Shaping Board or Fabric Board

If a lace shaping board is not available, a fabric board can be made from cardboard (cake boards, pizza boards or a cut up box) covered with fabric or paper. A child's bulletin board or a fabric covered ceiling tile will work. Just staple or pin fabric or white typing paper or butcher paper over the board before you begin lace shaping. Just remember you must be able to pin into the board, use a bit of stray starch and iron on it.

Tracing the Template

Trace the template on the fabric with a wash out marker. Margaret Boyles taught me years ago that it is simpler to draw your shapes on fabric by making dots about one half inch apart than it is to draw a solid line. This also means less pencil or marker to get out of the fabric when your lace shaping is finished. Mark

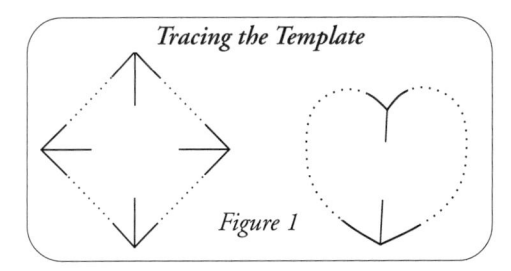

Tracing the Template

Figure 1

all angles with miter lines (a line dividing the angle in half). Sometimes it is helpful to make the solid lines at the angles and miter lines (**fig. 1**). Hint: If you do not want to draw the template on the fabric, trace the template on stabilizer or paper with a permanent marker. Place the template under the fabric. Because the fabric is "see-through" the lines can be seen clearly. Shape the lace along the template lines. Complete the design as stated in the lace shaping directions. Remember to remove the template paper before stitching so that the permanent pen lines are not caught in the stitching.

Shish Kabob Sticks

I first learned about using wooden shish kabob sticks from some of the technical school sewing teachers in Australia. By the way, where does one get these wooden shish kabob sticks? At the grocery store! If you can only find the long ones, just break them in half to measure 5" or 6" long and use the end with the point to push and to hold laces (or other items) as they go into the sewing machine. These sticks are used instead of the usual long pin or worse still, seam ripper that I have used so often. Using this stick is a safety technique as well as an efficient technique.

Shaping Lace Diamonds

Lace diamonds can be used almost anywhere on heirloom garments. They are especially pretty at the point of a collar, on the skirt of a dress, at angles on the bodice of a garment, or all the way around a collar. The easiest way to make lace diamonds is to work on a fabric board with a diamond guide. You can make your diamonds as large or as small as you desire. I think you are really going to love this easy method of making diamonds with the fold back miter. Now, you don't have to remove those diamonds from the board to have perfect diamonds every time.

Making Lace Diamonds

Materials Needed
- Spray starch, iron, pins, fabric board
- Lace insertion
- Diamond guide

1. Draw the diamond guide or template (**fig. 1**).

2. Tear both skirt pieces. French seam or serge one side only of the skirt.

3. Working from the center seam you just made, draw diamonds all the way around the skirt. This way you can make any sized diamonds you want without worrying if they will fit the skirt perfectly. When you get all the way around both sides of the skirt you will have the same amount of skirt left over on both sides.

4. Simply trim the excess skirt away. Later you will French seam or serge the skirt on the other side to complete your skirt. This is the easy way to make any type of lace shaping on any skirt and it will always fit perfectly (**fig. 2**).

5. The guide or template, which you have just drawn, will be the outside of the diamond. Draw lines going into the diamond, bisecting each angle where the lace will be mitered. This is very important, since one of your critical pins will be placed exactly on this line. These bisecting lines need to be drawn about 2 inches long coming in from the angles of the diamonds (**fig. 3**). If you are making a diamond skirt, it is easier to draw your diamond larger and make your diamond shaping on the inside of the diamond. That way, the outside points of your diamond can touch when you are drawing all of your diamonds on the skirt.

6. As I said earlier, you can shape the laces for diamonds on either the outside or the inside of the template. I actually think it is easier to shape your laces on the inside of the template.

7. Place your skirt with the drawn diamonds on a fabric board.

8. Place the lace flat and guiding it along the inside of the drawn template, put a pin at **point A** and one at **point B** where the bisecting line goes to the inside (**fig. 4a**). The pin goes through both the lace and the fabric into the fabric board.

9. Guiding the edge of the lace along the drawn template line, place another pin into the fabric board through the lace (and the fabric skirt) at **point C** and another one at **point D** on the bisecting line (**fig. 4b**).

10. Fold back the lace right on top of itself. Remove the pin from the fabric board at **point D**, replacing it this time to go through both layers of lace rather than just one. Of course, the pin will not only go through both layers of lace but also through the skirt and into fabric board (**fig. 5**).

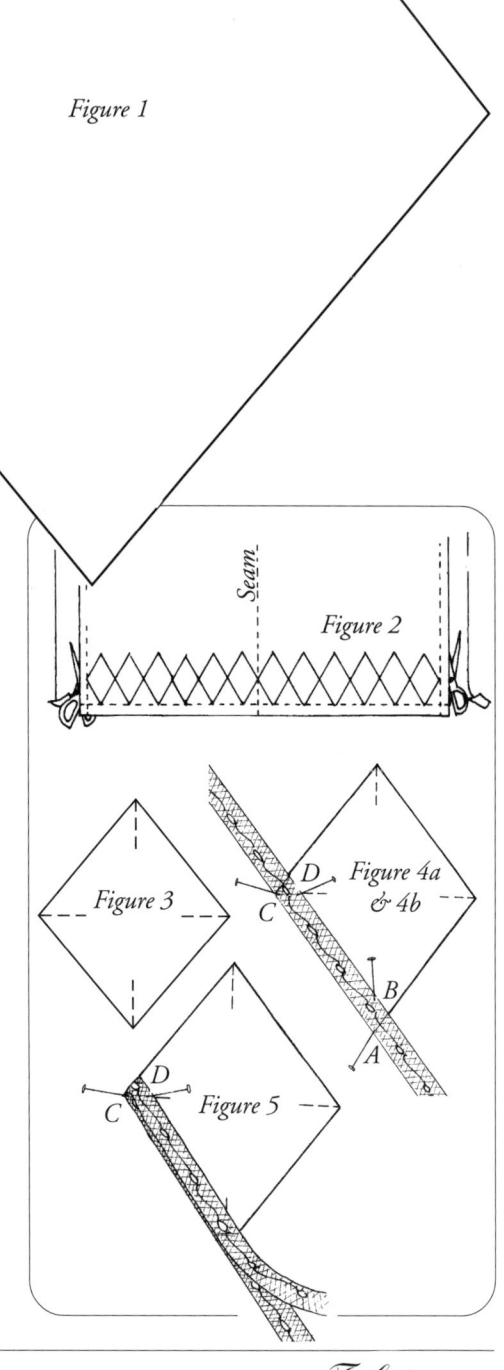

Figure 1

Figure 2

Figure 3

Figure 4a & 4b

Figure 5

11. Take the lace piece and bring it around to once again follow the outside line. You magically have a folded miter already in place (see fig. 6).

12. Guiding further, with the edge of the lace along the inside of the drawn template line, place another pin into the fabric board through the lace at **point E** and another at **point F** on the bisecting line (**fig. 6**).

13. Fold the lace right back on top of itself. Remove the pin at **point F**, replacing it this time to go through both layers of lace rather than just one (**fig. 7**).

14. Take the lace piece and bring it around to once again follow the outside line. You magically have a folded miter already in place (**fig. 8**).

15. Guiding further, with the edge of the lace along the inside of the drawn template line, place another pin into the lace at **point G** and another pin at **point H** on the bisecting line.

16. Fold the lace right back on top of itself. Remove the pin at **point H**, replace it this time to go through both layers of lace rather than just one.

17. Take the lace piece and bring it around to once again follow the outside line. You magically have a folded miter already in place (**fig. 9**).

18. At the bottom of the lace diamond, let the laces cross at the bottom. Remove the pin at **point B** and replace it into the fabric board through both pieces of lace. Remove the pin completely at **point A** (**fig. 10**).

19. Taking the top piece of lace, and leaving in the pin at **point B** only, fold the lace under and back so that it lies on top of the other piece of lace. You now have a folded in miter for the bottom of the lace.

20. Put a pin in, now, at **point B** (**fig. 11**). Of course you are going to have to cut away this long tail of lace. I think the best time to do that is before you begin your final stitching to attach the diamonds to the garment. It is perfectly alright to leave those tails of lace until your final stitching is done and then trim them.

21. You are now ready to spray starch and press the whole diamond shape. After spray starching and pressing the diamonds to the skirt, remove the pins from the fabric board and flat pin the lace shape to the skirt bottom. You are now ready to zigzag the diamond or machine entredeux stitch the diamond to the garment. Suggested zigzag settings are Width=2 to 3, Length=1 to 1 1/2.

Finishing The Bottom Of The Skirt

These techniques are for finishing the bottom of a Diamond Skirt, a Heart Skirt, a Bow Skirt, or any other lace shaped skirt where the figures travel all the way around the bottom touching each other.

Method One

Using Plain Zigzag To Attach Diamonds (Or Other Shapes) To The Skirt

1. First, zigzag across the top of the diamond pattern, stitching from **point A** to **point B**, again to **point A** and finish the entire skirt (**fig. 12**). Your lace is now attached to the skirt all the way across the skirt on the top. If your fabric and diamonds have been spray starched well, you don't have to use a stabilizer when zigzagging these lace shapes to the fabric. The stitch width will be wide enough to cover the heading of the lace and go off onto the fabric on the other side. The length will be from 1/2 to 1, depending on the look that you prefer.

2. Zigzag all of the diamonds on the skirt, on the inside of the diamonds only (**fig. 13**).

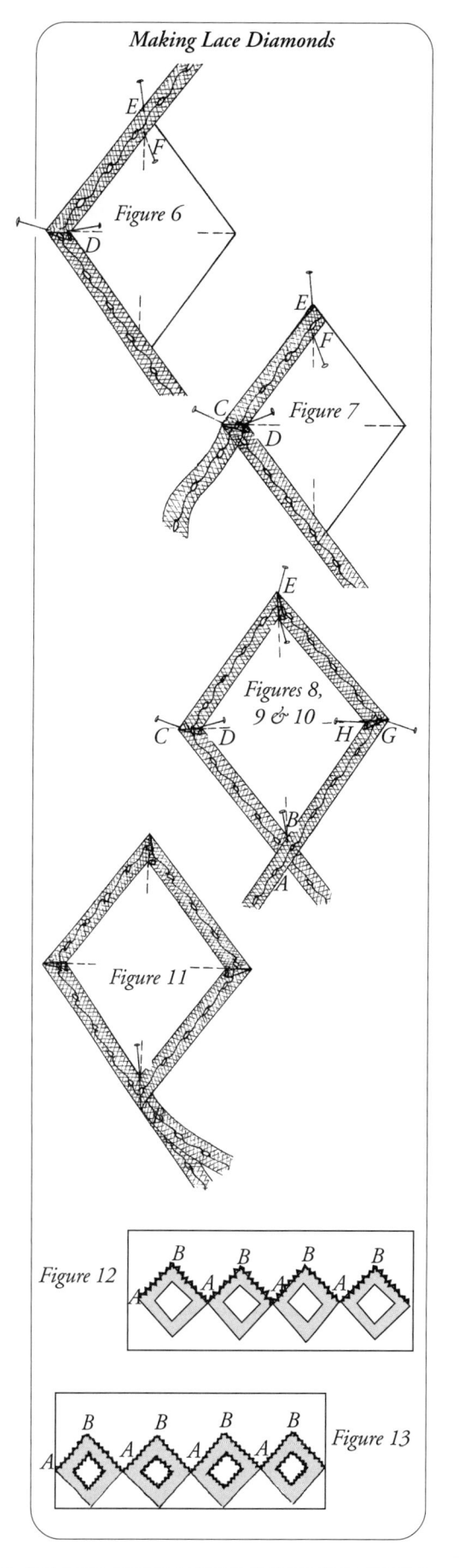

Making Lace Diamonds

Figure 6

Figure 7

Figures 8, 9 & 10

Figure 11

Figure 12

Figure 13

3. You are now ready to trim away the fabric of the skirt from behind the diamonds. Trim the fabric carefully from behind the lace shapes. The rest of the skirt fabric will now fall away leaving a diamond shaped bottom of the skirt (**fig. 14**). The lace will also be seen through the top of the diamonds.

4. If you are going to just gather lace and attach it at this point, then gather the lace and zigzag it to the bottom of the lace shapes, being careful to put extra fullness in the points of the diamonds (**fig. 15**). If your lace isn't wide enough to be pretty, then zigzag a couple of pieces of insertion or edging to your edging to make it wider (**fig. 16**).

5. If you are going to put entredeux on the bottom of the shapes before attaching gathered lace to finish it, follow the instructions for attaching entredeux to the bottom of a scalloped skirt given earlier in this lace shaping section. Work with short pieces of entredeux stitching from the inside points of the diamonds to the lower points of the diamonds on the skirt.

Finishing The Bottom Of The Skirt
Method Two

Using A Wing Needle Machine Entredeux Stitch To Attach Diamonds (Or Other Lace Shapes) To The Skirt

1. If you are going to use the wing needle/entredeux stitch on your sewing machine to attach your diamonds or other lace shapes to the skirt, use the entredeux stitch for all attaching of the lace shapes to the skirt. Remember **you must use a stabilizer** when using the entredeux stitch/wing needle on any machine.

2. Place your stabilizer underneath the skirt, behind the shapes to be stitched. You can use small pieces of stabilizer which are placed underneath only a few shapes rather than having to have a long piece of stabilizer. Just be sure that you have stabilizer underneath these lace shapes before you begin your entredeux/wing needle stitching.

3. First, stitch the top side of the diamonds entredeux stitching from point A to point B all the way around the skirt. (**fig. 17**).

4. Secondly, stitch the inside of the diamonds using the entredeux stitch (**fig. 18**). Do not cut any fabric away at this point. Remember to continue using stabilizer for all entredeux/wing needle stitching.

5. You are now ready to gather your lace edging and machine entredeux it to the bottom of the skirt, joining the bottom portions of the diamonds at the same time you attach the gathered lace edging. If your machine has an edge joining or edge stitching foot with a center blade for guiding, this is a great place for using it.

6. Gather only a few inches of lace edging at a time. Butt the gathered lace edging to the flat bottom sides of the diamonds.

7. Machine entredeux right between the gathered lace edging and the flat side of the diamond. Remember, you are stitching through your laces (which are butted together, not overlapped), the fabric of the skirt and the stabilizer (**fig. 19**). Put a little extra lace gathered fullness at the upper and lower points of the diamonds.

8. After you have stitched your machine entredeux all the way around the bottom of the skirt, you have attached the gathered lace edging to the bottom of the skirt with your entredeux stitch.

9. Trim the fabric from behind the lace diamonds. Trim the fabric from underneath the gathered lace edging on the bottom of the skirt (**fig. 20**).

10. Either zigzag your folded miters in the angles of the diamonds or simply leave them folded in. I prefer to zigzag them (**fig. 21**). You also have the choice of cutting away the little folded back portions of the miters or leaving them for strength.

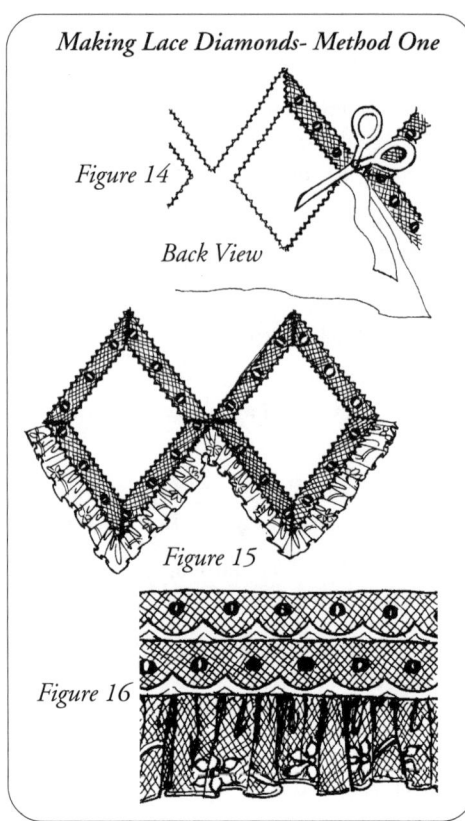

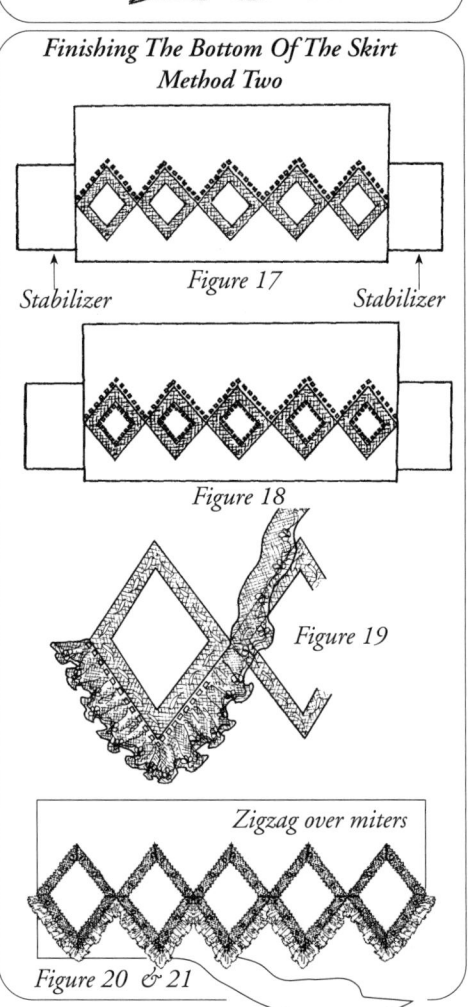

Making Lace Diamonds - Method One

Figure 14
Back View

Figure 15

Figure 16

Finishing The Bottom Of The Skirt Method Two

Stabilizer *Figure 17* *Stabilizer*

Figure 18

Figure 19

Zigzag over miters

Figure 20 & 21

Shaping Flip-Flopped Lace Bows

Figure 1

I make lace bows using a technique called "flip-flopping" lace — a relatively unsophisticated name for such a lovely trim. I first saw this technique on an antique teddy I bought at a local antique store. It had the most elegant flip-flopped lace bow. Upon careful examination, I noticed the lace was simply folded over at the corners, then continued down forming the outline of the bow. The corners were somewhat square. Certainly it was easier than mitering or pulling a thread and curving. I found it not only looked easier, it was easier.

Follow the instructions for making a flip-flopped bow, using a bow template. This technique works just as well for lace angles up and down on a skirt. You can flip-flop any angle that traditionally would be mitered. It can be used to go around a square collar, around diamonds, and around any shape with an angle rather than a curve.

Flip-Flopping Lace

1. Trace the template onto the fabric exactly where you want to place bows (**fig. 1**). Remember, the easy way to put bows around a skirt is to fold the fabric to make equal divisions of the skirt. If you want a bow skirt which has bows all the way around, follow the directions for starting at the side to make the bows in the directions given for a diamond skirt.

2. Draw your bows on your garment or on a skirt where you want this lace shape.

3. Place your garment on your fabric board before you begin making your bow shapes. Beginning above the inside of one bow (**above E**), place the lace along the angle. The template is the inside guide line of the bow (**fig. 2**).

4. At the first angle (**B**), simply fold the lace so that it will follow along the next line (**B-C**) (**fig. 3**). This is called flip-flopping the lace.

5. Place pins sticking through the lace, the fabric, and into the shaping board. I like to place pins on both the inside edges and the outside edges. Remember to place your pins so that they lie as flat as possible.

6. The lines go as follows: A-B, B-C, C-D, D-A, E-F, F-G, G-H, H-E. Tuck your lace end under E, which is also where the first raw edge will end (**fig. 4**).

7. Cut a short bow tab of lace that is long enough to go around the whole tie area of the bow (**fig. 4**). This will be the bow tie!

8. Tuck in this lace tab to make the center of the bow (**fig. 5**). Another way to attach this bow tie is to simply fold down a tab at the top and the bottom and place it right on top of the center of the bow. That is actually easier than tucking it under. Since you are going to zigzag all the way around the bow "tie" it really won't matter whether it is tucked in or not.

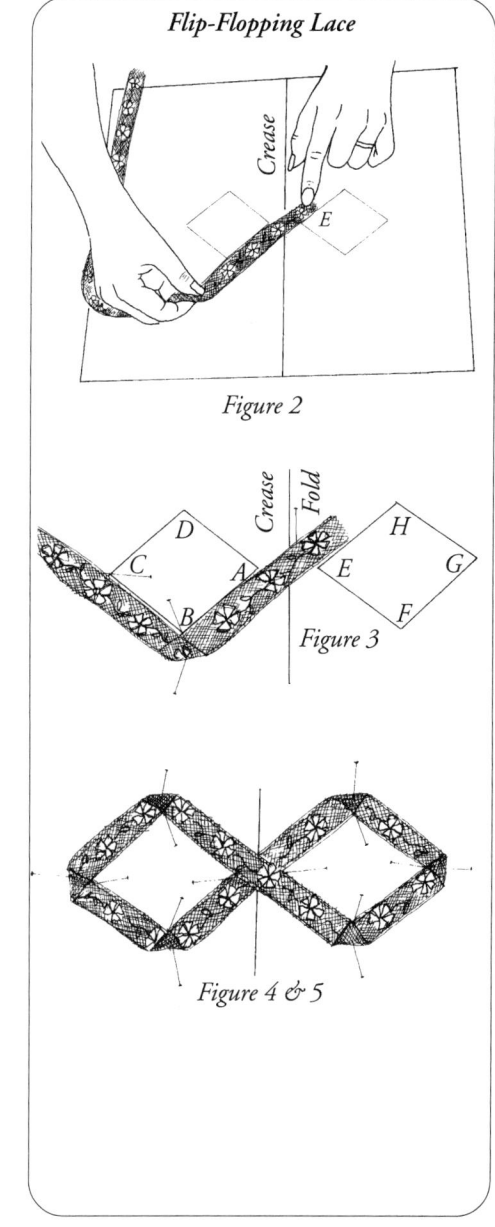

Flip-Flopping Lace

Figure 2

Figure 3

Figure 4 & 5

9. Spray starch and press the bow, that is shaped with the pins still in the board, with its bow tie in place (**fig. 6**). Remove pins from the board and pin the bow flat to the skirt or other garment. You are now ready to attach the shaped bow to the garment.

10. This illustration gives you ideas for making a bow two ways. First, the "A" side of the bow has just the garment fabric peeking through the center of the bow. Second, the "B" side of the bow illustrates what the bow will look like if you put a pintucked strip in the center. Both are beautiful (**fig. 7**).

11. If you prefer the bow to look like side (A), which has the fabric of the garment showing through the middle of the bow, follow these steps for completing the bow. Zigzag around the total outside of the bow. Then, zigzag around the inside portions of both sides of the bow. Finally, zigzag around the finished bow "tie" portion (**fig. 8**). The bows will be attached to the dress.

12. If you prefer the bow to look like side (B), which will have pintucks (or anything else you choose) inside, follow the directions in this section. (These directions are when you have bows on areas other than the bottom of a skirt or sleeve or collar. If you have bows at the bottom of anything, then you have to follow the skirt directions given in the diamond skirt section.)

13. Zigzag the outside only of the bows all the way around. Notice that your bow "tie" will be partially stitched since part of it is on the outside edges.

14. I suggest pintucking a larger piece of fabric and cutting small sections which are somewhat larger than the insides of the bows (**fig. 9**).

15. Cut away fabric from behind both center sections of the bow. I lovingly tell my students that now they can place their whole fists inside the holes in the centers of this bow.

16. Place the pintucked section behind the center of the lace bows. Zigzag around the inside of the bows, which will now attach the pintucked section. From the back, trim away the excess pintucked section. You now have pintucks in the center of each side of the bow (**fig. 10**).

17. Go back and stitch the sides of the bow "tie" down. After you have zigzagged all the way around your bow "tie," you can trim away excess laces which crossed underneath the tie. This gives the bow tie a little neater look.

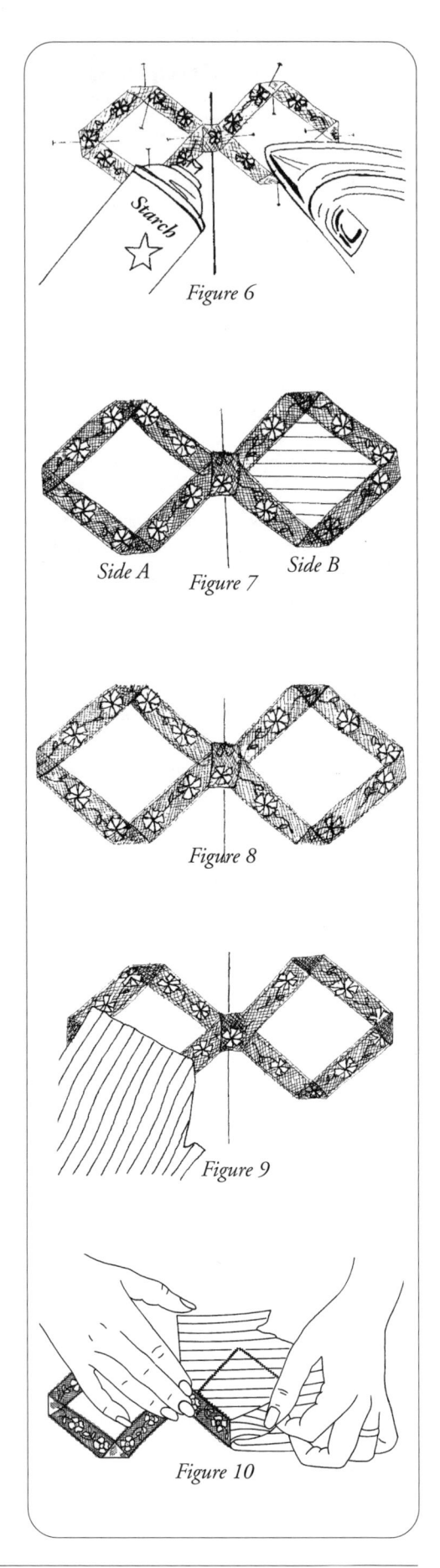

Figure 6

Side A *Figure 7* *Side B*

Figure 8

Figure 9

Figure 10

Tied Lace Bows

This method of bow shaping I saw for the first time years ago in Australia. It is beautiful and each bow will be a little different which makes it a very interesting variation of the flip-flopped bow. Your options on shaping the bow part of this cute bow are as follows:

1. You can flip-flop the bow
2. You can curve the bow and pull a string to make it round
3. You can flip-flop one side and curve the other side. Bows can be made of lace insertion, lace edging, or lace beading. If you make your tied lace bow of lace edging, be sure to put the scalloped side of the lace edging for the outside of the bow and leave the string to pull on the inside.

Materials Needed

1 yard to 1 1/4 yards lace insertion, edging or beading for one bow

Directions

1. Tie the lace into a bow, leaving equal streamers on either side of the bow.
2. Using a lace board, shape the bow onto the garment, using either the flip-flopped method or the pulled thread curved method.

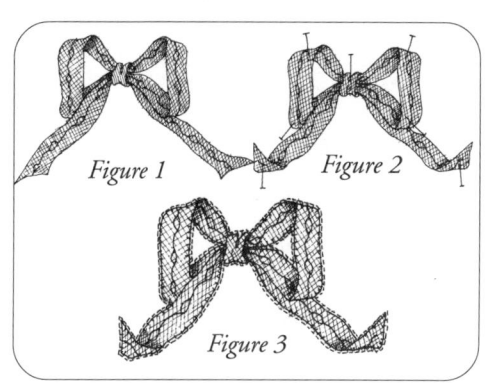

Figure 1

Figure 2

Figure 3

3. Shape the streamers of the bow using either the flip–flopped method or the pulled thread method.
4. Shape the ends of the streamer into an angle.
5. Zigzag or machine entredeux stitch the shaped bow and streamers to the garment.

Hearts-Fold Back Miter Method

Curving Lace

Since many heirloom sewers are also incurable romantics, it's no wonder hearts are a popular lace shape. Hearts are the ultimate design for a wedding dress, wedding attendants' clothing, or on a ring bearer's pillow. As with the other lace shaping discussed in this chapter, begin with a template when making hearts. When using our heart template, we like to shape our laces inside the heart design. Of course, shaping along the outside of the heart design is permitted also, so do whatever is easiest for you.

With the writing of the *Antique Clothing* book, I thought I had really figured out the easy way to make lace hearts. After four years of teaching heart making, I have totally changed my method of making hearts. This new method is so very easy that I just couldn't wait to tell you about it. After shaping your hearts, you don't even have to remove them from the skirt to finish the heart. What a relief and an improvement! Enjoy the new method of making hearts with the new fold back miters. It is so easy and you are going to have so much fun making hearts.

1. Draw a template in the shape of a heart. Make this as large or as small as you want. If you want equal hearts around the bottom of a skirt, fold the skirt into equal sections, and design the heart template to fit into one section of the skirt when using your chosen width of lace insertion.
2. Draw on your hearts all the way around the skirt if you are using several hearts. As always, when shaping lace, draw the hearts onto the fabric where you will be stitching the laces.
3. Draw a 2" bisecting line at the top into the center and at the bottom of the heart into the center (**fig. 1**).

   NOTE: I would like to refresh your memory on lace shaping along the bottom of a skirt at this time. You make your hearts (or whatever else you wish to make) above the skirt while the skirt still has a straight bottom. Later after stitching your hearts (or whatever else) to the skirt, you cut away to make the shaped skirt bottom.
4. Lay the fabric with the hearts drawn on top, on top of the fabric board. As always, pin the lace shaping through the lace, the fabric and into the fabric board.

Techniques   Three Best Friends   113

Curving Lace

Figure 2

Figure 3

Shaping Hearts

Figure 4

Figure 5

Pull thread to make heart lay down

Figure 6 & 7

Trim before stitching

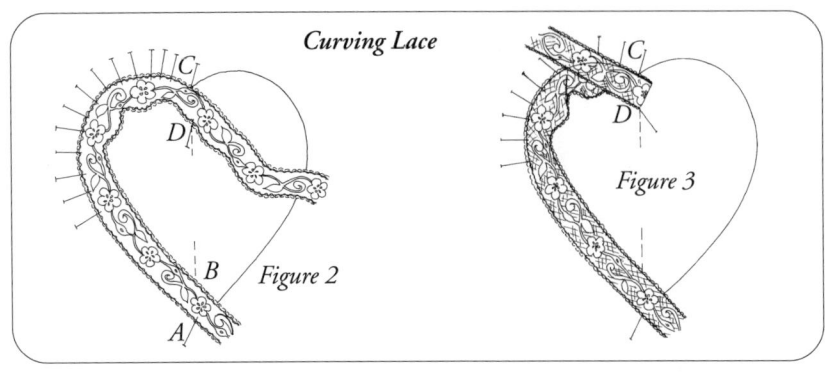

5. Cut one piece of lace which will be large enough to go all the way around one heart with about 4" extra. Before you begin shaping the lace, leave about 2" of lace on the outside of the bottom line.

6. Place a pin at **point A**. Beginning at the bottom of the heart, pin the lace on the inside of the heart template. The pins will actually be on the outside of the lace insertion; however, you are shaping your laces on the inside of your drawn heart template.

7. Work around the heart to **point C**, placing pins at $1/2$" intervals. Notice that the outside will be pinned rather tightly and the inside will be curvy. **Note:** One of our math teacher students told me years ago, while I was teaching this lace shaping, a very important fact. She said, "Martha did you know that a curved line is just a bunch of straight lines placed in a funny way?" She said this as I was trying to explain that it was pretty easy to get the straight lace pinned into a curve. Since I remembered as little about my math classes as possible, I am sure that I didn't know this fact. It makes it a lot easier to explain taking that straight lace and making a curve out of it to know that fact.

8. After finishing pinning around to the center of the heart, place another pin at **point D** (**fig. 2**).

9. Lay the lace back on itself, curving it into the curve that you just pinned (**fig. 3**). Remove the pin from **point C** and repin it, this time pinning through both layers of lace.

10. Wrap the lace to the other side and begin pinning around the other side of the heart. Where you took the lace back on itself and repinned, there will be a miter which appears just like magic. This is the new fold back miter which is just as wonderful on hearts as it is on diamonds and scalloped skirts.

11. Pin the second side of the lace just like you pinned the first one. At the bottom of the heart, lay the laces one over the other and put a pin at **point B** (**fig. 4**).

12. It is now time to pull the threads to make the curvy insides of the heart lay flat and become heart shaped. You can pull threads either from the bottom of the heart or threads from the center of each side of the heart. I prefer to pull the threads from the bottom of the heart. Pull the threads and watch the heart lay down flat and pretty. (**fig. 5**). After teaching literally hundreds of students to make hearts, I think it is better to pull the thread from the bottom of the heart. You don't need to help the fullness lay down; simply pull the thread. On other lace shaped curves such as a scalloped skirt, loops, or ovals, you have to pull from the inside curve.

13. Spray starch and press the curves into place.

14. To make your magic miter at the bottom of the heart, remove the pin from **point A**, fold back the lace so it lays on the other piece of lace, and repin **point A**. You now have a folded back miter which completes the easy mitering on the heart (**fig. 6**). You are now ready to pin the hearts flat onto the garment and remove the shaping from the fabric board.

15. You can trim these bottom "tails" of lace away before you attach the heart to the garment or after you attach the heart to the garment. It probably looks better to trim them before you stitch (**fig. 7**).

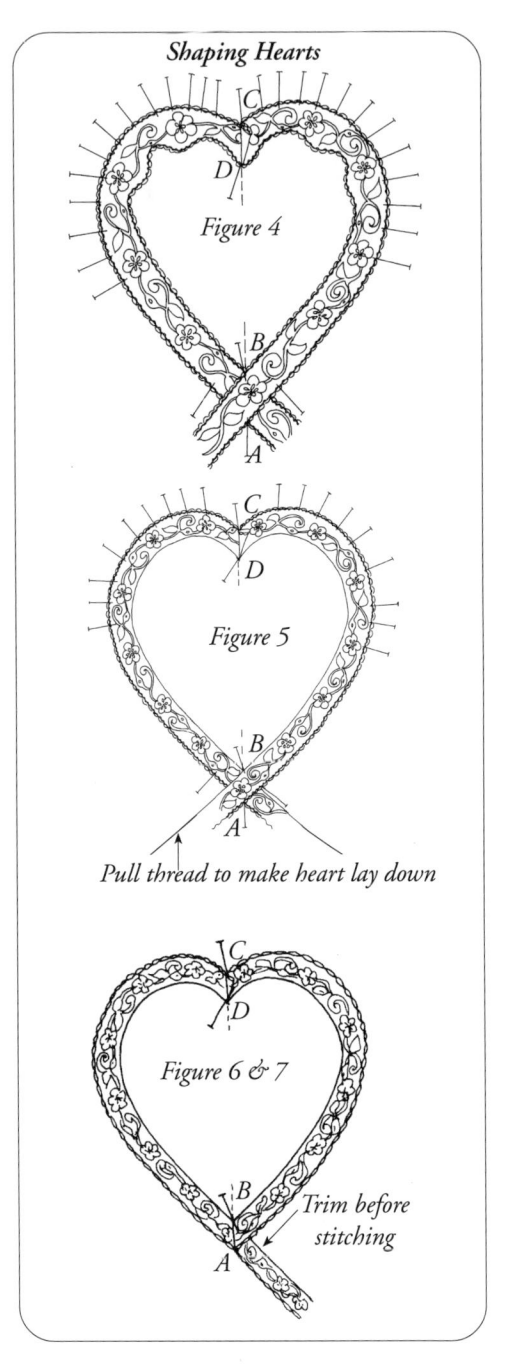

16. You can attach the hearts just to the fabric or you can choose to put something else such as pintucks inside the hearts. If you have hearts which touch going all the way around a skirt, then follow the directions for zigzagging which are in the diamond section.

17. If you have one heart on a collar or bodice of a dress, then zigzag the outside first. If you choose to put something on the inside of each heart, cut away the fabric from behind the shape after zigzagging it to the garment. Then, put whatever you want to insert in the heart behind the heart shape and zigzag around the center or inside of

the heart. Refer to the directions on inserting pintucks or something else in the center of a lace shape in the flip-flopped bow section.

18. You can certainly use the entredeux/wing needle stitching for a beautiful look for attaching the hearts. Follow the directions for machine entredeux on the lace shaped skirt found in the diamond section of this lace shaping chapter.

19. After you cut away the fabric from behind the hearts, go back and zigzag over each mitered point (**fig. 8**). You then have the choice of either leaving the folded over section or of cutting it away. Personally, I usually leave the section because of the strength it adds to the miters. The choice is yours.

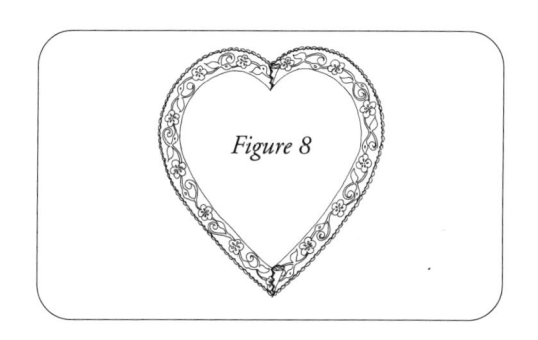

Figure 8

Scalloped Skirt

I have always loved scalloped skirts. The first one that I ever saw intimidated me so much that I didn't even try to make one for several years after that. The methods which I am presenting to you in this section are so easy that I think you won't be afraid to try making one of my favorite garments. Scalloping lace can be a very simple way to finish the bottom of a smocked dress or can be a very elaborate way to put row after row of lace scallops with curved pintucks in between those scallops. Plain or very elaborate - this is one of my favorite things in French sewing by machine. Enjoy!

Preparing The Skirt For Lace Scallops

Before I give you the steps below, which is one great way to prepare scallops on a skirt, let me share with you that you can also follow the instructions found under the beginning lace techniques for scallops as well as diamonds, hearts, teardrops or circles. These instructions are so that you can use any size scallop that you want to for any width skirt. How do you do that? Stitch or serge up one side seam of your whole skirt before placing the scallops.

1. Pull a thread and cut or tear your skirt. I usually put 88 inches in my skirt, two 44-inch widths - one for the front and one for the back. Make the skirt length the proper one for your garment. Sew one side seam.

2. Trace one scallop on each side of the side seam. Continue tracing until you are almost at the edge of the fabric. Leave a seam allowance beyond the last scallops and trim away the excess (**fig. 1**).

3. Now you are ready to shape the lace along the template lines.

Pinning The Lace Insertion To The Skirt Portion On The Fabric Board

1. Cut enough lace insertion to go around all of the scallops on the skirt. Allow at least 16 inches more than you measured. You can later use the excess lace insertion in another area of the dress. If you do not have a piece of insertion this long, remember to piece your laces so that the pieced section will go into the miter at the top of the scallop.

2. Pin the lace insertion to the skirt (one scallop at a time only) by poking pins all the way into the fabric board, through the bottom lace heading and the fabric of the skirt. Notice on (**figure 2**) that the bottom of the lace is straight with the pins poked into the board. The top of the lace is rather "curvy" because it hasn't been shaped to lie flat yet.

3. As you take the lace into the top of the first scallop, carefully place a pin into the lace and the board at **points C and D**. Pinning the D point is very important. That is why you drew the line bisecting the top of each scallop (**fig. 2**). Pin the B point at exactly the place where the flat lace crosses the line you drew to bisect the scallop.

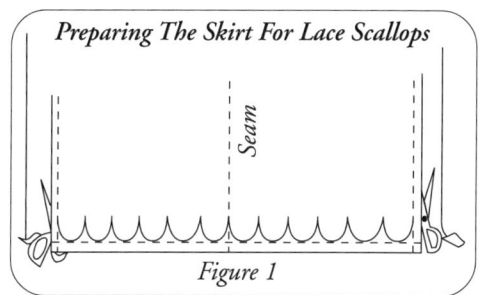

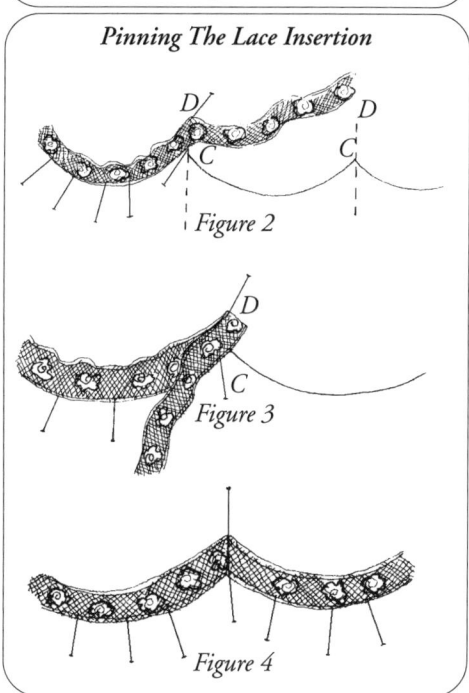

Preparing The Skirt For Lace Scallops

Figure 1

Pinning The Lace Insertion

Figure 2

Figure 3

Figure 4

4. Fold back the whole piece of lace onto the other side (**fig. 3**). Remove the pin at C and repin it to go through both layers of lace. Leave the pin at point D just as it is.

5. Then fold over the lace to place the next section of the lace to travel into the next part of the scallop (**fig.4**).

NOTE: If a little bit of that folded point is exposed after you place the lace into the next scallop, just push it underneath the miter until the miter looks perfect (**fig. 5**). I lovingly call this "mushing" the miter into place.

6. To shape the excess fullness of the top of the scallop, simply pull a gathering thread at the center point of each scallop until the lace becomes flat and pretty (**fig. 6**).

7. Place a pin in the lace loop you just pulled until you spray starch and press the scallop flat. Remember, it is easier to pull the very top thread of the lace, the one which makes a prominent scallop on the top of the lace. If you break that thread, go in and pull another one. Many laces have as many as 4 or 5 total threads which you can pull. Don't worry about that little pulled thread; when you zigzag the lace to the skirt or entredeux stitch it to the skirt, simply trim away that little pulled thread. The heaviness of the zigzag or the entredeux stitch will secure the lace to the skirt.

8. Spray starch and press each scallop and miter after you finish shaping them.

9. After finishing with the section of scallops you have room for on that one board, pin the laces flat to the skirt and begin another section of your skirt (**fig 7**). You have the choice here of either zigzagging each section of the skirt as you complete it, or waiting until you finish the whole skirt.

10. If you choose to use a decorative stitch on your sewing machine (entredeux stitch with a wing needle) you will need to stitch with some sort of stabilizer underneath the skirt. Stitch 'n Tear is an excellent one. Some use tissue paper, others prefer wax paper or adding machine paper. Actually, the paper you buy at a medical supply store that doctors use for covering their examining tables is great also. As long as you are stitching using a wing needle and heavy decorative stitching, you really need a stabilizer.

11. If you have an entredeux stitch on your sewing machine, you can stitch entredeux at both the top and bottom of this scalloped skirt (**fig. 8**). There are two methods of doing this.

Method Number One

1. After you finish your entredeux/wing needle stitching on both the top and the bottom of the scalloped skirt, trim away the fabric from behind the lace scallop.

2. Carefully trim the fabric from the bottom of the skirt also, leaving just a "hair" of seam allowance (**fig. 9**).

3. You are now ready to zigzag over the folded in miters (**fig. 10**). Use a regular needle for this zigzag.

4. Now zigzag the gathered laces to the bottom of this machine created entredeux.

Method Number Two

1. Machine entredeux the top only of the scallop (**fig. 11a**). Don't cut anything away.

2. Butt your gathered lace edging, a few inches at a time, to the shaped bottom of the lace scallop. Machine entredeux stitch in between the flat scalloped lace and the gathered edging lace, thus attaching both laces at the same time you are stitching in the machine entredeux (**fig. 11b**). Be sure you put more fullness at the points of the scallop.

3. After the gathered lace edging is completely stitched to the bottom of the skirt with your machine entredeux, cut away the bottom of the skirt fabric as closely to the stitching as possible (**fig. 12**).

4. Zigzag over your folded in miters (**fig. 12a**).

5. If you are going to attach the lace to the fabric with just a plain zigzag stitch, you might try (Width=1^1/$_2$ to 2, Length=1 to 1^1/$_2$). You want the zigzag to be wide enough to completely go over the heading of the laces and short enough to be strong. If you are zigzagging the laces to the skirt, zigzag the **top only** of the lace scallops (see **fig. 13**).

6. After you zigzag the top only of this skirt, carefully trim away the bottom portion of the fabric skirt, trimming all the way up to the stitches (**fig. 13**).

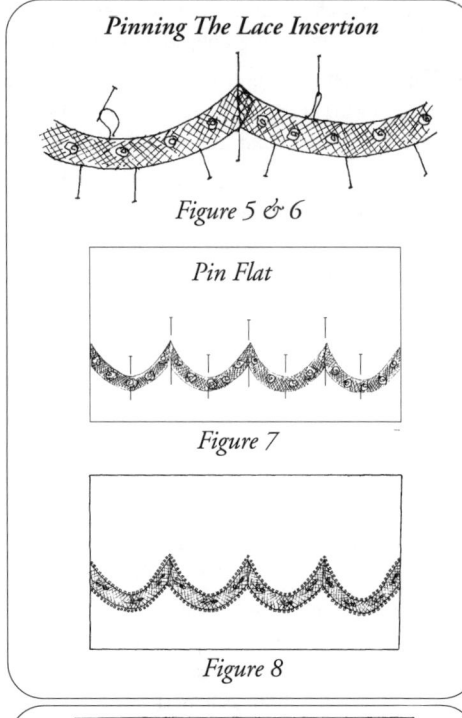

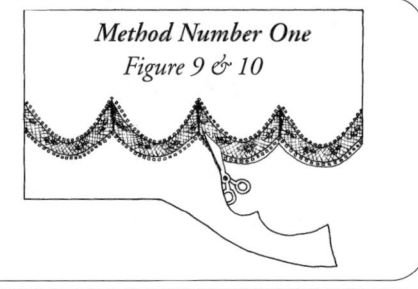

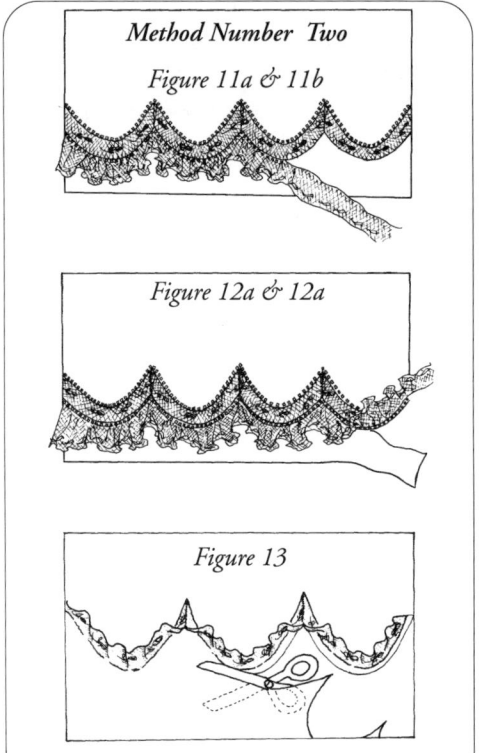

Pinning The Lace Insertion

Figure 5 & 6

Pin Flat

Figure 7

Figure 8

Method Number One
Figure 9 & 10

Method Number Two
Figure 11a & 11b

Figure 12a & 12a

Figure 13

7. Now you have a scalloped skirt. Later you might want to add entredeux to the bottom of the scalloped skirt. It is perfectly alright just to add gathered laces to this lace scallop without either entredeux or machine stitched entredeux. Just treat the bottom of this lace scallop as a finished edge; gather your lace edging and zigzag to the bottom of the lace (**see fig. 14**).

Finishing The Center Of The Miter
After Attaching It To The Skirt and Trimming Away The Fabric From Behind the Scallops

I always zigzag down the center of this folded miter. You can leave the folded lace portion in the miter to make the miter stronger or you can trim away the folded portion after you have zigzagged over the miter center (**fig. 14**).

Finishing The Center Of The Miter

Figure 14

Sewing Hand-Gathered French Lace To Entredeux Edge

1. Gather lace by hand by pulling the thread in the heading of the lace. I use the scalloped outside thread of the heading first since I think it gathers better than the inside threads. Distribute gathers evenly.
2. Trim the side of the entredeux to which the gathered lace is to be attached. Side by side, right sides up, zigzag the gathered lace to the trimmed entredeux (Width=1 1/2; Length=2) (**fig. 15**).
3. Using a wooden shish kabob stick, push the gathers evenly into the sewing machine as you zigzag. You can also use a pick or long pin of some sort to push the gathers evenly into the sewing machine.

Hint: To help distribute the gathers evenly fold the entredeux in half and half again. Mark these points with a fabric marker. Before the lace is gathered, fold it in half and half again. Mark the folds with a fabric marker. Now gather the lace and match the marks on the entredeux and the marks on the lace (**fig. 16**).

Sewing Hand-Gathered French Lace To Entredeux Edge

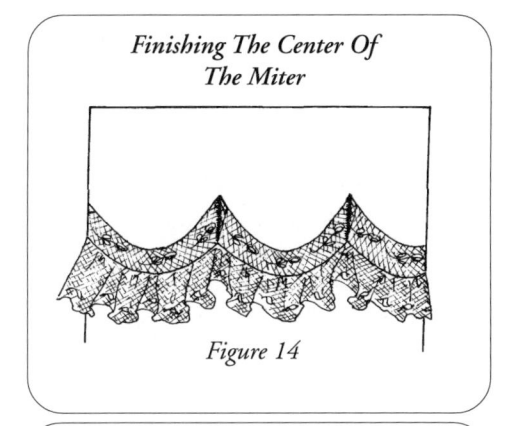

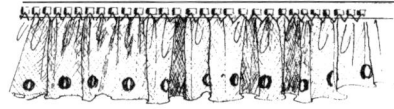

Figure 15

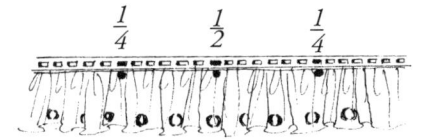

Figure 16

French Seam

1. Place the fabric pieces with wrong sides together.
2. Stitch a row of tiny zigzag stitches (L 1.0, W 1.0) 3/16" outside the seam line (**see fig. 1**).
3. Press the seam flat and trim away the seam allowance outside the zigzags (**fig. 1**).
4. Open out the fabric and press the seam to one side.
5. Fold the fabric along the seam line with right sides together, encasing the zigzag stitching (**fig. 2**).
6. Stitch a 3/16" seam, enclosing the zigzag stitching (**fig. 3**).
7. Press the seam to one side.

Note: A serged, rolled edge may be used for the first seam, when the fabric pieces are wrong sides together. No trimming will be needed, as the serger cuts off the excess seam allowance. If a pintuck foot is available, use it to stitch the second seam for either the zigzag or serger method. Place the tiny folded seam into a groove of the foot so that the needle will stitch right along beside the little roll of fabric (**fig. 4**).

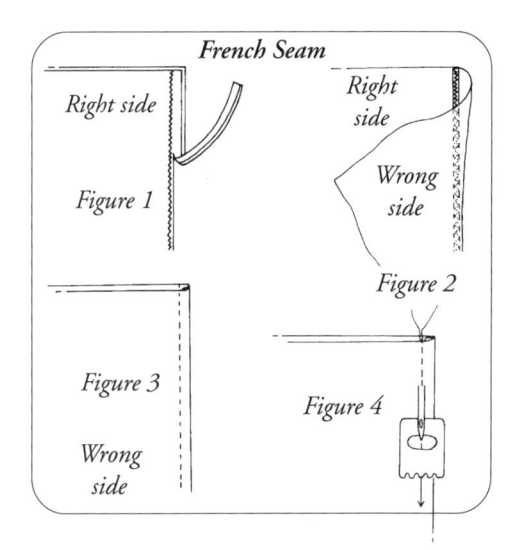

French Seam

Figure 1

Figure 2

Figure 3

Figure 4

Extra-Stable Lace Finishing

Extra-Stable Lace Finish for Fabric Edges

1. If the lace is being attached to a straight edge of fabric, pin the heading of the lace to the right side, ¼" or more from the cut edge, with the right side of the lace facing up and the outside edge of the lace extending over the edge of the fabric. Using a short straight stitch, stitch the heading to the fabric (**fig. 1**).

2. If the lace is being attached to a curved edge, shape the lace around the curve as you would for lace shaping; refer to "Lace Shaping" found on page 40. Pull up the threads in the lace heading if necessary. Continue pinning and stitching the lace as directed in Step 1 above (**fig. 2**).

3. Press the seam allowance away from the lace, toward the wrong side of the fabric (**fig. 3**). If the edge is curved or pointed, you may need to clip the seam allowance in order to press flat (**fig. 4**).

4. On the right side, use a short, narrow zigzag to stitch over the lace heading, catching the fold of the pressed seam allowance (**fig. 5**).

5. On the wrong side, trim the seam allowance close to the zigzag (**fig. 6**).

Note: Extra-Stable Lace Finish for Fabric Edges can be used for lace shaping.

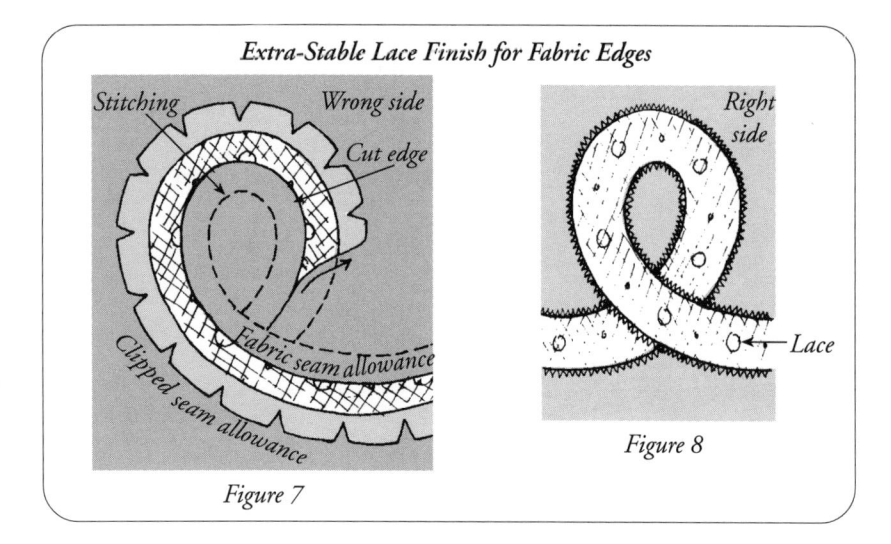

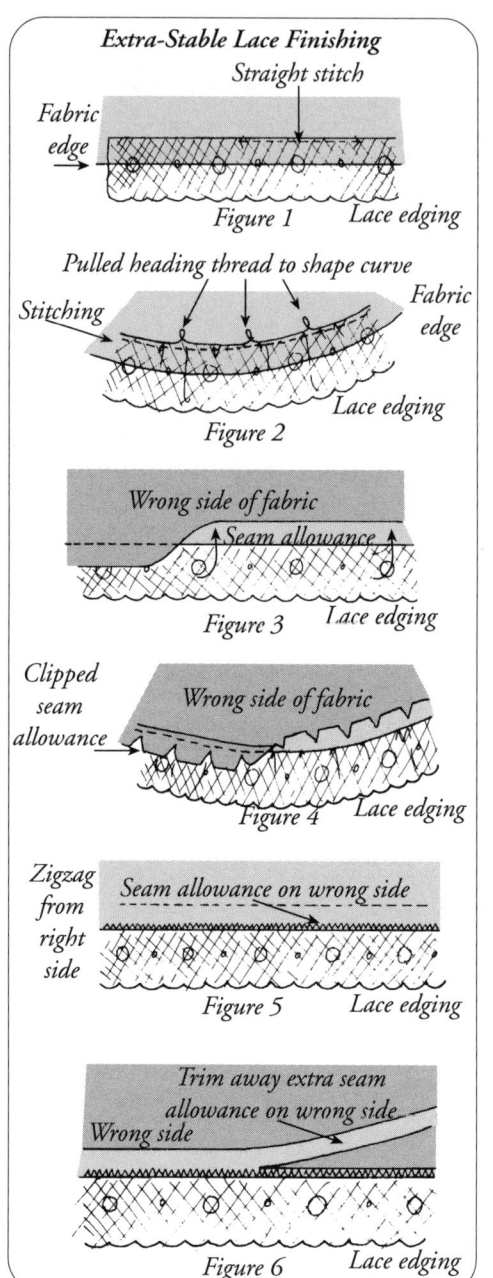

Extra-Stable Lace Finishing

Figure 1
Figure 2
Figure 3
Figure 4
Figure 5
Figure 6

Extra-Stable Lace Finish for Fabric Edges

Figure 7
Figure 8

Making Baby Piping

If self-made piping will be used, measure all of the places it will be applied and use these instructions for making it:

Cut a bias strip 1¼" wide by the length needed. Bias may be pieced so that the piping will be made in one long strip. Place tiny cording along the center of the strip on the wrong side and fold the fabric over the cording, meeting the long edges of the fabric. Use a zipper foot to stitch close to the cording (**fig. a**).

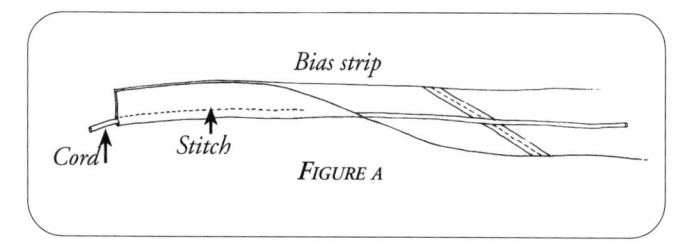

Figure A

118   *Three Best Friends*   *Techniques*

Ribbon Rosettes

Ribbon Rosette

Ribbon rosettes are used to embellish children's dresses, doll dresses, craft projects, pillows and other home decorating projects. Ribbon rosettes are most commonly made from double-faced satin ribbon or silk ribbon. The width and length of the ribbon will vary according to the project. Commonly used ribbon widths are $1/16"$, $1/8"$ or $1/4"$ while the lengths will vary from 18" to 5 yards.

1. Place dots on the ribbon evenly spaced apart, usually 1" to 2", leaving ribbon at each end un-dotted for the streamers. The directions for the project will give the length of the ribbon to be used and the dot spacing (**fig. 1**).

2. Thread a needle with a doubled thread and begin picking up the dots on the ribbon (**fig. 1**). Thread the dots onto the needle and pull them up tightly to form a rosette. Take a few stitches to secure the loops together (**fig. 2**).

3. Tack the rosette in place or pin in place using a small gold safety pin.

Knotted Ribbon Rosette

1. Make dots on the ribbon as described in step 1 of Ribbon Rosettes. At every other dot, tie a knot in the ribbon (**see fig. 3**).

2. Thread a needle with a doubled thread and begin picking up the dots on the ribbon. Thread the dots onto the needle (**fig. 3**) and pull them up tightly to form a rosette. Take a few stitches to secure the loops together.

3. Tie knots in the streamers, if desired (**fig. 4**).

4. Tack the rosette in place or pin in place using a small gold safety pin.

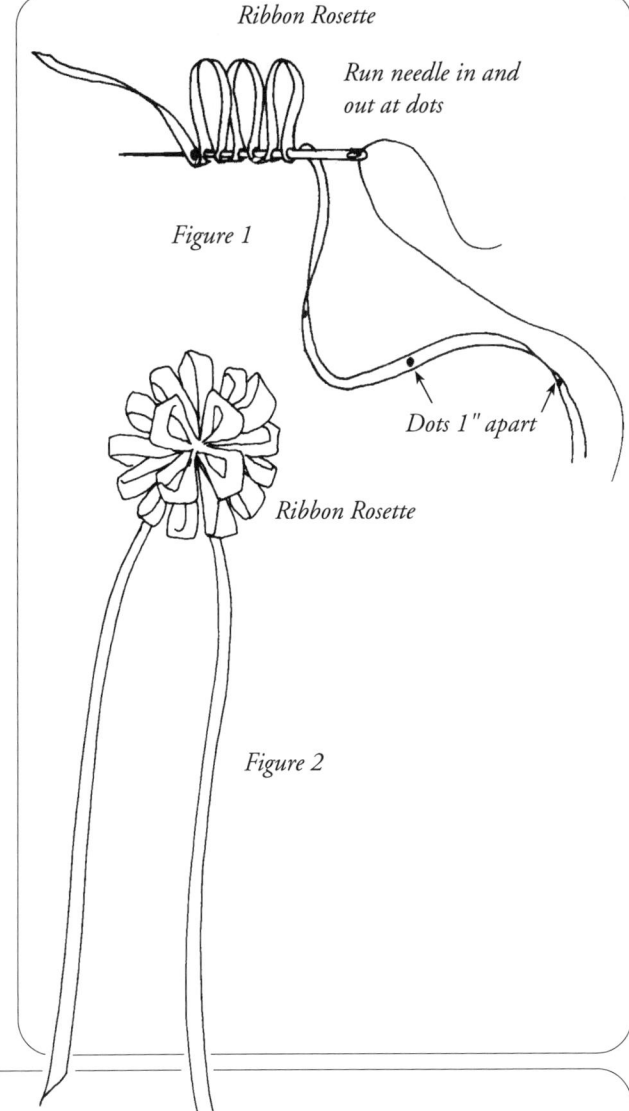

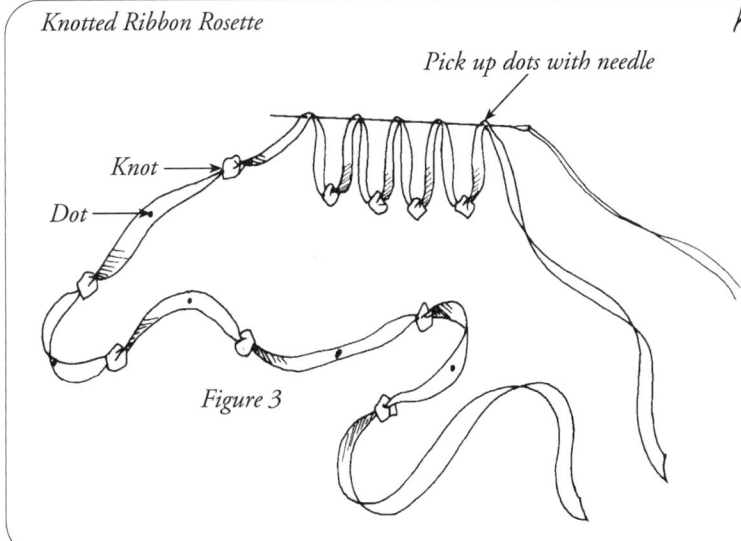

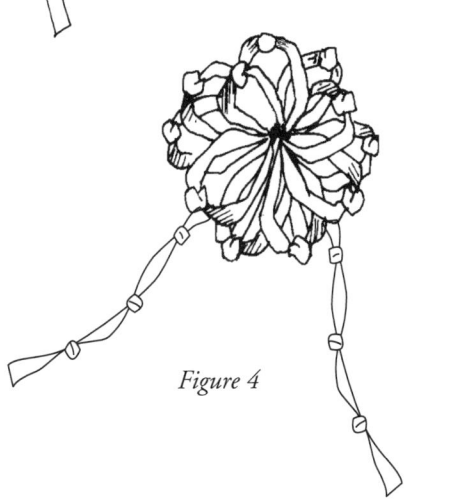

Ribbon Rosette

Run needle in and out at dots

Figure 1

Dots 1" apart

Ribbon Rosette

Figure 2

Knotted Ribbon Rosette

Pick up dots with needle

Knot

Dot

Figure 3

Figure 4

Techniques — Three Best Friends

Shaped Puffing

Narrow puffing strips can be shaped in many of the same ways in which wide lace insertion can be shaped. This technique for puffing should be used only for decorative effects, and not on sleeve cuffs, for yoke-to-skirt attachments, or any place where there is stress on the fabric, because it is not as strong as puffing made with entredeux. It is a lovely treatment for skirts or collars. The loops and teardrops shown here have a little Swiss embroidered motif in the center; however, you could use lace insertion or a lace rosette in the center.

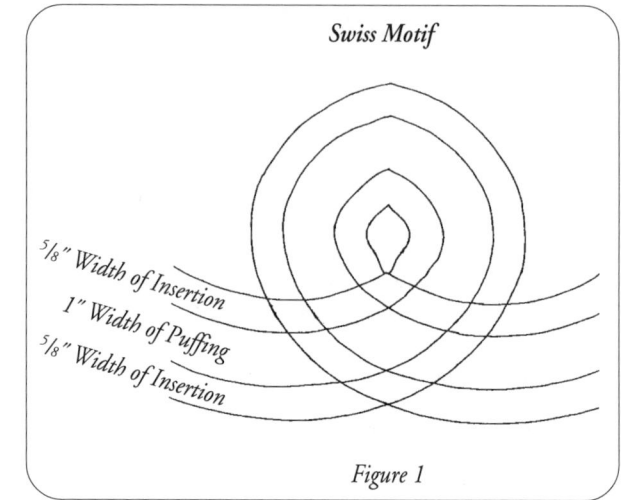

Puffing Directions

Method I

1. On paper, trace around the Swiss motif. Draw another line the width of the insertion away from the motif outline. Draw another line 1" (or desired width of puffing) beside second line. Draw another line the width of insertion outside the third line. Draw lines at the bottom to continue into smooth scallops (**fig. 1**).

2. Cut lots of puffing strips ¾" wider than your finished puffing. Run gathering threads ⅛" and ½" from each long edge. Use cotton covered polyester thread, loosened top tension, stitch length 2.5, stitch with bobbin thread on right side of strips (**fig. 2**).

3. Gather puffing strip to approximately 2:1 fullness and distribute gathers evenly. Place puffing strip over fabric (over fabric board), and pin in place as you would shaped insertion. Pull up gathering threads on inner curves to make puffing lay flat, just as you would pull the thread in the heading of lace insertion. Use your fingernail to distribute gathers (**fig. 3**).

4. Baste or pin puffing in place close to raw edges. Shape insertion along drawn lines. Remove pins from fabric board. Zigzag in place except for very center of loop (**fig 4**). Trim all layers from behind lace and puffing.

5. Place Swiss motif in center of loop and zigzag to lace.

Narrow Puffing With A Gathering Foot

Method II

You can use the gathering foot on your sewing machine to make this narrow puffing around the curves. Cut strip 1" wide than desired finished puffing. It really does work!

1. Using a gathering foot ½" from the edge. Trim the seam allowance to ¼". Using a gathering foot run a row of gathers down both sides of the strip.

2. Pin as shown in (**fig. 3**).

3. With your fingers, "mush" the inside gathers into place.

4. Follow directions as in 4 and 5 above.

Swiss Motif

⅝" Width of Insertion
1" Width of Puffing
⅝" Width of Insertion

Figure 1

Puffing Strip

Figure 2

Figure 3

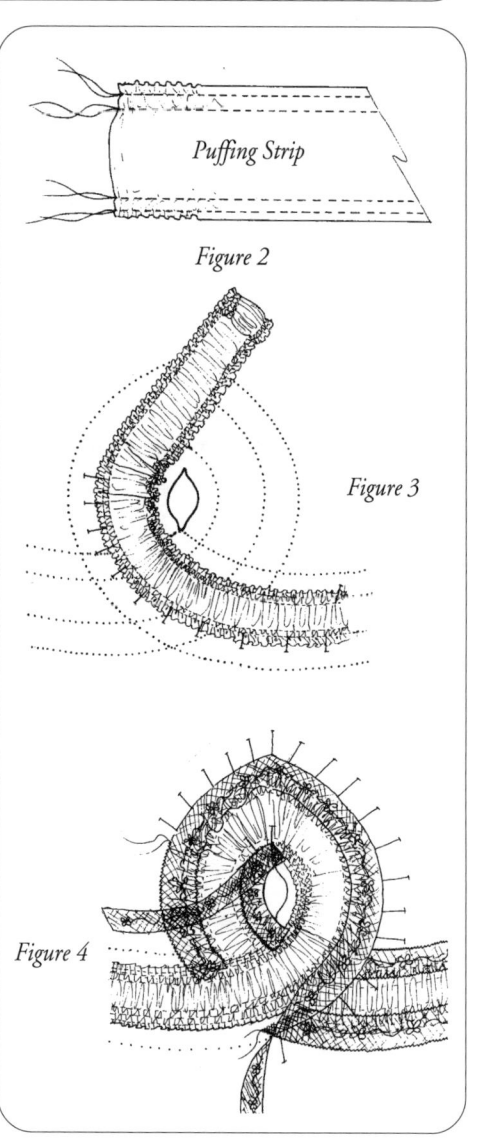

Figure 4

Teardrop Or Candlelight Puffing

Loop Puffing

Embroidery Techniques

Straight Stitch

Simply bring the needle up from under the fabric (fig. 1) and insert it down into the fabric a short distance in front of where the needle came up (fig. 2). It is an in and out stitch. Remember to pull the ribbon loosely for nice full stitches.

Japanese Ribbon Stitch

Use any size ribbon. Bring the needle up from under the fabric, (fig. 1) loop it around and insert the needle down into the center of the ribbon a short distance in front of where the needle came up (fig. 2). Pull the ribbon so that the end curls in on itself loosely so that it does not disappear.

Stem/Outline Stitch

Worked from left to right, this stitch makes a line of slanting stitches. The thread is kept to the left and below the needle. Make small, even stitches. The needle is inserted just below the line to be followed, comes out to the left of the insertion point, and above the line, slightly.

1. Come up from behind at "a" and go down into the fabric again at "b" (see fig. 1). This is a little below the line. Come back up at "c" (fig. 1). This is a little above the line. Keep the thread below the needle.

2. Go back down into the fabric at "d" and come up a little above the line at "b" (fig. 2).

3. Continue working, always keeping the thread below the needle (fig. 3).

French Knot

The most asked question about French knots is "How many wraps?". The number of wraps will depend on the size of the knot desired, the type of thread or floss being used, and personal preference. Generally, use one strand of floss or 2mm silk ribbon with one to two wraps per knot. If a larger knot is needed, use more strands of floss or larger silk ribbon. Often times, French knots will not lay flat on the fabric. To eliminate this problem, once the needle has been reinserted in the fabric (fig. 3), slip the wrapped floss or ribbon gently down the needle until it rests against the fabric. Hold the wraps against the fabric and slowly pull the floss or ribbon through the wraps to the wrong side. This will cause the knot to be formed on the surface of the fabric and not float above it.

1. Bring the needle up through the fabric (fig. 1).

2. Hold the needle horizontally with one hand and wrap the ribbon around the needle with the other hand (fig. 2). If you are using a single strand of floss, one or two wraps will create a small knot. If you are making French knots with 2mm silk ribbon, the knot will be larger. As stated above, the size of the knot varies with the number of strands of floss or the width of the silk ribbon being used.

3. While holding the tail of the ribbon to prevent it from unwinding off the needle, bring the needle up into a vertical position and insert it into the fabric just slightly beside where the needle came out of the fabric (fig. 3). Pull the ribbon or floss gently through the fabric while holding the tail with the other hand.

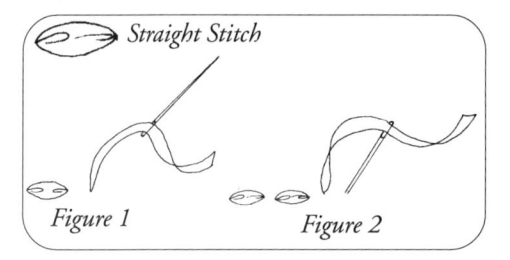

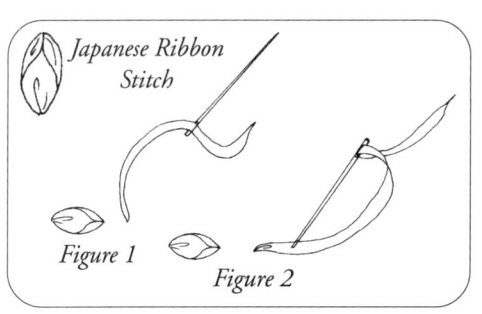

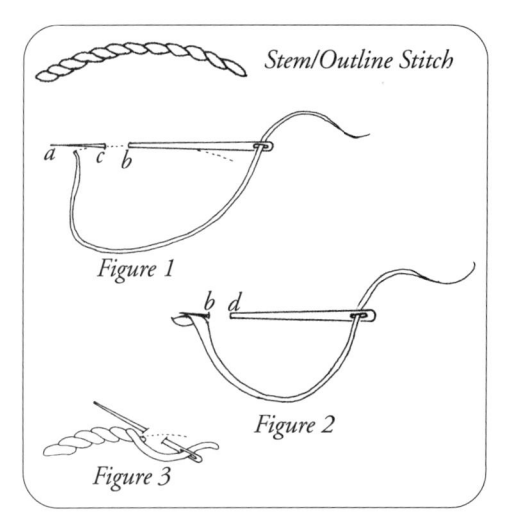

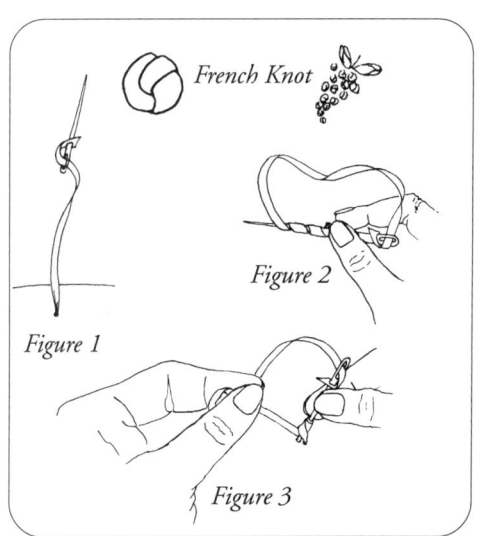

Lazy Daisy Stitch

1. Bring the needle up through the center point if you are stitching a flower, and up just next to a vine or flower for leaves (fig. 1).

2. Insert the needle down into the same hole in which you came up. In the same stitch come through about $1/8"$ to $3/8"$ above that point (fig. 2). Wrap the ribbon behind the needle and pull the ribbon through, keeping the ribbon from twisting (fig. 3).

3. Insert the needle straight down into the same hole or very close to the same hole at the top of the loop (fig. 4). Notice in the side view of figure 4 that the needle goes down underneath the ribbon loop. The top view of figure 4 shows that the stitch is straight and will anchor the ribbon loop in place.

Feather Stitch

1. Bring the needle up through the fabric at "A" (fig. 1). Insert the needle down about $1/4"$ to $3/8"$ across from "A" and into the fabric at "B". In the same stitch bring the needle out of the fabric $1/4"$ to $3/8"$ down and slightly to the right of center at "C" (fig. 2). With the ribbon behind the needle, pull the ribbon through (fig. 3). This stitch is much like the lazy daisy only the needle does not insert into the same hole in which it came up. Notice that the stitch is simply a triangle.

2. Now you will begin working your triangle from right to left, or left to right. "C" will now become "A" for your next stitch. Repeat the stitch as in step 1 (fig. 4).

3. Next time repeat the stitch on the other side (fig. 5). The trick is that "A" and "B" will always be straight across from each other and that "A", "B", and "C" will line up vertically (fig. 6).

Bullion Stitch

Use a 24 or 26 chenille needle.

1. Bring the needle up from under the fabric at point "A" and take a stitch down in "B" about $3/8"$ to $1/4"$ away and come back up through "A" beside (not through) the floss. <u>Do not pull the needle all the way through (fig. 1)</u>. Note: The distance from "A" to "B" will determine the length of the bullion.

2. Now, hold the end of the needle down with your thumb. This will pop the point of the needle up away from the fabric. Wrap the floss or floss coming from point "A" around the needle 5 to 6 times (fig. 2).

3. With your finger, push the wraps of floss to the bottom of the needle next to the fabric so that they are all lined up tight (fig. 3). With your other hand, place your finger under the fabric and your thumb on top of the bullion and gently pull the needle and floss through the wraps (fig. 4).

4. You almost have a bullion, but first you most lay the coils over to the opposite side and take up the slack floss (fig. 5). To do this, lay the bullion over and place your finger under the fabric and your thumb on top of the bullion and gently pull the floss until the slack is out (fig. 6). Insert the needle into the fabric at the end of the bullion (fig. 7) and tie off.

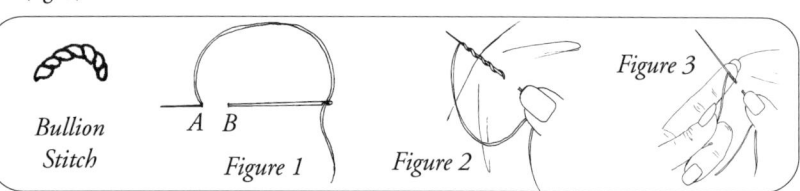

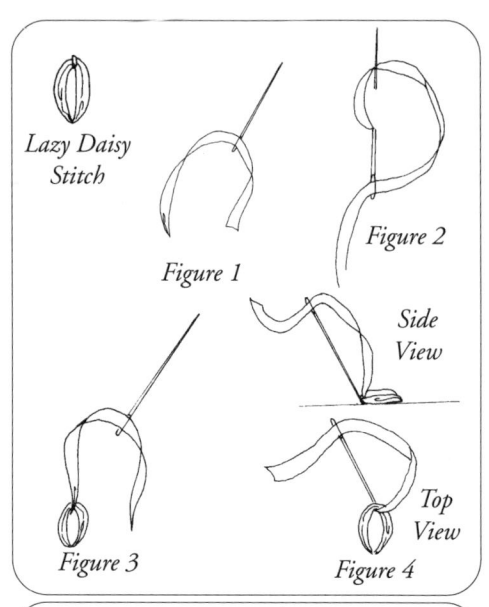

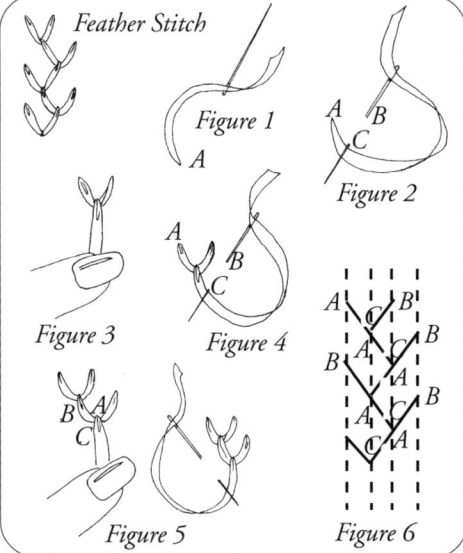

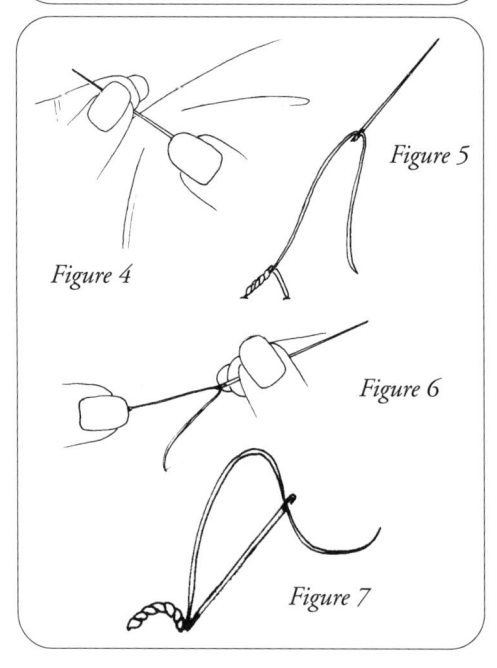

Chain Stitch

This is a glorified lazy daisy stitch that works beautifully on smocking and adds dimension to silk ribbon embroidery. It is a great outline stitch for stems and vines when done with one or two strands of floss.

1. Bring the needle up through the fabric at A. Swing the floss or ribbon around in a loop and hold the loop with your thumb (fig. 1).

2. While holding the loop, insert the needle in at B and out through C in one stitch. Keep the needle and floss or ribbon going over the loop (fig. 2).

3. Instead of inserting the needle to the other side like a lazy daisy, you will make another loop and insert the needle down, right beside C where you last came up, this will become a new A. In the same stitch, bring the needle through B and pull (fig. 3). Keep the needle over the loop.

4. Continue looping and stitching in an "A, B" - "A, B" sequence.

Fly Stitch

This stitch may be used for leaves at the base of flowers, it may be worked singly or in rows to give the appearance of ferns. This is an easy stitch to master and you will find many uses for it as fillers.

1. Come up at A. Insert the needle in the fabric at B, coming out of the fabric at C, making sure the loop of ribbon is below C (fig. 1). Keep the needle on top of the loop of ribbon.

2. The length of the anchor stitch is determined by the length of the stitch taken between C and D. The floss or ribbon comes out of the fabric at C and needle is inserted into the fabric at D. The longer the distance between D and D, the longer the anchor stitch. Gently pull the ribbon to the wrong side (fig. 2 & 3).

Side Stitch Rose

This rose takes careful placement and looks particularly good in 4mm variegated ribbon. It is made up of side ribbon stitch petals; instead of piercing the ribbon in the middle, pierce on either the left or the right side of the ribbon, depending on which way you want the petal to turn.

1. Start with an upright stitch, piercing the ribbon on the right-hand side (fig. 1). This is petal 1. The petal will turn slightly to the right (fig. 2).

2. Place a second petal, slightly longer, to the right of petal 1, piercing on the left-hand side (fig. 3). This is petal 2.

3. Place a third petal, slightly shorter, to the left of petal 1, piercing the ribbon on the right-hand side. Place a fourth petal, the same length as the third, to the right of petal 2, piercing the ribbon on the left-hand side (fig. 4).

4. Place petals 5 and 6 at an angle on each side, piercing petal 5 on the right and petal 6 on the left (fig. 5).

5. Petals 7 and 8 drop below, leaving a small space below the top petals (fig. 6).

6. Work petals 9 and 10 from the base of petals 7 and 8 and over petals 1 and 2. The length of petals 9 and 10 will be 2/3 the length of petals 1 and 2. There will be a small gap in between petals 9 and 10 (fig. 7).

7. Petal 11 is placed between petals 9 and 10 and is slightly taller than petals 9 and 10.

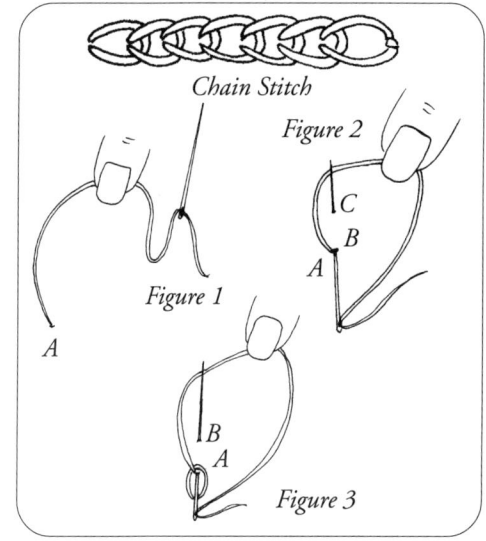

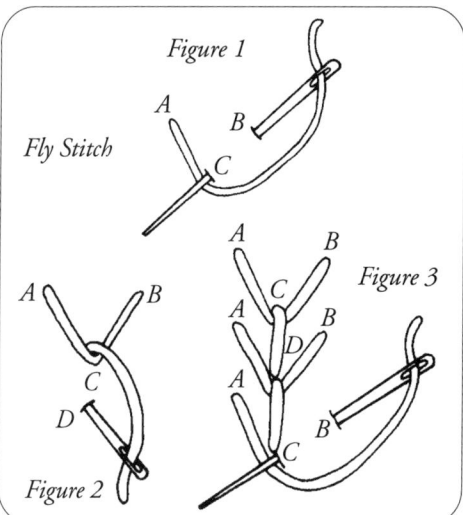

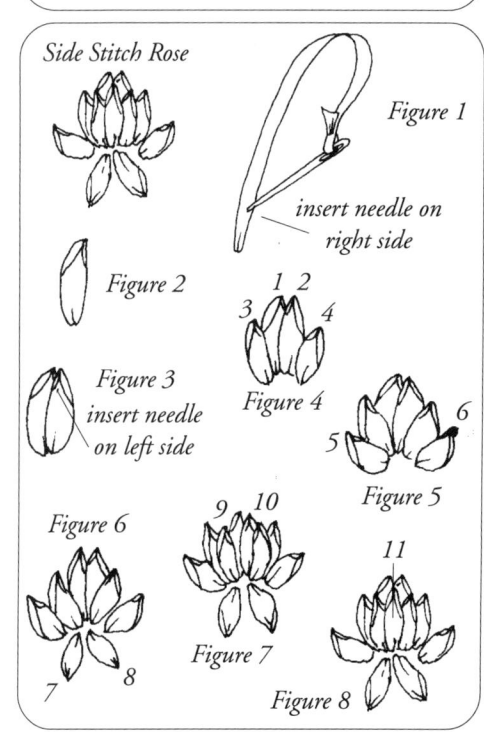

Techniques   *Three Best Friends*

Straight Stitch Rose

This is sometimes called a fish bone rose.
1. Start with a straight stitch. This will be the middle stitch of the flower (fig. 1).
2. Put a stitch at an angle to the left, crossing over the base of the middle stitch (fig. 2).
3. Put a stitch at an angle to the right, covering the base again and placing the bottom of the stitch slightly below the stitch done in step 2 (fig. 3).
4. Continue to work from side to side until the required size is achieved (fig. 4).
5. Add leaves by placing 3 shorter straight stitches at angles below the flower (fig. 5).
6. The more stitches used and the looser the tension will give greater fullness to the flower.
7. If you stop at step 3, this produces a lovely fat rosebud, especially if petal one is a dark color with a slightly lighter color for petals 2 & 3 (fig. 6). Using 7 mm ribbon for large flowers looks very nice.
8. A very pretty effect can be achieved if using 3 or 4 shades for the full rose — a little extra effort but definitely worth it.

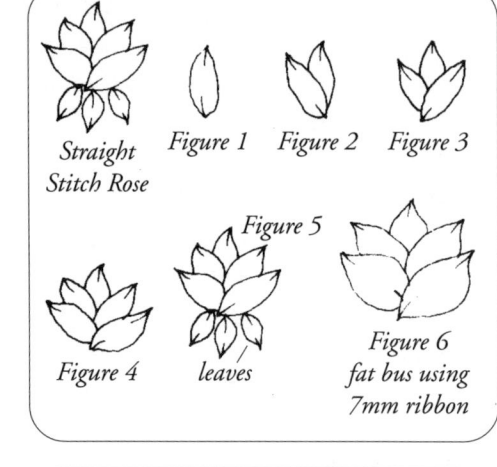

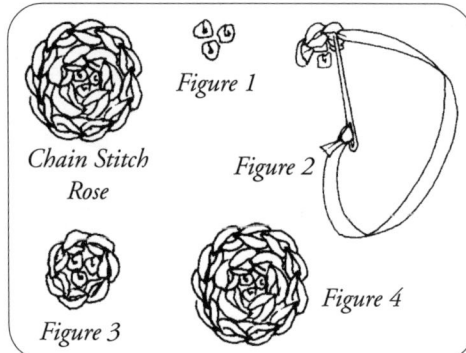

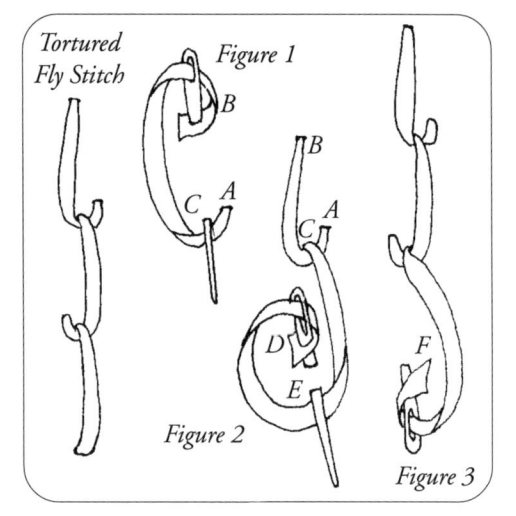

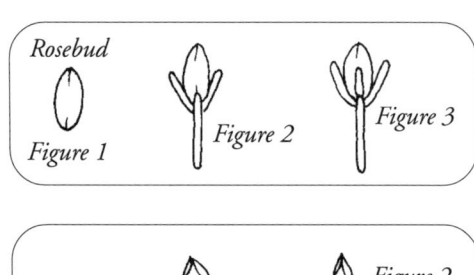

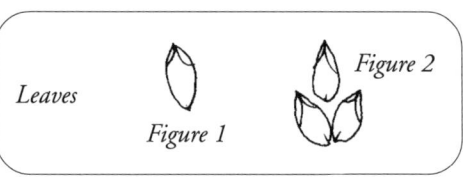

Chain Stitch Rose

1. Work 3 French knots in a dark color close together to form a triangle (fig. 1).
2. Using a lighter color, work chain stitches (fig. 2) around the French knot (fig. 3).
3. Continue working around until the size desired is achieved (fig. 4).
4. For greater shading effects, change to another color after the first two rounds.

Tortured Fly Stitch

This stitch is made very similar to the Fly Stitch. However, the stitches are not angled out as much and one side is much longer than the other giving the appearance of a fish hook.

1. Bring the needle to the front of the fabric at point A. Enter the needle at point B and out at C having the silk ribbon loop under the needle as it comes out at C (fig. 1).
2. Enter the needle at point D and out at E with the ribbon looped under the needle (fig. 2).
3. Continue this stitch alternating sides with the needle placement.
4. To finish the stitch, take the needle to the back of the work at F and tie off (fig. 3).

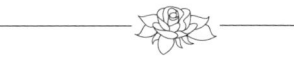

Rosebud

1. Stitch a straight stitch with 2mm silk ribbon (fig. 1).
2. Place a fly stitch at the lower point of the straight stitch with green DMC Flower thread or 2 strands of embroidery floss (fig. 2).
3. Work an extra straight stitch from the center of the rosebud to the base (fig. 3).

Leaves

1. Work the leaves using a Japanese Ribbon Stitch (fig. 1).
2. Cluster the leaves in groups of two or three according to the template (fig. 2).

Lady Bird

A little lady bird can look charming amongst a group of flowers.
1. Using red 4mm silk ribbon, work a ribbon stitch, piercing the silk ribbon on the right-hand side so it rolls to one side (fig. 1).
2. Work a second stitch to the right of the first stitch, piercing the ribbon on the left-hand side (fig. 2).
3. Using dark floss, work a large French knot for the head and slightly smaller ones for the body spots (fig. 3).
4. With the dark floss, work 2 pistol stitches for the antennae, and a straight stitch covering the join between the red stitches to mark the wings (fig. 4).

Stems and Branches

A silk ribbon and thread combination create nice flowing stems and branches for your flowers.
1. With 4mm green silk ribbon, work a ribbon stitch for the length of your stem (fig. 1).
2. When all embroidery is finished, take 2 strands of DMC floss or DMC Flower Thread and put long stitches down the center of the stems, taking a small back stitch approximately every half inch (fig. 2). Alternate from right to left as you stitch the length of the branch (fig. 3). This gives life to the stems and bridges the color jump between the sharp green of the leaves and the pale green of the stems.

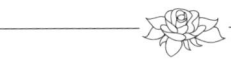

Beverly Bow

This lovely bow seams to dance its way over most things I do!
1. Allow approximately 16" of silk ribbon.
2. Make two loops in the ribbon holding one loop in each hand and having an equal amount of ribbon hanging below each loop (fig. 1).
3. Wrap one loop around the other and through the center. Pull the loops into a knot (fig. 2).
4. Place the bow in the desired spot and pin into place at the center knot.
5. Using pins, flip flop the ribbon to create a pretty bow (fig. 3). Do the same with the streamers of the bow. The more twists and turns, the more life it has (fig. 4).
6. If you don't like the shape reposition the pins until the desired bow shape is created.
7. When you have created the shape you like, stitch in place with French knots, using 2 strands of embroidery thread, or D. M. C. Flower thread (fig 5).

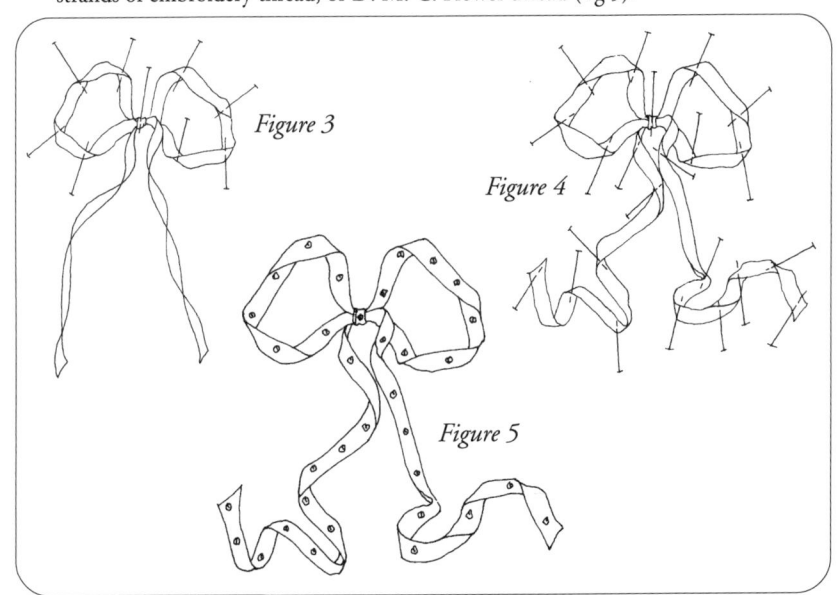

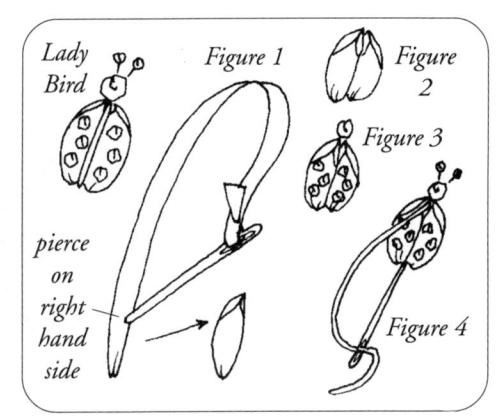

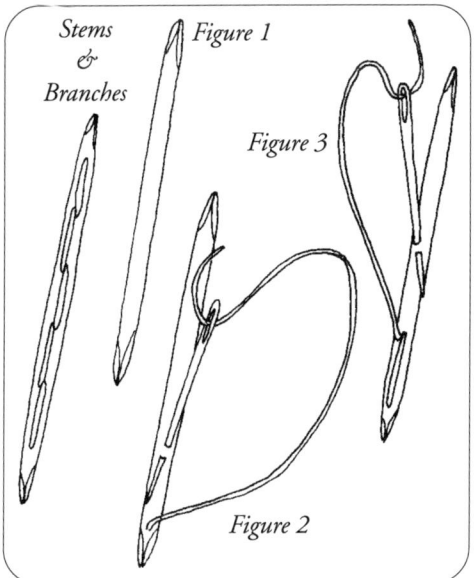

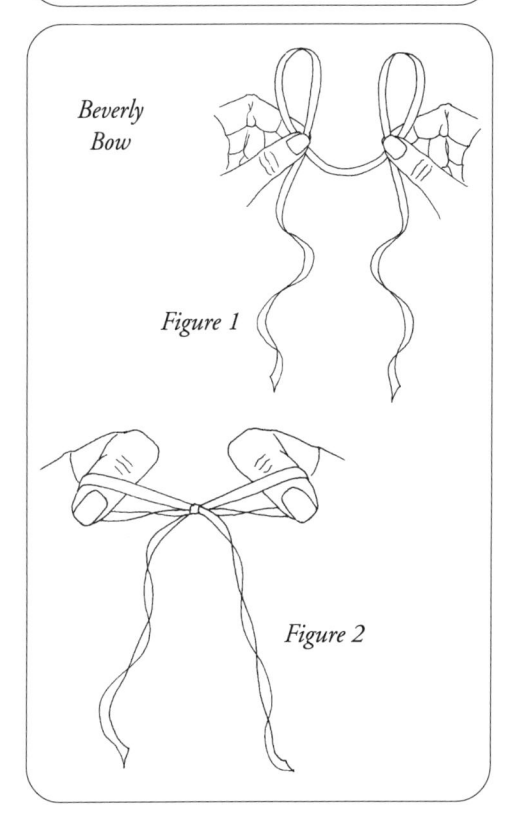

Techniques   *Three Best Friends*   125

About The Author

Martha Campbell Pullen, a native of Scottsboro, Alabama, is an internationally-known lecturer and author in the heirloom sewing field. After graduating with a degree in speech and English from the University of Alabama, she taught those subjects at almost every level of middle school and high school. Later, her studies led to receiving a Ph.D. in educational administration and management from the University of Alabama. She also attended graduate classes at Vanderbilt University, the University of Georgia, the University of North Carolina at Charlotte and the University of Florida. She has served on the faculty of the University of Florida and Athens State College. She did extensive consulting in the Dallas and Denver areas on using the newspaper to teach every aspect of the curriculum from kindergarten to high school. She especially enjoyed working for the *Fort Worth Star Telegram* and the *Rocky Mountain News*. She has done post-doctoral work in teaching reading to disadvantaged children at Vanderbilt University, Alabama A&M University, and the University of Alabama In Huntsville.

Her love of sewing and children's clothing encouraged the opening of Martha Pullen's Heirloom Shop in Huntsville, Alabama, August 1, 1981. Two months later, she opened Martha Pullen Company, Inc., the wholesale division. She has served on the board of directors of the Smocking Arts Guild of America and has presented workshops on French sewing by machine throughout the United States, Canada, Australia, England, Sweden and New Zealand. She has taught hand needlework in Brazil, Jamaica and Africa. Books she has written and published include *French Hand Sewing by Machine, A Beginner's Guide; Heirloom Doll Clothes; Bearly Beginning Smocking; Shadow Work Embroidery; French Sewing by Machine: The Second Book; Antique Clothing: French Sewing by Machine; Grandmother's Hope Chest; Appliqué, Martha's Favorites; Heirloom Sewing For Women; Joy of Smocking; Martha's Sewing Room; Victorian Sewing And Crafts; Martha's Heirloom Magic; Martha's Attic; Silk Ribbon Treasures; Heirloom Doll Clothes For Götz; Sewing Inspirations From Yesteryear, A Christmas to Remember, Beautiful Vests and All The Rest, The Princess Collection, Madeira Appliqué by Machine and The Australian Blouse.*

Martha is also the founder and publisher of the best-selling magazine, *Sew Beautiful*. *Sew Beautiful* is devoted to heirloom sewing by hand and machine and charms 110,000 readers worldwide. Her television series for PBS, *Martha's Sewing Room*, has appeared in 49 of the 50 states. Several times each year she conducts the Martha Pullen School of Art Fashion in Huntsville. She produced her first consumer show, *Martha's Sewing Market*, at the Arlington Convention Center in Arlington, Texas in June, 1998, which continues to be a success.

She is the wife of Joseph Ross Pullen, an implant dentist, mother of five of the most wonderful children in the world, and grandmother of the eight most beautiful, intelligent, precious and most adorable grandchildren in the world. She participates in many civic activities including the Rotary Club, Optimist Club, Gothic Guild and the Huntsville Symphony Orchestra board of trustees. She is an active member of her church, Whitesburg Baptist. She also volunteers with the Southern Baptist International Mission Board. In 1995 she was named Huntsville/Madison Chamber of Commerce Executive of the Year, becoming the second woman in the history of the award to receive this honor. She has been a nominee for the *Inc. Magazine* executive of the year award. She was nominated by the Huntsville/Madison County Chamber of Commerce for the Avon Award. She has finished her first business book, *Hobby to Profit with Grace*, which will be published in January, 1999 by the largest Christian publishing company in the world, Broadman and Holman. Watch for her new book in bookstores and sewing machine dealerships around the world.

The World's Largest Sewing Magazine

For Women Only and *Fancywork* combine with *Sew Beautiful* to bring you one bigger, better magazine!

In January, 1999, you will receive the first expanded issue (*up to 192 pages*) of *Sew Beautiful*; it will contain classic *Sew Beautiful* articles, *Fancywork* projects, and a new *For Women Only* section. We are now three magazines in one; this will be the largest sewing magazine ever published!

EACH NEW SEW BEAUTIFUL ISSUE WILL CONTAIN:
* 144 pages (increased from 112 pages)
* 2-3 pull-out pages (32-48 more pages), plus numerous templates, designs, and many full-sized patterns
* Columns by industry experts such as Margaret Boyles, Sandra Betzina, Sue Pennington, plus a new column from Carl W. Smith on fitting and pattern drafting
* An entire section devoted to garments and sewing for women using commercial patterns
* Women's full-sized patterns (sized 6-28) (every other issue)
* *Fancywork* embroidery projects for your home, yourself, and your children
* Embroidery by hand and machine
* Antiques to reproduce or adapt
* Projects suitable for every skill level
* All of the things you already love about *Sew Beautiful*; smocking, heirloom sewing, appliqué, doll clothes, gift ideas, baby items, and much, much more!
* Subscriber FREE one hour video ($5 s&h)

FOR SUBSCRIBERS ONLY!

Subscribers to the new *Sew Beautiful* will receive a discount coupon for Martha Pullen products with every issue, printed on the protective mailing wrapper. This coupon will be offered only to our subscribers!

Subscription price for a full year, six big issues, is only $29.99, a savings of 17% off the newsstand rate.

PLEASE CHECK ONE OF THE FOLLOWING:

____ I would like to subscribe to the new *Sew Beautiful* for one year for the low price of $29.99. I have enclosed my check or credit card number.

____ I would like to subscribe to the new *Sew Beautiful* for one year for only $29.99, and receive the Subscriber's video for only $5 s&h. Total for one year subscription and video is $34.99. I have enclosed my check or credit card number.

PLEASE PRINT
Name _____
Address _____
City _____ State _____ Zip _____
☐ Check ☐ Money Order ☐ MC ☐ Visa ☐ AmExpress ☐ Discover
Credit Card # _____

MAIL TO: Martha Pullen Company, Magazine Offer
518 Madison Street, Huntsville, AL 35801-4286 USA
(800) 547-4176 • (256) 533-9586 • fax (256) 533-9630

*Alabama residents add 4% sales tax. Madison Co., Al., add 8% sales tax. American VHS format does not work in all foreign video systems.

FOREIGN RATES: Visa or MC only! No Checks! All funds in U.S. dollars.
Canada/Mexico/S.America:
 $39 + $7 video = $46
Europe/Australia:
 $63 + $13 video = $76

DOLL99

DOLLS SIGNED AND NUMBERED BY MARTHA PULLEN
A NEW DOLL COLLECTION WITH ACCESSORIES
FROM MARTHA PULLEN COMPANY

Shown in dresses available in the book Doll Clothes for the Three Best Friends. Dolls come from the factory in gingham dresses.

The Three Best Friends

These brand new dolls with the traditional 13-inch Gotz cloth body come from the factory wearing a gingham dress, pantyhose, pantaloons, and shoes. *Morgan* is a brunette, *Emma* is a blonde, and *Bradley* has red hair. The first 2000 of these fine examples of German craftmanship will be signed and numbered by Martha Pullen.

$70.00 each (plus $5.50 s&h)

Three Best Friends Heirloom Doll Clothes
This delightful illustrated book is filled with patterns for clothing, hats and lingerie for 13" (fits Three Best Friends), 17$\frac{1}{2}$" (fits Martha), 18", and 19$\frac{1}{2}$" (fits Joanna) dolls.
Over 130 pages, color photographs, full-sized pull-out pattern, design templates

$24.95 (plus $5 s&h)

ALL MAJOR CREDIT CARDS ACCEPTED

Doll Trunk
This pink metal doll trunk, trimmed in white and gold, comes with 2 hangers, a drawer, and a place for one 13" doll to travel.

$50.00 (plus $6 s&h)

CALL TO ORDER
1 (800) 547-4176

Send Check or Money Order to:
Martha Pullen Company, 518 Madison Street, Huntsville, AL 35801

Summer Adventures of the Three Best Friends
COLORING/STORYBOOK
*Written by Joanna Pullen Hammett
Illustrated by Angela Cataldo Pullen*

$10.00 (plus $4 s&h)

(Shoes and hosiery available from Martha Pullen Catalog)

CALL FOR FOREIGN SHIPPING CHARGES